Urban Gun Violence

INTERPERSONAL VIOLENCE SERIES

Series Editors
Claire Renzetti, Ph.D.
Jeffrey L. Edleson, Ph.D.

Parenting by Men Who Batter: New Directions for Assessment and Intervention
Edited by Jeffrey L. Edleson and Oliver J. Williams

Coercive Control: How Men Entrap Women in Personal Life
Evan Stark

Childhood Victimization: Violence, Crime, and Abuse in the Lives of Young People
David Finkelhor

Restorative Justice and Violence Against Women
Edited by James Ptacek

Familicidal Hearts: The Emotional Styles of 211 Killers
Neil Websdale

Violence in Context: Current Evidence on Risk, Protection, and Prevention
Edited by Todd I. Herrenkohl, Eugene Aisenberg, James Herbert Williams, and Jeffrey M. Jenson

Poverty, Battered Women, and Work in US Public Policy
Lisa D. Brush

Child Victims and Restorative Justice: A Needs-Rights Model
Tali Gal

Battered Women's Protective Strategies
Sherry Hamby

Men Who Batter
Nancy Nason-Clark and Barbara Fisher-Townsend

When Men Murder Women
R. Emerson Dobash and Russell P. Dobash

Comparative Perspectives on Gender Violence: Lessons From Efforts Worldwide
Edited by Rashmi Goel and Leigh Goodmark

Religion and Intimate Partner Violence: Understanding the Challenges and Proposing Solutions
Nancy Nason-Clark, Barbara Fisher-Townsend, Catherine Holtmann, Stephen McMullin

Violence Against Women in the 21st Century: Transnational Perspectives of Empowerment and Subjugation
Edited by Kristen Zaleski, Annalisa Enrile, Eugenia Weiss, Xiying Wang

State-Sanctioned Violence: Advancing a Social Work: Social Justice Agenda
Melvin Delgado

Collaborating for Change: Transforming Cultures to End Gender-Based Violence in Higher Education
Edited by Susan B. Marine and Ruth Lewis

Women, Intimate Partner Violence, and the Law
Heather Douglas

Urban Gun Violence: Self-Help Organizations as Healing Sites, Catalysts for Change, and Collaborative Partners
Melvin Delgado

Urban Gun Violence

Self-Help Organizations as Healing
Sites, Catalysts for Change, and
Collaborative Partners

MELVIN DELGADO

Oxford University Press is a department of the University of Oxford. It furthers the University's objective of excellence in research, scholarship, and education by publishing worldwide. Oxford is a registered trade mark of Oxford University Press in the UK and certain other countries.

Published in the United States of America by Oxford University Press
198 Madison Avenue, New York, NY 10016, United States of America.

Library of Congress Cataloging-in-Publication Data
Names: Delgado, Melvin, author.
Title: Urban gun violence : self-help organizations as healing sites, catalysts for change, and collaborative partners / Melvin Delgado.
Description: New York : Oxford University Press, [2021] |
Series: Interpersonal violence series | Includes bibliographical references and index.
Identifiers: LCCN 2020031394 (print) | LCCN 2020031395 (ebook) |
ISBN 9780197515518 (hardback) | ISBN 9780197515532 (epub) | ISBN 9780197515549
Subjects: LCSH: Firearms and crime—United States. | Victims of violent crimes—United States. | Gun control—United States. | Self-help groups—United States.
Classification: LCC HV7436.D45 2021 (print) | LCC HV7436 (ebook) |
DDC 364.4/0450973—dc23
LC record available at https://lccn.loc.gov/2020031394
LC ebook record available at https://lccn.loc.gov/2020031395

DOI: 10.1093/oso/9780197515518.001.0001

9 8 7 6 5 4 3 2 1

Printed by Integrated Books International, United States of America

This book is dedicated to those who have dedicated their lives to ending gun violence and bringing hope to urban communities as they strive to achieve a violence-free life.

CONTENTS

This preface assists readers in understanding my approach to the topic of urban gun violence and why self-help organizations can play a role in finding a solution to this deadly challenge. We cannot talk about death without concomitantly talking about celebrating the life of those who have been killed. Those in the academy must uplift success stories and reasons to celebrate while not losing sight of tragedies and stories of losses. I endeavor to craft a narrative that walks an important line between trauma and hope.

We must strive to not allow gun violence to define and shape the identities of individuals or neighborhoods. I hope this book achieves this goal; such an identity compromises our outlook on life and what is good about living, hoping, and dreaming about a better future. Further, it should not define those of us who work in these communities because a balanced view of life is essential to be modeled—one that not only acknowledges pain and sorrow but also seeks to find what is good and hopeful in all of us.

Urban self-help organizations can play a pivotal role in brokering partnerships involving local community and community organizations and law enforcement; that is one of the central reasons for writing this book and why this collaborative potential is part of this book's title. A combination of local initiatives in collaboration with law enforcement, as the research and literature illustrate, must come together in effective partnerships not arduous to achieve.

This book relies on scholarly literature reviews, newspaper accounts, document analysis, interviews, ethnographic observations, drawing on personal experiences, and best practice reviews. No one method of gathering information can do justice to a topic as complex as urban gun violence. Time, scheduling, academic demands, and financial constraints were operative in writing this book. I hope that the content is able to surmount these limitations, allowing an important story to unfold.

Self-help organizations focused on urban violence are vehicles for the dead to speak to us and to let us not forget that they once lived among us. These voices are captured and amplified through these organizations—their family becomes our family. The headlines their deaths created are not allowed to be relegated to history and continue to live, giving meaning to a profound social justice cause. This book honors those who have died to continue to give voice to their lives and prevent others from joining this chorus. The theme that we must forgive ourselves before we can forgive the offender is strong and pervasive among those who are survivors and engaged in self-help initiatives.

Writing this book was a transformative process for me. I started out wanting to tell a story of the consequences of urban violence and guns and to act in the role of broker between urban gun violence self-help and a professional audience. In the process, I experienced a transformation of serving as a mega-voice to amplify a message about countless self-help organizations and the thousands of victims and co-victims of urban violence. This task took on immense importance to accurately portray the sorrow as well as the joy that surround those who have had to confront the unimaginable for the families of victims as well as those who committed the crime.

The advent of COVID-19 introduced a deadly virus that has had a disproportionate impact on urban communities of color, as both victims of this deadly virus and essential workers because people of color represent a significant percentage of these workers. Readers may rightly ask what a virus has to do with gun violence. The virus has dramatically impacted the mourning process, altering social and cultural norms of grieving for those lost to gun violence, and both have had a disproportionate impact on urban communities of color. Although this virus continues unfolding throughout the nation as this book goes to press, every effort has been made to bring to the fore COVID-19 dimensions, and its urban dimensions, highlighting important disparities that have existed in this country and have been exacerbated because of the virus.

ACKNOWLEDGMENTS

Countless individuals aided in this book coming to fruition by sharing their time and stories. I am singling out three because of how they went far beyond what I could rightly expect: Michelle Walsh, Clementina (Tina) M. Chery, and Ryane Nichols. I also wish to thank the anonymous external reviewers for the time and thought given to improving this book's readability.

Setting the Context

Self-help efforts related to urban gun injuries and fatalities introduce a new view of this violence, bringing valuable localized efforts into the national discourse on solutions in a more substantive and nuanced manner. This section grounds the world of self-help and the vast arena of gun violence in this country, specifically focusing on its city centers and the potential of self-help organizations as part of a delivery of services in solving this violence. Readers also have the benefits of being exposed to three case illustrations at the beginning of this book as a means of framing or grounding urban gun violence and indigenous efforts at preventing and treating this social problem. This contextual grounding amplifies aspects of this form of urban violence that generally are overlooked in a focus on statistics, including the immensely critical role that gender, in this case female, plays in reaching out to victims and their families in helping in a critical time of need. In many ways, this book is a testament to their compassion and leadership in this movement.

Setting the Context

Overview and Context

While violence of all kinds takes a tremendous toll on victims, gun violence is of particular concern because of the lethality, immediacy, and consequently, the ways it disrupts daily life.

—D. R. VOISIN, *2019, p. 20*

INTRODUCTION

How to start a book is never an easy decision for an author, and neither is ending it as readers will see; a book on gun violence is certainly not an exception because of the tragic toll it takes on communities. Gun violence often elicits strong reactions across a wide social-economic-political spectrum and touches all of us either directly or indirectly. It is appropriate to start this book with a quotation on the death of an urban adolescent of color who not only celebrated a birthday, but also reached the milestone age of 18, and it is so easy to get lost in numbers and lose sight that they represent human beings, with lives, personalities, families, hopes, and dreams.

When Davonte was asked what he wanted for his birthday, he didn't ask for a big celebration, he only said, "I'm glad I made it to see 18."

Urban Gun Violence. Melvin Delgado, Oxford University Press (2021). © Oxford University Press.
DOI: 10.1093/oso/9780197515518.003.0001.

He was shot and killed less than one week after turning 18. He had previously spoken before the Baltimore City Council on youth violence prevention. (Everytown for Gun Safety, 2019b)

Davonte's death symbolizes the early demise experienced by countless people of color who did not make it to adulthood and whose name we do not know and why we must increase the prominence of urban gun-related violence in our mission. The highly visible nature of Davonte's death and the message he sought to promulgate has reverberations across his community and country, touching on the lives of those who did not know him but can still relate to his challenge of living against all odds.

Gun violence, as it manifests itself in our urban centers, represents the death of an American dream for countless youth and young adults, primarily young people of color, across the nation's cities and communities. Simply put, a life span must extend beyond age 18. Living long enough to graduate from high school is a nightmare disguised as a dream. Unfortunately, we mourn his death because we are unable to celebrate his life and the potential future contributions he and others like him will simply not make because their lives were cut short or because their health was compromised due to a bullet. His family, and countless other families, are left to pick up the pieces left behind by gun violence.

The reach of gun violence encompasses wide geographical territory and crosses generations, with profound lasting repercussions that can deprive newborns of their parents and forever change their life trajectory in foreseeable and unforeseeable ways, as in the case of Davonte; judging from the magnitude of gun violence in our society, it may well span several lifetimes. Nevertheless, limiting the book's scope and goals is essential to do justice to the subject. Emphasizing the role of urban self-help organizations in interventions is the further evolution in community practice and research, helping to prevent gun violence and aiding those who survive. This chapter provides a road map for this book and, in the process, uplifts social issues of particular relevance for helping professionals and social scientists interested in urban gun violence.

URBAN SELF-HELP ORGANIZATIONS: ONE STORY

Self-help organizations, such as those associated with guns, are a vital part of the challenge in addressing urban gun violence, as readers will see here and in Chapter 3. In the case of this book, these organizations capture the phenomenon of indigenous efforts to help heal and prevent this form of violence; success at meeting local needs resulted in the establishment of more formal structures that resemble community-based organizations to the outside world but with roots that are locally based.

Chicago, Illinois's Mother's Healing Circle ("Mama's Circle") is a support organization for mothers with children in prison or who have been murdered, and Mary Thomas's thoughts and feelings capture a typical representation that members share as part of their experiences with these organizations (Conway, 2018):

Mary Thomas sits in an empty circle of chairs, waiting to talk about Ke'Juan. A clatter of silverware and bursts of laughter emanate from the room next door, which she just left, where a crowd of mostly middle-aged women hug and kiss while balancing plates of taco salad and cups of coffee. It's a change from the stillness of Thomas's home where she has spent most of her time since Ke'Juan's murder three months back. "It will be different to get out and talk to people today," she says.

It's the third Saturday of the month: time for the Mother's Healing Circle, or the Mama's Circle, as it's known among devoted attendees. Anywhere from 10 to 20 women meet each month at Precious Blood Ministry of Reconciliation, a tawny brick L-shaped building on a spacious lot just north of Sherman Park. Since its creation in 2013, some 50 women from mostly the Back of the Yards and Englewood neighborhoods have attended this "peace circle," where mothers who have lost sons to gun violence and the prison system can find peace, sisterhood, and community without judgment.

Holding her phone, Thomas scans through her late son's Instagram, a patchwork of dance videos and selfies punctuated by laughing smileys and devil emojis, ending abruptly on August 16, 2017. Together, they tell the story of 16-year-old Ke'Juan, who loved drawing and learning new dance moves from YouTube and dreamt of making it to college on a basketball scholarship.

"Come on Ke'Juan, show her how you can dance," the 40-year-old whispers to her phone, clutching a black sweater around her thin frame as her favorite video loads. She doesn't go out much these days. Sometimes she feels haunted by Ke'Juan—she'll feel her bed shake a bit while she's watching TV, as if he is crawling up to cuddle her like he used to.

Outside the window, a gray November sky frames the ministry's peace garden and labyrinth, a space Thomas's daughter helped plant a few years back in what was once an empty field near the corner of 52nd and Throop. On Thomas's phone screen, Ke'Juan appears, adjusting his tall, six-foot-two frame for the camera, then performs a dance routine in his socks on the family's living room floor.

"Dance, act silly, and play basketball—that's all my son did," says Thomas, touching the final still of Ke'Juan on her phone. "He really didn't deserve it."

"It" was Ke'Juan's murder. He died on the Bradley Park basketball court near 97th and Yates in South Deering last August—one out of the 3,457 shooting victims in Chicago in 2017. According to a Tribune report, prosecutors alleged that the shooter walked up to Ke'Juan, pulled out a gun, and shot him in the head. After Ke'Juan fell to the court, the other man stood over him and continued to fire as children as young as 10 years old watched, prosecutors said. Ke'Juan's older brother was there that day, too.

Farther down his feed, Thomas pauses on a photo of Ke'Juan and his brother, Kenny, deep in laughter, clutching one another in the bathroom after they begged her to relax their hair. "They almost killed their mama with all those chemicals and my asthma," she says, laughing.

She gets quiet again. "Really, you don't laugh like you used to. But today isn't for crying," she says, wiping fresh tears from her face.

Soon after the shooting, Sister Donna Liette, who leads the Mother's Healing Circle, called her to invite her to this special group. It took her three months, but finally, she's here.

The material cited captures the importance of a safe and affirming space where sharing is encouraged and resonates with others having similar experiences, allowing those seeking help to also assume helper roles, an essential element in self-help organizations. It also provides valuable insight into life after the death of a child. Urban self-help, as noted, started with an immediate and affirming response and evolved into more structured undertakings resembling community-based organizations. Their history and evolution, however, is unique. Although Chapter 3 specifically provides three case illustrations, short vignettes are used throughout to concretize self-help efforts in a more integrative fashion.

BOOK SCOPE AND GOALS

This book is really two books in one. One book provides information on guns and the multifaceted consequences of violence. The second book focuses on the incredibly important role that self-help organizations play in community healing and why they deserve more of our attention in understanding urban gun violence and support in their quest to heal communities in deep pain and frustrations. Although this book uplifts urban self-help organizations, their story cannot be told without a foundation on which to appreciate their invaluable work.

The scope and depth of urban gun violence defies a simple definitional narrowing process without losing sight of the broader context and magnitude of the social, political, cultural, and economic forces at work, making it a major national issue, including a historical grounding. Local contextual grounding also is essential. Any author writing on gun violence faces the challenge of outlining its scope in a manner that lends coverage to a preset number of printed pages. The importance of foreground and background necessitates that both receive sufficient attention to provide necessary details to substantiate or give meaning to a particular strategy, one seeking to support urban self-help organizations addressing gun violence and entering into partnerships with them. How well foreground and background perspectives are balanced is critical in this book, and readers will be the ultimate judge. For example, some readers may wish to have greater context of the factors setting the stage for gun violence; others may wish more emphasis on actual interventions. This requires a balancing act.

I have elected to go a very specific route on another dimension. Guns are used in rural areas of the country as well as urban centers. They are used for suicides and murders. They are involved in accidental deaths and armed robberies. (The threat of a gun is a form of violence and does not require its firing.) The association of domestic violence and guns has saliency, particularly when the onus of the consequences disproportionately fall on women. Veterans also are a group vulnerable to gun suicides (Stein, Kessler, & Ursano, 2019). There are mass and school shootings that defy logic but are still a part of the national landscape on violence in general. Guns are also used to target lesbian, gay, bisexual, transsexual, queer (or questioning) and other sexual identities (LGBTQ+), and other marginalized groups (A. P. Romero, Shaw, & Conron, 2019). Urban groups of color have all of these subgroups within the community.

Each of these groups and perspectives, as well as others, has a legitimate argument to make about why a book on gun violence must address the sociopolitical reasons giving rise to being a target. This book only touches on many of these perspectives in order to provide a contextual grounding for an urban focus on homicides and injuries resulting from guns. By limiting the scope of this book to intentional *urban gun violence*, it allows for sufficient context and depth to permit drawing research, policy, and practice implications for social scientists and helping professionals who want to make urban gun violence a part of their purpose or mission (Delgado, 2020b). I have elected not to include domestic violence because of a lack of space to do it justice rather than because it is not a reason for gun violence. The impact of COVID-19 on domestic violence, including use of guns, will no doubt be the focus of research in the future, as these two areas of pain converge and take a particular toll in communities of color.

Gun violence occurs across the entire nation, but there are sectors and segments within that experience this phenomenon more than others. The high concentration of people of color in the nation's cities brings this geographical entity to the forefront in social justice campaigns targeting violence in these communities, particularly when addressing guns, and that includes shootings by police of unarmed people of color, a dimension of urban gun violence with a prominent role in this discussion. Police shootings are often not part of the national narrative when discussing urban gun violence, and it must be discussed in this book because these shootings inhibit establishment of trust within communities, an essential element in any successful strategy to engage communities in gun violence initiatives (Dirlam, 2018; Spencer & Perlow, 2018).

I take the stance that intentional homicide is the most serious manifestation of violence and thus is worthy of a specific focus, while still acknowledging a plethora of other violence manifestations that fall short of fatalities but are still serious. Focusing on cities, some well known and others not readily associated with gun violence, will broaden the concern that many have about urban gun violence.

With this scope's rationale as a backdrop, the following goals further shape how this book unfolds: (a) provide a state of knowledge on urban gun violence in the United States, with specific attention to youth of color; (b) identify key factors commonly associated with intentional urban gun violence (primarily focused on African Americans/Black and Latinx); (c) issue a call for greater involvement of helping professions and social scientists; (d) identify a set of values and concepts guiding self-help community attempts at addressing gun violence, with lessons for other self-help efforts across the country; (e) provide a series of case illustrations of local efforts dealing with gun violence; and (f) identify key practice and research approaches shaping community interventions. These goals are highly interrelated because gun violence does not lend itself to a narrow interpretation and increases the flow and readability of this book.

As noted, readers can conceptualize this book as two books combined into one. The first book provides a highly detailed grounding on guns and victims, helping those new to this arena acquire the necessary grounding to appreciate the complexities and nuances associated with developing a picture of urban gun violence. This helps explain the extensive reference list. The second book focuses on urban self-help organizations and the inspiring and instrumental role they must play in any national comprehensive urban-focused solution. This second book is inspirational and a counter to the first book, which, admittedly, can be quite depressing, and is written in a more reader accessible language.

GUN VIOLENCE, SOCIAL SCIENCES, AND HELPING PROFESSIONS

The journey that we are commencing is one that it is hoped will make urban gun violence a central part of our mission, or in the case of those who have this as their mission, further reaffirms the wisdom of this choice. Putting our heads in the sand translates into professions increasing the likelihood of becoming irrelevant in the nation's urban centers and weakens potential influence in shaping the future of this nation and its urban centers. Further, it allows a major social issue to continue to take its toll on this nation's urban communities.

Being hypervigilant can translate into the expenditure of a high level of time and energy being diverted from other pursuits and can also result in high blood pressure, anxiety, and sleep disruptions, for instance, with educational and health implications that can often can go undetected but with long-term consequences (Short, Bartel, & Carskadon, 2019; J. R. Smith & Patton, 2016). I do not have to mention that sleep is underappreciated, and when disrupted over long time periods, it shapes our view of the day and life.

The health consequences can also be profound and far-reaching, such as with low-income urban youth of color who take insulin, particularly females, who can experience insulin resistance (Kliewer, Robins, & Borre, 2019). The onset of feelings of hopelessness among youth of color has also been found to predict future violence exposure risk in delinquent behavior (Burnside & Gaylord-Harden, 2019). Newcomer immigrant adolescents, who are having urban-based exposure to community violence that compromises their state of mental health (attachment anxiety and attachment avoidance), with corresponding internalizing and externalizing symptoms (Muller, 2019). Urban community violence exposure also negatively influences sleep patterns.

A community activist (Hitchcock, 2019a) described community violence as "a different experience. . . . It's kind of like a grenade goes off and the shrapnel hits everyone." "Silent" symptoms will severely compromise lifestyles. In Chicago, for example, there is a relationship between low birth outcomes and exposure to gun violence, along with residential segregation and the geographic inequities (Matoba, Reina, Prachand, Davis, & Collins, 2019). Many of these low birth babies are destined to a health-compromised existence and also are victims of gun violence. These families are destined to spend countless hours seeking medical and social services for their children, taking a financial and emotional toll. Children exposed to violence are also at increased risk of hypertension and cardiovascular events as they age (B. M. Kuehn, 2019).

The deaths of infants at the hands of gun violence is unimaginable in many circles, yet it is a reality in the nation's cities. However, they do not have to be shot to be killed. Infant mortality is positively correlated with neighborhood gun violence, yet another dimension of urban violence that has gone underreported (S. Levine, 2019). Gun violence must also be deconstructed to understand its multifaceted dimension and how interventions with an urban focus must materialize to maximize effectiveness (Abt, 2019a). Urban gun violence, for our purposes, focuses on homicides, injuries, and threats, highlighting aspects or dimensions that receive great attention as well as aspects that generally go unaddressed.

In the United States, gun violence has shortened the average life expectancy, disproportionally impacting people of color and low-income communities, making it a serious health issue worthy of national attention (Kim, 2019). Violence has assumed a public health crisis level, drawing the attention it deserves (Christensen, Cunningham, Delamater, & Hamilton, 2019; Freire-Vargas, 2018; Sood & Berkowitz, 2016). Thinking of a bullet as a deadly pathogen helps to recast gun violence as a public health issue

(Wintemute, 2015). The subject of violence, however, suffers from a lack of a coherent set of concepts and principles guiding its intellectual and consolidation of guiding development (B. X. Lee, 2019), challenging not only the social scientists but also helping professionals in addressing this issue and, from my standpoint, urban gun violence. It is against this backdrop that this subject is grounded and emphasizes the importance of personal narratives in shaping our views (C. Han & Brandel, 2019).

Gun violence has the enviable attribute of being attractive to a wide range of academic disciplines and helping professions, and that is both a blessing and a curse. It is a blessing because it attracts a range of perspectives and resources in enhancing our understanding of why gun violence is a national issue. The consequences of gun violence also attract a variety of helping professions. A multidisciplinary stance entails reconciling different conceptualizations. Language and academic biases stand as serious impediments to making significant progress in this realm and often require expenditure of considerable time in disciplining results and outcomes and narrowing potential audiences (Bunting, Benjamins, & Homan, 2019).

The broader category of violence is at the critical intersection of many disciplines, "intersecting analyses that traverse the micro and the macro, from individual psychosocial to structural societal dimensions" Mitton (2019, p. 135). Although this addresses violence in general but is applicable to gun violence, it notes the potential promise and pitfalls of a multidisciplinary approach:

> Violence lies at the juncture of many disciplines . . . despite categorical distinctions, focus and insights from these fields are often interconnected and indivisible, and taken together offer a sophisticated understanding of violence befitting its complexity. Regrettably, disciplinary rigidity has often impeded such exchange, and the in the worst of cases, commitment to a specialized methodology or interpretive framework has led to the blinkered exclusion of all others.

A note on the emerging controversy concerning the medicalization of violence is in order, as in the case of the "Cure Violence" campaign, which has been criticized in some academic circles, calling for further discussion concerning the premises on which this strategy is based (Riemann, 2019). Davidoff (1998) addressed this point over 20 years ago. Readers will need to make up their own minds regarding what the threat of medicalization of gun violence means to them and whether it has a place in their approach to this issue.

I, quite frankly, am more concerned with the magnitude of the problem and the necessity to rally all available resources in a coordinated fashion to address it. Criminalization, for instance, is well understood and has only further compounded what initially is a difficult social problem. A comprehensive approach to urban gun violence will necessitate a component that will involve deescalating gun violence while addressing the underlying causes.

Bringing medicine more substantively into the picture makes logical sense because of the role that medicine plays in the aftermath of a gun shooting, particularly in trauma centers, which are usually located within emergency rooms. However, medicine, and no other profession or academic discipline, can be the linchpin in any community coordinated gun violence initiative. Residents are the most impacted by gun violence, and they must have the major seat at the table, so to speak.

Joining the academic and community views together in pursuit of a common social change agenda may seem impossible (practitioners do face a similar challenge), but the gap may not be as great as many would fear (Abt, 2019b, p. 11):

Some might believe that the academic and community perspectives are too different to be reconciled, but that has not been my experience. Over the years, I have constantly compared what I learn from researchers with what I hear and see in neighborhoods. Perhaps surprisingly to some, social scientists and the street are largely in agreement on urban violence, one reinforcing the other as they see the same phenomenon through different lenses, with each perspective being necessary but not sufficient for a full understanding of the issue.

Those arguing against a life shortened because a person was at the wrong place and time is sufficient to serve as an impetus to find commonality in purpose. Many helping professionals have bridged this gap. Academics also can become active and well-informed voices in creating the change needed to end urban gun violence.

Self-help organizations on gun violence represent an ideal conduit for bringing together academics, helping professionals, concerned residents, and community institutions, such as houses of worship, and activists sharing similar concerns. These organizations have become focal points in creating coalitions or, in other cases, entering into established coalitions, providing a place and space for this to occur. They have provided the space for those grieving losses to come together.

LABELING GUN VIOLENCE

Labeling gun violence brings social-political consequences and helps determine the level of attention and funding of research and interventions. Do we label gun violence an issue, challenge, crisis, problem, or epidemic? (Bauchner et al., 2017, p. 1196):

> Guns kill people. More background checks; more hotel, school, and venue security; more restrictions on the number and types of guns that individuals can own; and development of "smart guns" may help decrease firearm violence. But the key to reducing firearm deaths in the United States is to understand and reduce exposure to the cause, just like in any epidemic, and in this case that is guns.

Limiting access to guns, which is addressed further in this book, not only brings an important added dimension, but also strikes a fundamental value in this country.

Hickner (2018) argued that the toll that gun violence takes necessitates that it be labeled an epidemic because of the extent and distribution of its consequences within particular geographical areas and social networks, with the causes of violence being multifaceted, acting as modulating factors causing increased rates for those exposed. There is no question that gun violence can be labeled an epidemic when focused on urban communities of color, and when we use this label judicially, it conveys the seriousness of the act(s). Gun violence's long history brings a time dimension that signals its entrenchment in this society and countless urban centers across the nation. Nevertheless, in some circles this form of violence is considered prosaic and therefore unconventional.

America was founded on a bedrock of violence, and it has continued throughout our history (See, 2018), illustrating how ingrained it is in the national social fabric, but it has taken a particular toll on those who reside in its urban centers (Delgado, 2020b). Why is it not surprising that this violence permeates our social fabric and represents an outlet for frustrations, structural inequities, and serious differences? Gun violence is symptomatic of this DNA. The nation is confronting a number of significant social issues, all competing for national attention and resources, and none with a consensus regarding their priority and the means for addressing them. Gun violence arguably leads this list, calling for a comprehensive strategy (Gabor, 2016; Webster & Vernick, 2014), but one that must contend with serious political differences and priorities. National issues such as racism, for example, are closely tied to other issues, with violence being but one manifestation.

The subject of gun violence nevertheless has had a high degree of saliency in this country because of the immense toll it has taken on the nation and in urban centers, particularly when the victims are youth (Everytown Against Gun Violence, 2016). Gun violence, as a result, radiates outward from the victim to include the immediate social network (co-victims) and that of their neighborhood and beyond. Its social, political, cultural, and economic ramifications are addressed in greater detail in Chapter 5, allowing readers to integrate case illustrations presented in Section I with a dynamic and multifaceted urban context.

TRAUMA AND POST-TRAUMATIC STRESS:
A BRIEF OVERVIEW

Urban violence is a broad concept, and there is no consensus definition on what it means (Pavoni & Tulumello, 2018). This lack of consensus challenges the development of responsive assessment and intervention strategies. Trauma, in addition, is often conceptualized as an individual phenomenon, but in communities with high violence, it brings a community-level manifestation that adds another level to this state of being and must be addressed through multiprong approaches (Lane et al., 2017, p. 454): "Community violence is more closely related to traumatic stress and PTSD than any other form of violence exposure, which has far reaching harmful effects on the entire community."

As social scientists and help providers, we see urban gun violence as a major concern, but do urban communities view it as so? More specifically, is gun violence a major concern among African Americans/Blacks and Latinxs? The answer is a resounding yes! A national telephone survey found 80% of African American/Black voters rated gun violence as an extremely serious problem, with 45% of Latinxs rating it as such (Beckett, 2016), illustrating the prominence of this issue in their lives. Black male trauma survivors (witnessing or direct victimization), for example, have been found to be significantly less inclined to seek and use mental health services than other sex–ethnic groups, highlighting a subgroup that will necessitate special outreach efforts (Motley & Banks, 2018). Potential access to these services will no doubt be a key factor in how this trauma is identified and addressed.

The trauma experienced by youth of color is not done in isolation of the trauma their family has experienced, that of their social network, and the broader community (Corazon, 2019). It is unreasonable to expect residents in high-violence communities to go through daily activities as if guns are not part of their lives, directly or indirectly, or having traumatic loss. Gun fatalities fall within the broad category of traumatic loss, along with other forms, such as death by house fire, accidents, car and plane accidents, drownings, falls, to list several. Their trials and tribulations of surviving violence often go unreported and unrecognized by the broader community and nation, thus minimizing their operative reality (Bidgood, 2019; Zakarian, McDevitt-Murphy, Bellet, Neimeyer, & Burke, 2019).

Monifa Akosua (Richmond, CA) discussed how loss stays with you and becomes part of a life's narrative ("It Takes the Hood," 2019):

> Loss is something that we all experience at some point, but in urban communities we experience it more often. When I was 10, my stepdad told me, "You need to start taking pictures with all your friends cause one day you're gonna look at them and say 'He's gone, he's gone, and he's gone. He's in jail, and he's in jail.'" At the time, I didn't know what he was talking about. Now, when I think of loss, I think about my friend in eighth grade. I'd [k]nown Lamar since we were five, we went to elementary school together. When I think about us being in class I remember him goofing off in the cafeteria. That's something that I always hold on to: him goofing off.

It is important to highlight that loss is not always associated with death because, as this illustration shows, mass incarceration and disproportionate contact with the criminal system also create legacies of loss, which can often be profound and with intergenerational consequences for individuals, families, and communities.

The significance of violence is greater if a person is a victim, or know someone who is, or could possibly be one, which can involve multiple possibilities. Forty-four percent of all Americans personally know someone who has been shot (intentionally or accidently), and a majority (57%) of African Americans/Blacks know someone, with Latinxs' 42% indicating so (Gramlich, 2018). It is estimated that 9% to 15% of the US adult population has experienced homicide or co-victimization, with between 8% and 18% of youth sharing this experience; those who are of color, who live in urban centers, and are low income have the highest reported experiences of homicide co-victimization (Bastomski & Duane, 2019).

Owning a gun increases the chances of knowing someone who has been shot in a nonhunting accident (51% vs. 40%) and may say a great deal about their social networks. Shooting-related trauma is usually associated with loss of family. However, when broadening the social network beyond kin to include friends, it introduces traumatic loss of friends and even peers who may be acquaintances (J. R. Smith & Patton, 2016).

Urban youth coping with violence through desensitization (emotional numbing) is a serious consequence (T. M. Kennedy & Ceballo, 2016). I would describe the symptoms of numbing as a form of dissociation that impedes building positive relationships and conjures images of battle fatigue experienced by soldiers with extensive wartime experiences, with children and youth assuming the role of child soldiers (N. J. Johnson, 2016). Urban violence fatigue is a form of cumulative trauma that can come across as depression and an inability to look toward the future. When we take into account cumulative grief and loss, there is a remarkable paucity of literature on the subject (Flippo, 2018).

Helping professions and social scientists must struggle with understanding how marginalized people experience loss, regardless of cause, but grief is unique and highly conditioned by the relationship one has with the victim, although there also are universal and highly particularistic aspects, as in the case of people of color. Interventions regarding gun violence must also address trauma at the victim and community levels (Pinderhughes, Davis, & Williams, 2015). Gun-related trauma must also be viewed from a collective viewpoint to mobilize communities to seek change (Ali, 2019b):

> "Connecting with each other through a shared trauma is not only good for grieving but effective to take action against gun violence," said Pam Bosley, an antigun activist from the South side who lost her son to gun violence almost a decade ago. "I want people to know that if we don't do anything about it, it [gun violence] will come to your door, no matter where you live," she said. "We can't let these moments divide us and weigh lives against each other to see who matters more. We're all in this together now."

Untreated or poorly treated grief results in a prolonged existence and becomes more complicated to treat successfully. It not only complicates the healing process but also can give those seeking help the impression that treatment simply does not work, dissuading them from seeking aid in the future. This lack of success, in turn, can influence others from seeking needed services within families and their social networks, making the impact of these actions far-reaching.

It is important to differentiate between grieving and mourning, although these two concepts are often used interchangeably. Rando (1993) distinguished between the two. Grief is conceptualized as a passive experience, and mourning assumes an active experience, thereby necessitating an active effort of working through the pain associated with the loss and adjusting to life without the individual. Grief results in a natural acceptance of one's loss; mourning, in turn, highlights, in the case of gun violence, dealing with an injustice if the perpetrator escapes justice.

The subject of post-traumatic stress disorder (Zakarian et al., 2019), for instance, has great relevance in urban neighborhoods with a high prevalence of gun violence (Stock, Bott, Villareal, & Carroll, 2016):

> Post-traumatic stress disorder is usually associated with soldiers returning home from war. But experts in psychological trauma say they now see the condition in residents of Oakland and other American cities with high rates of gun violence. Unlike soldiers returning home from the battlefield to relative safety, though, there is no safe place to escape for those traumatized by violence in their own community.

Drawing analogies to soldiers returning from combat is striking. Residents in high-violence communities, in similar fashion to mobilizing resources to help veterans, require special attention from helping professionals.

When this trauma goes unrecognized, it extracts a heavy toll on communities of color, with youth bearing a disproportionate burden, which often goes unrecognized and untreated (Ford, 2019): "When Black Americans experience gun violence or other traumatic events, we are rarely given time and resources to heal. Instead, we are expected to dry our tears and enter a world that is slow to connect Post Traumatic Stress

Disorder to gun violence in communities." This trauma is well recognized and treated as such in urban self-help organizations.

Much emphasis is placed on the capturing and conviction of a perpetrator and how it aids in the healing of a victim's family. Nevertheless, the process, both the legal and healing, is far more complicated. A perpetrator's arrest, conviction, and sentencing, if convicted, results in the continued traumatizing of the victims' family, and again, most likely mothers. The imprisonment results a loss for that family (McNeil, 2017) and introduces the concept of double grief to help capture the pain that the realization of another family, again most likely mothers, will see another lose their child to the criminal justice system. This grief has been referred to as "double grief" to help capture this pain.

Discussion of double grief requires addressing "survivor's guilt," a feeling that is universal. It can be applied to people of color who have lost a close family member or someone in their immediate social circle. How often this guilt is addressed becomes a key question in efforts to conceptualize family and close friends of those murdered. Outliving children is often a theme parents raise about how unfair and cruel life can be (DeBo'rah, 2016).

When talking with many colleagues who come from low-resourced communities and situations that drove them to the field of social work, for example, and those in other professions and academic disciplines with similar interests has shown me that survivor's guilt is quite powerful. Survivor's guilt related to gun violence is an underresearched and misunderstood topic and common when discussing urban gun violence. It may also have strong cultural roots, further strengthening its influence (Metz, 2019). We can, however, argue that no one really survives the violent death of a loved one.

How children and youth deal with the trauma of violent death of a member of their family requires age-appropriate approaches (Young, 1996, p. 11):

Children are particularly susceptible to the impact of traumatic death for several reasons. Children do not deny trauma; rather, they tend to record its full horror and impact. Trauma is terrorizing to them, rendering them helpless and unprotected. Death is unfamiliar. [Unless you are of color and urban based.] Their coping skills are often underdeveloped. They are still in the process of developing their own personalities and identities. They often do not have spiritual resources on which to rely.

Urban youth exposed to violence are at increased risk for internalizing problems that will result in mental health issues, which are further exacerbated by substance use/misuse (Khubchandani & Price, 2018). Adolescents of color are more likely to experience gun-related trauma and less likely than their White, non-Latinx, counterparts to receive quality mental health to help them or trauma-informed services (Cromer, D'Agostino, Hansen, Alfonso, & Frazier, 2019).

SOCIAL SCIENCES AND HELPING PROFESSIONALS AND GUN VIOLENCE

Why is there a need for another book on gun violence? The American College of Physicians is one of countless helping professions calling for an end to gun-related violence in this country (Butkus, Doherty, & Bornstein, 2018). The "stopping the bleeding" argument made by surgeons (Masiakos & Warshaw, 2017) can also be embraced by social workers (M. E. Brown & Barthelemy, 2019) and other helping professionals, such as those in public health, where research funding does not match the severity of the problem when compared to other health issues (Peetz & Haider, 2018). Although this stance has proven controversial, it is gaining wider acceptance within the medical profession (Konstam & Konstam, 2019).

Social workers will never be accused of eschewing any social issue as part of our mission. Mind you, that does not mean that we embrace all social issues with equal favor or commitment. The field of social work has an obligation to address gun violence (Sperlich, Logan-Greene, Slovak, & Kaplan, 2019). Addressing gun violence is the latest challenge in a sea of challenges, and so it will be for other professions, but one with immediate deadly consequences. Successfully helping professions in the center of this struggle necessitates that we be prepared for the challenge. Urban gun violence brings all of the isms associated with socially oppressed groups and does so from a distinct urban geographical stance, which in the broader society is stigmatized.

Social work's mission, and that of other helping professions, cuts across the entire nation, with particular relevance in the nation's urban centers. Gun violence and its consequences must be deconstructed, as will happen in the following chapters, identifying which aspects of gun violence must resonate for them and their organizations, and no one helping profession should be expected to embrace all the elements associated with this phenomenon—gun safety versus gun control, gang-related individuals versus single actors, youth versus adults, male versus female, and so on.

Urban stigma? Yes, there is an antiurban attitude in this country, and it was reflected in the presidential election of 2016, but it is certainly not limited to that time period. It can be traced to the founding of the nation because cities were viewed as hot beds of activism, home to the nation's unwashed, non-English speakers, religions, and people of color. This stigma or bias against cities shapes discourse on gun violence, such as President Trump's threatening to send the National Guard into a northern city such as Chicago, as well as other disparaging remarks about that city (Bosman, 2019).

Do trauma centers and other institutions dealing with the consequences of gun violence have an institutional duty to address the prevention of gun violence in a planned manner (Scarlet & Rogers, 2018)? How helping professionals answer this question will dictate a provider's marching orders and ability to join forces because no one profession can adequately address urban gun violence; a national issue or epidemic is all our responsibility (Sadat & George, 2019).

As social workers, we have an important role to play in addressing gun violence, and we bring unique perspectives and skill sets, as do other professions, which allow us to carry out roles with particular relevance for addressing this form of violence, increasing our influence in working with other professions. For those who practice in urban communities, it is very easy to answer this question. Those who focus our research and scholarship also have no difficulty in answering the question of why social work, for example, has an instrumental role to play in this area. Barksky (2019) discussed how social work can approach gun violence:

> People who commit gun violence do so within a social context. We can help others understand the role that families, teachers, communities, and social policy play in either raising or lowering the risks of a certain person committing gun violence. . . . We can also contribute to the use of social workers and allied mental health professionals to develop evidence-based strategies to identify people at risk and to implement strategies to reduce the risks of suicide, homicide, and accidental death.

Social work, for example, must collaborate with others sharing our values and commitments, as with public health, with implications for research and interventions (Bulger et al., 2019; Hardiman, Jones, & Cestone, 2019; Neville, Goodall, Gavine, Williams, & Donnelly, 2015). Collaborations across professions on guns are the latest new frontier for the profession.

This call to action also involved the academic community. *Health & Social Work*, for example, and the journals of other helping professions, has devoted a forthcoming special issue to gun violence, which it is hoped will lead to other social work journals devoting issues to various aspects of this problem:

> This special issue is intended to spark action among social work practitioners and researchers to address gun violence across the micro, mezzo, and macro systems. We welcome manuscripts that attend to topics such as the role of guns in intimate partner violence, firearms in community violence, unintentional death, efforts to increase social worker knowledge about gun violence and safety, programs to identify at-risk kids in schools, firearm suicide prevention, and effective responses to gun violence incidents.

The call for papers is broad and expands the scope of gun violence.

There is a paucity of data on preventing urban gun violence (Vlahov, 2018). Funding spent on gun violence research is under 1% of that spent on liver disease research, even though the disease is responsible for a relatively small number of deaths in this country (Joint Economic Committee Democrats, 2017). Ending the moratorium on gun research funded by the Centers for Disease Control and Prevention (CDC) (Jaffe, 2018; Kellermann & Rivara, 2013) is not considered enough; there is a call for having this governmental agency set a budgetary agenda (He & Sakran, 2019). Although the CDC has not played a major role in advancing gun-related research, the National Institutes of Health has (Rubin, 2016b), and there is a renewed and more vociferous call for increased research (Rosenberg, 2019).

Helping professionals understand that there are many causes of gun violence, necessitating multifaceted intervention strategies. A consensus exists that any comprehensive understanding of gun markets cannot be separated from drug markets, for instance. Today's urban gun violence is not a recent phenomenon and is best understood from a historical perspective that elucidates the challenge we face in addressing its presence. Gun violence cannot be understood without this context or foundation from which to examine it; the future, in turn, is tied to the present and the past. These time periods, in essence, are interconnected. The interrelationship between gun violence and drugs, such as crack cocaine in the 1980s and 1990s, sets a foundation for today's gun violence, even though considerable time has passed since that era.

Gun violence does not limit itself to innocent victims that happen to be at the wrong place and time; it is also part of life for those who are not law-abiding residents (Jacobs, 2017). They also can become victims with all of the same consequences found in their innocent counterparts. Are they any less worthy of our indignation because they were not law abiding? The answer to this question raises profound ethical issues for how we think of urban gun violence.

Gun possession increases the odds of becoming a victim. Not surprisingly, owning a gun increases the possibilities that one can commit suicide using it as the primary weapon of choice. Again, it is not a stretch that it increases gun-related accidents in the home (Stroebe, 2016). The tendency to embrace gun-carrying laws has also been found to be positively associated with a corresponding increase (13% to 15%) in violent crime a decade after a state adopts them, with Pennsylvania increasing by over 24% in 10 years, and an almost 17% increase occurred in Texas (Vergano, 2019).

Screening for youth risk for violence as well as protective factors has taken on greater saliency because of their precarious status (Juarez, 2019, p. 127): "Understanding these risk and protective factors may help primary care providers identify various opportunities to incorporate screening questions to identify youths at risk for youth violence perpetration and to identify community resources for referring youths who possess these trait."

Restrictions on gun access by individuals assessed at high risk for future acts of violence have shown promise in reducing gun violence (Zeoli & Webster, 2019). While cities are the focus of gun violence, they are often blocked by state laws from attempting to curb gun access, such as Dayton, Ohio (Davey & Hassan, 2019), calling attention to national and state efforts to curb it. An extensive review of the state of science on primary prevention of gun injuries among youth with access to firearms in storage, concluded that few evidenced-based programs exist addressing schools, healthcare settings, and community settings to prevent (Ngo et al., 2019). The subject for promoting safe firearm storage in urban neighborhoods has been advanced, as in Chicago, as a means of reducing accidental child injuries and deaths (Haser, Yousuf, Turnock, & Sheehan, 2020). Social workers also have initiated gun safety programs (Jennissen, Evans, Karsjens, & Denning, 2019).

Suicides are a violent form of death, and the leading cause of violent deaths in the country (Hanlon, Barber, Azrael, & Miller, 2019; B. Kuehn, 2018). The gun violence prevention field is cognizant that gun availability makes suicide attempts more likely to occur, as well as assaults more likely to become homicides (Cukier & Eagen, 2018). The likelihood of dying (suicide, accident, murder) due to a gunshot is increased if the victim also is in possession of a gun (Mathews, 2018).

States with restrictive gun access also have a reduced likelihood of lower gun carrying among White, non-Latinx youth, but this is not the case among youth of color (African American/Latinx), which raises profound questions about strategies that are intended when attempting to reduce this phenomenon among urban youth of color (Xuan & Hemenway, 2015). States with restrictive gun access laws and have reduced fatalities have not had reduced gun fatalities among African Americans/Blacks in nearby states with less restrictive laws (Olson et al., 2019). The movement of guns from less to more restrictive states has been labeled as "gun migration" (Coates & Pearson-Merkowitzz, 2017).

Gun availability is a major piece of the gun violence challenge, but with many other pieces also, some self-evident and others less so, with local circumstances wielding great influence in dictating how guns wind up in violent crime. Fatal police shootings, for example, account for 1,000 deaths in the country on an annual basis, with firearm availability considered a key factor in this high rate (Hemenway, Azrael, Conner, & Miller, 2019) and a form of state-sanctioned violence (Delgado, 2020a). Reduction in the costs of "entry-level" guns increased the supply in the 1980s and 1990s and has been attributed to the increase in gun violence during this period (Bartley & Williams, 2015).

Although mass shootings, such as those occurring in schools, have taken central stage in garnering popular attention on guns, these are few but generate considerable national and international attention, as in the 2019 mass shootings in El Paso, Texas, and Dayton, Ohio, and noted by Wong (2019): "Gun violence has killed nearly 1,200 children in the United States since the school massacre in Parkland, Florida, one year ago. Few of these deaths became the focus of the nation's attention. Maybe that's because these killings were so mundane, so normal, in the 21st-century United States." Mass shootings account for approximately 0.1% of gun fatalities (2000–2014) but receive disproportionate media and political attention (Siegel & Boine, 2019).

The same weekend that the nation experienced mass murders in El Paso and Dayton, Houston had 12 deaths, 9 of which were murders (Blakinger, 2019). Although mass killings have become prosaic in this nation, the families of victims must contend with the emotional ramifications after the initial publicity and indignation subsides, and the same can be said for their social networks and the key institutions with which they interact. The nation has simply become numb to shootings that are not mass shootings (Fleegler, 2019; Hagan, 2018), although rare when viewed from the shootings occurring on a daily basis (R. M. Cohen, 2015):

> For public policy experts, though, the fact that national discussions around gun violence seem to reawaken only after mass shootings—not counting those in urban cities like Baltimore, Philadelphia, and Chicago, of course—is incredibly frustrating. Tens of thousands of people die in America every year from gunfire, homicide, and suicide, and mass shootings are responsible for just a fraction of those deaths.

When "ordinary" shootings and fatalities are viewed from a clustered and urban community trauma stance, they should easily attract the attention that mass shootings receive because of their magnitude and frequency (Beard et al., 2019). However, race and social economic class complicate such a stance because gun violence victims are invariably low income and of color, expendable, and therefore not considered tragic (Delgado, 2020a). National indifference to gun violence in these communities translates into a nation willing to tolerate this form of gun violence.

Many people in this country know someone who was a victim of gun violence, but that personal level of knowledge is higher among people of color (Kalesan, Weinberg, & Galea, 2016). Stories of gun violence have particular saliency within urban communities of color for very good reasons, and that is why gun violence as a social issue has particular relevance in these communities. These narratives often serve as the basis or impetus for creating local efforts to address gun violence in neighborhoods across the country, as in the case of urban self-help organizations. Best practices, not surprisingly, advance the need for the capturing and use of urban youth trauma narratives into treatment of violence-related experiences among this population group (Corrado, 2016).

The multifaceted consequences of gun violence must be cast against the backdrop of violence in general because of how it permeates so many layers in society. Of course, violence can manifest itself in a variety of forms, with various degrees of impact and involving weapons other than guns. However, when it involves guns the consequences are far more severe and long lasting than when using a knife or other weapons (Centers for Disease Control and Prevention, 2016; L. Cohen, Davis, & Realini, 2016; Sheats et al., 2018).

Gun violence, as manifest with murder on an individual scale, excluding suicides and accidents, is far more frequent and damaging from a death numerical standpoint and its impact on the social network of the victims (Justice Policy Center, 2016, p. vi):

Gun violence inflicts a devastating double blow to communities of color. First, shootings shatter families and neighborhoods. In 2014, homicide was the leading cause of death for African American boys and men ages 15 to 34 and the second leading cause of death for Hispanic boys and men ages 15 to 34. Compared to the rate of gun homicides for white boys and men of the same ages, the rate for African Americans was 21 times greater and the rate for Hispanics was nearly four times greater. Too often, however, the justice system response to this violence inflicts a second blow; intrusive policing tactics and overreliance on incarceration destabilize neighborhoods and damage police-community relations.

Social networks generally refer to a set of individuals who may consist of "familial, domestic, and interpersonal relationships and specifically in terms of formally measured social and behavioral ties" (M. Tracy, Braga, & Papachristos, 2016, p. 70).

Police–community relations are best understood within a broader context of polities ("systems of authority" or "of domination") and the state (Roché & Oberwittler, 2018). The police, it bears noting, have been referred as a "legal gang" within urban communities, highlighting how they negotiate community interactions and legally exercise power and authority to maintain public order, bringing to the fore the importance of fairness in how they carry out their roles (Novich & Hunt, 2018; Weaver, Prowse, & Piston, 2019). There is greater sociology attention being paid to identifying and preventing potential violent interactions between police and residents (J. W. Collins, 2019).

In Boston, for example, it is estimated that 1% of its gang members are either perpetrators or victims in 70% of the city's homicides (Field, 2019). Social networks, of course, cover gangs, but they should not be automatically associated with this group. Urban informal street crews or networks, as opposed to gangs that symbolize formal relationships, play influential roles in gun violence. Although Chicago is usually associated with gang-related shootings, New York City also is experiencing a deadly outbreak of such killings, with 32 killings this year, double that of 2018, with many involving crews rather than formalized gangs (Sandoval, 2019).

Microcommunity-specific scales for interventions based on the concentration of crime according to addresses, streets, and neighborhoods, rather than broader geographical perspectives, is complimentary with a social network viewpoint (O'Brien, 2019). "Hotspots" indicate a concept that has introduced a highly geo-concentrated dimension to crime and is often used by the police, but not restricted to them, in deploying law and concentrating enforcement resources (Kochel & Weisburd, 2017; Papachristos & Kirk, 2015; Schnell, Grossman, & Braga, 2019).

This focus does not generally single out social networks that can cross narrow geographical definitions (Abt, 2019c). Research, however, has found that it is possible to alter peer influence and the structure of networks to maximize gun violence reduction efforts (Wood & Papachristos, 2019). Highly focused gun violence interventions that take into account zip codes (Borg, Krouse, McLeod, Shanti, & Donoghue, 2019) can be further enhanced through the use of social network data, allowing for identifying high-risk interactional contexts.

"Public space violence," with the extraordinary distress or trauma associated with these places and acts, has guns playing a prominent role in the vicious cycle of race, inequities, and deaths and injuries of people of color. An emphasis on urban geographical space (street networks) as a strategy broadens the conventional approach focused on social networks to include structural changes that have been found to reduce gun violence, such as taking care of the land (trash removal and maintaining green spaces) (Blais, 2019). For example, in late 2019, Jacksonville, Florida, was on pace to record the largest number of homicides since 2009, with 50% of these occurring in four zip codes (zip 32209 at 23, 32210 at 13, 32208 at 11, 32254 at 10), illustrating how geographic or community centered these killings are (Frazier, 2019). Street networks can be conceptualized as a complementary perspective on social networks, adding a dimension to this discourse, as in the case of a Newark, New Jersey, study of liquor stores, grocery stores, bus stops, and residential foreclosures as shooting attractors, adding further credence to a social ecological view of gun violence (Xu & Griffiths, 2017).

A word of caution is in order. The association between low-income urban housing and gun violence is one that is quite strong in the average person's mind, which has more to do with stereotypes than reality. This form of housing must not be automatically associated with crime because there may well be variability across this system within a city (Tillyer & Walter, 2019), or labeling a low-income housing development as a hotspot would be inaccurate.

Youth of color witnessing gun shootings also, cannot be ignored in capturing the broad impact of this act the moment it occurred, as well future developments. A focus on victims must be expanded to include witnesses and not just those showing physical injuries. In addition, how victims of gun violence who require medical attention are handled by the police and emergency personnel also adds to the discourse on the consequences of gun violence, and when handled in a manner that is experienced as racist, it adds to the trauma and further alienates victims and their families from the police (Jacoby, Richmond, Holena, & Kaufman, 2018).

Violence intentionality is often highly congruent with group or social network norms (Neville et al., 2015). M. Tracy et al. (2016, p. 84) summarized an extensive literature review of social networks and gun violence that showed the importance of these networks in fostering gun violence and why interventions must take them into account: "The results of our systematic review demonstrate that one's risk of violence, including victimization and perpetration of gun or other weapon violence, is increased through close connection with someone who has either perpetrated or been a victim of violence, with transmission demonstrated across family ties, intimate partner relationships, peer networks, and co-offending networks." Interventions targeting gang violence are increasingly using a social network approach and have benefited from technological advances (Sierra-Arévalo & Papachristos, 2017).

A social network lens is supported by social learning theory (social norms providing information and skill sets, shaping attitudes, and providing material/logistical support), peer influences and socialization influencing behavior, and victim–perpetrator association with others with similar experiences (Pineo, Zimmermann, & Davies, 2019). The possibility of a victim turning around and becoming a perpetrator is influenced by their relationship to the victim, family, and ith peers, with a gang member being the most influential in this transformation (Zimmerman, Farrell, & Posick, 2017). Traumatic loss due to violence (direct and exposed), as well as having witnessed or been threatened with abuse, is particularly heightened when being a member of a gang, presenting an opportunity to further engage in violence or shift focus and seek a more constructive path (Dierkhising, Sánchez, & Gutierrez, 2019).

Engaging in bullying as a perpetrator, victim, or both is associated with negative outcomes, with a small subset of studies finding bullying leading to gang involvement (Shelley & Peterson, 2019). Although social network analysis has shown promise in increasing our understanding of gun violence, the promise of this approach also brings limitations, particularly the nature and strengths of these ties (Faust & Tita, 2019).

Violent victimization's impact is associated with a decrease in youth friendship networks, and this is magnified among females, occurring at a time when there is an increased need from this network to help socially navigate hostile environments (L. N. Wallace & Ménard, 2017). Tapping an organization or network with similar positive experiences takes on added meaning in the lives of these youth and increases the likelihood of living a life free of gun violence.

When gun-related deaths are due to police shootings, particularly where the victims are of color and unarmed, and the officers are White, non-Latinx, it further introduces a different dimension to the reactions of family and community and is indicative of a major problem beyond gun availability and violence, which is national in scope and often sparking community outrage. If we view police killings of unarmed people of color as a form of a racial control mechanism, gun carrying by these individuals for self-protection (self-help) takes on a highly politicized and rational meaning (Cazenave, 2018). The paucity of data on police-inflicted injuries limits our comprehension of police–community relationships (E. J. Evans & Thompson, 2019).

Distrust of the police and feeling unsafe are major factors in gun-carrying motivations. Owning a gun is perceived as a necessity, as a means of self-protection, as in the case of Chicago (Nettles, 2019):

Jaron Jones, 29, was shot in the leg in 2018. The injury required multiple blood transfusions, and it took him 10 months to recover. Today, Jones sees living in Chicago without a gun as a way of tempting fate. He's convinced that not having one would make him more likely to be shot—again. "It's dangerous every day walking in Chicago. . . . You can have no affiliation with nobody and you can die innocently, so be prepared." He added that if being prepared "means carrying a gun— Hey, it means that."

Even when communities file complaints with the police (Chicago), they generally go without a formal response for 74%; when responding, stylized narratives were the norm, or what has been referred to as "perfunctory policing," resisting significant changes in behaviors, or what we would consider inactions (Cheng, 2020). Lack of trust in the police compounds implementation of any coordinated local strategy addressing gun violence (Bieler, Kijakazi, & Vigne, 2016):

We learned that gun violence is a multifaceted challenge that demands a holistic set of solutions. In communities of color, gun violence is interconnected with issues of policing and prosecution, disinvestment, and marginalization of community voices. Limiting access to deadly weapons must be part of the solution, but it's not the only part. Improving police-community relations and enhancing law enforcement accountability, investing in community-based supports, and creating opportunities for the community to engage in violence prevention are critical in a comprehensive approach to reducing gun violence in communities of color. (p. vi)

Several major national models have police playing key elements in these strategies, but success is contingent on the trust that they enjoy within communities, necessitating taking local circumstances into account in developing these strategies.

Urban people of color must contend with gun violence, as well as with the police who are entrusted to keep them safe, placing families in the middle of what has been considered war zones (Currie, 2017, p. 24): "But those two kinds of violence—the unjustified killings of black Americans by police and the tragic killings of black Americans mostly by each other—are two sides of the same coin. Both reflect the same underlying reality." Nevertheless, police will be expected to be a part of any comprehensive solution to local gun violence (D. R. Armstead, 2019; Prowse, Weaver, & Meares, 2019; Rivers, 2018). Increasing police accountability is an essential element in any systematic effort at establishing much needed trust levels (Boyles, 2019; Harris, 2020; Morton, 2018; Nolan, 2019).

The increased recognition of gun violence in urban community life, which can be part of countless family histories, with some communities standing out because of the excessive toll it takes, can also involve multiple family members. This violence has prompted a call for innovative approaches to this social and public health issue because of its consequences on the health and well-being of victims and their communities (Dzau & Leshner, 2018; Rajan, Branas, Hargarten, & Allegrante, 2018; van Dijk et al., 2019; Wamser-Nanney, Nanney, Conrad, & Constans, 2019). When focusing on domestic gun violence, African Americans/Blacks are disproportionately killed or injured in this country, making this community a prime focus for gun violence interventions (Violence Policy Center, 2016), while raising social justice issues that help us understand the interrelationship between this violence and other forms of violence in their lives.

These small social networks are responsible for a high percentage of gun and other forms of violence, which means that community-centered research be undertaken to pinpoint how local circumstances dictate the nature and composition of these networks. Approximately half of all criminal complaints and gun violence has been concentrated in 5% of a city's streets or blocks, calling for emphasis on social networks within a concentrated geographical areas (Lurie, 2019). Chicago's gun violence can be traced to a small social network that consists of 6% of that city's population, yet is responsible for 70% of nonfatal gun victims (Lurie, 2019).

Communities, particularly parents, relatives, and social networks of those killed have roles in preventing future gun deaths or helping heal when individuals survive and must be highlighted to inspire other communities facing similar challenges. Stories of victims and their families are powerful and play an influential role in this movement against gun violence, as with other movements (Polletta, 2016, p. 43): "Activists, like prophets, politicians, and advertising executives, have long recognized the power of a good story to move people to action. The tale of a chosen people's wanderings that end in the promised land becomes a clarion call to revolution." Capturing narratives and having them serve as motivators for action is a skill well familiar to the helping professions.

URBAN GUN VIOLENCE

The United States is the gun violence world capital for a nation not at war, and this should not surprise readers or anyone on the street, let alone professionals. It is estimated that in the United States, there are approximately 393 million guns in private hands, or 46% of the world's gun stock (857 million civilian firearms), yet we represent 4% of the population (Ingraham, 2018). That statistic is overwhelming and indicative of the enormity of the goal this nation faces in reducing gun ownership and corresponding violence. The majority of gun owners, not unexpectedly, are men (Cassino & Besen-Cassino, 2020).

The topic of violence is one that urban practitioners are well versed with based on how it permeates life throughout this country. Guns also permeate this society. Bringing these two subjects together and grounding them within a place such as cities, shapes the contours of practice in profound ways. Bringing together violence, youth/young adults, and guns, shapes how practice transpires, with overlaps and significant differences between these two geographical places.

Gun violence, regardless of location and victims, is a dimension of society that is endemic to the American way of life, which we often take for granted as just a price we pay for living in this country. Its manifestation among a small percentage of urban youth and their social networks takes on immense significance for social work and other helping professions and those very isolated communities from the broader society.

There are certain geographical places (cities) that symbolize this level of gun violence for the nation, with Chicago (Fraser, 2018) serving as a social and politically convenient poster child of this symbol of violence. There is a propensity to localize gun violence, but it is a national problem, with no section of the country exempt from its consequences, although there are some areas that bear the brunt. We must focus locally without losing sight of the national implications.

There are approximately 38,000 (more than 100 per day) violence-related deaths annually occurring in this country, of which 13,000 are homicides and 25,000 are suicides by guns, with an additional almost 85,000 suffering injuries each year (over 230 per day), illustrating the extent of this national problem (Team Trace, 2018). For every death to gunshots, there are six who are wounded (Fairchild, 2016), with a call for greater reliability on injury-related data (Hink et al., 2019). Injuries are discussed again in the next chapter. The need to uplift the heterogeneity of gun violence within certain subgroups/networks and local circumstances cannot be lost in crafting community intervention strategies (Gill, 2016). Gun violence, as readers can no doubt surmise, is a major and complex social problem that necessitates a variety of approaches.

SOURCE OF URBAN GUNS (LEGAL AND ILLEGAL)

Determining how guns enter the community may seem a legal matter best left to local and federal law enforcement. We must understand how guns enter urban communities in order to successfully address gun violence. The answer to the question of how and where guns used in urban violence come from, including ammunition, not surprisingly, has many responses, requiring localities to provide answers in order to individualize intervention approaches and avoid generalized responses that will not succeed (M. E. Collins, Parker, Scott, & Wellford, 2017). Much myth and confusion exist on legal and illegal gun ownership (Legault, Hendrix, & Lizotte, 2019), complicating our understanding in developing intervention strategies, urban focused and otherwise.

There are various terms that elucidate the source of guns, legal and illegal. One popular term is the "iron pipeline," which refers to the routes taken by gun smugglers, primarily from 10 southern states (legally purchased and stolen), which wind up in the nation's cities. Thinking about this pipeline as capillaries, based on new research, illustrates local with social networks influencing the nature and extent of gun transactions (Chesnut et al., 2017).

The concept of "time to crime," is another example that captures the source and travels of a gun from the time of legal purchase, which is the primary source of eventual illegal guns, to its use in a crime, with our knowledge based on the final stage (the elapsed period from the final transaction that places the gun in the hands of the perpetrator) necessitating further research in crafting interventions (P. J. Cook, Pollack, & White, 2019).

The source of guns used in crime and violence also bears attention in this chapter and book, requiring a distinct and highly focused approach that is urban, gender, and age specific to be successful. It does not take away from the argument concerning gun control in general because guns are manufactured by a multibillion-dollar industry and supported by banks and credit card companies since it is rare to purchase a gun and ammunition with cash, but the guns take a very different path when involved in urban gun violence, although still a part of this industry, whether obtained legally or most likely illegally.

Further, a states' rights approach to gun control translates into states with tough gun laws contending with nearby states with lax gun laws, as illustrated in California's 2019 Gilroy Garlic Festival murders. California is a state with one of the nation's strongest gun laws, with the shooter obtaining an assault rifle in nearby Nevada, a state with lax gun control (Olson et al, 2019; Oppel & Arango, 2019). Similar conclusions can be made about the Indiana–Chicago pipeline. Examining the long-term trends in the sources of Boston guns used in crime found they were obtained from legal sources in the South and the bordering states of Maine and New Hampshire, states with lax gun laws (Braga, 2017). States with stricter gun control laws also have fewer children dying as the result of gunshots (Goyal et al., 2019) and also fewer in other age groups (Jehan et al., 2018).

W. N. Evans, Garthwaite, and Moore (2018) addressed the historical antecedents to today's gun violence and how it has exacerbated the gap in life expectancies between African American/Black and White, non-Latinx males:

> Access to guns by young black males explains their elevated murder rates today compared to older cohorts. The long run effects of this increase in violence are large. We attribute nearly eight percent of the murders in 2000 to the long-run effects of the emergence of crack markets. Elevated murder rates for younger black males continue through to today and can explain approximately one tenth of the gap in life expectancy between black and white males.

It is estimated that there are about 250,000 to 500,000 gun theft incidents per year, with about 380,000 guns stolen, with the southern region of the country responsible for 37% of US households, 43% of gun owners, and most importantly, 66% of all gun thefts in the nation (Driskoll, 2018; Hemenway, Azrael, & Miller, 2017). Stolen guns have found their way to the northern states and their cities, with approximately 30% of stolen guns eventually being used in the perpetration of a crime.

A study of Chicago gun crimes concluded that stolen guns could account for a high percentage of those used, but there may be other forces operating in gun availability (E. Cook, 2018b):

The current theft rate is sufficient to provide the weapons for every violent gun crime committed each year. Yet a quite different possibility is that guns, once they are stolen, are not necessarily acquired by violent offenders, but rather enter the stream of stolen merchandise of all kinds, including everything from jewelry to cell phones. It may well be that criminals are overrepresented among the buyers of all kinds of stolen merchandise, but there is no reason to think that they constitute the majority of buyers, or that many of them are involved in serious violence. So what about buyers of stolen guns?

Another Chicago study of one high-violence neighborhood found that obtaining fresh produce is more difficult than obtaining a gun, with 69% of young adults in one neighborhood indicating they could secure one within hours, with 86% obtaining them from street dealers, 78% from friends and family, and 76% stealing them (Robertson, 2018). That city's underground gun market (Ludwig, 2019) found that ammunition was also primarily obtained from street sources, although 15% was obtained by having someone else purchase it from legal businesses (Ludwig, 2019). One study found that interstate movement of guns was closely tied to migration of individuals carrying guns, with the two closely tied together (Kleck, 2018).

When guns are an integral part in urban youth masculinity, it signifies a depth to violence that extends beyond conventional views of violence prevention, highlighting how ease of pathways to gun access is integral to identity formation. Guns can even be obtained as gifts from peers or adults and viewed as a rite of passage, transitioning youth into adulthood (Marano, 2015). Guns also can be obtained at home (Kagawa et al., 2019). When guns are obtained in the home, it signifies a cultural grounding that necessitates a family-focused conceptualization of this violence, adding a new layer to intervention strategies, which may typically focus on age groups and communities, to include family-focused strategies.

Gun availability is a core violence factor and its use to resolve urban conflicts, which can turn deadly (Allchin, Chaplin, & Horwitz, 2018; Kleck, 2017a, 2017b; Lu & Temple, 2020). It has been established that most guns involved in crime were obtained from private hands, but we cannot ignore the potential of purchase from licensed dealers (P. J. Cook, 2018a), necessitating a comprehensive approach to cover major categories of gun availability.

We can get around restrictions (loopholes) by buying a gun through online private sellers and buyers (Franks, 2019; Oppel & Hassan, 2019), including having intimate partners buying a gun. These are business transactions unlike any other. We must have a broad concept of gun accessibility to appreciate the challenge in preventing gun violence (Kessler, 2015):

> "If you want a gun in this part of the city, you can usually get one, despite California's strong gun laws. As in years past," says George Tita, a criminology professor at UC Irvine who's conducted research on black-market firearms sales for the RAND Corporation, "The illegal gun markets remain local. People aren't going out of state to buy them surreptitiously. In fact, they're not even going to gun shows and pawn shops. A nontrivial number of guns," Tita says, come from another family member, "A gift, so to speak."

If legal gun ownership is closely tied to domestic homicides (women bearing the onus) and suicides, then where are the guns used on city street violence coming from (Mervosh, 2019)? How many urban families living in highly dangerous and low-resourced communities are willing to use funds to go to a gun store to legally buy and register a gun? Legally obtained guns and ammunition are expensive (Willis, 2018):

> Conversations about gun policy rarely consider how the sticker price of hardware might affect ownership patterns. But the nonpartisan

Pew Research Center has found that NRA membership rates are highest among gun owners who report household incomes of greater than $100,000. A 2014 analysis published by NORC, a nonpartisan research organization affiliated with the University of Chicago, found that 44 percent of respondents with incomes above $90,000 had a gun in the home. For those making between $25,000 and $49,999, the rate fell to 32.1 percent. Below $25,000, it was only 18.2 percent.

Purchasing a gun and ammunition is a luxury, with an estimated cost of $300–$400, with registering a gun adding hundreds of dollars, such as in New York City, where this fee is $340, not including fingerprinting (Willis, 2018).

The use of legally purchased guns in urban and low-resourced communities is not the issue that it is in more highly resourced and White, non-Latinx communities. Individuals considered at a high risk of gun violence victimization are usually prohibited from owning a gun by federal law. Further, those most likely to become gun violence fatalities have criminal justice histories and an extensive number of police arrests (Roberto, Braga, & Papachristos, 2018).

Another aspect of gun access is starting to emerge and take on significance: the availability of "ghost guns" (Lotan, 2019). Ghost guns (unserialized weapons) are considered to have been manufactured outside of the traditional sources (parts from different countries), are homemade and undetectable (built without the government's knowledge), and thereby untraceable, and largely attributable to hobbyists and backyard tinkerers. Further, some guns can be modified to be fully automatic.

In California, ghost guns represent 30% of all guns acquired by the Bureau of Alcohol, Tobacco, and Firearms and are unable to be traced in criminal investigations. Ghost guns are but the latest evolution in gun availability and are frequently acquired with the intention to commit a crime. The cost of these guns is considerably higher than legally purchased weapons and can range from $1,500 to $2,000, compared to a legally store-purchased AR-15 for approximately $500 (Stephens, 2019).

Urban gangs can consist of multigenerations, showing what seems as an intractability of this problem. Gangs play an instrumental role in illegal gun availability, with the costs of illegal guns being inflated by them and drug dealer purchases, further shaping the market for guns (Hureau & Braga, 2018). Those carrying guns who are not gang affiliated or in the illicit drug business must either pay more for carrying one or be in a position to borrow a gun when deemed necessary.

An underground gun-lending system varies between communities and is worthy of greater attention (Cunningham, 2016). It is almost the equivalent of a lending library, but instead of books, one can get a loaded gun, without identification no less, and takes economic motive over gun access. The emergence of what are referred to as "community guns," which can be rented for a price, usually $100, brings an added dimension to gun access (Sandoval, 2019).

Gangs play a significant role in Chicago's gun violence (Aspholm, 2020). A Chicago study of gun sources by those considered dangerous found that it is rare when they are purchased from a gun store or stolen, with social networks being a prime source and gangs assuming a prominent role within this network, avoiding transactions with strangers for fear of undercover agents or "snitches" (P. J. Cook, Parker, & Pollack, 2015). However, the propensity to label the vast majority of gun injuries and fatalities as "gang related" or "gang involved," as in Chicago, simplifies gun violence in a manner that precludes finding effective solutions to this problem (Doering, 2020).

This book's focus is on intentional violence, how communities address it, and the factors that enhance our abilities in understanding and helping the communities achieve desired outcomes. We must have an understanding of the multiple factors associated with gun violence, including how guns enter and move within urban communities and the forces at work to facilitate or hinder access to them. In Chicago, illegal guns have flooded neighborhoods, and it has exacerbated curtailing gun violence (S. Cohen, 2018):

The Auburn Gresham neighborhood is flooded with illegal guns: .40-caliber pistols, .380 semi-automatics, .38-caliber revolvers.

Police recover as many as they can, searching apartments, stopping cars, cornering people on the street. A buy-back in June brought in hundreds of firearms. And in September, the mayor and other dignitaries gathered to mark a milestone: Police in the 6th District had recovered their 1,000th gun this year. It was a triumphant moment, but it also offered a glimpse into the overwhelming task faced by law enforcement—and the wounds inflicted on just one Chicago community—when guns are readily available and violence so common that, one study found, an estimated 1 in 2 young men had at some time carried firearms, almost always illegally. Most did so to stay safe. . . . Chicago police regularly recover more illegal firearms than officials in larger New York and Los Angeles. Last year, the city-wide haul was 7,932 firearms. The 2018 tally exceeds 9,100, and police say it could surpass 10,000 by year's end.

Neighborhoods must contend with the influx of illegal guns because of the laws of the economics of supply and demand, with demand most easily and profitably met through illegal means. This means that it is much more difficult to address gun violence, particularly since illegal gun markets are highly localized (Tita & Barragan, 2018). The presence of Dark Web gun vendors further challenges efforts at stopping illegal gun sales (Copeland, Wallin, & Holt, 2020).

Social factors are associated with gun-carrying behavior. Research has shown a close relationship between male adolescents involved with drugs, interacting with peers who are prone to delinquent acts, engaged in behavior that is aggressive, will also be inclined to carry guns, particularly for African American/Black youth (Docherty, Beardslee, Grimm, & Pardini, 2019). This is addressed in various sections of this book.

MOTIVATION FOR CARRYING AND USING A GUN

We must differentiate between motivation for carrying and using a gun and mindset. The former focuses on obtaining specific details. Obtaining a mindset is far more complex, necessitating gaining historical knowledge on an individual carrying and exercise using one. For our purposes, motivation receives attention in this book.

Understanding shooting motivation takes on great significance in crafting solutions (Kukharskyy & Seiffert, 2017). There are motivational differences for carrying or possessing a gun, for example, a specific threat of assault and diffusing a threat (dangerous world we live in), and depending on the motivation, the threat requires a corresponding intervention focus (Stroebe, Leander, & Kruglanski, 2017). Urban youth gun carrying is positively related to higher levels of psychological distress for those exposed (victim or witness) to violence, with each additional exposure increasing the likelihood of gun carrying (Reid, Richards, Loughran, & Mulvey, 2017). Youth gun carrying (usually driven by fears of becoming a victim, peer pressure, or reputation building), as manifested in schools by students with mental health (depression) and delinquency histories, is influenced by level of school attachment (Watts, Province, & Toohy, 2019).

Emmert, Hall, and Lizotte (2018) provided an excellent summary of adolescent gun-carrying behavior as a basis from which to pursue greater awareness of specific categories. Perceived gun access is strongly related to a higher probability of future gun carrying (Keil, Beardslee, Schubert, Mulvey, & Pardini, 2020). The following typology is illustrative of prevalent gun-carrying motivations and does not address those who seek guns to carry out self-harm. Someone who shots in self-defense is different from someone who is protecting a drug business and carries a gun as part of their responsibilities; someone who shoots seeking revenge is different from someone who wants to build a reputation as being dangerous; someone who shoots because they enjoy hurting people, and is a form of tension relief, is different from a hired killer who has chosen this as a profession.

Urban communities can have these types of shooters and more in their midst. If I carry a gun for self-protection because I am fearful of being hurt, I will benefit from a gun violence strategy that increases my sense of security (S. Cohen, 2018). If I carry a gun to protect my business or territory, as with drugs and gangs, that requires a targeted police enforcement strategy, one that also addresses my belonging to a violent gang enterprise, assuming that I joined as self-protection, since there are multiple reasons for joining them.

Although gun violence motivation is essential in understanding and stopping gun violence, its complexity often defies a simple categorization (Dong & Wiebe, 2018). The categorization presented is meant as a starting point rather than an endpoint. The nuances attached to shooter motivation must be captured and categorized whenever possible, although no two shooters and shootings will ever be the same, requiring a nuanced understanding, such as history of gun carrying and violence within the family and events leading up to acquiring a gun. Yet, we can capture and ground these incidents and place them into broader groupings to shape our institutional and community responses.

CO-VICTIMS OF URBAN VIOLENCE

Violence has the profound power of defining urban communities of color in a manner that cuts across generations (Rich, 2009). For social scientists and helping professionals with extensive urban violence experience, there is an appreciation for the broadening of the category of what constitutes a "victim." A narrow conceptualization of victim may be easier to address. Nevertheless, there is always an implicit understanding that countless others also are victims. Co-victims address a concept that needs far more attention now because for every direct victim of gun violence there are numerous others not shot but also victims, and they often fade into the background as the spotlight focuses on direct victims (Robertson, Bastomski, & Duane, 2018):

> The sudden and violent loss of a loved one is one of the gravest experiences anyone can have. CVR researchers have identified three major challenges co-victims commonly experience: 1. They can experience substantial **psychological harm**. Losing a loved one can be devastating, and when that loss is because of violence, it can lead to

prolonged or complicated grief. 2. In the aftermath of the homicide, co-victims must often **interact with the criminal justice process**, which can be lengthy, cumbersome, and difficult to navigate. Co-victims sometimes look to the conclusion of a criminal trial for a sense of closure, but that doesn't always happen, even once the case is resolved. 3. **Media and society at large** react to homicide cases in ways that are often sensationalized or lead to heightened interest from co-victims' communities. This can force co-victims to deal with increasing attention as they are experiencing grief, leaving loved ones isolated from or stigmatized by their community at a time when they need support the most.

When co-victims are taken into account in a comprehensive picture of urban gun violence, it highlights the reach and importance in addressing these victims quickly and in an affirming manner.

Self-help organizations often represent an oasis in a sea of turmoil and trauma for the families and friends of loved ones whose lives were either lost or dramatically altered due to gun violence. The services provided by these organizations are culturally based and often delivered by individuals who also live in the community and represent the racial backgrounds of the victims they seek to help.

GUN VIOLENCE AND JUSTICE?

Gun violence and justice? This question is not meant to be provocative. Rather, how can we not separate gun violence from justice? Albert Einstein understood this relationship, although making reference to war but equally applicable to urban gun violence: "Peace is not merely the absence of war but the presence of justice." Death by gun is not a natural way of dying, as with cancer and other deadly diseases. Thus, why is it occurring and why are we not stopping or stomping it out? Why don't we see television campaign ads requesting money be sent to a charity devoted to making sure no one person dies because of gunfire?

Gun violence and justice can be two separate but highly interconnected viewpoints. The first involves the experiences residents have with police when a crime has been committed, and the second involves the criminal justice system. Police response to shootings, and not just the apprehension and eventual conviction of those found guilty, is a dimension of community–police relationships that must be addressed in any comprehensive effort at addressing gun violence (Jannetta, 2019, p. 2): "In my career, I've learned that most people don't expect law enforcement to solve every crime, or to catch every perpetrator, or even to bring everyone to the traditional, state defined concept of justice. What I have found is that everyone expects people to care, and the way you show that is through active communication, both in the short and long term."

A government's ability to solve a crime and bring perpetrators to justice is the second viewpoint, and it is seen as a critical function in a society (Reed, Dabney, Tapp, & Ishoy, 2020). What does gun violence have to do with justice? A great deal! When a murder transpires, what is the likelihood of it being solved, and how does race play into this deliberative process? Disparities in bringing the guilty to justice vary according to the race and economic status of the victim and location, and this cannot be dissociated from a fearless mentality of committing a shooting (Tuerkheimer, 2017).

No justice translates into injustice; when this injustice is part of other injustices, communities have no trust in the authorities to ensure that they are protected (Amnesty International, 2018, p. 44):

> Excessive use of force by police, racial profiling and low homicide clearance rates are all factors which contribute to a lack of trust between law enforcement and communities of color. The lack of trust also means that communities may be reluctant to cooperate with law enforcement in solving homicides that have taken place.

Social justice is never an abstract concept; it has very real life implications for life in urban centers.

Murders, often involving guns, are not equally distributed in this country because of how people of color bear an undue burden (Giffords

Law Center to Prevent Gun Violence, 2017, p. 10): "Murder inequality in America is real. . . . It's staggering to consider that black men make up 6% of the US population, yet account for more than half of all gun homicide victims each year. Latino men are also disproportionately impacted. Of America's 13,000 gun-related homicide victims in 2015, over 8,500 were men of color." Murders are also unequal because certain cities, communities, and social networks are subject to increased odds of experiencing gun and other forms of violence.

Bringing perpetrators to justice also is not equally distributed in this country, and disparities engender distrust of the police, complicating a comprehensive and coordinated response involving law enforcement along with community institutions (Justice Policy Center, 2019, p. 1):

> Police play a critical role in reducing community violence, but their legitimacy can be undermined by a lack of community trust, particularly in high crime communities where intervention is needed most. Mistrust of law enforcement is especially acute among young men of color, especially those living in neighborhoods afflicted by crime and disorder associated with gang activity. . . . The absence of trust reduces the public's willingness to report crime, engage with law enforcement on crime control efforts, and abide by the law, since trust is a fundamental component of police legitimacy.

Research showed that the probability of becoming a gunshot victim is greatly increased when one's social network consists of members who also have been shot, and this is particularly the case when the victims are African -American/Latinx (B. Green, Horel, & Papachristos, 2017; Papachristos, Wilderman, & Roberto, 2015; Ulrich, 2019). Murders and injuries tend to be highly concentrated within small networks, increasing the needs and importance of these networks being identified for research and intervention. There is an ongoing debate on the role and influence of retaliatory and nonretaliatory gun shootings, rather the consequences for those subscribing to a contagion stance of this form of violence (Loeffler & Flaxman, 2018).

One has only to focus on the nation's largest cities ($N = 52$) to see that 26,000 murders occurred between 2008 and 2018, which witnessed 18,600, or 71%, of the victims being African American/Black (Lowery, Kelly, & Rich, 2018b). When this statistic is compared with White, non-Latinxs, it also shows a much higher likelihood of resulting arrests (63%). Twenty-five percent of the population was African American but accounted for 68% of the victims. When focusing on Baltimore, Chicago, Detroit, and Philadelphia, cities typically associated with murders and gun violence during the same period, there were over 7,300 murders (39%) not resulting in arrests.

Extrajudicial killings have a long history within communities of color (Sacks & Chow, 2018) and their place in lynchings. Lack of trust and co-operation with the police are key factors in urban communities (Brunson & Wade, 2019):

> Police administrators often hold press conferences after particularly heinous street violence, surrounded by victims' inconsolable loved ones. Routinely, while standing at the podium, city officials will decry the lack of eyewitnesses willing to come forward with valuable information. Although much has been written about bystanders' reticence to cooperate with investigators as a result of reduced police legitimacy, "stop snitching" campaigns, and fear of retaliation, we have little firsthand information from those at considerable risk for becoming victims and perpetrators of urban gun violence.

Reasons for not cooperating invariably center on a lack of trust in the police and in the judicial system, and this mistrust has deep historical roots (Kochel, 2018). Reluctance to cooperate with the police on solving the murder of a relative may be largely due to a family's past experiences with law enforcement and the criminal justice system. Cooperating with investigators and a system that historically has been viewed as oppressive is a major hurdle for families to overcome, particularly since they believe that sharing this information will not result in justice. We must not lose sight of the role police can play in criminal activities, bringing an often-missing dimension to any discussion regarding the lack of trust between urban communities and law enforcement (Stinson, 2020).

Boston, a city not usually associated with murder but more so with institutions of higher learning, led all major cities in the gap between White, non-Latinx and African American/Black arrests (Lowery et al., 2018a): "Since 2007, Boston police have made an arrest in nearly 90% of the homicides with white victims but 42% of the homicides with black victims, who account for the vast majority of the city's killings. Of the 435 homicides with black victims, 254 remain unsolved. Of the 57 homicides with white victims, only six are unsolved."

Clearly, this picture is disturbing and conveys a law enforcement and justice stance as either uncaring or incompetent; neither perspective is optimal in creating a sense of caring and a deterrent against gun use and other acts of violence. Solving urban homicides, particularly when involving African American/Black victims, decreases as the number of open cases each investigator is expected to carry increases, reducing the time devoted to each murder (LoFaso, 2020). Unsolved murders also can result in family and friends seeking revenge because justice is impossible and further compounds the grieving process.

Boston leads all major US cities in the gap between White, non-Latinx and Black murder arrest records, with the majority of victims being Black. Further worth noting, although racial statistics were not reported, there are significant differences between gun murders and nonfatal gun assaults, which are rarely compared, as in the case of Boston (43% for gun murders vs. 19% for nonfatal gun assaults), and is primarily due to sustained investigative efforts within the first 48 hours of a murder (Cook et al., 2019).

Since 2007, Boston, a city steeped in racism, had arrested 90% of perpetrators when the victim was White, non-Latinx, but only 42% when the victim was African American/Black. There were only four cities that had no racial disparities between murders and arrests—Birmingham, Alabama; Durham, North Carolina; Fort Worth, Texas; and Wichita, Kansas. One can wonder if these cities would appear on any reader's list because they simply are not part of those on the national radar on murders. A lack of faith in law enforcement or fear of retaliation disengages victims of color from the broader society. Gun violence normalization translates into gun fears going unreported to the police (Calamur, 2018).

Regarding understanding what causes anger and potential responses from the relatives of gun fatality victims (Milliff, 2019),

> Evidence [Chicago] suggests that cognitive clarity about the identity of the perpetrator, the perpetrator's motive and the nature of the violence as unjust are necessary for an individual to become angry at the perpetrator. . . . Certain contextual conditions—like the political narrative of conflict—might make it easier for victimized individuals to achieve cognitive clarity, become angry, and desire retribution.

Hope of justice prevailing, even if it does not, can weigh in on revenge seeking (Heffernan, 2019, p. 39).

> In turning from theory to practice, it's essential to begin with the most basic of questions concerning social organization: how to resolve grievances about harm. Grievances fester: they originate in resentment and they culminate, at least sometimes, in retaliatory violence. The challenge they pose has to do with the containment of violence—with identifying and adopting procedures that forestall retaliation by persuading parties their grievances will be fairly resolved. Retaliation can be resolved if grieving parties expect that their assailants will be punished. In this way, punishment—even the prospect of punishment—can serve as a mechanism for averting retaliation.

Chicago symbolizes urban gun violence in the national consciousness. It is estimated that only 17% of that city's murders were solved in 2017, which is considered an all-time low, down from 41% in 2000 (Main, 2018). Voisin's book (2019), *America the Beautiful and Violent: Black Youth and Neighborhood Trauma in Chicago,* provides invaluable insights into the historical, social, economic, and political forces shaping how gun and other forms of violence have shaped some neighborhoods struggling with violence, with stories to share with common and unique themes and lessons for those interested in social justice.

Alex Kotlowitz's (2019) *An American Summer: Love and Death in Chicago* also provides an insightful account of that city and how violence gripped one neighborhood, with some meeting untimely deaths and others carrying out perpetrator roles, with countless others as collateral damage, suffering lifelong trauma, including those who cooperated with the police to bring justice for a relative being killed, and they, in turn, were killed as a result. He also raised critical questions about how victims and their families address the present and plan for the future with trauma a vital part of their lives, including the perpetrators.

Understanding local trends and patterns in police clearances of lethal violence takes on significance in cities with high homicide rates and must be part of any comprehensive solution (Regoeczi, 2018). Degree of investment in investigative resources is positively correlated with homicide case clearances, but gang and drug-related cases are the most challenging to solve when compared to other forms of murder (Braga, Turchan, & Barao, 2019).

Gun violence impacts must not be viewed from an individualistic standpoint, which is a tall order in a nation that values individualism. They must take into account the trauma it causes a victim's loved ones, and, for those surviving gunshots, the care and rehabilitation required depending on the type of injury suffered (Patton, Sodhi, Affinati, Lee, & Crandall, 2019) and the role of their families in helping them during this care period. A collectivistic stance highlights how the ripples of gun violence are manifested in neighborhoods. Neighborhoods with high levels of gun violence have heightened climates of fear, disrupting lives from being lived to their fullest extent. Gun victim race also influences whether a crime is reported or there is cooperation with law enforcement, with White, non-Latinxs more willing to report when compared to individuals of color (Hipple, Thompson, Huebner, & Magee, 2019).

Urban youth who perceive high levels of racism and poor relationships with local law enforcement have a higher propensity for gun violence, calling for interventions that increase positive relationships with adults and the police (Beck, Zusevics, & Dorsey, 2019). Reluctance to cooperate with law enforcement leaves victims of color with no legal recourse in obtaining justice, making them and their social network more likely to engage in revenge. However, revenge as a motivator requires an in-depth understanding because of its complexity (Jäggi & Kliewer, 2016).

Feeling unsafe can translate into gun carrying as a means of protection (self, family, and friends), as in the case of Chicago's West and South Sides (Fontaine et al., 2018): "The justification of carrying because of safety concerns is well supported by the fact that young adults who reported having carried a gun were more likely to experience violent victimization than those who reported never having carried a gun. Those shot or shot at in the past 12 months were 300 percent more likely to have ever carried a gun." Being shot or shot at increases the likelihood of gun carrying as a means of self-protection (Robertson, 2018). A high level of belief that they will not be apprehended often accompanies and compounds this need for safety. Adolescents carrying guns are at an increased risk of becoming victims of guns (Watts, 2019).

The probabilities of being a victim of gun violence will likely involve a friend, relative, or an acquaintance as a perpetrator rather than a lone violent "psychopath," highlighting how social networks shape this violence (Abt, 2019b; J. M. Metzl & MacLeish, 2015; Rubin, 2016a; M. Tracy et al., 2016). Gun violence, more specifically within select urban neighborhoods, is further concentrated within small social networks (Everytown for Gun Safety, 2019c): "Gun violence is further concentrated in small social networks. Within these social networks, the spread of violence looks much like the spread of a contagious disease—when an individual is victimized by or exposed to violence, it increases the likelihood that they will be victimized again or resort to gun violence themselves." This concentration exacerbates the consequences, making it easier to understand and address local causes and solutions if these small networks can be effectively identified.

Unfortunately, entire cities, including neighborhoods with low gun violence rates, have their reputations compromised when there is no effort to specify the geographical location with high levels of gun violence

(Mirabile & Ness, 2019): "If some scholars of crime had their way, discussions of murder rates would focus not on cities, but on the few urban neighborhoods battling vastly disparate murder levels: Travel a few city blocks, and rates of violence can fluctuate dramatically." This stance requires a very focused and nuanced understanding of local violence and a highly coordinated approach involving all pertinent parties, including law enforcement, which can prove problematic in areas with histories of distrust with local police.

This calls for a site-specific and nuanced approach on gun violence lends itself to better understanding local forces at work, as well as local-based initiatives involving formal or informal resources, and an opening for service providers to become active parts of these efforts. Although most community intervention research to reduce violence has focused on individuals, the potential of altering environments (e.g., vacant lots, abandoned buildings, and other environmental factors) also is increasingly finding this approach in curtailing violence (Kondo, Andreyeva, South, MacDonald, & Branas, 2018).

There is an increasing consensus that green space is widely associated with positive health outcomes, but our understanding of its impact on urban violence is only recently being paid attention, with much theoretical and empirical analysis to be undertaken to maximize its potential in urban centers (Bogar & Beyer, 2016). An extensive review of the scientific literature found that the presence of urban green spaces reduces violent crime (Shepley, Sachs, Sadatsafavi, Fournier, & Peditto, 2019). The sponsoring of community gardens, for example, brings the healing power of green space to address trauma (Hoffman, 2019), and it does so in a place that is often large enough to accommodate large groups of participants.

Abandoned buildings are ubiquitous in low-resourced urban areas, as are vacant lots, which often symbolize despair and a focus for interventions as a means of reducing gun violence (Jay, Miratrix, Branas, Zimmerman, & Hemenway, 2019). Converting urban vacant land that is blighted into green land or for other purposes has reduced the likelihood of gun violence (Moyer, MacDonald, Ridgeway, & Branas, 2019), calling attention to the interplay of urban blight and this violence (Valasik, Brault, & Martinez,

2019). An urban asset perspective views this as an opportunity rather than a liability in addressing gun violence and a tall order when systems rallied to deal with urban violence only embrace a deficit stance.

MEDIA, VIOLENCE, AND PEOPLE OF COLOR

There are numerous books devoted to illustrating how media wields such an important role in shaping all aspects of society, including public opinions on major social issues. Thus, why not influence public perceptions of guns, violence, and people of color residing in the nation's cities (Sege & Augustyn, 2019)? Ironically, gun violence is not a silent killer and quite public, making it easier for media to galvanize public support (Spinrad, 2017). Although mass killings receive public attention, the vast majority of gun deaths do not fall into this category. Rather, they often occur on a one-on-one basis (Crifasi, 2018), and when involving people of color, they receive different coverage (Frisby, 2017; Koepke, Thomas, & Manning, 2019) and appear as a common daily occurrence, generating less sympathy and resulting policy discussions (Zhang et al., 2019).

Media has the propensity to downplay "ordinary" murders, highlighting sensational ones, and killings that occur in urban America fall into the former (O'Kane, 2017). Media's indifference to Black suffering, although applicable to other people of color, is manifested on a daily basis when covering gun fatalities, exacerbating the trauma experienced by the family and friends of victims, making healing that much more arduous to achieve (Baker-Bell, Stanbrough, & Everett, 2017). These deaths can be cynically called "nothing murders" or "population control" (Leovy, 2015). Neely (2015) argued that the murder of Black women is often ignored by media and considered low priority by law enforcement because these women are devalued according to race, economics, and gender.

Racial bias goes beyond television and print newspaper coverage, manifesting itself in online coverage, emphasizing a moral interpretation, and in the case of police shootings of unarmed victims, minimizing police responsibility and advancing localized and nonsystemic solutions when structural changes across this nation's law enforcement system are warranted (Smith, 2020; Stone & Socia, 2019). General public distancing from these tragedies occurs to minimize these acts.

Psychological distancing is a key factor in numbing the nation to day-to-day gun violence and a major obstacle in mobilizing the nation to take urban gun violence seriously. This numbing is also occurring with mass killings (Fleegler, 2019). A *Los Angeles Times* editorial (Williams, 2019) addressed this distancing:

> Psychological distance from these shootings does not lessen our responsibility to act. All concerned residents can and should prioritize the safety of their neighbors by fighting against misrepresentations of gun violence victims and perpetrators—including in the media—and learning more about the social injustices and traumas at the root of our cycles of violence. . . . One's own sense of safety *should never lead to complacency* when it comes to shootings in our American cities.

Gun violence media attention captures the alarm and anguish felt in communities and the political ramifications it has caused across the political spectrum, such as the case with gun control and police brutality. Nevertheless, it also faces the challenge of how best to address the causes and consequences of this coverage and to sustain it over an extended period of time in a search for solutions that take into account local needs without losing a national perspective and instilling hope. Gun violence cannot be examined without attention to how the media addresses these acts and to what extent it is racially biased (Y. T. Mitchell & Bromfield, 2019), ultimately negatively influencing social policies and interventions, such as an emphasis on tough law and order as the solution. The Center for American Progress (2018) undertook an analysis relevant to this book:

> Black Americans, and black men in particular, are overrepresented as perpetrators of crime in US news media. This is especially true

when looking at the incidence of violent crime. For example, one study of late-night news outlets in New York City in 2014 found that the media reported on murder, theft, and assault cases in which black people were suspects at a rate that far outpaced their actual arrest rates for these crimes. The news media also vilifies black people by presenting black crime suspects as more threatening than their white counterparts. It does this in several ways, such as by showing the mug shots of black suspects more frequently than those of white suspects; depicting black suspects in police custody more often; and paying greater attention to cases where the victim is a stranger.

A comprehensive picture of gun violence requires attention to media and how victims and perpetrators are portrayed and how they are responded to by governmental officials and care providers. Further, media should spotlights successes to counter prevailing attitudes that there is nothing than can be done to prevent gun violence.

Success stories must be covered and a concerted effort made to highlight lessons learned, providing hope for the public (Reichel, 2018). Obtaining sound bites does little to inspire hope and encourage engagement in solution seeking. Providing a detailed coverage of a victim's life, including integrating perspectives of loved ones and how they have been traumatized by the killings, would be a public favor and bring integrity to the stories.

Media attention rarely focuses on solutions because they do not fit nicely into a 2- or 3-minute segment. Social workers and other practitioners understand the complexity of seeking and maintaining active family and community cooperation to prevent gun violence through multifaceted participatory interventions (Delgado, 2019, 2020b; Lanyl, Gonzalez, & Wilson, 2018; Logan-Greene, Sperlich, & Finucane, 2018). Latinxs also face similar struggles as African Americans/Blacks in obtaining fair representation in the media, further casting them to a marginalized and compromised racialized status (Center for American Progress, 2018):

Latinos are similarly maligned in the news media. A study found that 66 percent of the time, news coverage between 1995 and

2004 showed Latinos in the context of either crime or immigration rather than in other contexts. More recent analysis confirms these findings. This treatment of Latinos as criminals and outsiders is especially concerning given that Latinos are otherwise rarely represented in the news media. A recent study found that between 2008 and 2014, stories focused on Latinos and issues concerning Latino communities composed just 0.78 percent of coverage on national evening network news. To put this in perspective, CBS, NBC, ABC, and CNN dedicated an average of just 87 seconds of coverage on Latinos per day—combined—from 2008 to 2014. In the same way that it over represents black people in its coverage of crime, the news media's overrepresentation of Latinos as lawbreakers and outsiders is troubling considering the overall lack of coverage of Latinos.

Prominently introducing race into national narratives on urban gun violence has compromised the lives of youth and adults in obtaining a fair justice outcome for them as victims and those accused of these crimes.

The argument has been made that it is only when both victim and perpetrator are White, non-Latinx, and middle class will there be extensive media coverage (R. M. Cohen, 2015): "This disparity in coverage showcases how a few high-profile shootings can dominate the discourse around gun deaths in harmful ways, as the public focuses on extreme events rather than the everyday tragedy of firearm-related suicides, homicides, and accidents." Everyday gun violence is far more consequential from a national perspective when compared to the number of fatalities and injuries of mass shootings.

When media coverage is racially biased, acts of violence, when followed with a lack of justice, only compound the trauma and healing that is necessary when media provides biased coverage, adding insult to injury for the families and loved ones killed and their respective communities. This bias means that justice is beyond the reach of these communities, calling for their needs being met internally, as in the case of gun carrying for self-protection.

STREET WORKERS AND GUN VIOLENCE

Street worker outreach has been proposed to curb gun violence, introducing a model that brings together institutional and community spheres (Hardina, 2012; Maguire, Telep, & Abt, 2018). A review of interventions (1996–2013) on urban youth gun violence found two distinctive themes: (a) use of outreach street workers and (b) targeting and supporting individuals with high probabilities of engaging in violent acts (Petrosino et al., 2015).

Outreach workers have been effective bridging the gap between formal and informal systems of care (Delgado, 2020a; Gay & Cosey, 2019). They bring high levels of energy and creativity, key in responding to local circumstances and often want to give back to their communities, increasing their community legitimacy among residents (Cosey Gay, 2019, p. 140): "Outreach workers initially can connect because they possess respected cultural capital. That is, outreach workers understand the worldview of high-risk men because they have 'lived the life they lived.'" These workers must be supported because of the trauma that they encounter in outreaching victims (Free & Macdonald, 2019). Self-help organizations invariably involve outreach workers who live in the community, and they also have faced the consequences of gun violence in their lives.

Urban families must assume a more protective role in protecting their children from gun violence (Culyba, Ginsburg, et al., 2019; Culyba, Miller, Albert, & Abebe, 2019), setting the stage for joining a modern-day ("new") self-help movement, which is international in scope (Matzat & Estorff, 2018). The level of parental monitoring in families of color is a protective factor, as with African American (Giovanelli, Hayakawa, Englund, & Reynolds, 2018; Hong, Ryou, Wei, Allen-Meares, & Espelage, 2019) and Latinx families (Rios, Friedlander, Cardona, Flores, & Shetgiri, 2019), and is associated with violent peers and violence, with low involvement increasing the likelihood of negative associations. Parental disengagement in male upbringing has influenced youth engagement in behavior that is more likely to engage in gun carrying (Beardslee, Docherty, Yang, & Pardini, 2019). Helping families with monitoring strategies is a role that self-help organizations can fulfill in minimizing the reach of gun violence.

Who assumes the role of helping these families and youth? More specifically, what are the expressive and instrumental benefits that they derive from participation? How can these benefits be enhanced? How can we support them? These and other questions must be answered. Further, the answers must mobilize institutional resources to help ensure these organizations thrive and continue to respond to local needs. A key question is how to bring these resources to bear without severely compromising the mission and unique sociocultural character of self-help organizations.

The answer to this question necessitates delicate balancing between trusting and respecting local cultural customs and professional responsibility. It also necessitates that we enlist a community's voice in crafting interventions of any kind, but more so in the case of gun violence; this not only is empowering but also makes sense from a political standpoint in order to obtain valuable buy-in (Forrest, Wallace-Pascoe, Webb, & Goldstein, 2017). Local ownership of interventions helps ensure that residents shape priorities and methods. Professionals become valuable partners, but we are not the experts of their lives—they are the experts of their own lives and what it means to live with gun violence.

Self-help organizations have filled a critical vacuum of help provision and social action across the country, and more so in its urban communities. Use of "violence management strategies" by youth of color is common and indicative of the world that they must socially navigate to avoid physical/emotional injuries or even death (Dill & Ozer, 2016). These skills must be included in educational systems and be part of health-enhancement courses if schools are to be relevant in the lives of urban youth. Schools are called on to offer trauma-informed services (Dutil, 2019). School, after all, is considered the first environment that purposely influences a student's abilities to socially negotiate the outside world (Sims, 2018). Community efforts to fill this vacuum is discussed further in this chapter.

Home is where most of us learned how to love; it is also where we started to learn how to socially navigate our way through the world, starting in our immediate neighborhood. Negotiating and navigating neighborhoods involves a litany of visible and invisible obstacles, and corresponding skill sets, particularly when are attempting to reconcile aspirational goals with the operative realities of urban life that act as barriers (Brooms, 2015). M. Armstrong and Carlson (2019) developed the concept of "anticipatory trauma" applied to factors surrounding gun violence, which include parents' conversations with their children on their heightened fear of gun violence.

If the neighborhood is so violent, why not leave and get the children out? Protecting youth of color from violence can take many different manifestations depending on viable options (D. Voisin, Berringer, Takahashi, Burr, & Kuhnen, 2016): (a) "sheltering" (entails keeping children off the streets); (b) "chauffeuring" (transporting or accompanying children to and from places); (c) "removal" (enrolling children in schools outside of the neighborhood); and (d) focusing on "rebuilding the village." It can also entail using a strategy of exiling (moving) youth of color, often males, out of the neighborhood (J. B. Richardson, Van Brakle, & St. Vil, 2014). Urban self-help organizations, as readers will see, emphasize rebuilding the village approach, which is a key focus of this book, with women assuming pivotal roles within these villages.

The community, in these instances, undergoes a sustained period of disinvestments, further exacerbating dangerous situations. Sharkey's (2013) *Stuck in Place: Urban Neighborhoods and the End of Progress Toward Racial Equality* illustrates the power of intractability in moving out of neighborhoods that are high-violence prone, in addition to a host of other social ills, for all but a few. Violence is often the primary reason why there is a desperate attempt to move out of an urban neighborhood (Graves, 2019). If people are successful in moving out, it will likely be to another community that is either high-violence prone or on the verge of becoming so, destroying the illusion of a geographical cure because of financial limitations.

Understanding how urban youth navigate their way through daily activity spaces provides insights into violence victimization and how interventions can be targeted to decrease the likelihood of this occurring (Dong, Morrison, Branas, Richmond, & Wiebe, 2019). The chances of urban youth finding themselves in high-risk circumstances were found to increase systematically over the course of the day up to the time when they were shot (Dong, Branas, Richmond, Morrison, & Wiebe, 2017). Urban youth can use virtual means to socially navigate their neighborhoods as well as express condolences on the premature deaths of their friends and acquaintances (Mullings-Lawrence, 2017).

Urban gun violence perspectives (insights and attitudes), and other pressing community issues, must be sought in any community-based and systematic attempt at addressing local concerns if they are empowered to engage in social change (Bettencourt, 2018; V. J. Lee, Meloche, Grant, Neuman, & Tecce DeCarlo, 2019; Nutt, 2019). Soliciting these inputs and actions also helps ensure they develop a sense of being respected and valued. Self-help organizations have assumed the role of teaching these skills as part of their mission, including having youth play a prominent role in teaching these skills, including listening ones, to others. Case illustrations also identify challenges and setbacks because self-help groups' and organizations' insights learned from how these experiences were encountered and addressed can be of tremendous aid to other organizations and social workers working with them (Posner, 2018).

STRENGTHS, RESILIENCY, AND ASSETS

This section is strategically located in this chapter for good reason and is addressed again in Chapter 6. A book on urban gun violence can easily devolve into despair because of attention to deaths and injuries. Those with interests in risk and protective factors on youth firearm violence with have no problem finding information on risk factors but will be challenged to find comparable information on protective factors (Schmidt et al., 2019). This book seeks to maintain a balance between the stark realities of this issue and uplifting local efforts that encapsulate much that is good about these neighborhoods.

The "concrete killing field" of urban centers have much in common with the killing fields of other countries at war (Bourgois, Hart, Karandinos, &

Montero, 2019), but with the intersection of structural barriers to contend with service delivery (Bourgois, Holmes, Sue, & Quesada, 2017). Sadly, COVID-19 has added another deadly dimension to this killing field in the nation's urban communities. Although it is tempting to describe these communities as war zones, they still experience joy, celebrations, hope, and faith about the future. Gun violence is not the only issue they are dealing with. They must contend with state-sanctioned violence that takes far more lives than guns in their midst and compromises their dreams (Delgado, 2020b). Many communities have marshaled internal resources, as with gun violence self-help organizations and other institutions, such as the faith based, have rallied to help the community if we take the time to see this and engage them.

Although this book focuses on one specific form of violence, polyvictimization of children and youth is more of the norm than exposure to one form of violence (Richards et al., 2015; Seal, Nguyen, & Beyer, 2014). This is a policy and funding challenge because of how funding for interventions generally has a very narrow focus when violence permeates their almost entire existence. Complex problems necessitate broader and all-encompassing approaches to take into account how local circumstances influence how gun violence is manifested.

Polyvictimization is a reality that compounds the lives of victims (Miller-Graff, Howell, Scheid, & Schaefer, 2019). Nevertheless, the conceptual shift from a polyvictimization (total cumulative burden of violence) to a polystrengths stance opens the door to focusing on violence perpetration and ways youth draw on inner and local resources to help them (Hamby et al., 2018). This shift, in addition, facilitates a wide range of helping professions to come together because of a shared view on maximizing strengths, even when they focus on different consequences of violence. Self-help organizations have taken a tragedy as an opportunity to tap strengths and assets.

All those wishing to make a difference in these communities must eschew taking a deficit approach on gun violence; blaming–the-victim approaches are not needed, welcomed, or effective. What is needed is an affirmation that gun violence is unacceptable in any form and that solutions will require that these communities play an active and meaningful role in shaping their approaches to this problem. Eliminating all forms of gun violence will still leave these communities underresourced and facing multiple forms of oppression, and we must lose sight of this in a rush to address gun accessibility, for example. The violence engendered by guns is social, political, and economic in origin. Getting rid of guns still leaves the factors and conditions that originally led to this violence. The challenge and reward are how we can stamp out gun violence without losing sight of community assets and other pressing needs (Singer & Gorman, 2018).

The coalescing of academic disciplines and helping professions brings tremendous promise, but it will take a domestic Marshall Plan the likes of which this country has not applied to any social problem, and more so when it involves communities of color and its cities. We must never lose sight of strengths, resiliency, and assets in addressing gun violence. There is a natural tendency, which can be quite powerful when discussing urban gun violence, to focus on problems associated with this form of violence. We have the requisite values and tools to make important contributions to applying this affirming and empowering paradigm to urban gun violence.

Contextually grounding gun violence necessitates understanding resiliency in order to develop a comprehensive snapshot of this community issue in the development of strategies (Cantor & Haller, 2016, p. 5): "The goal in developing a portfolio of strategies is not to create a laundry list of disconnected activities, but rather a balanced, mutually supportive approach that is an integrated response to a complex set of factors." Enhancing self-regulation, family, school, and peer support has been found to increase protective or resiliency in violence exposure (Deane, 2018; Hill & Adesanya, 2019; J. E. Logan, Vagi, & Gorman-Smith, 2016; Yule, Houston, & Grych, 2019). This calls for comprehensive gun violence strategies.

What on the surface appears as pain and a hopeless future may even go deeper and require a more nuanced scrutiny to find communities resilient against incredible odds (F. Walsh, 2019). Ralph's (2014) *Renegade Dreams: Living Through Injury in Gangland Chicago*, although ostensibly addressing gangs and violence, including gun-related themes, is really about how urban communities with a wide range of violence are resilient if we use an asset lens. Ralph (2014, p. 17) noted, "I saw how injury could be crippling, but could also become a potential, an engine, and a generative force that propelled new trajectories." A key challenge is how we see communities in pain without losing sight of their hopes and dreams.

African Americans/Blacks and Latinxs are two major urban groups of color that must shape how these paradigms are operationalized in community initiatives targeting gun violence. Resiliency (cohesion across family, school, and community contexts) among African American adolescents moderates adverse consequences following violence exposure (DiClemente et al., 2018). Latinx youth with high levels of religion and spirituality have protective factors when exposed to community violence (Jocson, Alers-Rojas, Ceballo, & Arkin, 2020).

A community strengths/resiliency/assets paradigm allows the placing and understanding of self-help organizations within a multifaceted strategy addressing gun violence (Furman, 2018; McCrea et al., 2019). It also creates a language that is affirming and embracing, away from a language emphasizing victim blaming and deficit focused. Shifting from a deficit and a blame–the-victim paradigm to an assets stance introduces a human rights paradigm with far-reaching ramifications for how best to address urban gun violence (Jumarali, Mandiyan, & Javdani, 2019).

CONCLUSION

Books on painful aspects of life must not solely focus on pain and why it is a major social issue. They must also capture the prospects of a better future, introducing hope. These two views are not mutually exclusive and must be realistic and balanced. In all likelihood, readers have a profound understanding of urban gun violence, personally, professionally, or both. This introductory chapter provided a road map on how this book unfolds. The next chapter introduces readers to the concept of urban self-help organizations.

2

An Overview of Urban Self-Help Organizations

Black people care about the violence that confronts their communities. It is also true, as I frequently heard in community meetings I attended, that "Black babies are dying" still as a consequence of the persistence of gun violence in the city.

—Nikki Jones, *2018, p. xiii*

INTRODUCTION

Self-help goes by many names, including peer support, volunteer care networks, mutual support/aid, reciprocal assistance, self-care groups, peer support, support groups, to list several, showing its wide appeal across spheres when using different labels to capture this phenomenon. Sadly, there is even an argument that possessing a gun is a form of self-help (Klofas, Altheimer, & Petitti, 2019; Kwak, Dierenfeldt, & McNeeley, 2019). Self-help, it is important to note, can also have different meanings depending on the field. In criminal justice, for example, it generally refers to efforts on the part of formerly incarcerated individuals to get on with their life crime free. Self-help, in essence, means helping oneself without expressive or instrumental assistance from others. That form of self-help or mutual aid is not what this book addresses. For our purposes, self-help

Urban Gun Violence. Melvin Delgado, Oxford University Press (2021). © Oxford University Press.
DOI: 10.1093/oso/9780197515518.003.0002.

embraces a unique set of values that stress solutions that are syntonic with local customs and norms, are highly participatory, and bring an appeal for addressing the cumulative grief and loss that accompanies gun violence. Further, readers will see women assuming prominent roles in this movement, both as members of support groups and as leaders of these efforts.

The self-help literature is almost half a century old, attesting to its longevity, and reviewing this literature is beyond the scope of this book. Its evolution now encompasses urban gun violence, introducing a new need and geographic context. Although gun violence does not have to have heavy racial overlays, in this instance, it does, making it significantly different from its predecessors, which ostensibly were a-racial and nonurban specific. It brings a geographical setting that historically was not emphasized by previous self-help movements.

Self-help reliance is a value with deep cultural and historical roots in this country and is attractive because of the control it gives to groups without financial and emotional ties to formal caregiving organizations, as is the case with urban groups of color. "Pulling oneself up from our own bootstraps" conjures up an American image that we must rely on oneself before turning to professional help, which can result in being labeled and stigmatized. However, there is a counter-prevailing force that values the importance of receiving help and helping others (reciprocity) that creates a strong social bond. That is often not the case with formal caregiving organizations.

Self-help organizations are attractive because of the power of using local resources within a highly racialized state and geographically grounded, shaping initiatives congruent with local values, as well as led by people who share much in common beyond the presenting need. This ability to channel cumulative grief, as in gun violence, into constructive outcomes makes their contributions unique in a field desperate for coherence and purposeful actions, not to mention innovation. The role of women as leaders of these efforts and members of support groups and other services provided by these organizations provides them with a role that helps them and their families cope with the far-reaching consequences of urban gun violence.

Local efforts (informal sources of social control and support) at controlling violence must not be an excuse for external sources withdrawing support, and more so when discussing gun violence. Rather, these efforts call for extensive collaboration on agreed goals for local initiatives (collective efficacy), but with the potential for crossing geographical areas to encompass other communities facing similar challenges. Mutual trust is critical in these efforts, within and between internal and external groups (Sampson, Raudenbush, & Earls, 2019).

Not everyone dealing with gun violence benefits from turning to a self-help organization. These organizations are part of a network of other help-providing organizations, formal and informal. Although self-reliance can involve self-help organizations, it can also mean not turning to outside sources for support, placing victims and co-victims in a very precarious state of dealing with the immense consequences of trauma within a highly racialized existence, further marginalizing them at a critical and vulnerable moment in their lives.

BRIEF DEFINITION

The term *self-help* is part of any community practitioner's language. However, a brief self-help definition is in order at the beginning of this chapter (Ahmadi, 2018):

> Self-help groups, also known as mutual help, mutual aid, or support groups, are groups of people who provide mutual support for each other. In a self-help group, the members share a common problem, often a common disease or addiction. Their mutual goal is to help each other to deal with, if possible to heal or to recover from, this problem. (p. 1)

Although this definition is brief, we must not be fooled by its simplicity because self-help organizations are complex and ever evolving in mission and structure, with gun violence an example. Consequently, readers must be prepared to embrace a broader and more encompassing definition of self-help to take into account local circumstances and issues and the unique aspects related to urban gun violence. As addressed further in the chapter, self-help can go by numerous other names, so local factors will dictate the preferred term to be used.

KEY ELEMENTS

Self-help influence is multifaceted, with several key elements standing out in shaping how self-help organizations unfold, particularly with gun violence as a focus:

1. Goals and mission of urban self-help organizations;
2. Prevention;
3. Providing an avenue for community participation;
4. Validating and empowering;
5. Blending formal and informal (experiential) education;
6. Culture in help-seeking and help-giving;
7. Victim as helper;
8. Social activism;
9. Community engagement and assets;
10. Constructing new identities;
11. Obtaining help without stigmatization; and
12. Participation at the level sought.

These elements cover wide terrain, which is necessary to do justice to self-help organizations with gun violence missions.

Urban self-help organizations refocus attention on finding solutions within neighborhoods and cultural contexts, but not without connecting with external sources of potential support in dealing with gun violence. This is an important distinction representing a fundamental shift in the philosophy usually associated with self-help movements.

Brokering outside resources based on an explicit vision and set of values guides which resources should be invited is a deliberative process, one that this book seeks to enhance. Importantly, these self-help organizations expand the circle of those who care. Surviving urban violence individually and collectively is hampered by the general public's indifference to these acts (Wright, 2019). How can you effectively heal when you and your social network are the only ones who do? Self-help organizations expand the circle of caring for these individuals and families.

Goals and Mission of Urban Self-Help Organizations

Although it is understandable that urban community self-help efforts are viewed as providing a therapeutic service, they also fill a vacuum created by inadequate policing (over- and underpolicing) or a lack of trust in the police (Stolzenberg, D'Alesso, & Flexon, 2019), an often overlooked dimension to the emergence of urban self-help. Broadening our conception of self-help beyond therapeutic services allows for capturing how local circumstances shape their missions in order to remain viable within their respective communities.

An instrumental part of a self-help organization's mission is to provide a place and space for sharing of pain without fear of being judged, and this is typified by the Kansas City's Mother's Cry for Life mission (https://www.motherscryforlife.com/):

> After the loss of a child, it's hard to find a mother whose heart doesn't bleed when hearing that another life was taken. Losing a child penetrates your very soul! We at Mother's Cry for Life Inc. have made it our mission to turn pain into purpose. We support any type of loss, missing children, loss at birth, etc. Let us help!

The killing of African American/Black children marginalizes their mothers by taking away the opportunity to raise their child and compromising a community's social fabric (Killen, 2019). Women have ascended in importance in developing and participating in gun violence support groups, although men can be a part of these efforts. The presence and prominence of women is stark.

The ability of self-help organizations to be flexible and responsive to changing local circumstances quickly is a product of their size, mission, and understanding that immediate needs necessitate immediate responses. This observations may appear as simplistic. However, service organizations are generally very slow in shifting resources to meet emerging community needs. Responding quickly is often a part of their mission. Organizational connectedness takes on added significance with self-help organizations. Interventions early after the death of a child, as self-help organizations have recognized, are highly advisable, and this is facilitated when these organizations have close working relationships with local police authorities and emergency rooms so that a referral can be made quickly and efficiently.

When does a self-help organization stop being self-help and assume the position of a service organization, following all the rules and regulations associated with these organizations? When the focus remains on empowering the victims, and survivors play a central role in shaping the mission and daily operation of the organization, it remains a self-help–centered organization. This definition is open to challenge. However, maintaining the central purpose (values and principles) is a key factor in this conceptualization.

Prevention

The prevention field has evolved over the past quarter century, largely fueled by academic programs and funding supporting research and knowledge creation. As a cadre of graduates enter their respective fields, they, in turn, influence those around them. Prevention takes on added significance in undervalued urban communities and with population groups that are highly marginalized and prone to becoming victims of gun violence.

Coming across prevention experts is no longer a rare occasion. Prevention has found the gun violence field and self-help organizations, opening the door for exciting innovation. It is worth highlighting that these organizations often have dual purposes: (a) providing assistance to those in need; and (b) preventing future gun violence from occurring. This dual purpose challenges organizations balancing immediate with long-term needs, requiring coordination of staffing (paid staff and volunteers), activities, and fundraising. Creating a cadre of specialists also has emerged as part of some of their missions to meet the unique needs of their respective communities.

Kansas City's Mother Cry understands the importance of prevention and the multifaceted forces at work in causing gun violence (https://klcjournal.com/mother-of-kansas-city-gun-homicide-victim-seeks-to-turn-pain-into-purpose/):

> She [Sims] believes that modest gun regulations might cut into those numbers. So she supports policies that require more thorough background checks, longer wait times and lock boxes for guns. But she does not actively advocate for these things. Rather, she focuses on social issues, beginning with the simple need to teach children to value and respect every life, beginning with their own. As it stands, she sees too many broken lives. Kids grow up seeing violence at home, at school, on the streets. They become desensitized. "It's just one revolving circle of brokenness and hurt and pain," she says. Her hope is that Mothers Cry can do its part to break that cycle. In time, she wants Mothers Cry to do more than create support networks, and to encourage the survivors to tell their stories publicly. Once they've begun to heal, Sims believes those mothers can raise their voices to promote peaceful conflict resolution and raise awareness about how deeply and broadly a single violent death affects the community.

Kansas City, it should be noted, is considered one the country's most gun-violent cities (Winfield et al., 2019).

As addressed in Chapter 3, the cases reflect an understanding of this balancing act and in highly creative fashion, with many lessons to teach social scientists and helping professionals. Each case operationalizes gun violence prevention and interventions in a different way, and that is not surprising concerning the breadth and depth of the field and the multifaceted nature of gun violence, including how local pressing needs may differ. This focus helps organizations obtain needed expertise, which often is academic, in crafting curricula in educational prevention efforts and targeting different age groups. It is hoped this revelation spurs further collaboration to address gaps in needs and services.

Providing an Avenue for Community Participation

The following quotation by a mother who lost her child to gun violence sums up a key motivation for establishing self-help groups and organizations (CBS 58, 2019): "What are we gonna do different? Each one of us, we gotta stop blaming each other, waiting for someone to come and save us." Stopping gun violence necessitates community participation in various forms, including establishing self-help organizations to reach hidden or difficult-to–reach populations.

Trauma can be responded to with self-destructive attitudes and behaviors; others may see this as an opportunity to seek a positive and constructive life (McClintock, 2019). A desire to give back is a key element for engaging in self-help organizations, although not initially. Much more needs to transpire before individuals can actually become part of this movement. They, for example, must undergo training, close supervision, and support during the initial period to ensure they are carrying out an organization's mission, as well as not being retraumatized in the process. The transition from grieving to giving can be enhanced when there are structured opportunities to do so, as in the case of former bereavement campers who return to act as volunteers (McClatchey, King, & Domby, 2019) and in the case of self-help organizations.

Helping gun victims is a voluntary act of love and caring, rather than a professional duty. Sharing by providers of how they experienced gun violence is openly done and encouraged, and this is very different from a professional stance, where sharing of oneself is generally frowned on. This stance allows helpers to bond with those seeking assistance. Further, by living in the community they serve, as is often the case, there is an increased likelihood of coming across those seeking help in other settings, socially engaging with them in worshipping at the same house of worship, and that is viewed as perfectly fine and would not be with professionals.

There are exceptions to this focus. *Mothers of the Movement* is another self-help organization example with women assuming leadership roles, but one with a national scope of influence. It was inspired by George Zimmerman's acquittal in the murder of Trayvon Martin in Miami, Florida, in 2013, and addresses killings by the police and gun violence. This organization took a social activist approach and helping others with coping after their loss. Many mothers in this movement experienced a child killed, and the mothers achieved nationwide media attention because of the egregious nature of the killings.

Validating and Empowering

Empowered individuals are in a position to help themselves (Tice, Long, & Cox, 2019) and validate others in the process. Providing victims, such as gunshot survivors, and co-victims, with an opportunity to break their silence and isolation, supporting and giving them a voice with a collective potential, provides self-help organizations with an important motivation for recruiting them to be part of their mission. This sense of purpose takes on great significance within their families and communities.

A flood of mixed emotions will be expressed by parents, including feeling shame, embarrassment, and a profound sense of failure as a parent. These intense feelings cannot go unaddressed. On May 16, 2014, the weekend after Mother's Day, Sybrina Fulton, Trayvon Martin's mother, established the *Circle of Mothers* for uniting grieving mothers who lost their children to gun violence (Welch, 2018):

> Two years after her 17-year-old son Trayvon Martin was killed—and nine months after <u>George Zimmerman, the man who shot him was acquitted</u>—Sybrina Fulton had a dream. "It was so vivid that I woke up in the middle of the night and wrote everything down," she says. In that dream, she saw a room full of women, all wearing her favorite color purple—laughing, crying, and embracing one another. The Circle of Mothers, a retreat for women who have lost a child to gun violence, was born. "When I went through my journey, there was no sorority of mothers who said, 'We're here to support you. To guide you,'" Fulton says. "My dream had a purpose: not only to help me heal, but to help other mothers heal as well."

Forming a parents group of individuals with similar experiences and purpose validates their experiences and is a familiar theme in tracing the origins of self-help gun violence organizations. Ironically, we can ask any mother in this or any other self-help effort whether the loss of their child is an event that makes them bond and fill a void in their lives. The opportunity to do so will rarely be turned down.

Any journey that validates traumatic experiences of loss, as with gun violence's pain and sorrow, also empowers by connecting perfect strangers in pursuit of a common social change agenda that ties tragic individual experiences with others sharing similar experiences. Empowerment is a value that resonates regardless of the group and takes on even greater significance when applied to disempowered groups. It certainly has a prominent place within the profession of social work.

An opportunity to make good, as with those who have committed violent acts and paid through incarceration, presents a group with tremendous potential that has generally been overlooked in general, but more so from a self-help perspective. Redemption takes on added meaning when the formerly incarcerated who committed serious violent crimes return to communities where they lived before incarceration (Jones, 2018).

Giving back to communities (expressive and/or instrumental) in a structured and purposeful manner, either formally or informally, increases a community's assets and integrates these helpers into a community's social fabric.

Setting the groundwork for redemption is an important step in this process. Helping others with children killed does not require a helper to personally have experienced the death of a child, as in the case of San Diego's Bevelynn Bravo's work as a volunteer first responder for the San Diego Compassion Project and a cofounder of Mothers (Trabulsi, 2019). However, the death of a son can occur. Bravo's 21-year-old son (Jaime Bravo Jr.) was killed (stabbed) (Trabulsi, 2019), and she took on the mantle to help others and those incarcerated for their crimes:

> She spent 5 years in court until two men were finally convicted of Jaime's murder. "I went into court crying for the son that I had lost, and I left crying for these young people that decided to take my son's life." Just as she had helped grieving mothers before becoming one herself, Bravo used her own tragic story to effect change. Together with other moms of murdered sons and daughters, she formed a group called Mothers with a Message. "It is a mother's pain. We carry our child for nine months and when that child is taken at whatever age that may be, something inside of you dies," said Bravo. The women took their grief into the community, hoping to divert youth before more murders took place. But they always wanted to reach out to men who had already gone down that path—and ended up in the correctional system. And that is where Dennis Martinez [Operator of Training Center, San Diego] knew their message would be taken most to heart.

Forgiveness does not mean that self-help organizations such as Mother's With a Message wait for a perpetrator's release, it can start during the trial process and extend into incarceration and release from prison. Paving the way for possible redemption must start as early as possible, including posttrial and while incarcerated.

Self-help organizations are ideally situated to bring these individuals within their aegis because their past crimes may prevent them from being hired or allowed to volunteer in formal caregiving organizations but are not restricted within self-help organizations. Forgiveness is the other part of this equation, allowing violence victims and co-victims to accept perpetrators' quest to be reintegrated as contributing members and role models and assets.

Blending Formal and Informal (Experiential) Education

Self-help invariably elicits images of individuals leading these efforts that bring a wealth of experiences divorced from their formal education. This perspective, at least regarding gun violence, must be opened to question. Urban self-help organizations bring unique and attractive aspects to addressing gun violence, with their leadership playing an important role in shaping this worldview. This does not mean that they do not also bring in the latest developments in knowledge and approaches based on the scientific literature and training. Leaders of these organizations often bring expertise legitimacy—formal, which is based on academic training, and experiential as a result of having lived through a shooting and killing of a loved one. Bringing together these two worlds increases the effectiveness of these leaders in galvanizing support within and outside of their communities. The case illustrations in Chapter 3 are examples of this stance.

Dorothy Johnson-Speight, PhD, MHS, LPC, for example, is the founder and national executive director of Philadelphia's Mothers In Charge Inc. (MIC), typifying this background:

A licensed family therapist, Dorothy is a proponent for the rights of children and families. She has a distinguished career in victim advocacy. Following the tragic murder of her son Khaaliq Jabbar Johnson in 2001 over a parking space dispute, Mrs. Johnson-Speight along with other grieving mothers founded the non-profit organization Mothers In Charge, Inc. (MIC). Based in Philadelphia, MIC is a grassroots organization whose mission is violence prevention through education.

Educational/training efforts are a form of community investment and preparing future generations, serving to bridge at what times may seem as two nonintersecting worlds.

Many founders of urban self-help organizations bring extensive formal education credentials to their roles as leaders, facilitating the integration of formal and informal knowledge gained through personal tragedy. The development of Philadelphia's MIC, for instance, was precipitated by the convergence of a mission to aid victims of violence with the tragic death of a son to gun violence. In this instance, her son, Khaaliq Jabbar Johnson, was killed in 2001 over a parking space dispute, and the impetus to embrace gun violence as a cause.

Education can be operationalized along other formal lines, such as in mentoring and support of volunteers, as in Kansas City's Mother's Cry for Life (https://www.motherscryforlife.com/a-child-is-worth-saving):

> Learn to value education because it plays a major role.
>> Learn ethics of hard work.
>> Learn to forgive and not to hold any grudges.
>> Set short and long term realistic goals.
>> Create a vision, and implement it.
>> Make a weekly goal and try to accomplish it by the end of the week.
>> Team and staff are provided to help you gather resources.

Mentoring and other educational supports enhance a community's assets through investment of resources, highlighting the interconnectedness of this chapter's major themes and book.

Culture in Help-Seeking and Help-Giving

Culture's influence is acknowledged to be a major factor in how self-help is conceptualized and operationalized (Lavoie & Gidron, 2014). This point is only emphasized more when discussion of people of color and how cultural values and norms shape worldviews and behaviors, including structural violence and law enforcement, as with gun violence.

Riley, Evans, Anderson, and Robson (2019), using a cultural lens, argued that the process of providing and receiving self-help in the broadest and most encompassing sense is gendered, with women being more willing to seek help outside of the immediate family. Gun violence self-help organizations also are quite gendered with women, often African American/Black, playing prominent roles, facilitating women seeking assistance and even becoming members and leaders in the cause.

It is tempting to think of grief as specifically focused on a parent. However, it is broad in reach and may differ from victim to victim (Wiebe & Bloos, 2019):

> Sims is quick to note that the grief created by her son's death affected a large circle of close friends and family, including a brother, a sister, uncles, aunts and cousins. One of those cousins, Sada K. Jackson, was especially close. Separated in age by just a few months, the two grew up together, played together, rapped and sang together, and as they got older, supported each other.

Immediate family is defined by the individual seeking solace, and this can be strongly influenced by cultural values and traditions, including how family is defined.

Groups historically played important roles in urban communities, and it is a natural extension to have them play instrumental roles in self-help organizations, as with Mothers United Against Violence (https://muavct.org/), based in Hartford, Connecticut, which are called Circles of Compassion:

> What Is Circle of Compassion? This is a group which is designed to provide direct support to our Mothers and families impacted by the loss of a child or family member. How do you provide Support to Families? This group specializes in providing compassion, grief support and direction for other support services required. We offer group dynamic sessions to help our families with the healing process. Okay. But what do you really do? This group is special and maintains

a communication network with our core group of mothers, dads and families to help keep them involved in celebrations of special days, healing and support retreats and other work focusing on maintaining their peace and a level of comfort.

The prominence of groups in helping grieving family members and close friends will no doubt be impacted by the presence of COVID-19 because of the social distance that it requires to minimize contracting the virus. It has implications for space, for example, as there is greater need for reduced participation and large physical spaces. It further complicates grieving by restricting hugging, shaking of hands, and other forms of physical contact, which may have significant cultural roots.

Denver's *Enough Is Enough* also uses groups called restorative justice circles (Saunders & Kilmer, 2019):

"Every time you hear a shooting or [that a] young person has lost their life, it's like an old scar that don't go away. It opens back up," Angela Lee, another co-founder of the non-profit said. Angela Lee lost her son to gun violence in 2016. She decided to turn her pain into purpose. "I was just like, 'I have to do something.' . . . I just kept saying, 'Enough is enough,' and me and Doretta was like, 'Yeah, that's what we'll call it, Enough is Enough. We are basically supporting moms, families that have lost their children to gun violence.'" Tootle said. "We're doing restorative justice circles with them, and in those restorative justice circles, we have moms and families that have lost their children to gun violence. And with that, they're telling their stories." This modality is often used later on in the grieving process after initial work is accomplished one-to-one, setting the stage for group participation.

African American/Black mothers will undergo profound changes in relationships with family and friends following the death of a child to gun violence, leaving them isolated during the grieving process and in need of positive coping strategies (Hannays-King, Bailey, & Akhtar, 2015; E. J. Jenkins, 2002). How grieving Black mothers cognitively and emotionally construct the loss (meaning-making) of a child due to gunshots has not received the scholarly attention it warrants, particularly social, cultural, spiritual aspects, essential elements in the crafting of interventions targeting them that results in new meaning structures (A. Bailey, Hannays-King, Clarke, Lester, & Velasco, 2013). There is no established timeline for meaning-making to occur, complicating the grieving process. If the death of a child can spur parents to take an active and prosocial approach, which self-help organizations provide, the process of meaning-making is facilitated.

Helping mothers embrace life without their child and move forward, and more so when there are remaining children in the family, has a strong cultural dimension. The example of Georgie Dixon, *Mothers Against Murders Association* (MAMA), West Palm Beach, Florida, helps them transition in roles from victim to helper, as addressed in the following section (Hitchcock, 2019a):

> Dixon spent years in a fog of grief. Then one day, her oldest child looked at her and said, "You have one more son." Manuel had died in his brother's arms. Her oldest son was hurting, too, but Dixon said she never had realized it. In that moment, she moved from being a victim to becoming a survivor and, now, an advocate. She's had to forgive without justice. She said she knows who killed her son; in fact, he was a regular at their home growing up. But she also knows that she can't live with the hate that once consumed her. Anyway, a conviction would be an imperfect justice, she said. Her son still would be gone. So she concentrates on what she can control, namely sharing her experience of gun violence. Dixon is among a group of MAMA members who visits the county's juvenile assessment center and tells them about Manuel. Dixon sees how those kids hurt. Many have lost relatives, friends or neighbors to gun violence. But she wants them to hear a mother's pain.

A sense of purpose in preventing the consequences associated with gun violence assumes a prominent role in the lives of these mothers that uplifts resiliency in the face of extreme pain.

Victim as Helper

Victim status, directly or indirectly, is a catalyst and legitimacy (experiential) for establishing and becoming a part of a self-help organization and in the process providing a purpose for dealing with grief and trauma and providing much needed hope for a violence-free future. It also empowers victims in the process. Role shifting from victim to advocate is transformative, with possibilities for positive change at individual and collective levels, including aiding others facing similar life challenges, as in the example that follows.

Continuing a life worth living must also incorporate the realty of a life with a child lost to guns, as articulated Sybrina Fulton, mother of Trayvon Martin (Hahn, 2019):

> I didn't feel like I would ever enjoy life again, but slowly I started incorporating the things that I used to do before into my life again, and I started to tell myself it was okay for me to enjoy life, to continue to enjoy life. . . . Yes, I lost my son, but I had to keep living or I would have lost my son and lost my life, too, because it would have been like I'm walking around with no life. . . . I'm really just continuing my life, my second part of my life. . . . I mean, nobody knows what the future holds, but these are just the cards that I was given and I'm just playing the hand that I'm given.

Sybrina Fulton found a cause developing a self-help organization on gun violence, and that is not unique, enhancing or creating a community's assets in the process.

Self-help is an attractive vehicle for addressing highly interrelated and difficult to disentangle community issues, allowing responsiveness to local circumstances in immediate time (Shafique & Abdulaziz, 2019, p. 21):

> Self-help groups will come together the members to participate and going toward the common purpose, in this regard, the members

will enhance their strengths and help together to enhance their weaknesses. These groups help to strength the unity of society and all activities undertake to reach a big purpose which is the community development. . . . Self-help group is also helpful to improve the social concepts and remove the barriers such as racism, home violence and also increase the knowledge of people which is the critical issue to go toward a more developed society.

Families of color play a critical role in self-help efforts addressing gun violence (Delgado, 2017a; S. Logan, 2018).

The emergence of "victim narrative criminology" emphasizes the benefits that homicide co-victims derive from sharing their stories to audiences in a variety of settings and occasions, such as social action demonstrations, fundraisers, memorials, self-help group meetings, advocacy events, and celebratory gatherings (Hourigan, 2019b). Telling the stories of those killed by gun violence by sharing their joys takes on so much importance when they reside in urban communities of color. The Giffords Center recognized this importance and sponsored a project to do just that (Baum, 2019):

We had to convey the profound loss of youth, not just on a personal level, but on a massive, nationwide scale. We had to make our readers care about each and every one of the kids we wrote about in a time when viral videos of shootings are so commonplace that our generation has become oversaturated with grief. But if murders go uncovered, imagine what happens with injuries? The stories of those injured by guns are rarely newsworthy and this viewpoint is simply lost to the general public (Turner & Wise, 2019):

Corie Davis has been in a wheelchair since Aug. 30, 1999, when a physical altercation ended with a gunshot. "When the bullet hit me in my neck, I just went to the ground," Davis said. "My eyes closed and I went to the hospital, woke up [and] I was paralyzed." In the 20 years since, Davis has become a de facto mentor to many of the young men, including Gay, at the NRH's Urban Re-Entry Group, a

support group for people with disabilities who are survivors of violence. "You just gotta take it one day at a time, and do what you gotta
do to make yourself happy," Davis said. "I mean, you're going to have
your ups and downs, but it is what it is."

Cory Davis's story is newsworthy with a profound life lesson to share of
how a victim becomes a helper and the power of resiliency. His story, as
readers will see in other chapters in this book, will be replicated countless
times throughout this book.

Sharing of narratives is facilitated when co-victims affiliate with self-
help organizations by finding mutual support and enhancing their storytelling competencies. These "storytellers" have taken it upon themselves
to assume healer roles even though this will introduce great demand and
stress in their lives. Urban self-help organizations are in unique positions
to both capture and share these stories with the public.

Bevelynn Bravo (San Diego, CA), discussed previously in this chapter,
commented on how helping those convicted of murder unexpectedly
transformed her (Trabulsi, 2019):

For her, Mothers With a Message has transcended its original purpose
of changing the hearts and minds of murderers. "I thought I was going
there to see what I could give them, but they actually did something for
me because my heart was in a lot of pain, and they offered me a little bit of
a peace," she said. "And it just heals your heart."

The topic of who is the victim emerges in conversations with self-help
organizations. The following case highlights why defining victims must be
expansive. The death of a victim, and with the perpetrator brought to justice, does not mean that two chapters in a book are closed, as in the case
of two mothers. A guilty verdict and lengthy prison sentence does not
necessarily translate into "closure." The case shows two mothers coming
together, one involving a daughter shot and the other a son killed while
incarcerated (Ceballos, 2014):

Viruegas visited her son's grave almost every day. She noticed that
Peraza's tombstone was on the same lot. After that, when Viruegas went

to the cemetery she began laying flowers on both graves. For months, remorse gnawed at Viruegas. She felt a burden from the loss of her son, and from the life her son took. She couldn't sleep. One night, Viruegas decided to contact Ortiz. She hoped she held the key to finding peace.

"Mother, I know you're hurt. So am I. My nights are sleepless since 2009," Viruegas wrote in an email. "I put flowers all the time. Please know I feel your pain every day and hope you can forgive." Ortiz responded a few days later. Viruegas had expected her to be angry. Both mothers had attended Sanchez's trial, eyeing each other warily from across the courtroom. They had never spoken before. But Ortiz's email was kind.

"All was forgiven since the beginning," Ortiz wrote back. "The anger you seen in me was for the denial, and not letting us put it to rest immediately." The emails continued. The pair exchanged phone numbers and eventually agreed to meet face to face at Peraza's grave. The day of the meeting, Viruegas brought with her a poem Sanchez wrote for Peraza while at prison. He had expressed feelings of regret and guilt. In person, both mothers fed into nostalgia and talked about their shared past for hours. Eventually, a cemetery worker walked up to tell them it was closing time. It was then that they realized there were so many more things that needed to be said. They needed more than just one day to talk.

They started sending each other text messages and became friends on Facebook. They shared stories about their children and how they used to be. They talked about how they cope with their passing and how it has affected their families. These days, they talk about three times a week, and try to see each other once a month. When they're together there's no trace of the anger and guilt they used to feel. For Ortiz, there's no one that can empathize with her pain like Viruegas. Their friendship has given Ortiz the closure she was missing after Sanchez's conviction.

"It's not a matter of who did what, both families are suffering," Ortiz said. "Find it in your heart to find a place for both families, only then you will find peace." One topic tends to dominate Viruegas and

Ortiz's conversations: This shouldn't have to happen to anyone else. "No mother should ever have to bury their child," Ortiz said. "It's not natural." Today, they're members of an advocacy group called Mothers With a Message. They're two in a group of six mothers who have all lost a child to a violent death. They share their experience of loss with troubled youth across San Diego County. The mothers use their grief as an example of the consequence of any crimes they might commit.

Ortiz and Viruegas vividly illustrate gun violence consequences and how a terrible act can unite those in severe pain, with the eventual joining of Mothers With a Message serving to help them heal.

Social Activism

Social activism, when based in serious loss, suffering, and injustices, can be manifested into movements, such as those related to gun violence (E. Cook, 2018, p. 13):

> Victim movements, such as bereaved family activism, vary in shape and scope, each characterized by different means and geared towards different ends. Each represents a diversity of voices, needs and strategies at one historical and cultural moment in time and emerging in response to a particular form of violence.

Mothers who lost children to violence have assumed an activist role by running for elected office to establish laws that curb the availability and use of guns. This theme is given added coverage because it has not received the attention it deserves in the scholarly literature.

Shute's (2016, p. 173) "bereaved family activism" concept has applicability for this book:

> Naturally, each death presumes one direct victim, however, the effects of an untimely and violent death on the networks of actors

connected to the deceased by ties of family, friendship and work are often profound and enduring . . . the effects of violent bereavement on family members—defined as any self-identifying relation by blood or partnership—and attempts, among the normal range of responses, to understand the organised attempts of some to address publicly aspects of their experience: what will be termed "bereaved family activism."

The responses of loved ones in establishing and supporting self-help organizations are a significant contribution to their communities, and as readers will see in the following chapter, one that illustrates their contributions to their communities and cities.

There is a growing consensus that efforts addressing gun violence cannot succeed without the active involvement of communities (P. Bailey, 2018; Butts, Roman, Bostwick, & Porter, 2015; Perez, 2019; D. Wilkinson et al., 2018), sometimes referred to as a "ground-up" approach (Byrdsong, Devan, & Yamatani, 2016). As social workers, for instance, this recommendation rings true because residents are the ultimate experts of their lives and living situations. Local efforts take on significance when embracing a capacity enhancement paradigm that seeks to have providers work with communities, and they must have a central role in these initiatives to be successful (Delgado, 1999, 2000). Community empowerment is not possible without community-driven development or capacity enhancement (B. Anderson, 2019).

Gun deaths require difficult conversations (Frerichs et al., 2016), necessitating safe places for these to occur, with expert help that often has had to deal with the same feelings (experiential legitimacy), and urban self-organizations (organizational legitimacy) are such places, with personnel with the requisite experiences to help victims. The unexpected nature of the death impacts the bereavement process and necessitates having helpers with similar experiences to recognize and address it (McNeil, 2017, p. 2): "The bereavement trajectory of homicide survivors is unique because the suddenness of the death predisposes survivors to complicated grief and the possible development of post-traumatic stress disorder."

The suddenness of death is matched with the circumstances, further complicating this process.

The term *unexpected grief* can be found in the literature to capture the feelings associated with the sudden death of a loved one, complicating the grieving process. The context in which this term applies may appear as sudden and unexpected in some communities. However, in a large number of urban neighborhoods, it does not carry the same meaning or significance because of the frequency in which these deaths occur.

The concept of "suffocated grief" also has emerged to help capture the state that African Americans/Blacks and other people of color encounter as they navigate the loss of a loved one due to violence, which entails interacting with helping, law enforcement, and judicial systems that further complicate their grieving process (Bordere, 2019). When these systems are indifferent or hostile to their plight, their state of mental well-being is severely compromised, enhancing the importance of self-help organizations.

Self-help necessitates introducing a social activism and social justice stance to achieve structural changes to help grieving families and prevent future gun violence, while still dealing with the trauma associated with gun violence. Gun violence survivors often seek justice, not revenge, in memorializing their lives and those of others killed; the rhetoric surrounding these calls is important in putting together a compelling narrative for self-help and social justice (Rood, 2018). It is imperative that youth not be forgotten, however. Fostering urban youth's sense of social justice, and an opportunity to acquire skills and knowledge to carry out such a goal, is essential in urban violence initiatives (Aviles & Grigalunas, 2018).

It is not out unusual to have public marches and demonstrations that result in a gun violence episode, and these acts often garner important publicity and bring together local organizations, established antiviolence groups, elected officials, and faith-based organizations, for example. These events can spark efforts to establish more permanent organizations, such as those with a self-help focus, because there is a recognition of a gap in services and the social connections needed to facilitate establish these organizations.

The quest for institutional resources to address urban violence is ever constant, with a focus on the governmental and private sectors. Human service providers, not surprisingly, are increasingly embracing the need to be a significant part of the solution for gun violence (Shelly & Battista-Frazee, 2018):

> It's striking how gun violence now plays a prominent role in social work practice, from surviving the trauma and grief, to how one's mental health is considered or not considered for gun ownership, to many other touchpoints. Social workers are now tasked with the almost impossible. We will apply common sense in the most ethical way possible against the growing stockpile of guns in our culture, with Americans owning nearly half of all guns worldwide. Loopholes after loopholes make it harder to deem gun buyers a danger to themselves or others, and gun shows sell firearms sans background check. Also, it is not the "bad guy with a gun" that we have to worry about when nearly two-thirds of deaths by gun violence are suicides.

Professional practice covers many different arenas. However, we must coordinate our efforts to maximize data gathering and proposing interventions based on a common knowledge base, local context, and introducing informal resources (local and self-help) to combine with formal resources to advance a social justice mission.

Urban communities are not standing by and fostering gun violence, which is a common stereotype. Those living in neighborhoods with high gun violence do not enjoy living under those circumstances. It is important to assess what actions have been, or are being taken, within neighborhoods to stem this violence. A savior mentality is counterproductive and even harmful for those wishing to make a difference in these communities. These communities do not need saviors; they need partners in this quest.

Self-help organizations are such an example and worthy of attention and a vital part of community efforts at stemming gun violence bringing a single focus on this issue. Are these organizations the only parties that should be at the table? Absolutely not because this problem's magnitude is so immense that it reaches the lives of countless millions of people who live in high-violence communities. Helping professionals also must assume a prominent role in shaping solutions to gun violence and assume a chair at the table.

Urban gun violence self-help organizations are found across the nation, such as the following examples, with some discussed in this book:

1. The Louis D. Brown Peace Institute (Boston, MA)
2. Enough Is Enough (Denver, CO)
3. Telling the Truth (St. Louis, MO)
4. Mothers With a Message (San Diego, CA)
5. MASK (Mothers/Men Against Senseless Killings) (Chicago, IL)
6. Women Against Gun Violence (Los Angeles, CA)
7. Mothers Fighting for Justice (Miami, FL)
8. Mothers Standing Against Gun Violence (Greensboro, NC)
9. Crown Heights Community Mediation Center (Brooklyn, New York)
10. Wear Orange Campaign (Chicago, IL)
11. MIC (Philadelphia, PA)
12. Community Justice Reform Coalition (San Francisco, CA)

The geographical range in this list illustrates the national appeal of urban self-help movements with strong advocacy and social action components, offering lessons for the rest of the country on community engagement. Self-help efforts can probably be found in every major city with sizable percentages of people of color and gun violence as a major concern. They may consist of small efforts from an organizational point of view or major undertakings, as in Boston, as addressed in Chapter 3. Residents without formal organizational affiliations may be providing a wide range of healing services that can go unnoticed by formal organizations, for example.

Community Engagement and Assets

Urban self-help organizations are founded on experiences of pain and injustice, galvanizing communities because they share these violent experiences, and are a significant and often overlooked dimension to civic engagement. Any comprehensive effort to achieve success, and increasing our knowledge of how they emerged and evolved over time, is valuable in informing academics and providers in supporting these community efforts.

Community engagement efforts can be found in the self-help scholarly literature. Civic engagement enhances resiliency when addressing violent acts (Hayhurst, Hunter, & Ruffman, 2019). Finding positive avenues to engage youth in civic projects (Delgado, 2016) on violence offers much promise for their communities and country (Jain, Cohen, Kawashima-Ginsberg, Duarte, & Pope, 2019, p. 24):

> Exposure to community violence and low civic engagement co-exist for many youth and are often compounded by socioeconomic disadvantage. Many have documented growing cumulative disadvantage and community violence in cities. . . . Meanwhile, others have studied the experiences of structurally marginalized urban youth, finding they are less likely to be civically engaged, but that those who do engage benefit more than their structurally supported peers. . . . At the intersection of these two strands of inquiry, we highlight the importance of considering civic engagement among youth living in structurally marginalized communities with higher incidences of violence. Civic engagement may serve as a coping mechanism youth of color (and perhaps other marginalized youth) use as they navigate contexts of inequality. . . . Since civic engagement among youth of color in urban areas with concentrated violence was associated with reports of better mental health and well-being . . . , we posit that civic engagement could help youth cope with disproportionate exposures to community violence.

Civic engagement is not limited to youth; projects can target them as well as engaging them alongside adults. Self-help organizations can craft activities/projects that accommodate both age groups, as well as other groups depending on local needs.

Broadening understanding of community assets to include youth taps various age segments in playing an important role in addressing urban gun violence, with civic engagement projects representing potential vehicles for various settings to channel their energy and creativity on gun violence because they are the best experts of their lives (Jain et al., 2019). Youth expertise must be integrated into self-help organizations and their efforts to reach other youth. Their perspectives, unfortunately, are rarely sought by human service organizations.

Are urban self-help organizations infallible? Absolutely not! Much can be learned from their successes and failures in shaping gun violence initiatives. We can argue that formal systems of service or care cannot continue to operate as if in separate universes. Acknowledging the importance of self-help organizations is the first step in the process of developing collaborative agreements. Supporting these organizations is immensely important and must be done without compromising their integrity and effectiveness, which is a perennial concern when professionals help communities with complex social problems. None of us is exempt from this warning.

Self-help organizations encapsulate values of identifying and enhancing strengths, resiliency, and community assets, all cornerstones that many helping professionals and social scientists embrace, particularly in urban-focused community practice and scholarship. Identifying what is good about a community as the initial step shapes the dialogue and path that follows, regardless of the difficulties that will be encountered. Our ability to implement these values minimizes local opposition for achieving social justice in this nation's urban centers.

Organizations establishing collaborative agreements with self-help organizations open the door for innovative initiatives combining the power of these institutions to maximize resources and having formal organizations learn from these organizations in the process. Collaboration is not new to social scientists and helping professions, introducing a dimension that brings immense rewards and challenges also because of potential distrust between these two worldviews and outsiders.

Self-help organizations born from the pain and sorrow of gun violence that seek to create acceptance and change it into peace and self-efficacy have much to offer the field of gun violence prevention. These local efforts can conceptually be traced to the self-help movement that historically addressed a variety of social problems, with behavioral, substance misuse (particularly Alcoholics Anonymous), and veterans standing out in importance (Katz, 1981, 1993; Shatan, 1973), illustrating a long and distinguished history that has continued its evolution to today. As already noted, self-help can go by various names and can consist of various formal or informal efforts. It is important to emphasize that self-help does not mean "go it alone."

Rather, it signals a centrality of approaches involving lay/professional assistance as well as governmental and private resources, including possible collaboration between these two formal and informal mutual systems of assistance (Francis, 2018; Hutchison, 2018). Gun violence's magnitude extends beyond sole reliance through self-help community efforts. Why? Local communities do not manufacture guns, and curtailing their availability is a critical step in comprehensive gun violence initiatives that does not rest at the community level, necessitating a national approach to prevent the influx of guns. Communities cannot rely on local law enforcement to protect them and may also be a source of fatalities, requiring external interventions to correct these injustices.

Constructing New Identities

The topic of identity is well understood to be significant, regardless of context. The quest for a new identity is one that most of us have desired at one point in our lives. The desire for a new identity is probably often in response to some event or tragedy that has made us question the old self and why a new identity is called for. Tragedies have the power to make us question our state of being and the place we have within the surroundings of our families and communities.

Urban self-help groups and organizations can evolve into important settings for the construction of new identities for victims and co-victims that is affirming, with the organizations sponsoring this approach also developing identities and reputations that enhance a community's sense of social agency. They serve to counter gun violence's power to extinguish hope and destabilize communities by being an anchor in a stormy sea, to use this metaphor. This transformation will not happen overnight, but there are examples in this book where self-help organizations are addressing gun violence in a purposeful and sustainable manner, serving as role models for other urban organizations and providing lessons that can cross disciplines and helping professions, in the process transforming the self-identities of help seekers.

Some of these identities can be activist, crusader, and helper, for example, and can be compared to a book (Hahn, 2019):

"For a lot of moms, we kind of stay in that position of loss, of disappointment, of sadness, of hurt, of pain, but we need to move to the next chapter. . . . I always tell them that if you wrote a book about my life, you could not leave out Chapter 5, the chapter that my son was shot and killed. . . . But it's also important of what happened in Chapter 6, 7, 8, 9 and 10 about my advocacy work, about me putting time and the energy in myself and making sure that my mind is right, making sure I'm right spiritually and making sure that I'm helping others. . . . You can't leave out those chapters, just like you can't leave out Chapter 5." Books on lives never consist of one chapter; they have a beginning, a middle, and an end, and tell a story, in this case, both the joys and sorrows.

Opportunities for constructing new and positive identities must be available at the community level—new identities that are positive, using the experiences of victimhood to craft identities and corresponding roles that are constructive, community focused, and evolving, with an opportunity to take on leadership, if so desired to do so. This point cannot be emphasized enough, and this theme is discussed throughout this book. Trauma can be a destructive force if unattended in a manner that resonates with the lives of victims. If properly recognized, affirmed, and an avenue provided to turn this tragedy into a positively transformative role, in honor of victims, and even take on religious overtones.

Religious or interfaith institutions can help fill the void created by lack of adequate formal local responses:

> Mothers United Against Violence is a faith based voice of hope founded by Rev. Henry Brown and Henrietta Beckman, promoting justice through community responses to violence, poverty and need for education and through bringing families spiritual support! MUAV brings the message of safety, love and unity within our community. We stand for making positive change by offering support services for victimized families and community members who have lost loved ones through violence.

Self-help organizations bring that potential to gun violence.

Obtaining Help Without Stigmatization

Stigma is alive within urban communities of color and comes in many different forms; its presence is always felt because of where they live, go to school, and are affected by the organizations serving them. Finding formal organizations that are nonstigmatizing can be a quest, and this is particularly challenging in gun violence, where parenting skills and values can be a subject that emerges. Obtaining help in what may be the deepest point in one's life, as in the case of burying a child, without feeling stigmatized cannot be minimized. For these organizations to be effective, they must accomplish this goal.

The transformative potential of urban self-help organizations addressed in the previous section is possible if those using their services can do so without fearing being looked down on, blamed, and even stigmatized. Urban self-help organizations destigmatize help-seeking and foster reciprocal social relationships (Munn-Giddings et al., 2016). These destigmatizing efforts take on added significance with highly marginalized groups that are not having their needs met by existing organizations, calling on their own members to fill this gap in services.

Self-help organizations effectively connect parents to form new social networks, or families, and create a community with shared histories, further validating their feelings of pain. The power of shared wisdom based on experiences, including the ownership of strategies that are essential in addressing common challenges, is enhanced through collectivity, and self-help efforts are a mechanism to achieve this goal, and more so when viewed from a group process perspective. When this wisdom is shared without passing judgment, it takes on greater significance because it allows for a frank conversation or exchange to occur.

Although self-help can be a vehicle to help anyone, women stand out as the primary beneficiaries. Self-help, for example, has been a powerful vehicle for enhancing women's health and empowering them (Narasimha, Anand, Ravish, Navya, & Ranganath, 2017). When self-help is grounded within a solid organizational context, its reach and power are further enhanced at a community level because of the ability to marshal internal and external resources under one roof. How these organizations respond to emerging needs and new issues will have much to offer us in the social services realm.

Participation at the Level Sought

The uninitiated in the self-help literature may be surprised by the inclusion and importance of the concept of participation in this chapter. Self-help organizations are dependent on having a high level of community participation to survive and thrive. However, they must provide a high level of flexibility to allow various degrees of engagement by those seeking services. There is an explicit understanding that no two individuals seeking help share the same resources, expectations, levels of pain, and expectations for what constitutes help. Consequently, organizational flexibility to accommodate varying demands is essential.

Those seeking aid from self-help organizations have different goals. Some may simply want validation and assistance with making funeral arrangements; others may seek help when realizing they are still in mourning a considerable time after the burial. Others may find that they are still angry, and this interferes with carrying out roles and functions within their families and at work. There is a group that goes through all of the stages, wishing to prevent gun violence from depriving other parents of their children.

Reliance on participatory learning, which has generally been overlooked, and action to heal and mobilize individual and community action, particularly in women-led efforts, hold great appeal (Preston et al., 2019). This learning and healing takes time and must be individualized for maximum impact. This aspect is very attractive because individuals seeking help may go through various starts and stops in the help-seeking process, which is highly frowned on in formal organizations. This requires a helper's patience, which is conveyed in a manner that is normalized because no two individuals searching for help are the same.

CONCLUSION

Self-help capacity is vastly underestimated in importance and no more so than when it is applied to urban communities of color. It has persisted and addressed major social issues over history and has not waned in the present day as case illustrations highlight in the following chapter. In a society where membership in organizations is often sought for the purposes of prestige or the seeking of connections to move careers forward or get one's child into an exclusive school, membership in a self-help organization is not one that parents and others desperately want to join. However, it is an organization that fills a community and society void that no other organization can possibly match and that makes it stand out and worthy of attention because of the services they provide and the lessons they can share.

This chapter provided a broad conceptual grounding and illustrations on a very complex and evolving subject, one that can be compared to an expanding universe approach addressing a multitude of urban ills that can benefit from this approach. These themes are addressed throughout the rest of this book to reinforce the role self-help organizations are playing in the field of gun violence prevention and intervention. The three case illustrations selected for analysis in the next chapter ground readers in the operative reality of gun-focused urban self-help organizations and the tireless efforts undertaken by women in seeking to prevent and heal within their respective communities. The emergence of COVID-19, however, must be kept in the back of our minds as we read about the important work undertaken by these organizations in addressing gun violence.

Three Case Illustrations (Boston, Chicago, and Washington, D.C.)

> We need to stem the tide of against the loss of precious and inno-
> cent lives, and only the lives of those who are innocent. We need
> to work to give new meaning and purpose to the lives of those
> people who take control by picking up a gun. Far too many people
> on both sides of the gun are losing their lives.
>
> —C. C. Thompson, *2018, p. 45*

INTRODUCTION

We have reached the central purpose for this book. I usually include case
illustrations far later in a book, after the establishment of a solid foundation based on theory and statistics. However, I have made an exception in
this book and included cases very early to tap reader interest and to serve
as a grounding for better understanding theory and research on the subject. Readers, as a result, will be able to weave together a plethora of material covered in the remaining chapters to enhance their understanding
and appreciation of the important role that urban self-help organizations
play in the life of their communities, including the prominent leadership
role that women have assumed in the process of meeting the community
crises resulting from gun violence.

Urban Gun Violence. Melvin Delgado, Oxford University Press (2021). © Oxford University Press.
DOI: 10.1093/oso/9780197515518.003.0003.

Obviously, urban self-help organizations rest on a mountain of history and legacies of inequities that must be acknowledged to understand their birth and importance in cities across the country. Their birth is one associated with pain and suffering, as well as mutual support and faith in a better future built on an embrace of a social justice value. This hope that victims are not alone is critical in their DNA and is best created internally within the communities that they serve. In addition, how and why they have focused on gun violence rests on a body of scientific knowledge that helped them conceptualize this violence within an urban context.

Self-help organizations not only are exciting and full of hope; embrace a wide range of missions, sizes, and staffing; and represent an often overlooked dimension in solutions for gun violence, but also face a host of challenges. These organizations bring passion for work on a complex social issue. It is hoped the cases receiving focus in this chapter will inspire hope, with the passion they bring being contagious beyond their geographical confines, and facilitate the integration of theory for addressing urban gun violence.

These illustrations are not representative or generalizable across the country; they highlight key findings specific to the sites, although themes are highlighted, combined with the scholarly literature in the chapters that following chapters, with implications for practice and disciplines interested in urban gun violence. They represent different budgets, missions, developmental histories, staffing, and futures. Self-help organizations are best appreciated within a historical context. Healing and caregiving are topics rarely associated with communities of color, and nothing could be further from the truth. Even in the most dangerous communities, there are people who are fearless and have taken the challenge of helping, and sometimes risking and losing their lives in the process, and there are institutions that have also assumed this role.

One does not have to be a historian to understand how healing and caregiving were present during this country's enslavement period (Logan, 2018; Mbilishaka, Mitchell, & Conyers, 2020; Porter, 2018). Other groups of color also have traditions of providing care, primarily driven by an unselfish need to make a difference and make their communities better places to live in by taking a tragedy and converting it into an opportunity to help; these individuals are community assets and attract others with similar concerns who seek to make a difference (Delgado, 2017a). Although these opportunities to serve others are open to all demographic groups, women have seized these opportunities and filled an important void.

Urban communities have nontraditional settings (Delgado, 1999), which are places within a community where residents can go to receive assistance, such as houses of worship, grocery stores, funeral homes, botanical shops, folk healers, to list several. Self-help organizations are the latest evolution in this source of healing and caregiving, although with a different conceptual foundation but sharing many of the same values. Again, in similar fashion to what has happened historically, they have not received the attention and appreciation that they deserve, which must translate into instrumental and expressive support of them and can play an instrumental role in addressing community gun violence. Self-help organizations have much to offer the field of gun violence if we take the time to pause and listen to them and follow their advice. However, we first must acknowledge that they exist.

CASE SELECTION PROCESS AND CRITERIA

The case selection process unfolded in a rather predictable manner. Added elements and decisions entered to take into account input from a variety of sources, logistic concerns, and availability of access. Without question, more time, funding, and pages could have expanded the number and range of cases, including depth of coverage, and this limitation is always a frustration but a reality for authors. The case selection criteria covered three realms: The first involved a children/youth focus (two) and adult focus (one), and second was related to length of existence. The two children/youth-focused cases involved children under 5 years old, and the adult-focused organization was over 20 years old. The third realm was geographical region: Boston, Massachusetts, in New England; Washington, D.C., representing the mid-Atlantic; and Chicago, Illinois, in the Midwest). Each illustration has a website that allows readers to follow the cases over time.

CASE ILLUSTRATIONS OUTLINE

Case illustrations allow the integration of information and theory in a manner that defines key lessons. Cases have always played important roles within social work education and practice, concretizing situations and practice responses to allow the application of theory to live situations. This book uses cases to help readers understand similarities and differences between gun violence self-help organizations across the country, setting the grounding for examining statistics, issues, and interventions addressed further on in this book.

This section has three case illustrations. Case illustrations, unlike case studies with substantially more depth of detail, highlight key points that allow practitioners to obtain an important contextual understanding to inform their initiatives based on local circumstances, including norms and dynamics of street groups (Contreras, 2018a; Egley, Howell, & Harris, 2014; Huebner, Martin, Moule, Pyrooz, & Decker, 2016; Jennings-Bey et al., 2015; Nakamura, Tita, & Krackhardt, 2020). Integration of theory into current-day examples makes important bridges between theory, research, and practice.

G. Nelson, Ochocka, Griffin, & Lord (1998), well over 20 years ago and still salient today, advanced participatory action research to enhance our knowledge base on self-help/mutual aid, with direct applicability to self-help organizations on gun violence, because both share a common value base or DNA: (a) empowerment, (b) supportive relationships, (c) social change, and (d) learning as an ongoing process. These case illustrations embrace these values and provide approaches and services to bring them to realization.

The following outline was used:

1. General introduction
2. Precipitating incident and history of organization
3. Organization development stages
4. Values and principles guiding mission
5. Organizational goals, structure, funding, governance, and staffing
6. Programming
7. Key challenges
8. Observations and concluding thoughts

This outline gives the impression of discrete categories; in reality, there is a great deal of overlap, as readers will witness.

Readers are warned that although these categories were applied to all three self-help organizations, the level of detail will vary based on organization longevity, detailed record-keeping systems, interviewer accessibility, and recall level of key personnel. Particular attention was paid to public records, newspaper coverage, Internet sites, and other documents available to the general public, as noted, and were thus material available for further review, minimizing possible distortion or bias on my part.

Every effort was made to rely on provided documents and organizational web pages to minimize potential errors in reporting essential aspects of the organizations. The interpretations shared in these case studies, however, are mine. Although these case illustrations attempt to present a comprehensive picture, they, as already noted, elucidate the role that youth play throughout all aspects of these endeavors since the youth are often the targets of gun violence.

THREE CASE ILLUSTRATIONS

Boston: The Louis D. Brown Peace Institute

I traditionally have avoided selecting Boston for inclusion in any of my writings, although exceptions have been made. Nevertheless, the selection of Boston was a logical choice for a variety of reasons:

1. Boston is not a city typically associated with gun violence, and its selection is intended to illustrate that all cities must contend with this violence.
2. The logistics of conducting this case illustration was facilitated because of this organization's proximity to me.
3. Boston University School of Social Work had established a collaborative relationship through a student placement, with two faculty members playing instrumental roles in facilitating this, and a faculty member (Prof. Walsh) having undertaken a case study of the organization and published a book that prominently included the Louis D. Brown Peace Institute.
4. The Peace Institute is probably this nation's oldest gun violence self-help organization, providing a picture of an organization that has gone through various key developmental stages, with many lessons to offer other communities.

1. General Introduction: Gun violence has a long history in Boston, setting the stage for the birth of the Louis D. Brown Peace Institute in response to one particular death but still capturing the impact of this violence on countless others. In 1990, there were 152 murders in Boston (M. Walsh, 2017). In 2018, there were 56 killings, with victims ranging in age from 17 to 77 years old, and a reduction of almost two thirds fewer murders (Universal Hub, 2018). However, the 2018 statistics represent an increase from 2017 (Lou, 2018). Thus, it is fair to say that gun violence is a serious social and public health issue in that city's neighborhoods of color.

I have been well aware of the Peace Institute's work over the past two decades and more so recently because a student in one of my classes did her second-year placement there. The fact that it is probably one of the oldest self-help organizations devoted to urban gun violence only heightened my interest for including this self-help organization in this book. This is because of how it provides valuable insights into what many can consider a "mature" self-help organization, and this longevity will prove attractive for readers.

2. Precipitating Incident and History of Organization: The death of gun victims often remains as numbers without any sense of who the individuals were within their families and communities. All too often we know how someone died but know nothing about how they lived. In the case of the Louis D. Brown Peace Institute, we have the benefit of knowing the person who was the impetus for its creation:

Who was Louis D. Brown? Louis D. Brown, 1978–1993, was a champion of peace whose legacy lives on. Louis D. Brown dreamed on a wide screen. He was 15 and a 10th grader at West Roxbury High School in the fall of 1993. He had already decided he was going places. College was high on his agenda, then graduate school, where he intended to earn a doctoral degree in aerodynamic engineering. However, his long-term goal—the one he talked about the most with his family and friends—was to become the first African American (and youngest ever) president of the United States. Louis attended the Boston public schools: John Marshall Elementary and the Richard Murphy School for advanced studies. His teacher said, "He fit in beautifully with this group of talented peers, and he was often described as a special kid, warm, talented, personable, and polite, a boy who was kind to others, who told the truth even when it was difficult, who had a curious mind, and who wanted to learn and do well." Louis was an intelligent, capable student, who, like many teenagers his age, was still finding his way. He wasn't perfect, though as his teacher said, he was pretty close to it. There were times he didn't always do his homework. He also struggled with the image of being smart and being called a "nerd" in a culture where sometimes it was not "cool" to be too smart. Through it all, Louis believed that he would be famous someday. Louis dared to dream big. In the eighth grade, at the Martin Luther King Jr. Middle School, he was a student in the First Class Prep Program, where he "learned to make the impossible become possible." He also realized that "it was fun to be a preppie." His advice to incoming eighth graders was "to work smart, not hard; try to do the best you can do and not what people expect to see."

At home, he enjoyed his Nintendo games. He spent most of his time after school at home with his family and devoted a considerable amount of time to his hobbies, which included music, reading, and creating projects. He spent most of his young life in his third-floor bedroom surrounded by his things and by stacks of books that he read for pleasure and to fulfill class assignments. His reading was eclectic and included titles such as *Charlie and the Chocolate Factory; Oprah; To Be Popular or Smart; The Book of Presidents; I Am Third; The Story of Brian Piccolo and Gale Sayers; The Adventures of Huck Finn;* and the *Lexicon Universal Encyclopedia.* He also loved comic books like Archie and the Marvels, and collected the Sunday TV week, Matchbook cars, and caps.

In 1993, just before he was taken from us, Louis had another important life transformation. He wanted to do something to make his community a better place. He wanted to change the image that some people had of African American teens—that they could not succeed at anything. He wanted to be a role model to other teens, that they could work to change their circumstances, and most importantly, that they could work for peace. He joined the Teens Against Gang Violence, a place for teenagers who view peace and justice as a means of reducing violence. Often, Louis would say, "I want young people I went to school with, and from my community, to be active in my government. However, if things don't change, I'll be alone in the White House, because by the time I become president, my peers will all be dead, addicted to drugs, or in jail."

The origins of the Peace Institute would resonate with numerous other self-help organizations throughout all regions of the country: a tragic death results in a gift to a community, city, and generation.

We too often narrow our attention on the circumstances surrounding the death of gun victims and overlook their dreams and aspirations, leaving a much distorted vision of who they were:

Louis dared to dream a better future for his peers and his community and demonstrated the commitment to work toward realizing his dream. Louis would have been 31, this year, had he survived the cruel irony of being caught in the crossfire of a gang shootout while on his way to a Teens Against Gang Violence meeting. Louis might be looking down on us, now, dispelling the irony of why things happened for him the way they did. Despite all of the pain and sorrow of the loss of someone with such great promise, he has indeed achieved his goal of becoming "famous." Louis's life work began as a teen and continues. Louis's short life has become an inspiration for all young people who dare to dream big and work for peace. He has become a symbol for peace in his community, which he persistently worked to achieve.

Dreams are important in all lives regardless of demographic circumstances. Not much attention is paid to the dreams of victims, and victimizers for that matter. Urban self-help organizations must capture these dreams because they serve as a vital source of motivation for undertaking very difficult work.

Louis was an avid reader a total bookworm. He was caring and compassionate. He loved Chinese food and hated doing the dishes. At 15, he was committed to making his community a more peaceful and just place through the Teens Against Gang Violence group to which he belonged.

Louis believed that all young people had the potential to be peacemakers—regardless of what side of the streets they come from. He had the long-term goal of becoming the first Black president of the United States. Louis was killed in the crossfire of a shootout in 1993. Louis's parents, Joseph and Clementina (Tina) Chéry, founded the Peace Institute in 1994 to carry out the peacemaking work that Louis started. Their goal was to teach young people the value of peace, focus on the assets in community, and transform society's response to homicide.

Urban youth have dreams, and when they die, their dreams also die, for them and their families. Readers can certainly have an appreciation for Louis's life and the irony that he died on his way to an antiviolence meeting. His death and dreams were not in vain, inspiring the development of an organization that has existed far longer than his short life span and spurred countless efforts to reduce gun violence in Boston and throughout other cities that have benefitted from the experiences garnered by the organization that bears his name. His legacy has lived on because of the noble goals of this organization to share the meaning of his life with others.

3. Organizational Development Stages: Organizational development stages provide a window through which to understand and better appreciate the rewards and challenges faced in carrying out the organization's mission. Organizational longevity is a key factor for assessing an organization's viability. The longevity of the Louis D. Brown Institute is reflected in the sophistication of their website, and the immense details provided are accessible to others wishing to develop their own self-help organizations and range of services. Readers will be able to compare the other organizations addressed in this chapter in order to appreciate the uniqueness of this institute because of its long and distinguished history within a city that also has a long history, although not very distinguished when discussing race relations.

The Peace Institute turned 25 years old in 2019, and this history is reflected in how the organization has evolved and its ability to codify many of the elements found in community organizations with similar longevities, including developing a detailed history of the organization, which is an important step in the history of this organization and the community it serves. "The first project of the Peace Institute was to develop peace education curriculum to help students learn how to deal with murder, grief, trauma, and loss. This curriculum was nationally recognized as an innovative effective primary prevention strategy." This step highlights the importance of a model of service delivery that goes beyond grief counseling and emphasizes prevention. Preventing future gun violence, particularly that tied to revenge, is critical in breaking the chain that often accompanies this violence and introduces the need for a homicide response protocol.

Such a protocol introduces an intervention stance presented in stages, which increases the chances that important steps are not overlooked in the heat of the moment, allowing for deployment of necessary resources to increase the likelihood of success:

> "Prior to Louis's murder, there were no homicide response protocols in the city of Boston. In 1996, the city of Boston, the Boston Police Department, and other agencies began referring survivors of homicide victims to Tina to walk them through the crisis and chaos after a homicide. Tina witnessed the way families were denied access to needed support and services if their loved one was 'known to police' or had a 'criminal history' and worked to be sure that all survivors were treated with dignity and compassion, regardless of the circumstances. With support from the Boston Public Health Commission, Tina founded our core program, Survivors Outreach Services (SOS), to deliver consistent, coordinated services to survivors." Turning to outside community sources for assistance is another way of mobilizing external resources and increasing the connection of a self-help organization to the surrounding environment, and to do so in a manner that enhances its mission.

Self-help organizations must actively undertake outreach and do so in a way that is both respectful and welcomed. Grieving families are in a vulnerable stage and may have difficulty problem-solving how best to respond to an unexpected tragedy. Being there at a very critical stage, if handled well, will forever shape that family's response to healing.

Helping survivors with burials, for example, is a concrete action but with heavy emotional overtones that those not involved with gun violence may simply overlook as significant for a grieving family and community. "In 2009, the Peace Institute began convening the Serving Survivors of Homicide Victims Network to improve service delivery and coordination to families impacted by murder. In 2013, the Peace Institute published *The Survivor's Burial and Resource Guide* that codifies the best practices we have developed over twenty years of serving survivors of homicide victims. *The Survivor's Burial and Resource Guide* has been purchased by four level-one trauma centers in Boston and other service providers across the city. In 2016, the Peace Institute launched the Statewide Survivors of Homicide Victims Network for family members of murder victims using their experience and expertise to shape public health and safety policy.

This society emphasizes an individualistic perspective, and this carries over to gun violence. Viewing gun violence interventions from a family stance helps ensure that they are equally informed, minimizing misinformation, and allowing families to share similar information and responses:

> In each family, there are 8–10 relatives who are profoundly affected by the murder. All those relatives have friends, co-workers, and classmates who share in their grief. The way society responds to homicide is often so inadequate it's referred to as "secondary victimization." Families on both sides of homicide undergo emotional, physical, and financial stress. This leads to instability that has a negative impact on entire communities. Addressing the impact of homicide requires a significant investment, yet not addressing it is even more expensive.

Life has meaning and we must endeavor to "promote the goodness of everyday people." All families matter. "Hurting people hurt people; healing people heal people." This quotation emphasizes the humanity in us and why it must be fostered to heal others; self-help organizations understand this important point.

Having extensive experience has led the Peace Institute to develop a series of best practices that are supported by research and scholarship on the subject of gun violence:

> With more than twenty years of experience serving families impacted by murder, the Peace Institute has developed the best practices in the field of homicide response. We have become the go-to community-based agency when a homicide happens. The Peace Institute remains committed to transforming society's response to homicide so every family impacted with murder is treated with dignity and compassion regardless of the circumstances.

The Peace Institute's lessons must be analyzed and disseminated across the nation and modified according to local circumstances where appropriate.

As already noted, the Peace Institute's 25th anniversary did not go unnoticed in Boston, and this is a testament to the prominence of this organization in that city (Horn, 2019):

> The Louis D. Brown Peace Institute in Dorchester, which aids families and communities touched by violence, marked its 25th anniversary Thursday with a call to broaden its message of healing beyond Massachusetts. Chaplain Clementina M. Chery, who founded the center and named it for her 15-year-old who was killed in a gang crossfire in 1993, said the first step of the campaign was to establish Survivors of Homicide Victims Awareness Month as a national observance. Boston already recognizes the month during from Nov. 20 to Dec. 20. "We are taking our focus beyond ending violence and gun control, to building a national movement of waging peace and transforming society's response to homicide," Chery said at a news conference attended by Mayor Martin J. Walsh, Attorney General Maura Healey, and community leaders.

This accomplishment is deserving of national attention and efforts to apply lessons learned during this tenure that can help self-help and formal organizations develop interventions in this arena.

4. Values and Principles Guiding Mission: The shaping of the Peace Institute is largely due to two models—a public health model and an antioppression stance—providing a conceptual base and language for conveying their mission and influencing why community participation was so critical in its evolution (M. Walsh, 2017). Readers may have a preference. Both are essential. "The Louis D. Brown Peace Institute is a center of healing, teaching, and learning for families and communities impacted by murder, trauma, grief, and loss." This role is unique and indicative of the extent of the seriousness surrounding urban gun violence, with gun deaths and injuries being one dimension of social inequities.

An examination of this statement highlights the immediate consequences of a murder and the ripple ramifications of trauma, grief, loss, and bringing obvious and invisible consequences, to the outside world (Horn, 2019):

> Such services as survivor workshops and a survivors' burial and re-source guide that weren't available for Chery during her mourning now exist because of the institute's efforts, she said. "When I left the hospital [the night of Louis's death] I left empty-handed physi-cally and in my soul. There was no resources, no one to turn to," she recalled. Shannon Tangherlini received a grant from the institute to present a memorial site for survivors of homicide in Brockton, where her son, Richard Matthew Tangherlini Jr., was murdered in 2015. He was 27. "The Louis D. Brown Institute was there for me during the worst time of my life," Tangherlini said tearfully. "Three and a half years later, they are still here with me with great love and support for my family and I." The Rev. Ronald Odom Sr., a Dorchester res-ident whose 13-year-old son, Steven, was killed by a stray bullet at age 13 in 2007, joins the institute's Mother's Day Walk for Peace each year. Chery felt hopeful that the work the community would con-tinue to effect change. "There is more good than there is evil, that's what I want to be able to promote," she said. "There's goodness that's happening in this community. Peace can overcome evil, but only if we make the commitment."

Burials and all of the decisions that accompany this final ritual take on great significance, with assistance in making necessary arrangements bringing a level of relief, and having an organization there to aid, particu-larly one staffed with people who also have had similar experiences, brings much needed relief—emotional and instrumental in form.

The Peace Institute principles are easily understood and addressed, as manifested in Chapter 2 and other sections of this book: "Love, Unity, Faith, Hope, Courage, Justice, and Forgiveness." These principle are based on a set of values stressing the importance of a self-help organization bringing inspiration and hope to a community that suffers from the undermining of faith and hope in a future free of violence. Valuing life and equity is a core value of this organization.

Vision: An ability to clearly articulate an organizational mission aids an organization in public relations, enlistment of support, and conveying the most salient values that they hold dear. "The Institute vision on projects is 'We work to create and sustain an environment where all families can live in peace and all people are valued.' This vision is supported by a fundamental belief that 'all families impacted by murder deserve to be treated with dignity and compassion, regardless of the circumstances.'" Again, viewing trauma from a broader lens, and in this case the family, fortifies them in addressing grief and possible action helping them demonstrate their commitment to social justice and community.

(5) Organizational Funding and Staffing: The Peace Institute only accepts funding that does not blame or revictimizes/retraumatize the community and will not compete with other organizations for funding; it must adhere to the Peace Institute's values and ethical principles. Charting this navigational course is undertaken by the North Star mentioned previously, and is survivor centered and offender sensitive. This organization's ambitious goals reflect on its ability to obtain necessary funding, financial and in-kind, and this is as critical to self-help organizations as to their formal counterparts: In fiscal year January 1, 2019, to December 31, 2019, projected income was $1,612,165.00, with projected expenses $1,612,314.00. In fiscal year 2017, it devoted 70.7% of revenues to programming, 23.4% to administration, and 6% to fundraising. Setting aside a specific funding category devoted exclusively to fundraising is an accomplishment worth noting.

Holidays are troubling for families of victims. However, Mother's Day takes on great significance among mothers because it highlights a loss on a day of celebration. Mother's Day marches and vigils take place on this popular day for community actions seeking to gain greater awareness on gun violence (Fox 17, 2019). Father's Day generally does not elicit the same reactions. This observation saddens me because as a father of two daughters I am as committed to social justice as my partner.

Boston's Mother's Day's March for Peace, which in 2019 celebrated its 23rd anniversary, is an occasion when the Peace Institute organizes a march and fundraiser that draws wide participation (https://www.ldbpeaceinstitute.org/mothers-day-walk-for-peace/):

The Mother's Day Walk continues to be a powerful way to honor our loved ones who have been murdered and embrace our partners in peacemaking. The Mother's Day Walk is also the Peace Institute's most important fundraising event. We hope you will help us raise our goal of $400,000 so we can continue to work to tip the scale toward justice for families and communities that are stigmatized by murder.

This march is the Peace Institute's biggest annual fundraiser. It generates funding that is flexible in how it is spent and generates immense publicity, providing an opportunity for participation from within and outside the community on a cause that rarely has such a major annual event devoted to it. Readers may wonder whether this march transpired in 2020 because of COVID-19? Yes, it did. However, it was altered and done virtually (T. Logan, 2020).

6. Programming: The Peace Institute's approach is multifaceted and includes aspects generally are not addressed by other self-help organizations; this is largely due to the length of existence in serving the community.

Our programs and services are grounded in the Center for Disease Control's social-ecological framework that interventions are needed at multiple levels in order to interrupt cycles of violence. The heart of our work is with families impacted by murder on both sides. Our impact extends to community and society through tools, training, and technical assistance.

The Peace Institute has devoted valuable space to provide a library of books on loss and grief that can be borrowed and do not have to be returned and shared with others. These books geared to address a range of age levels and views of violence, loss, grief, and forgiveness; the books include the Bible. Those wishing to read can use the library as a sanctuary and a means of informing themselves in a space that is affirming and shared by others with similar quests.

A family-centered approach means that all family members in grief can express themselves, including children of all ages. A specific room has been set aside for children. This therapeutic room is filled with toys to help children express their feelings. The toys line several bookcases and were donated by families who have been part of the Peace Institute's work. These toys, including sand, help traumatized children to express their thoughts and feelings without fearing adults will be judgmental.

Prevention must never be lost in the quest to address the immediacy of gun violence and all of its manifestations. True, a focus on the present will translate into activities addressing the immediate needs of grieving families, but we must maintain a dual focus with prevention activities occurring at the same time as active gun shooting interventions. Self-help organizations do not have the luxury of addressing one without also addressing the other.

7. Key Challenges: A number of challenges stand out for attention. Ensuring that those who assumed the mantle of fighting gun violence must be ever vigilant that their self-care needs do not fall by the wayside in service to others. It is impossible to help others if we cannot take of ourselves. Being centered on oneself and our grief does not mean that a person is self-centered or selfish. It does highlight that it is impossible to help others when we cannot help ourselves. Giving license to do so is a fundamental step in the healing process and journey of becoming a helper.

The Peace Institute recognizes this challenge and has a yearly summer weekend retreat when they rent a house on Cape Cod, and the time spent with staff and their families is focused on self-care and not work. The institute hires a cook and meals are provided, freeing participants to engage in self-care. Workdays start at 9 a.m. with a moment of mediation; lunch is at noon, and no cell phones are allowed. Each year, $300.00 are allocated to each staff for a self-care act that they normally would do. It is important to emphasize that organizational sustainability goes beyond an emphasis on financial resources, with attention paid to staff and volunteer capacity enhancement, which can be enhanced by external organizations through provision of trainings, consultation, and valuing self-care.

Countering stereotypical media images of victims as unworthy because they have a criminal justice system history is a perennial challenge and one not unique to the Peace Institute. When victims have criminal justice backgrounds, this is often emphasized in news coverage, making them a less worthy victim, further adding to the sorrow a family feels. All lives must be treated with dignity, and this must not be lost in pursuit of a story to lead an evening news program.

A challenge confronting the Peace Institute is one that many organizations, self-help or otherwise, would love to have. A growing organization is always in need for additional space, and the Peace Institute is in need of more space. Finding space that is sufficiently large to accommodate an expanding staff must contend with geographic and physical accessibility. This is challenging within highly dense urban communities.

Maintaining a viable working relationship with the Boston Police Department necessitates walking a thin line, which is a challenge that all urban self-help organizations must contend. The Peace Institute has worked with five police commissioners and will not publically criticize the department; however, the criticism is provided in private meetings. Building and maintaining a professional working relationship with Boston Police commissioners has been taken seriously by Tina. This is a challenge that the Peace Institute has managed quite well. To prevent community disturbances from occurring, the Peace Institute is informed by police when there is an officer-involved killing. Police family resource officers also work closely with the Peace Institute to facilitate connecting services with those in need.

Founder-led organizations with longevity are unique within the self-help movement. The Peace Institute has had one leader over almost three decades. However, according to Tina, being a founder and director does not make one's identity, and she has no fear of eventually moving on and turning the leadership of the institute to someone else. Finding a Peace Institute successor will not be easy.

Finally, there is a challenge that is not unique to the Peace Institute, but it is one that was articulated during my visit. The criminal justice system has escaped accountability in how this system retraumatizes those who are incarcerated because of gun violence. The vicious cycle endemic to anyone touched by the criminal justice system further dehumanizes those who have been convicted for gun violence, and those fortunate enough to live to re-enter their community. The likelihood of perpetrating or being a victim of gun violence goes up dramatically when a person has a criminal justice background. Changing correctional institutions to prevent future violence is an immense challenge for the Peace Institute or any other organization.

8. Observations and Concluding Thoughts: One must be impressed with the tenacity of Tina after 25 years at the helm of this organization. This organization's rise from humble beginnings out of a tragedy to an organization that wields tremendous influence within and outside of Boston. Readers have a rare glimpse into a "mature" self-help organization to appreciate a developmental history spanning this period of decades of service, rewards, and challenges.

Readers will be struck by the Peace Institute's reach across multiple sectors and most notably the importance placed on self-care, which is also a theme in social work and other helping professions. Based from its position of 25 years of service, it is a beacon for other self-help organizations for learning and connection.

Chicago: MASK (Mothers/Men Against Senseless Killing)

Chicago has been a city near and dear to me for well over 50 years, going back to my time at the University of Illinois (Urbana) and the many friends I made while there and made that city home. Chicago has a gun violence reputation that at times it does not deserve and at times it cannot simply escape because of a rash of deaths and injuries resulting from guns (Diamond, 2019, p. 149):

> Chicago is currently a flashpoint for discussions of race, class, gun violence, and education. It has been used as a symbol of out-of-control "urban" crime in right-wing propaganda about Black criminality. It has been referred to as "Chiraq" in popular music, media representations, and major motion pictures. Gun violence in Chicago is also used by people seeking to score political points about gun control and to cloak their antiblackness in flawed statistical legitimacy.

Death in some of Chicago's neighborhoods comes in many different forms, with gun violence being one, although a prominent form; it is slow or fast, but still ever present and an integral marker and part of the developmental life cycle of residents (Fredrick, 2019). When children and youth lose faith in adults and the institutions serving them, they turn to alternatives that can embrace violent tendencies as forms of self-protection.

Large cities often have more than one gun violence self-help organization. Chicago, as one of the nation's largest cities, is not at a loss for self-help groups and organizations. The following are examples: Chicago Survivors, Kids Off the Block, MAAFA Redemption Project, Mother's Healing Circle, Mothers of Murdered Sons, Parents for Peace and Justice, Purpose Over Pain, and Sisterhood. These efforts represent a range of organizational capacities and purposes. I have selected to focus on Mothers/ Men Against Senseless Killings (MASK) because of its approach to violence and the importance it places on creating social connections to ground children within their neighborhoods.

Chicago has the unenviable status that an entire set of chapters can be devoted to gun violence and the attention it has received throughout the nation and within the city itself. Chicago's gun homicides, from 2005 to 2010 had high variation in rates in communities with high concentrations of African Americans/Latinx residents (Walker, McLone, Mason, & Sheehan, 2016), and that is a theme that continues to today.

1. General Introduction: Chicago's prominence in any discussion of urban gun violence necessitates that at least one of the self-help organizations featured in this book involve that city. Readers, up reading the case of Chicago's MASK will be impressed with the power one person can possess to tackle urban gun violence, particularly when the causes of gun violence are viewed from a community-centric stance. Chicago's gun statistics, as this book unfolds in subsequent chapters, are covered in a variety of manifestations, highlighting why this city symbolizes urban gun violence.

2. Precipitating Incident and History of Organization: Chicago's MASK origin follows a dissimilar path from other self-help organizations in this book, and this is why it was selected for inclusion. Unlike most gun violence self-help organization founders, Tina Maskchi, MASK's founder, did not have a child killed by gunfire. Her daughter's friend was killed, and her daughter asked her mother to help do something and did not want her friend's death to go unchallenged. Adults must never fear children, and that is what has happened when guns are introduced into a community. Children must not have their childhood stolen from them, and MASK seeks to prevent this. Although Tina has not personally lost children to gun violence, she has said, "I'm a mom who hasn't lost her kids, and I don't want to" (Dockray, 2019).

As a concerned community resident, she witnessed its devastation across her neighborhood:

> ' "I'm not an activist; I'm just a mother." I used to think my greatest accomplishment was raising two happy, healthy children in Chicago, where so many other mothers are denied that right. Then I sat in a lawn chair on a street corner and extended the love I have for my kids to someone else's. I have been enriched and deeply fulfilled by all of my children. I hope that one day you get to experience the same level of purpose that I have. See you on the block.

Eschewing an activist label does not diminish Tina's role in community social change. Her strategy would fall under the issue consensus and collaboration approach to social change.

Tamar brings a unique background to fighting violence in Chicago and is worth noting in discussing this case illustration (B. Rothschild, 2019):

But Tamar Manasseh is more than just a concerned mother—she's a 41 year-old black rabbinical student. Her unique background and upbringing give her a perspective that few people can claim. Tamar credits her Judaism for her activism: "Jewish people don't see problems, we see cracks that need fixing," she likes to say. To her, gun violence is just another crack to be fixed, albeit a pretty big one. As a Jew and an African American Tamar brings an understanding of these communities, even as she struggles for acceptance in each one. For years, Tamar has been trying to get ordained as a rabbi by the International Israelite Board of Rabbis, but the powers that be are resistant; after all, she is a woman and there has never been a woman rabbi in this stream of Judaism. But in many ways Tamar is already a rabbi—she's held Yom Kippur services, Passover Seders, and Sukkoth celebrations on the block. As a matter of course she settles disputes, dispenses advice and welcomes all guests with a smile and a meal.

The convergence of a strong embrace of faith with a deep community commitment shaped her unique perspective on preventing gun violence in her Chicago neighborhood.

MASK (Mothers/Men Against Senseless Killings) was established in 2015 as a way to put eyes on the streets, interrupt violence and crime, and teach children to grow up as friends rather than enemies. A group of caring individuals in the community began to simply hang out on the block, cook food, and emanate love. Our presence was felt. People began to notice neighbors were watching out for each other, and it was contagious. Now this method of injecting good vibes in troubled areas is catching on in more communities. Our primary mission is to build stronger communities through a focus on: Violence Prevention. Food Insecurity. Housing. Additionally, MASK partners to ensure that community members have access to necessary city services, opportunities for education & professional skills growth, and economic development.

MASK embraced a multifaceted mission on gun and other forms of violence, creating a collective sense of responsibility, seeking to build trust and social bonding. MASK's goals are simple and significant at the same time according to Tamara (L. Williams, 2018):

> I'm trying to keep them alive. That's what I'm trying to do. And for the past four years, I have been successful with hot dogs and hamburgers and chicken and hugs and love, and consistency. That's what I have been doing. Nobody gets shot there. And it's not just about the kids. It's about the wellness of the entire community. So we not only feed children there. We feed adults as well. So we're feeding upwards of 150 people every night.

Communities of color must contend with structural inequities that lead to despair and violence, a disconnectedness from the immediate family, and joining a social network engaged in crime. Providing constructive alternatives that create positive social networks and a sense of community is the primary route that MASK has taken on gun violence. This approach seeks to heal a community's social fabric through connections within and across generations. Although self-help organizations attempt to create a sense of community among gun violence victims, MASK does not specifically target these victims, although they are participants. They are not in the middle of a war zone but in the middle of a community. Residents must have viable options to killing. Engaging children year round keeps them alive by providing an alternative and becoming part of a social network that shares similar goals. Space for a community center is an active goal that will allow MASK to carry out its mission year round.

MASK's summer street corner daily events (positive loitering) do not gather huge crowds, with an estimated 20 participants. Residents show up and help in all aspects, such as cooking or supervision, becoming a community center without walls and located in the heart of a community.

Food costs average $28 per person. "No one wants to kill the people you eat dinner with." There are no membership requirements; residents just show up. This open membership allows participation without the anticipation of making a long-term commitment. Nevertheless, there is a core group that can be counted on. There is one member who is 90 years old playing a central role in managing the food and is a prominent figure in this organization.

3. Historical Organizational Development Stages: MASK, unlike the previous case illustration, has a relatively short history, which if placed within a life cycle continuum (4 years) would be classified as a toddler. However, its location in the city of Chicago, and the amount of attention it has generated in the brief period of its existence, warrants a place in this book.

4. Values and Principles Guiding Mission: MASK has embraced a mission that is more encompassing than only focusing on gun violence but also drawing attention to the social context in which this form of violence occurs: "Our primary mission is to build stronger communities through a focus on: Violence Prevention. Food Insecurity. Housing. Additionally, MASK partners to ensure that community members have access to necessary city services, opportunities for education & professional skills growth, and economic development." Partnering with other organizations increases the likelihood that necessary resources are brought to bear on these social issues.

MASK, according to its founder, is not only an organization but also a movement, and this stance speaks to the basic premises underpinning the establishment of gun violence urban self-help organizations. Manasseh noted:

It's not just necessarily stopping the violence as it is about building community. You build community [and] violence stops—that's how that goes. You don't want to underestimate the power of a mother. MASK is a force that empowers us to be the voice of change, safety, and presence for our families and communities. As individuals joined together, our many voices are amplified as one.

It is important to emphasize, because it is very different in how its mission has been conceptualized, the organization must not be thought of as part of an antiviolence movement. Further, mothers must not be thought of as activists because building a community is simply the "right thing to do."

5. Organizational Structure, Funding, Governance, and Staffing: MASK relies on small grants from foundations, donations, and in-kind resources and has been creative in seeking operating funds. A GoFundMe page was established to generate funds and to generate reward money for the capture and conviction of the gunman who killed two members in summer 2019. In the summer of 2019, it ventured into establishing a business, a pizza restaurant that could also serve as a job training program for the neighborhood and the operating budget of a proposed neighborhood school. The PEACE of PIZZA restaurant was opened as a source for generating MASK funding, but it was closed before its official opening (Golden, 2019b):

> Days after its soft opening, a new Beverly pizza restaurant that aims to fund for programs Englewood kids has been forced to close up shop because of nearby Metra construction. Owner Tamar Manasseh, who recently opened Peace of Pizza, 1801 W. 95th St., said the Metra construction project that began last week is three days away from completion, but the damage has already been done. Instead of a grand opening sign, she's contending with a "sidewalk close" sign inches from the restaurant's front door, and is now worried a July 31 grand opening celebration won't happen. Manasseh, founder of Mothers Against Senseless Killing (MASK), had hoped that the profits from the pizzeria would help defray the cost of the school the organization is opening in Englewood later this year but said that the construction has already eaten away at her inventory. Metra crews are working on a nearby railway crosswalk as part of the project. "This has slowed everything down. I've got bread growing mold, sausages and vegetables going bad," Manasseh told Block Club Tuesday. "I've lost about $10,000 in inventory and $3,000 in advertising."

Although MASK did not succeed in this social enterprise, it does highlight how they are willing to think outside the box to fund ambitious goals. Lessons learned in this failed effort will serve the organization well in future undertakings, although these types of setbacks take a very heavy toll on an organization.

6. Programming: MASK's founder explained what makes its programming so different from other community efforts at stemming gun violence, and one holding great appeal for bringing others, residents as well as organizations, into this effort (PBS NewsHour, 2019):

Kamar Manasseh: OK, first off, MASK, we are moms who occupy a corner. We don't have a membership. It's not like that. If you show up on that corner, you show up to dinner, you bring your kids, they show up to play, paint faces, jump rope, play hopscotch, then, yes, we are there, all momming together. And so as far as them being members or not, because there has been a lot of discussion about that, is neither here nor there, because Chantel was someone who would bring her kids to the corner and mom and just—she would just play with them and hang out with them, because that is what we do on that corner. And she was a loving and patient mom. She was a good mom. And Andrea, she had older children, so we didn't see her in our space as much, but we saw her around the neighborhood every day. And she was fiercely protective of the young women in the neighborhood. And there was certainly a way that she thought the young women should have been treated, that women should be respected.

Their presence on Chicago's Englewood streets de-emphasizes the need for police presence, which can be a source of contention because of the high level of distrust residents have toward them (Dukmasova, 2015). Police–community lack of trust, as highlighted throughout previous portions of this book, is also a reality in Chicago. MASK seeks to promote positive social relationships and activities while trying to deter gun violence, and introduces adults in a position as potential mentors for those who seek this guidance. Manasseh's "Army of Moms" seeks to bear witness, share food, and engage in conversation as the formula for stopping gun violence, and this has shown results; it is the community equivalent of community policing (Alexander, 2018).

MASK fills a critical vacuum within a Chicago community that combines education, meal provision, social networking, and emotional support. Helping youth control their emotions and eschew rash decisions that can escalate into violent acts is one of the goals for their presence. Interrupting the escalation of conflict is one effective means used in other parts of the country, and the strategy has a long history in Chicago.

One major project that seeks to rectify a lack of connectedness will be undertaken by obtaining shipping containers and establishing classrooms within these structures in response to local schools being closed and children not being able to attend schools in their neighbors. Block Academy gives adolescents and young adults an opportunity to complete their high school education and find internships, an essential step in climbing the economic ladder (Tucker, 2019). These "minischools" also fill a social network vacuum in the lives of children and will allow parents to volunteer, as well as serve as a focal point for the introduction of external resources and potential volunteers.

MASK (4 p.m. to 8 p.m.) has volunteers wear bright pink T-shirts with the words "Mom On Patrol" conducting a patrol of the streets to highlight their presence. They view themselves as a "supplemental force" to law enforcement to the Chicago Police Department. MASK has undertaken other projects, such as the Abel Project, which plants trees in memory of children and other victims of street violence, with tree leaves symbolizing the blood that was shed by the victims; the project was inspired by the Jewish holiday of Tu B'Shevat, which celebrates the bloom of trees and signals the awakening of the earth (Nelson, 2016). Trees, and in other places gardens, do fulfill more than a symbolic role within urban communities.

MASK is seeking to rectify policies that have eliminated neighborhood schools and the social cohesive role that they play in creating a sense of neighborhood (L. Williams, 2018).

Well, you're seeing the violence on the West Side and the South Sides of Chicago because, about 20 years ago, in the early 2000s, the city of Chicago implemented some very, very bad public policy. The most damaging of those policies was the policy of Renaissance 2010, when Chicago basically privatized, through charter schools, neighborhood public elementary and high schools. It became a serious problem, because many of the high schools and communities that had long traditions of street organizations caused young African-American males to be afraid to leave out of their communities, going to new schools throughout the city of Chicago. So, basically, from the early 2000s, too many young African-American males haven't been going to school, meaning that they don't have life prospects. They can't get jobs. They're self-medicated to deal with the stress in their community. And it's driving a lot of the violence.

MASK has uplifted the importance of schools in their quest to stem gun violence by acknowledging the central role that they play in the lives of children and youth and the neighborhood as a whole. Schools are considered to be a vital element in any comprehensive effort at stemming gun violence.

7. Key Challenges: The work that self-help organizations undertake is not without the threat of danger, and that was tragically the case with MASK (Yin, 2019):

The usually bustling corner of Stewart Avenue and 75th Street seems emptier now without Chantell Grant and Andrea Stoudemire. The two mothers were familiar faces at the Englewood intersection, where the group Mothers Against Senseless Killings has camped out every day during the summer since 2015—hoping to break the cycle of violence in the neighborhood by transforming a corner with a history of bloodshed into a lively hangout for mothers and their children. Just before 10 p.m. Friday, Grant and Stoudemire were standing at the corner when **a blue SUV passed by and someone opened fire**, according to Chicago police. Both women were shot several times in the chest and died at University of Chicago Medical Center. A man was hit in the arm and was stabilized at St. Bernard Hospital. Police had no motive and have made no arrests.

The death of two mothers, who were not considered targets, introduces a perspective on the work that is undertaken by residents in high-violence neighborhoods in pursuit of healing and peace. How the media handled these killings raised important questions about the role of victim blaming. Victim blaming is common when media describes deaths of those perceived as innocent, as the case with these mothers; no one can be killed without challenging the reasons why it is commonplace. In essence, all lives matter.

On a final note, organizational setbacks, unfortunately, are part of MASK's year. In late December 2019, a container filled with toys and decorations for a Christmas party and material for the Block Academy was towed away to a city pound under the misguided impression that it had been abandoned (Golden, 2019a). Presents to MASK, such as a tree to be planted and other items, were part of the content in the container. The container was eventually returned. This incident, in many ways, symbolizes the challenges that urban self-help organizations face.

8. Observations and Concluding Thoughts: MASK's multifaceted goals require an agenda that purposefully seeks the support and partnership with countless other organizations. Such an agenda necessitates considerable establishment of partnerships that will require strategic decisions and time and effort to establish and maintain collaborative agreements. Filling the gap caused by local school closings will prove an immense challenge.

A funding strategy requires staff with these competencies and appropriate fiscal control mechanisms. This organizational development phase is extremely important if it wishes to seek major foundation and corporation funding. Establishing grassroots funding campaigns must also be a part of this effort, requiring staff with specialized skill that can generate community engagement through special projects, as in the case of the other organizations highlighted in this chapter. These types of fundraising efforts are labor intensive but generate goodwill and connectedness, as well as necessary funding. The success of these campaigns rests with community participation. Writing proposals to foundations, for example, do not rest with such participation.

MASK seeks immense goals by addressing gun violence through creation of community. These goals address many key elements that social scientists have highlighted and how inequities compromise community well-being and the importance of social connectedness. The immensity of the goal translates to a corresponding immensity of challenges from a funding and operational standpoint.

MASK addresses violence by creating social bonds through activities highlighting a fundamental premise of the importance of connectedness in creating bonding and a sense of community (A. Wilkinson, Lantos, McDaniel, & Winslow, 2019). This approach is labor intensive and requires the leadership of someone who possesses experiential and community expertise. Living the life and being a resident translates into street credit. Expanding beyond a street corner to establish key institutions, such as local schools and businesses as sites for training and generation of funding, will be an organizational challenge. Although an expanding organization is always far better than a contracting one, it is still challenging because eyes must be kept on the immediate tasks while positioning for the future.

Finally, Tamar's personality and media understanding combine to get MASK's message out, and this publicity casts her into a central role in any discussion of Chicago's gun violence problem. This media aspect must never be underestimated in shaping public opinion on gun violence. Media attention, particularly when carefully and strategically crafted, is a dimension of a self-help organization's mission that increases in importance as it continues to grow and wield greater influence within and outside of the community. Having a grasp of public relations and the ability to craft central messages places this important function within the community as opposed to having to respond to external media, which is often victim blaming and insensitive to the community's needs and issues.

Washington, D.C.: TraRon Center

1. General Introduction: Selecting an organization in the nation's capital, one focused on children, introduces the specific needs, challenges, and rewards of this age group. Such a specialized focus highlights the importance of a place specifically devoted to their unique circumstances and the use of art as a central vehicle for helping participants to express themselves and connect with others. Their needs warrant specific attention rather than these needs being subsumed under a broader agenda.

Children are the forgotten voices in urban gun violence. Killing any person makes it tragic. When it involves a young person considered a role model, it brings another dimension to sorrow and fear (Wise, 2019a):

> Several children at the Langston Lane Apartments in Southeast Washington, D.C., saw the body of 15-year-old Gerald Watson after he was chased down by two assailants, shot, and killed in December. The shooting happened just a short walk away from the TraRon Center after-school program, a community anti-gun violence resource and refuge for some two dozen children. It's housed in the same apartment complex where Watson lived and was killed. The circumstances of the high schooler's death—he was chased down and shot 17 times in the stairwell of his apartment building—were especially unnerving for neighborhood residents, but served as an unfortunate reminder of the routine nature of violence in the area. Some 160 people, including 13 minors, were killed last year in the District of Columbia. A majority of the deaths occurred east of the Anacostia River, where Langston Lane Apartments is located.... But the shooting death of Watson, a high school freshman and role model to many of the young boys at the TraRon Center, had a sharp impact on neighborhood children, who are now struggling with the trauma of losing one of their own.

The death of anyone due to a gunshot is tragic. However, when the victim is a child, the enormity of the act takes on great significance within a community because it conveys a climate that no one is safe regardless of their age. The innocence that children bring within a family and community is well understood and appreciated, and this creates a greater reaction.

In Washington, D.C., children going to school experience a higher likelihood of being victims of gun violence. Schools, as a result, are often patrolled by the police. Making their streets safer through keeping children and youth off the streets is essential in keeping them alive and an essential element in any gun violence initiative.

2. Precipitating Incident and History of Organization: Ryane Nickels, the founder, was born and raised in Ward 8 of Washington, D.C. Ryane's personal experience with gun violence has guided her efforts to ensure families and communities affected by gun violence have resources to help them deal with their trauma. It was the murders of her Uncle David (mistaken identity), sister Tracy (9 months pregnant), and brother Ronnie (shot in a parking lot and whose body was found by a schoolboy on the way to school) and the shootings of her mother and sister Danielle that sent Ryane's life into a tailspin when she was a youth. Her parents sent her to therapy, which assisted Ryane in developing healthy coping mechanisms to deal with the trauma.

After graduating from North Carolina Central University, she returned home shortly after, and, through her church, began engaging in mission/advocacy work in Ward 8. As Ryane worked in the community and deepened her relationship with God, she felt a call to minister, leading to enrolling at the Howard University School of Divinity. Religious education, in similar fashion to the two other self-help leaders highlighted in this chapter, played a significant role in Ryane's mission.

3. Historical Organizational Development: The TraRon Center is in its infancy compared to Boston's Peace Institute.

The TraRon Center was founded in 2017 by Ryane B. Nickens, a native Washingtonian who was raised in the Ward 8 section of the city. Her life was impacted by gun violence on several occasions. First, in 1990 her uncle was murdered walking home from a relative's house, the gunman believed her uncle was someone else.

Then in 1993, her family was rocked again when an argument between her sister, Tracy, and a neighbor escalated into gun fire. The neighbor's son killed Tracy, who was nine months pregnant, and wounded her mother, other sister, and brother. In 1996 Ryane's brother, Ronnie, was murdered and found by a little boy on his way to school. And so, The TraRon Center was birthed out of Ryane's desire to help families that have endured the pain of gun violence find healing, and to empower them to change the culture of violence in their communities.

Ryane began laying the groundwork for The TraRon Center while a student at the Howard University School of Divinity and an intern with the Washington Interfaith Network. While organizing a Gun Violence campaign, Ryane gathered 15 mothers of murder victims for a conversation around community safety. That initial meeting of mothers turned into quarterly meetings for families. During these sessions, it became apparent that deep emotional wounds were still open, and that the survivors needed a safe space to deal with their personal traumas before they could effectively address violence in their own communities.

The quest for a community free of gun violence found an outlet through the TraRon Center.

4. Values and Principles Guiding Mission: In reviewing its mission and vision, a distinct set of values emerged that can be found with other self-help organizations and can be conceptualized as critical DNA shaping how an organization evolves: "Our Mission is to expose gun violence survivors to therapeutic modalities that may be absent from their current grieving and coping methods. With a focus on the inclusion of creative arts, we will equip survivors with strategies to healthfully endure the complexities of loss—while promoting community health and solidarity." This mission was shaped by a vision stressing safety and support.

The TraRon Center provides a model for organizations and groups to aid victims, survivors, and their communities with the structures and supports necessary to healthily endure the complexities of loss. While promoting community health and solidarity, it provides platforms that effectively engage affected individuals in their political arenas such that it fosters and empowers their participation in local and citywide political processes, from policy conception to implementation.

This mission is shaped by the following vision:

> Our Vision is to provide a safe, supportive space for affected members of the community to express themselves—such that it fosters an environment of openness, honesty, and critical reflection of the factors contributing to gun violence in our communities. By openly addressing gun violence, we will empower community members to collectively engage in dialogue that will produce viable solutions for gun violence prevention.

The TraRon Center views gun violence as a systematic and not one that simply has people wanting to kill each other. How governmental and law enforcement authorities responded to the urban crack epidemic several decades ago is still felt today and illustrates the long reach of systematic responses to today's gun violence in the District of Columbia and other cities across the nation. Intervening early in the lives of children of color helps increase their probability of not getting caught in a gun violence cycle.

5. Organizational Structure, Funding, Governance, and Staffing: Resources must be broadly conceptualized as monetary and nonmonetary. The TraRon Center has an extensive network of small funders providing monetary and in-kind support from conventional and unconventional sources. From an organizational structural perspective, it can be classified as a primary-based organization. This translates into a flat structure, highly flexible in deployment of resources, low level of bureaucracy, and with informal and personal relationships.

As expected with a primary-oriented organization, grassroots fundraising, including individual contributions, is the prime source of funding. There are major individual donors, such as one who donates $20,000 annually, that aid in covering operating expenses. The faith community ($80,000) stands out as a major source.

6. Programming: Programming is multifaceted and covers the entire age continuum even though there is an emphasis on children and youth. Children's voices are the forgotten voices of urban gun violence. Children are a group suffering in silence, calling for a special place they can feel comfortable and safe in sharing their concerns about gun violence in their lives. Providing children with a place of refuge where their voices are not ignored assumes a prominent place in its mission.

Possessing and carrying a gun is equated with respect and power among many, particularly youth. When these sentiments are socially ingrained, it requires a multifaceted strategy that involves all segments of a community, starting with children as the building block of a strategy for reducing gun violence, as epitomized by the TraRon Center. Crafting innovative and child-centered strategies is one approach to prevent future gun violence.

The TraRon Center "offers the community and after school program that provides 'a place and space' for those with gun violence experiences by providing them with an opportunity to be affirmed and loved. Helping children deal with trauma, often manifested through bouts of rage, sorrow, difficulty sleeping, anxiety, and even suicidal attempts. The immediate and long-term consequences of these symptoms are well recognized by mental health professionals."

A focus on children brings very unique age-related needs, and in a neighborhood with gun violence it is hard for them to express their feelings (Wise, 2019b): "Even before the shooting, the program incorporated art and group therapy to help the kids, mostly elementary and middle school-aged, deal with the trauma of what Nickens called 'generational gun violence.' But in the months since Watson was killed, Nickens and volunteers there say they have seen more unpredictable bursts of rage, sadness, and anxiety from the students."

The TraRon Center sees children with guns versus the conventional views of them as thugs or criminals (D. R. Voisin, 2019). Children have basic human needs that have universal qualities. When parental needs go unmet, their connectedness to the family is replaced by connecting to a newly constituted family that can be violence prone. This situation creates a vacuum in these children's lives, and gun violence prevention is not possible without responsible adults entering their lives. Parenting, in essence, is taken from an individual responsibility to a collective responsibility and a version of the "It takes a village" saying. Children get overlooked if they are not shot, yet they suffer invisible wounds that must not go unattended. They will eventually become adults and represent a threat to their communities if their needs go unmet.

The TraRon Center's Treatment Model: Peer Support: Through her journey, Ryane Nickens realized that much of the gun violence in her own community springs from the pain of unaddressed trauma over the life span, with children often bearing the onus. Yet, African Americans residents are often not well served by traditional mental health services. The TraRon Center uses evidence-based, culturally specific, peer-to-peer approaches to serve this population.

> Peer support is a common way for people of similar backgrounds and challenges to help one another. Typically, people with more experience overcoming a particular challenge provide guidance, inspiration and emotional support to those still struggling. Of course, the more experienced person also often benefits by helping others. Well-known peer support groups include Alcoholics Anonymous, Narcotics Anonymous, Gambler's Anonymous and other 12-step programs. The group Compassionate Friends helps grieving parents. Other peer support programs connect people recovering from mental illness or chronic disease.

Reliance on peer support taps into cherished values and is attractive to urban self-help organizations because it creates a sense of group, and a community and participants see facilitators as peers sharing their background and experiences. Further.

> The program is easy to access and responds quickly to clients. The program is confidential; the program offers clients a safe

environment; Peer supporter and client are well-matched; Peer supporters are carefully selected; The program partners with mental health professionals; Peer supporters are thoroughly trained; Peer supporters are monitored and cared for; The TraRon Center works to meet all these goals.

Accessibility and quick response are essential to be effective.

The TraRon Center offers a comprehensive program of individual and group counseling, therapeutic arts, and programming designed to raise community consciousness about the impact of gun violence. We currently offer two adult programs that meet bi-weekly for 90-minutes each: Journaling to Inner Peace where individual reflection, meditation, and journaling help gun violence survivors express their thoughts, feelings, and suppressed reactions to traumatic violence; and, Circles of Exhaling which are group sessions (supervised by licensed clinical therapists) where survivors discuss topics that directly and indirectly address their experiences of gun violence.

As evidenced with other cases in this chapter, groups, because of the power they wield in shaping social networks, can carry over beyond group meetings.

The survivors in our adult groups shared that their children, extended families, and communities also needed support, so in 2018, The TraRon Center launched an Arts & Healing program for school-aged children via after-school programs and a summer camp. We are also developing a series of training sessions on conflict resolution, emotional intelligence, peer pressure, and leadership for the community-at-large.

Summer is a time period of high activity by self-help centers because it brings together high temperatures, high humidity, and people on the streets.

Creative Arts Summer Camp and Afterschool Programs: From Tragedy to Triumph: The TraRon Center provides children with a safe space and tools to help them manage their emotions, exposes them to creative arts, and provides a vehicle to help express their emotions in a constructive manner (Delgado, 2018).

The effects of gun violence are reverberated within and amongst the members of our communities. Loved ones are abruptly forced to navigate one of life's most challenging experiences. The mental and emotional complexities of loss are—too often—suppressed, subdued, and ignored, especially within communities of color. From Tragedy to Triumph seeks to provide loved ones of gun violence victims with the mental and emotional outlets to start and continue their paths to healing.

Providing mental, emotional, and spiritual outlets for gun violence survivors is essential to our overarching goal of facilitating grief processing and healing. The fusion of creative and artistic channels allows all participants, in addition to those with exceptional needs, the opportunity to access and benefit from the offered therapies. Summer sessions will offer full day programming from July 2 to August 10th and afterschool sessions offered Monday–Friday after Labor Day. The summer and afterschool programming will integrate Arts Education and therapies such as journaling, discussion circles, and meditation.

The summer camp and afterschool programs are centrally located and operate at the Atlantic Garden apartment's community center, which is a block from the Hendley Elementary School, where most of the children attend, and geographically accessible. This seasonal time period seeks to engage youth during periods where there is an increased likelihood of gun violence occurring. Engaging youth in adult-supervised activities is a goal that is shared by MASK, as described in the previous case illustration. Enhancing positive adult–children/youth relationships is a core value and principle.

The TraRon Center Consulting: A self-help organization can aid other organizations and interested parties in furthering their mission, as well as providing needed consultation from sources that are trusted:

> While fighting gun violence and healing its survivors is among the TraRon Center's primary platforms, addressing the host of underlying factors is paramount to its reduction and prevention goals. Tackling counterproductive policies, integrating supports for at risk youth, and engaging returning citizens are a few ways to produce real change for victims, survivors, and their communities. Maintaining the effectiveness of these programs and structures requires support from those who are directly affected. TraRon Center Consulting seeks to guide community groups/organizations with two sources of support: (1) Provide loved ones of gun violence victims with the mental and emotional outlets to start and continue their paths to healing; (2) Educate, engage, and empower the community through political education and activism.

Enhancing the capacity of other organizations increases the TraRon Center's reach beyond its immediate focus on its neighborhood. The provision of consultation also provides an opportunity to develop mutual trust, a key element in any successful effort at establishing collaborative projects.

Putting the Act in Activism: Community Engagement for the People, by the People: The primary method financing this organization is grassroots fundraising efforts at local businesses, concerts, in-kind and individual donations, and small grants. This necessitates a year-round fundraising campaign that is labor intensive and competes with other organizational and operating development efforts.

7. Key Challenges: Self-help organizations confront challenges on a daily basis, including addressing a problem with very limited resources. However, in this case, one main challenge is financial, particularly when applying for grants focused on young children. Funding sources often target preventing gun violence with interventions aimed at 15- to 20-year-olds, and this is much too late. Instead, we should provide funding for research and interventions targeting children 3 years and older in order to prevent any violence cycle from taking hold. This age group is not a priority. Ideally, interventions should start while babies are still in the womb to maximize breaking the gun violence cycle.

Although having a center as a home (scared place) that TraRon controls is a priority, this does not mean that it will pull back services from being embedded throughout key places within the community. Not having a building of its own is a mixed blessing, requiring activities to be carried out throughout the community. This enhances their integration into community daily life, as well as more actively involving local settings in the mission addressing gun violence. This need broadens the social fabric of a community to become involved in this campaign.

It also means that the TraRon Center is dependent on other settings to provide space for activities. This makes the planning of activities contingent on availability of space rather than on the schedule preferred by the center. The TraRon Center is without a center to call its own, which can serve an important role as a beacon for a community and the centerpiece of a campaign to address gun violence.

The TraRon Center's goal is ambitious in the way it targets the social fabric of the community and seeks to change social norms. Such an approach is arduous to achieve, even without limits to funding. However, this goal, although inspirational, and rightly so, requires many key aspects of community life to be addressed. Focusing on children is one way of limiting normalization of gun violence in future generations.

8. Observations and Concluding Thoughts: A key element in organizational survival and eventual expansion often rests in an ability to reach out and engage other organizations across a wide continuum. This is certainly the case as evidenced with the following arrangements:

(a). **Institutions of Higher Learning:** The TraRon Center has
    benefitted from being in a city with many institutions of higher
    learning, which have been a valuable source of volunteers and
    internships that have supplemented the mission. One relationship

that stands out is involvement of a George Washington pediatric professor and his team, which has focused on generating data on the role and importance of early intervention on gun violence through the use of the arts and music. This partnership typifies the potential benefits that collaborative partnerships can engender. Institutions of higher learning represent a vital source of resources that can be mobilized in service to communities and addressing gun violence.

(b). **Faith-Based Institutions:** Several religious institutions stand out in importance in helping to carry out the mission of this self-help organization: Washington Ethical Society; New Life Ministries; Adas Israel Congregation; Washington National Cathedral; National United Methodist Church; Metropolitan AME Church. Ryane's religious education no doubt facilitates this level of engagement and collaboration with religious institutions. Religious influences have helped shape urban self-help organizations across the nation and do so in this and the other cases highlighted in this chapter and throughout the book.

(c). **Nonprofits/Government Agencies:** Collaborations are a key to TraRon's mission, as readers will see in other chapters of this book, and the following are an example of its outreach to other organizations in pursuing its mission (East of the River Clergy Police Community Partnership; United Planning Organization; 6th District Community Outreach Office for the DC Metropolitan Police Department; Moms Demand Action–DC; Man Power DC A Hand Up). These organizations represent a range of types illustrating the broad reach of gun violence in the District of Columbia, including the police department. TraRon's collaborations highlight a wide range and tap local resources and strengths; other communities will be presented with a different set of opportunities that take into account local circumstances. These collaborations, as argued elsewhere in this chapter and book, benefit self-help organizations, their collaborators, and the community.

Ryane, in part based on her formal professional education (master of divinity), and as director of this self-help organization, is often called on to share her insights and offer suggestions on the subject of gun violence. The following are some examples. She co-chairs Washington Interfaith Network's (WIN's) Community Safety/Police Accountability team and represents WIN on the Metro-Industrial Areas Foundation's Do Not Stand Idly by Campaign and serves in an advisory role with the Washington National Cathedral Church's Gun Violence Group. Ryane is on the board of directors for Brighter Day Enrichment Academy and the Wesley Foundation at Howard University.

Assuming a vital and integrative role within a broad social network is essential in grounding self-help organizations and not isolating them within this world of human, governmental, and religious-based organizations. Joining in a common but highly emotional struggle helps ensure that these organizations have each other's back, so to speak, from political and social standpoints. Although self-help organizations can be found within Washington, D.C., reaching out and connecting with similar organizations outside of the geographical area serves many different functions—sharing of information and lessons learned, enhancing political support to pass legislation, and generating publicity on gun violence stand out as obvious benefits.

Developing organizational collaborative relationships facilitates the TraRon Center's mission in many different forms. One form of relationship that stands out is how effective the center has been in generating grassroots fundraising efforts with local businesses and service organizations. This type of funding is labor intensive from an organizational viewpoint and often only generates modest amounts of funds. However, the funds generated come without typical "strings," providing flexibility in how they are expended. Further, and arguably more important, it helps integrate organizations into the social fabric of a community, in both business and human service dimensions. The sponsoring of a music event, for example, draws residents who normally would not go to a self-help center, generating greater awareness of the goals of the fundraiser, opening the door for potential volunteers and financial contributions.

Any effort to focus attention and resources on one population age group means that it is challenging to address the scope of gun violence. Focusing on young children places an emphasis on preventing future gun violence by providing them with tools to use in understanding their emotions and finding constructive outlets rather than relying on the use of guns, for example, in settling disputes. Young children, with rare exceptions, are not the perpetrators of gun violence but the victims. This calls for a comprehensive strategy where all age groups are targeted through active collaborations and partnerships that bring other community resources together to ensure that no single age group is ignored.

Such a goal will necessitate more active outreach and strategic partnerships with other organizations, which requires considerable expenditure of time and effort to plan, establish, and maintain agreements. Nevertheless, gun violence is a pressing issue that interacts with other social justice issues, necessitating a comprehensive approach toward addressing inequities, and more so when focusing on children and youth.

The TraRon Center, due not only to a limited budget but also based on its commitment to community participation, relies heavily on volunteers. The TraRon Center's call for volunteers, who must undergo a police clearance, sign a confidential agreement and complete a Child Protection Registry application, illustrates the unique nature of this center's approach to gun violence. These volunteers include artists; authors/writers; actors/actresses; art instructors; licensed clinician/art therapist; psychology majors; education majors; dancers; dance instructors; drama instructors; music instructors; and musicians. Relying on volunteers not only helps ensure a deep connection to the community, but also requires a huge expenditure of time and effort.

"Good" volunteer programs just do not happen, and when they are successful, it is not by accident. Recruiting, vetting, supervising, supporting, and celebrating their involvement is often best addressed by someone specifically assigned to direct a volunteer program. That is a goal for any service-oriented program and a rarity among self-help organizations. Having a vibrant volunteer dimension opens the door for involving a wide range of groups, including youth.

Gun violence is so stark in the nation's capital, elected representatives can see it on a daily basis. TraRon Center's specific focus on children is unique. Children's voices are the forgotten voices of urban gun violence. They are a group that often suffers in silence, calling for a special place where they can feel comfortable and safe to share their concerns about violence in their lives. Providing children with a place of refuge, or sanctuary, where their voices are not ignored and come together, while assuming a prominent place in the mission of the organization, is certainly the case with the TraRon Center. The power of the group also must not be ignored in this process.

Generating publicity on gun violence statistics helps self-help organizations further their reach, and the TraRon Center's local media coverage certainly has shown it can accomplish this task with great acumen, interjecting this organization into the gun violence narrative beyond the neighborhood. This center's effort to target young children and families stood out for me. The active use of creative arts as a method for helping children living with trauma and in high-violence neighborhoods has been a key method used by the TraRon Center. Arts are a mechanism to address trauma, and it will increase in importance in the near future because it increases accessibility.

Startup organizations always face myriad challenges. The TraRon Center will encounter many of the challenges of any startup self-help organization—establishing procedures, developing necessary networks and partnerships, finding funding streams, and securing its own space, to list a few. Nevertheless, these challenges are also motivation for addressing gun violence and investing in young children and communities to preventing future violence.

CONCLUSION

This chapter's case illustrations are uplifting and illustrate the power that rests within urban neighborhoods to help alter their life circumstances by rallying local leadership and using the diverse approaches toward urban gun violence. Clearly, local circumstances wield great influence in shaping how the mission of self-help organizations are conceptualized and implemented. These organizations, nevertheless, are an inspiration because of how they defy the odds against them and are examples of how valuable assets exist in communities that are generally viewed as incapable of helping themselves. I am sure readers would have loved more extensive coverage of each of these case illustrations, but due to limited space, it simply was not possible.

It is impossible to examine urban social problems without acknowledging how gun violence permeates all aspects of life in these centers and the challenges self-help organizations face in implementing their missions. These data reinforce why gun violence cannot be ignored and why grasping facts is essential in setting the foundation for community initiatives with this focus. In this book's next section, readers are provided with a prodigious amount of information on gun violence and my vision for how social work, other helping professions, and social scientists can assume prominent roles in preventing gun violence in the nation's cities. My focus is on crime, particularly gun related, and how a community's future is compromised in a multitude of ways in achieving the American dream for this and future generations.

The next and subsequent chapters introduce readers to a multitude of perspectives and data on the subject of urban gun violence that will further contextualize the immense importance of the work undertaken by self-help organizations. Section II brings quantitative and qualitative dimensions to gun violence and its prominence on the national stage, competing for attention in a vast array of major social issues. Urban gun violence must be viewed from a multifaceted perspective to understand its origins and how best to address it, with self-help organizations playing an instrumental role in shaping local responses.

Multifaceted Dimensions

Urban gun violence is complex and necessitates a multifaceted perspective; this is attested to by the plethora of scholarly articles, books, and reports. It touches all aspects of urban life, and its consequences cannot be limited to a small segment. The case illustrations provided in Chapter 3 allow readers to apply material in the remaining portions of this book to situations within their respective communities. This section builds on material provided in the previous section and provides a multifaceted view of how urban gun violence is manifest through various lenses, further developing a well-rounded picture of how guns dramatically alter urban life. Material is drawn from various academic disciplines and helping professions to present a comprehensive understanding.

Social sciences and helping professions founded on bringing change at the individual, family, community, and national levels places them in a propitious position for addressing gun violence. Understanding a social problem is not sufficient without a full-fledged effort at achieving positive change. This goal can be achieved when we assume an active role in shaping how we prepare future practitioners for the field and crafting requisite research and scholarship to inform other professions with similar goals. This section addresses how best to understand and address urban gun violence and make it a prominent part of a mission. Lessons learned in major gun violence initiatives are reviewed, including the most promising approaches.

4

Understanding the Crisis
of Urban Gun Violence

I suffered from Shock in the beginning. I wouldn't wish this pain
on any other mother. My son's murder has put a big strain on my
marriage, my husband and I argue all the time since that night
14 years ago. I feel empty, I suffer from severe depression, I have
tried to commit suicide several times. I have been in and out of
psychiatric hospitals so many times, I can't count them all. No one
cares about our Black boys being murdered on the streets, somebody had to see or hear something.

—Parent of a 15-year-old (DeBo'rah, *2016, p. 94*)

INTRODUCTION

Death is deeply embedded in the social fabric of society and everyday
life, and as a result has many manifestations in how it shapes the lives of
those that were part of a victim's social network (Holmberg, Jonsson, &
Palm, 2019). It stands to reason that how it occurs also takes on significance. When it is the result of a violent act, such as a gunshot, it must
make us pause. In urban communities, premature death, particularly
when gun related, is too common a phenomenon, and self-help organizations have emerged to fill a gap among families of those lost to violence.

Urban Gun Violence. Melvin Delgado, Oxford University Press (2021). © Oxford University Press.
DOI: 10.1093/oso/9780197515518.003.0004.

Deaths due to COVID-19 have added another layer to this phenomenon. The interactions of deaths due to guns and COVID-19 will bring prodigious stress within urban families of color, with immediate and long-term consequences.

The prodigious and multifaceted consequences of gun violence are well known and are only touched on in this chapter, and reasons why urban self-help organizations are well positioned to understand these nuances in creating interventions are presented. Effort is made to highlight overlooked ramifications to broaden our understanding and appreciation of why urban gun violence must assume a prominent place in our missions as professionals. For example, urban gunshot injuries and fatalities are not limited to human beings, with dogs and cats also not immune (Manojlović, Vnuk, Bottegaro, & Capak, 2017). Trauma from sudden death of pets takes a back seat to their human counterparts. Anyone who has lost a pet will attest to the sorrow that it elicits. If life is very circumspect because of violence, pets take on added significance in a person's life.

There is a natural tendency to discuss gun violence from a standpoint of fatalities because it illustrates long-lasting consequences for the victims and their families and how it is covered by the popular media. Gunshot wounds simply do not warrant the same level of media coverage that a death necessitates, yet wounds bring lifetime consequences for victims and their loved ones. Broadening discourse beyond fatalities to include nonfatal victims, which can be defined in a variety of ways, further emphasizes the broad reach of consequences with a potential to cover a long-term life span. This more encompassing view has implications for gun violence prevention and early interventions.

Gun violence is complex because of so many different interacting causal factors, although there seems to be a propensity to simply call them things such as "drug deal gone bad" or "gang related" (Alvarez & Bachman, 2016; House, 2018; Lauritsen & Lentz, 2019; Wheeler, Worden, & Silver, 2019). This chapter examines different dimensions of guns and the violence they generate. Further, it often relies on providing a quantitative picture of gun violence, and effort is made to introduce narratives, personal stories, and rarely covered nuanced perspectives to humanize these statistics to appeal to a cross section of social scientists and helping professions. Mind you, quantitative data bring inherent limitations. For example, reporting practices can skew statistics, as with crime, emphasizing the importance of local-based circumstances dictating local responses (Asher, 2019).

Some readers may be tempted to skip this chapter because of the level of detail on a range of gun violence topics. I hope this does not happen because gun violence is deeply rooted in this nation's history and covers a wide range of topics. This information, in addition, helps us better grasp the challenges that self-help organizations face. Grasping the magnitude and intricacies of gun violence necessitates using quantitative and qualitative data to fully capture how this phenomenon is manifested on a daily basis and over an extended period of time, introducing a historical perspective that helps us better appreciate the present and plan for the future. A multifaceted picture ensures that no significant aspect is overlooked, including capturing very important personal narratives.

Flexibility in eliciting urban youth narratives, in turn, allows them to use their own vocabulary, metaphors, and sequencing of traumatic events in their lives (Garo & Lawson, 2019). Digital storytelling, for instance, is promising for capturing the pain of youth of color in a manner that reduces stigma and facilitates sharing with others who have similar experiences (K. M. Anderson & Mack, 2019). What professionals view as logical sequencing may not be how youth of color feel most comfortable in sharing their stories. A trusting and accepting climate, with someone who shares their background, enhances this therapeutic process. I made a judgment call that this information is necessary to understand and appreciate the immense challenges that self-help organizations face in meeting their community's needs.

This is not to say that statistics do not carry their own weight in any national gun violence discussion because they help capture the magnitude of this major social problem. For example, violent deaths in the United States, which invariably involve guns, and accounts for 83.7% of the world's firearm deaths, and more specifically with 91.7% of all women and 98.1% of all children being killed by guns (Grinshteyn & Hemenway, 2019). Personalizing gun casualties, deaths, and injuries must never be lost in any comprehensive picture of this violence. Most helping professions are much more comfortable in reading a scholarly article that places emphasis on narratives of those impacted by gun violence as opposed to a statistical report.

These stories introduce nuances often lost in a statistical view of the problem. Human interest dimensions are powerful in concretizing why gun violence qualifies as an epidemic, and no more so than when focused on urban communities of color and youth. I favor qualitative research because of the nuances that are revealed, such as those related to dreams, inspirations, depth of despair, and guilt, for example. The guilt a mother experiences from the loss of a child to gunfire is profound, but so is the resilience that they are capable of displaying (Edmonds, 2019).

Nevertheless, there is a place for a statistical portrait of urban gun violence, particularly when deconstructing how it is manifest at a neighborhood or community level, and this chapter provides it. This portrait provides the backdrop or canvas on which to better place and understand the stories associated with gun violence. Numerous publications provide a statistical portrait of gun violence to further pursue if interested. This chapter highlights key aspects from national and urban perspectives, including subjects that must be a part of any urban gun violence strategy, setting the stage for the introduction of key constructs in the following chapter that influence urban practice, research, and scholarship.

This chapter's statistical portrait is one dimensional but critical in shaping our argument about the saliency of gun violence in the communities we serve. This picture can best be conceptualized as a backdrop to the social, economic, political, and cultural perspectives, allowing for a more in-depth appreciation for the challenge ahead for those embracing this social justice mission. The narratives we embrace to bring this subject to light can use statistics as a backdrop.

INTENTIONAL HARM—INJURIES

Why is a section on injuries needed when fatalities are such a significant issue and source of so much trauma, and self-help organizations seem to be focused on fatalities? True, fatalities generate considerable attention from these and other organizations and within respective communities, including law enforcement. Addressing injuries also is part of their mission, and we cannot fully appreciate the importance of these organizations by narrowing their scope to fatalities, thereby missing an important aspect of their work. Further, gun violence consequences extend far beyond fatalities, as discussed in the Chapter 5.

Firearm injuries have been referred to as a silent epidemic (Beard et al., 2019), and no age group has escaped its consequences, including very young children and youth (Brewer et al., 2019; L. K. Lee & Schaechter, 2019; Veenstra, Schaewe, Donoghue, & Langenburg, 2015). One has only to read Durando's (2018) *Under the Gun: A Children's Hospital on the Front Line of an American Crisis* on the Children's Hospital in St. Louis to comprehend the profound consequences of gunshot injuries on children and their families and how this children's hospital and others have been transformed because of gun violence.

It has been argued that gun violence prevention would be advanced with more information on nonfatal shootings, particularly motives (Hipple & Magee, 2017). This section's title highlights the importance of developing a picture of the consequences of gun violence going beyond fatalities to also include injuries, a complex topic with immense ramifications for social scientists, helping professions, and self-help organizations, with all age groups having to contend with the consequences of guns. Gunfire injuries fall within the broad category of penetrating injuries. Violence-related injuries, as in the case of Atlanta, Georgia, which also include gun violence, disproportionately impacts youth of color (Akinleye, 2016).

There has been a dramatic increase in civilian brain injuries caused by penetrating gunshots. An extensive review of the literature with an emphasis on cervical spine immobilization, seizure incidence and prophylaxis, infection incidence and antibiotic prophylaxis, coagulopathy vascular complications, and surgical management concluded that there is a paucity of literature, which is highly biased and of overall low quality (Loggini et al., 2020). We must keep in mind that surgeons are expected to play a critical role in reducing fatalities.

An extensive literature review of long-term youth exposure to firearm injury found a lack of evidence on best practices for preventing mental health and behavioral consequences (Ranney et al., 2019). This conclusion is profoundly troubling because youth represent the future of their communities and nation; when they are injured, immense family and social networks are marshalled to aid in the youth's recovery. Being shot at but missed is still traumatic without any physical scars to show. This experience is rarely captured by authorities or reported and often is overlooked, underestimating the extent of injuries. Nevertheless, it leaves an emotional scar, that is hard to compete with for the attention of those victims with physical scars to show. The high percentage of females and younger children hearing and seeing gun violence calls for special attention to be paid to these groups, typically not a focus of prevention and early intervention programs.

Urban youth exposed (witnessing and/or hearing) to gunshots in public places will react in a variety of ways. One study found that 50% took protective action to keep safe, and 58% reported an extreme emotional response (very or extremely afraid, sad, or upset), with specific attention on young children (K. J. Mitchell et al., 2019). Research on hearing gunfire unfortunately has generally focused on adolescents, and the importance of focusing on younger groups with interventions is one recommendation of this study.

Community violence exposure is a profound stressor in early adolescence and has been found to have a physiological result by predicting brain structure and resting state connectivity; it may also be associated with the size of the amygdala and hippocampus, impacting learning and memory (Saxbe et al., 2018). These consequences carry over to all aspects of the lives of children and youth, including school performance. Gun violence exposure is a cause of and obstacle to educational equality by being a constant disruption, trauma, and source of fear that interfere with learning and teaching (D. D. Stevenson, 2019).

One Denver, Colorado, study of gun fatalities and injuries at a hospital emergency room found rising severity and number of injuries (2000–2013) (Sauaia, Gonzalez, Moore, Bol, & Moore, 2016). Trauma centers are increasingly under pressure to develop approaches to achieve pediatric relief, recovery, and rehabilitation (Olufajo et al., 2020; Romo, 2020; E. H. Rosenfeld & Cooper, 2017; Wolf, 2019). Although violence prevention is a trauma center programming requirement, our knowledge of the effectiveness of these programs is limited, particularly regarding longitudinal studies (Mikhail & Nemeth, 2016). An assault injury presented at an emergency room is a critical intervention point for preventing youth from further gun use escalation (P. M. Carter et al., 2015).

Emergency rooms have assumed a prominent place for gun violence interventions (Betz et al., 2019), and this increases the need for research and data generation to inform practice. This is particularly the case in pediatric cases at the initial point of entry, placing emergency room physicians as key stakeholders in violence prevention initiatives (Abaya, 2019). When gunshots involve pediatric brain injuries, the mortality rate is 45%, with hypotension, cranial and overall injury severity, and suicidal intent resulting in poor prognoses (Deng et al., 2019). Pediatric palliative care is yet another dimension that we generally do not read or hear about when discussing children and introduces another potential intervention point for helping parents find avenues to derive meaning from the eventual death of their children (Vente, 2020).

Distance to trauma centers in transporting victims, with shorter distances associated with increased survival chances, as in Detroit, Michigan, calling for faster transport procedures (Circo, 2019). The odds of dying on arrival at a trauma center from a gunshot prior to seeking medical assistance have increased multifold, including those involving knife wounds (Sakran et al., 2018). Violently injured patients often bring histories of physical and emotional trauma that have an impact on emergency room caregiving, requiring a treatment approach that rests on several pillars: "knowledge of the effect of trauma, recognition of the "signs and symptoms of trauma, avoidance of retraumatization," shaping policies and procedures (Fischer et al., 2018, p. 193).

Untreated childhood trauma is lifelong trauma, increasing the importance of addressing it early in the life span (Leasy, O'Gurek, & Savoy, 2019; Soyer, 2018). Youth violence exposure can cause feelings of being out of control over their future, and this comes on top of feeling insecure about the future to begin with, thereby increasing engagement in delinquent behavior and stressing the importance of fostering coping behavior in dealing with the immediacy that perceived danger poses (So, Gaylord-Harden, Voisin, & Scott, 2018).

There are proximal individual-level and sociocontextual predictors for adolescent male gun violence, such as witnessing non-gun violence, not being oriented to the future, and being perceived as having status and financial rewards from crime involvement (Rowan, Schubert, Loughran, Mulvey, & Pardini, 2019). Witnessing violence as an adolescent increases development of a host of emotional symptoms and engaging in aggressive behavior (Cooley, Ritschel, Frazer, & Blossom, 2019). The interplay of these factors shows how community climate shapes gun violence attitudes and behavior and the challenge community's face in stopping this violence.

A lack of a national surveillance system has hampered our understanding of children and adolescent nonfatal firearm injuries (Zeoli et al., 2019). The lack of research on the long-term consequences, for example, is quite serious because injuries far surpass fatalities among youth, and this lack limits our ability to plan based on evidence, compromising the future of these youth and their families (A. Brooks, 2019). Further, there is a call for meaningful engagement of those with violence-related injuries in shaping research questions and minimizing professional biases (J. W. Collins, 2019).

The likelihood of being wounded by a gunshot is higher than becoming a fatality; becoming a wounded victim, in turn, increases the chances of becoming disabled, further stressing the lifelong health, social, and well-being consequences (Ralph, 2014). Although pediatric gun injuries represent only 5% of all pediatric injuries, they account for the highest associated fatality rate (Feldman et al., 2017). Upper body pediatric proximity gunshot wounds generally result in severe health consequences (Dabash, Gerzina, Simson, Elabd, & Abdelgawad, 2018). Gun violence knows no holiday, as with Chicago, Illinois' West Side (Little Village neighborhood), where a 7-year-old girl was shot in the neck while trick-or-treating on Halloween (Ortiz & Zaveri, 2019). This injury has long-term health consequences.

The most common site for fatal gunshot injuries is the thorax (containing the chief organs of circulation and respiration), followed by the upper and lower extremities (Patil, Kumar, Wankhede, Tekade, & Kaulaskar, 2019). One study of gunshot victims found that 30% who are shot die, while another 30% live to get to an emergency room and released, but the remaining 40% fall into the category of having complicating conditions requiring prolonged hospitalization (Kalesan et al., 2018). Children who go to a hospital with gun wounds face different levels of survival probability. Young children (5 years and under) are 2.7 times more likely to be fatalities compared with older children (15.3% vs. 5.6%); those under 1 year old had the highest hospital mortality (33.1%) (A. J. Cook et al., 2019). Surviving an injury while hospitalized is a critical juncture for reaching out to them, and it becomes a profound life-shaping experience when the individual reaching out was in a similar situation, showing the potential of this period to be positively transformative. The case of Sherman Spears spotlights the importance of helping gun violence victims while they are hospitalized (Van Brocklin, 2019):

Sherman Spears was shot at a friend's apartment complex in East Oakland, California, in 1989. Someone from the neighborhood had been seeking revenge on his friend, but found Spears first. He was struck by three bullets and hit his head as he fell to the ground, leaving him paralyzed. As the 18-year-old lay in a hospital bed recuperating, he felt disoriented and scared about his future. His parents were distraught, his friends wanted revenge, and he didn't feel like he could relate to the doctors and nurses. "I really didn't have time to process what I was going through," Spears recalled. "There was nobody I could really talk with about what was happening to me." While Spears adjusted to his new life, the experience of feeling lost in those first days remained vivid. A doctor connected him with Youth Alive, then a fledgling violence prevention organization in Oakland. With encouragement from the organization's director, he began going to the hospital and meeting with other young victims of violence. He talked to them about what they were going through, physically and emotionally, and let them know what to expect. Before leaving, he'd give them his phone number and tell them to call any time. The idea that Spears pioneered, of mentoring and supporting gunshot and stab-wound victims immediately after they are injured, is today known as hospital-based violence intervention.

Sherman Spears could have taken his injury and embraced a revenge-seeking mission. There is such a powerful lesson that we can learn and translate into service provision to help victims and increase the likelihood of turning a tragedy into life-saving actions, and this is greatly increased when there is a self-help organization readily available.

There is an increased chance that substance-using youth admitted to an emergency room for assault injuries are at increased risk of being arrested during a 2-year period following discharge for criminal violent acts (Carter et al., 2018). This population group, as a result, warrants intensive intervention in any comprehensive effort to address community violence. Incidentally, race is not a predictor of medical discharge against medical advice among trauma patients (Jasperse et al., 2019). This topic needs further research using a more nuanced racialized viewpoint. Emergency rooms, as a result, represent an important portal into addressing urban gun violence (Kazemi et al., 2017).

Helping professions understand the pain suffered by survivors of those killed by guns. However, how they cope with the injured also extracts a tremendous toll on their loved ones, particularly where wounds leave them in a compromised state of health, such as those who are paralyzed or require highly specialized care. Further, we usually think of gunshot wounds as isolated events (Turner & Wise, 2019):

"I know of like 70 people that got shot . . . personally. . . . I probably seen about . . . 30 people get shot." In 2017, a week after his older brother was shot and killed, Sergio Hill woke up in a hospital bed suffering from a gunshot to the leg. "I didn't even notice that I had got shot until somebody had walked up to me and told me," Hill said. "I was so drunk because my brother had recently passed away . . . taking the stress out [with] just drinking." The next year, Hill, who had been working to improve his life and be a better role model for his younger siblings, would be shot again. As he was walking to hang out with friends after a day of work, a bullet ripped through his other leg in an incident that also injured two of his friends. "It was like 60 rounds [of bullets] that went off that night," Hill said. After being shot randomly for the second time, Hill found himself feeling discouraged about his efforts to better his life. "I was thinking about just saying fuck everything. . . . It don't matter what I do right, it's like something's always going to happen. It don't matter where I go, something's always going to happen to me. So I might as well just go back to the streets," Hill said. "But I thought about my brother. Me thinking about my brother not being here made me not want to break [the] law, or go back to the streets, go back to my old ways."

Hill's experience with urban gun violence has more in common with returning war veterans than civilians in urban streets across the country. The trauma, both physical and emotional, makes it challenging to feel secure and trust the future.

The likelihood of being wounded and surviving translates into an increased chance of another gunshot wound occurring. One incident does not take into account other symptoms of being a violence victim, introducing the potential role of a cumulative index. Consequences of surviving a gunshot wound are only now starting to be understood (Zebib, Stoler, & Zakrison, 2017). The emergence of the Urban Injury Severity Score has been found to be a better predictor of mortality resulting from gunshot wounds, shaping services and increasing our understanding of gun violence consequences (Tobon, Ledgerwood, & Lucas, 2019).

Recidivism from wounds increases the chances of more severe outcomes and prognosis, particularly when compared to victims of knife wounds, raising the importance of targeting intervention to these victims because of the potential of violence to escalate (Nygaard, Marek, Daly, & Van Camp, 2018). African American/Black men's emotional responses to repeated intentional traumatic injuries compromises their abilities to enter into trusting relationships and engaging their support system in time of need (T. Jiang, Webster, Robinson, Kassam-Adams, & Richmond, 2018). These situations increase self-help organizations' importance.

A gun violence focus de-emphasizes other weapons, such as knifes, as in other countries that do not have a tradition of gun use (Astrup, 2019). High-velocity air weapons, commonly known as air rifles or starter guns, have been overlooked in the discussion of gun violence, but these weapons also can cause injuries and even fatalities when diabolo pellets are used (Apelt et al., 2020; Mogni & Maines, 2019; Simon, Heckmann, Tóth, & Kozma, 2019; Uyeturk, 2019). Knives, or machetes, as in the case of MS 13, is still prevalent. Being shot is often associated with being knifed, although the latter can often get lost through a focus on gun wounds (Maki, 2015). Surviving a cut or stabbing leaves physical scars, and depending where located, similar to gunshots, it has physical and emotional repercussions.

Gun lethality and consequences far exceed those of other weapons and thus are worthy of focus. According to the Centers for Disease Control and Prevention (CDC), between 2015 and 2016, firearm-related injuries increased by 37% (from 85,000 to more than 116,000), the biggest single-year increase in over 15 years (Campbell, Nass, & Nguyen, 2018). Gunshot wounds often require multiple surgeries over an extended period, prolonging the physical healing process (Ignatiadis et al., 2019), which extends emotional healing, more so when poorly treated. The following gun injury descriptions illustrate challenges in categorization and why they significantly alter the lives of those surviving this violence (Amnesty International, 2018):

> The key to saving a gunshot victim is usually to stop the internal bleeding, often from multiple sites inside the chest and abdomen. This is one reason why survivors of a gunshot to the trunk typically have such large scars—running from the base of the sternum, around the belly button to just above the pubic bones—they need to be split open for the surgeon to get the best view of all possible sites of blood loss. Damage to the intestines is common, and dangerous; a perforated intestine can spill its contents into the abdominal cavity,

possibly leading to a lethal infection. The abdomen may be left open between procedures, to facilitate further surgery, to prevent infection or because it is too swollen to close. (p. 96)

There is a call to develop standards and processes for equipping public spaces for rapid point-of-injury hemorrhage control (Goolsby et al., 2019) and will be addressed again.

Gun violence can often result in homicides, which garner the bulk of publicity, and injuries (visible and invisible) do not. Gun injuries have more severe short- and long-term consequences when compared to other forms of injuries (Foran et al., 2019; Vella et al., 2020), and manifestations may not conform to conventional expectations associated with physical symptoms. Injury statistics far exceed fatalities, increasing the likelihood that helping professionals will encounter a gun-injured victim than a gun fatality. Depending on the wound, this experience may not be shared because of shame or other reason.

Knowledge of gun injuries is very limited when compared to fatalities, complicating development of interventions based on clarity of thought, theory, and appropriate data (D. S. Bernstein, 2017):

Fatal gun violence is often categorized in ways that make it easy to track and study. That's how researchers know that the murder rate in the United States has declined steadily over the past three decades. But what about gun violence that does not result in death? That is far trickier to measure. That's because nonfatal gun violence has mostly been ignored. As a result, policymakers, law-enforcement officials, public-health experts, urban planners, and economists are all basing their work on information that is unproven or incomplete.

"Code red" is rarely used with major hemorrhage injuries among urban children presenting at trauma centers, calling for a change in the use of vital signs because they are inadequate indicators of hypovolemia and recommended ratios of blood to plasma (Randhawa, Edwards, & Cantle, 2016).

The CDC's quantitative data on gun injuries are not considered reliable by leading social scientists, complicating obtaining a comprehensive understanding of the toll it extracts (Campbell & Nass, 2018). Other major gun violence quantitative data sources are also deficient, limiting our comprehension of this problem's magnitude (Y. Jiang et al., 2019), essential in crafting interventions. Gun violence requires a nuanced approach to allow full comprehension of its multifaceted significance because a broad picture will overlook local factors that are nuanced. Altheimer, Schaible, Klofas, and Comeau (2019), for example, identified six potential outcomes of a shooting, bringing a public health and lethality perspective to this event: (a) the number of shots fired; (b) the caliber of the bullet; (c) the number of times the victim was hit; (d) where the victim was hit; (e) the number of victims; and (f) whether the shooting resulted in a fatality or injury.

These categories bring a degree of depth that is generally described numerically. An increase in firearm caliber/capacity causes a higher likelihood of death or a more severe gunshot injury for those surviving a shooting (Braga & Cook, 2018; Koper, Johnson, Nichols, Ayers, & Mullins, 2018; Manley et al., 2019). If injured, the location and severity of the injury, and whether it is hidden or used as a badge of courage, also must be taken into account. There are various types of gunshot wounds. For those shot and the bullet is impossible to remove, it is a constant reminder of being lucky; it can also be a reminder to seek revenge or can result in a moment of clarity, bringing a change in lifestyle.

Nonfatal gun injuries have generally been ignored when compared with fatalities, with six of seven victims surviving, excluding suicides, resulting in underestimating and misunderstanding shooting consequences, including economic and social costs (D. S. Bernstein, 2017). Cranial gunshot wounds, for example, have the highest mortality of all gun injuries (Crutcher, Fannin, & Wilson, 2016), with corresponding severe long-term consequences (Menger et al., 2017). Are the injuries suffered in mass shootings more severe than those occurring on a daily basis in the nation's streets? Although mass shootings receive the bulk of the headlines in media outlets, injuries resulting from these shooting incidents are no more severe than what is experienced on an everyday basis (Maghami et al., 2019).

The physical trauma of a gunshot injury has a psychological consequence (Buchanan, 2014). If part of a bullet fragment remains within the victim's body, it can bring increased post-traumatic stress disorder and depression (R. N. Smith et al., 2018, p. 138):

> The most important finding of our study is that the presence of a retained bullet was associated with more severe depressive symptoms in Black men who sustained firearm injuries. Specifically, men with retained bullets had depressive severity scores 3.5 points higher than those without retained bullets when controlling for other variables. Our results suggest that there may be value in removing retained bullets.

A gun injury can be more consequential than a physical injury from another cause (Tasigiorgos, Economopoulos, Winfield, & Sakran, 2015). However, this type of injury brings with it stigma, even when the victim is an innocent bystander.

Bone fractures are rarely associated with gun injuries. Children's and adolescents' bone fractures, for example, are common comorbid injuries associated with firearm-related fractures in males, with youth of color disproportionately affected (Blumberg et al., 2018). Injuries have not benefited from in-depth research, which is a key theme in this section and book, providing an important opportunity for providers and academics interested in making a contribution to this field.

Finally, although gun fatalities and injuries are more male focused, females also are not immune from gunshots. A recent trend analysis of gun violence in Chicago's West Side between 2005 and 2016 found a significant 74.7% increase in female nonfatal hospitalizations from 2009–2012 to 2013–2016 (Fitzpatrick et al., 2019) and a disturbing trend expanding casualties to involve females. An extensive review (13 years) of Pennsylvania's gunshot hospitalizations found that assaults were most frequent among young African American/black males (Gross et al., 2017).

INTENTIONAL HARM—HOMICIDES

The United States is the world's most violent country not in the midst of a civil war (Gellert, 2019). A slow-moving massacre, in similar fashion to a slow-moving hurricane or tornado, is still as devastating as one that is fast moving. In the end, the casualties may be equal in number, but the speed of death will either garner national attention or be ignored in the reporting of the deaths. Mass gun violence is the fast-moving massacre, and daily killings are the slow version. On an average day, there are 300 shootings, with 100 dying (Hemenway, 2017). One estimate has almost 1,300 youth 17 years old and under killed by guns in homicides and suicides each year, and almost 5,800 are injured and treated in hospitals (Shaull, 2016).

One hundred deaths in any one event and location would make world news. When spread out nationally, these deaths simply are overlooked. Gun violence is associated with males; women and guns are an afterthought in discussions of gun violence (Mullins & Lee, 2020). If women of color embrace guns and use them for self-protection or to settle arguments, the gun violence scene will undergo a dramatic seismic shift, further challenging addressing this urban epidemic.

Homicides are best understood within national and international contexts. Understanding US gun violence requires it to be cast internationally because of how disproportionately prominent this violence is when compared to other countries. Pallin, Spitzer, Ranney, Betz, and Wintemute (2019) summarized the epidemiology of gun violence, setting the foundation for this section: Risk for firearm-related homicide is highest for adolescents and young adults and then decreases, but suicide risk increases with age. Firearm-related homicides and suicides rank among the 10 leading causes of death for Americans for most of the life span.

There are profound differences in firearm mortality rates by sex and race/ethnicity, with young African American men representing almost 90% of gun deaths, with gun-related suicides a greater threat among middle-aged, White, non-Latinx men with 90% using guns (Pallin et al., 2019). The premature deaths of young Black males in this country is alarming and constitutes a national epidemic; these deaths are on the verge of replacing the birth-to-incarceration pipeline with the birth-to–premature death pipeline for those 15 to 24 years of age (Jones-Eversley, Rice, Adedoyin, & James-Townes, 2020). Dying while on society's margins is the ultimate outcome of social injustice (Moller, 2018).

In 2016, the United States had the distinction of having the highest rate per capita of firearm-related deaths among all industrialized nations, with an average of 5 children killed per day in 2016 alone (Amnesty International, 2018). US gun fatality rates are 25 times higher than other high-income countries (P. Bailey, 2018), and this is due in large part not only because of the availability of guns but also because of the power of these weapons. What appears as typical here is atypical elsewhere in the world.

American guns, it bears noting but the discussion is beyond the scope of this book, also cause carnage abroad, as with Jamaica and other neighboring countries, introducing an overlooked international perspective on the topic (Ahmed, 2019).

[In Jamaica] law enforcement officials, politicians and even gangsters on the street agree: It's the abundance of guns, typically from the United States, that makes the country so deadly. And while the argument over gun control plays on a continual loop in the United States, Jamaicans say they are dying because of it—at a rate that is nine times the global average.

In Mexico, it is estimated that between 2011 and 2016, of the 106,000 guns seized in criminal investigations, 70% originated in the United States (Ramos, 2019). The reach of guns goes beyond our borders but still manages to kill people of color, and it should not be viewed as strictly a domestic issue.

We will not have difficulty in obtaining gun statistics for any state, and depending on particular interests, also group-specific information. For example, it is fair to say that African Americans/Blacks have received considerable scholarly attention; Latinxs also face gun violence. Although much of the gun violence literature emphasizes African Americans in cities such as Chicago, the Latnix community also, must struggle with gun violence there and other cities (Vargas, 2016). Taking a state perspective, such as that of California, highlights how gun violence is a serious issue within this community. The 1999–2016 period witnessed almost 17,000 Latinxs killed by guns—16,600, of which 12,912 were due to murder, 3,042 to suicide, and 319 to accidental shootings (Violence Policy Center, 2019b). Forty-five percent were in the 10- to 24-year-old category. Gun deaths and injuries are not evenly distributed across the country, with, for example, 2.0 deaths and 4.6 injuries per state (Everytown for Gun Safety, 2019a):

> One analysis found that in 2015, half of all gun homicides in the U.S. took place in just 127 cities, which together contain less than a quarter of the country's population. 31 percent of gun murders occurred in the 50 cities with the highest murder rates, though only 6 percent of Americans live in these cities. Individuals in these cities are 5 times more likely to be murdered with a gun than Americans overall. In some cities, the risk is much higher: residents of Jackson, MS are 9 times more likely to be the victims of a gun murder than Americans overall. In New Orleans, residents face a gun murder rate 11 times greater than other Americans.

Unequal distribution means that the entire country does not experience the same level of pain and expense. Further, murders are not evenly distributed within urban communities, highlighting how certain death zones stand out for focus.

An examination of 2015 data has half of these killings transpiring in cities with only a quarter of the nation's population (Aufrichtig, Beckett, Diehm, & Lartey, 2017). More specifically, almost one third of the nation's murders transpired in the 50 cities with the highest murder rates, with residents in these cities having a 500% greater chance of being murdered with a gun when compared to Americans overall (Federal Bureau of Investigation, 2019). The concept of "concentrated disadvantage," including traumatic expressions (J. R. Smith & Patton, 2016), is generally applied to urban communities of color and is best replaced by "concentrated gun death," one more deadly, less sanitized, and best understood by communities contending with this history and threat.

Contextual grounding of gun violence is attractive to helping professionals, who benefit from the research and scholarship undertaken by social scientists. There is a call for social scientists to further develop theory that can inform crime prevention (Welsh, Zimmerman, & Zane, 2018), setting the requisite foundation for community interventions and group-specific targeting and facilitating debates based on theory and research. An extensive gun death study found that although restrictive gun legislation does decrease pediatric, unintentional, suicide, and overall firearm deaths, it does not have a corresponding impact on homicide and African-Americans/Blacks, calling for initiatives that specifically target this group (Resnick et al., 2017).

Guns are often the weapon of choice in fatalities when used in criminal activities (Pizarro, Holt, & Pelletier, 2019). Further, a multifaceted snapshot of gun violence entails gathering information on the source of the gun/ammunition; caliber; how often carried; its use in prior criminal violence; when (day, time, month) the shootings occurred; weather at the time of shooting; demographics of victim/perpetrators; whether cohorts or groups were involved; outcome of the shooting; and location where the gun violence transpired are but a few perspectives on this violence.

Does time of day of gun violence differ between youth and adults? A Detroit study of offender age (youth and adults) found no differences in time and space (temporal, situational, and spatial patterns) involving gun use between these two age groups (Circo, Pizarro, & McGarrell, 2018). A similar understanding of time of day must be considered in understanding the circumstances leading to gun violence, including when and where it is, and when it is propitious to focus interventions.

For the first time in over 100 years, the *New York Times* editorial board (2015) published a front-page editorial on gun violence in response to the San Bernardino, California, mass shootings:

It is a moral outrage and a national disgrace that civilians can legally purchase weapons designed specifically to kill people with brutal speed and efficiency. These are weapons of war, barely modified and deliberately marketed as tools of macho vigilantism and even insurrection. America's elected leaders offer prayers for gun victims and then, callously and without fear of consequence, reject the most basic restrictions on weapons of mass killing, *as they did on Thursday*. They distract us with arguments about the word terrorism. Let's be clear: These killing sprees are all, in their own ways, acts of terrorism.

Gun violence, according to the CDC, is at a 40-year high (Charlton, 2019), an upswing after a period of declines (K. Smith, 2018):

During 2015–2016, the federal agency says there were 27,394 homicides involving firearms and another 44,955 gun suicides—the highest levels recorded since 2006–2007. In 2015–2016, the latest year available, homicide was the 16th leading cause of death among U.S. adults and the third leading cause for children between the ages of 10 and 19, according to the report. Guns were used in 74% of all recorded homicides, and used in 87% of homicides involving youth.

Increased urban gun fatality rates are felt throughout the entire health system, most notably emergency rooms. Trauma centers have experienced increased rates of gun fatalities because of gunshot wound cases (P. J. Cook, Rivera-Aguirre, Cerdá, & Wintemute, 2017; Kent et al., 2017). It is impossible to dissociate gun-related murder and suicides from loved ones left to deal with the aftermath.

Finally, the subject of organ donation has escaped systematic research and scholarship on urban communities of color and is worthy of more attention because it represents another avenue for someone in need benefitting from a tragedy, particularly the ethical issues that it raises (Prabhu, Parker, & DeVita, 2017), allowing someone to live as an act of giving. Studies showed that organ donation is relatively low related to homicide victims (Bilgel, 2018). However, no research could be located on victims of color engaging in this selfless act. People of color have suspicions of organ procurement and transplantation system fairness, complicating raising this question, let alone proposing policies on this subject (Annas & Grodin, 2017).

URBAN SCOPE

Recent urban gun violence trends generally fall into two categories (R. Rosenfeld, Gaston, Spivak, & Irazola, 2017, p. iii):

> Big-city homicides rose in 2015 and again in 2016, although not all cities experienced a large increase, and homicides fell in some cities. We consider two explanations of the homicide rise as guides for future research: (1) expansion in illicit drug markets brought about by the heroin and synthetic opioid epidemic and (2) widely referenced "Ferguson effects" resulting in de-policing, compromised police legitimacy, or both.

De-policing's impact on homicide rates, more specifically increasing murder rates, has not increased these rates (R. Rosenfeld & Wallman, 2019).

This book's focus is reinforced by national anti–gun violence organizations, and it is appropriate to start this section touching on two that have specifically recognized the impact it has on urban communities (Giffords Law Center to Prevent Gun Violence, 2016, p. 6):

> Gun homicides in America are disproportionately concentrated in urban areas, particularly in impoverished and underserved minority communities. Such neighborhoods are too often plagued by homicide rates on par with warzones. As one mother in a high-crime area of Chicago put it, "At night you had to put your mattress on the floor because bullets would be coming through the windows. It was like Vietnam."

Each new death revives the deaths of others who also died, creating a life that consists of a mosaic of pain and sorrow that simply refuses to go away, as evidenced in Reynolds's (2017) book *Long Way Down*. Life is measured by number of deaths rather than by accomplishments. In some urban neighborhoods, residents can name more gun deaths than high school graduates.

Everytown for Gun Safety (2016) and Moms Demand Action for Gun Sense in America, another group headed by women, address cities bearing the brunt of gun violence: "Urban gun violence touches on issues central to American life: safety, equality, opportunity, and community. As thousands of city residents are killed or injured with guns each year, mayors and other community leaders face an urgent challenge: finding effective solutions to make a difference now and into the future." We can create narratives increasing the importance of overlooked dimensions of gun violence in community life, and what can be done to address this problem is within our grasp.

We cannot obtain comprehensive community health status without gun violence as part of this picture and, more specifically, the status of young men of color, particularly African Americans/Blacks (Formica, Rajan, & Simons, 2019). Gun violence research shows it disproportionately impacts communities of color that also experience social and economic inequities, concentrated poverty, and racial segregation (Santilli et al., 2017), in what is a deadly combination. The level of community economic and social distress is related to urban youth violence (B. M. Tracy et al., 2019).

Gun violence is a symptom (a deadly one) of other social issues (Amnesty International, 2018, pp. 43–44):

> Firearms violence and the toll it takes on communities of color in urban settings is a symptom of a broader problem, one rooted in failures of federal, state and local government to address institutional racism and its multigenerational impacts. In the absence of jobs, investment in at-risk communities, adequately funded and resourced violence reduction and youth mentorship programs, and

other support networks and services that can provide stability, gun violence remains prevalent.

Mass shootings garner attention because of the sheer magnitude of concentrated killings in a single time episode (Ali, 2019b):

> Although any gun violence is traumatic, the narrative surrounding mass shootings is much different than that of deadly shootings in poor neighborhoods, said Laura Wilson, a psychology professor at the University of Mary Washington in Fredericksburg, Virginia. "The narrative is typically that mass shooting victims are innocent people who were just living their lives, while other gun-related deaths are wrongly assumed to be deserved," she said. "They are seen as gang-related or drug-related violence, but in actuality, when you read more closely, it's typically innocent bystanders that are just going to church or going out shopping."

A deserving versus undeserving victim stance is disturbing because no one should be a gun victim, but victimization is racialized, with corresponding social consequences.

Urban centers experience a far greater number of killings, but in a different pattern, and unless there is a high number of concentrated deaths over a weekend, violence is not considered newsworthy from a national or even state standpoint, as in Chicago. When a nation focused on the 2019 mass gun killings in El Paso, Texas, and Dayton, Ohio, Chicago experienced the worst weekend of killings (Ali, 2019b):

> As the nation mourned the deaths of 31 people in mass shootings in El Paso, Texas, and Dayton, Ohio, some Chicago neighborhoods experienced their most violent weekend of the year with 59 people shot, seven of them killed. While many Americans are expressing fear and anxiety about mass shootings in public places, residents of Chicago's West and South sides say they have lived with an epidemic of gun violence for decades and know the loss the rest of the nation

is experiencing. "We deal with this every day," said Edwin Taylor, 43, who lives in the Austin neighborhood on Chicago's West side. "Mass shootings are terrible and my heart goes out them, but what people need to understand is that it happens over and over in our neighborhoods."

Readers can appreciate how the slow cadence of death due to guns over a long period of time influences the character of a neighborhood.

Major media urban centers have a propensity to make national news when covering gun violence. One New York City resident of a neighborhood with high gun violence compared this violence to being in prison (P. J. Cook & Ludwig, 2002, p. 91): "[It] controls you. It does not allow you to be. It makes you feel like a prisoner when you have not committed a crime." The concept of prisoners has great relevance in communities with high percentages of residents with histories of incarceration.

It is important to examine gun violence in cities that do not capture the national limelight, such as Birmingham, Alabama, with approximately 211,000 residents. In 2018, Birmingham had 107 homicides, the majority gun related. Over 700 gun injuries were treated at the University of Alabama at Birmington Trauma Center, compared to 331 in 2010 (Sher, 2019). This center has three active duty US Air Force surgical teams assigned to it because it provides valuable experiences that they encountered in a war zone, and they benefit from experiences not found on the battlefield. In late 2019, Jacksonville, Florida, a city that generally goes under the radar on gun violence, was on pace to record the largest number of homicides since 2009, with 50% of these occurring in four zip codes (32209 at 23, 32210 at 13, 32208 at 11, 32254 at 10), illustrating the geographic-centeredness of these killings (Frazier, 2019).

Although urban violence unfolds through a variety of instruments, guns are without question the primary mechanism of choice. In 2017, guns and homicide were highly correlated (72%) according to the Federal Bureau of Investigation (2017). Urban violence cannot be understood without a historical context (Abt, 2019b, p. 5): "Urban violence can occur in the course of other street crimes. . . . In 2017, 64% of all homicides where a motive was identified were the result of disputes of some kind, and with stronger data the percentage would probably be higher. Many of these conflicts are connected to cycles of retaliatory violence that go back years, even generation."

Community social norms supporting violence as retribution (vigilante theory) are stronger where the police cannot be counted on to support justice, although this is not easily measurable (Kochel, 2018). Latzer (2018), in discussing the tension between structural theorists and cultural theorists, concluded that when combined, it provides the most propitious explanation for crime, particularly among subcultural groups. When conflicts leading to gun violence are historically based, it highlights the challenge in what appears as the intractable nature of this problem and what we face in addressing this pressing urban issue, requiring a highly coordinated campaign.

PEOPLE OF COLOR SCOPE

It is important to focus specific attention on people of color. Urban White, non-Latinx shootings of people of color are very rare, with the exception of police shootings of the unarmed. Types of gun violence casualties are essential in developing a picture of this epidemic. Gun violence can be conceptualized as falling into two categories: criminal and noncriminal (Drayton, 2019). We will not be hard-pressed finding evidence about the disproportionate impact of gun violence on communities of color.

In the United States, over the last three decades, young African American/Black men have been killed at an alarming rate, double that of any other group, leaving a lasting impression on an entire generation and a public concern focused on mass killings and underfunding gun violence in the nation's cities (Carswell, 2019; Freeman, Bachier-Rodriguez, Staszak, & Feliz, 2017). Urban gun violence introduces the sensitive and controversial subject of "Black on Black" crime (Abt, 2019b; Latzer, 2019b), and one can add the often overlooked topic of "Brown on Brown" violence, which has been complicated by data collection limitations (Violence

Policy Center, 2019a). Viewing urban gun violence from a racialized state brings a perspective on prevention funding that challenges us in pushing this agenda (Van Brocklin, 2019):

> Yet for all their promise, programs targeting community gun violence have struggled to win funding and support from local, state, and federal officials. When cities have implemented these strategies, they've often done so inconsistently. Activists and organizers of color say there is a clear reason for the shortfall: The gun violence prevention movement, up to this point, has largely been defined by white progressives responding to mass shootings, and the deaths of white victims have overwhelmingly garnered more attention, resources, and sympathy than those of black and brown people. The disparity has left evidence-based approaches to bring down community gun violence lacking political and financial support.

I agree with this assessment and makes it much more important to conduct a community assessment to identify resources (formal and informal) that decrease reliance on external sources of funding.

These racialized forces are not new to anyone who is committed to urban-focused social justice. Gun violence death rates display a strong racial disparity based on 2010 data (Payton, Thompson, Price, Sheu, & Dake, 2015): overall, 3.62 per 100,000; African Americans, 13.76 per 100,000; Latinxs, 3.40 per 100,000; and White, non-Latinxs, 1:41 per 100,000. The Giffords Law Center to Prevent Gun Violence (2016) provides another perspective on gun violence vulnerability, noting the African American men are particularly vulnerable. They constitute 6% of the population but are responsible for half of all gun fatalities each year. African American children have a 62% higher probability of dying from a gunshot than a car accident. Incidentally, in a similar manner to gun violence, COVID-19's disparity rates have an alarming impact on communities and people of color (Eligon & Burch, 2020; Jordan & Oppel, 2020).

YOUTH SCOPE

Sadly, there is a market for coffins for children that has surged; these coffins are often decorated with an array cartoon characters and angels (Rawlings, 2019). A search of the Internet on the words *coffins for kids* will uncover over 2.5 million sites. Gun violence has created an expanding market for these caskets, setting the stage for why children and youth cannot be subsumed within the broader category of gun violence. This subject is often overlooked, including the funeral services that are specifically youth centered, which differ from their adult counterparts.

Urban childhood within the context of gun violence is unlike that found in other areas of the children: Outdoor play is done at great peril (Knoll, 2019); schools are not sanctuaries; hospitals are not healing and wellness centers; friends and siblings can be here one day and dead another; houses of worship stress the afterlife at the expense of the current life; the future is now rather than some distant time; feeling safe is not taken for granted; and pain and suffering are the norm rather than health and joy. Life without respect, as in the case of law enforcement, cannot be surrendered (Kerrison, Cobbina, & Bender, 2018).

Simply summarized, children and youth of color are miniature adults, facing the strains and stressors that adults face without the benefits. This assessment shows the urgency before the nation. A sign being carried by a youth demonstrator is a sad statement on how youth think about becoming a gun violence victim: "I want to leave high school in a cap and gown not a body bag." A generation is on the verge of being lost to their families, communities, and country.

Infants and young children are not bulletproof. In fall 2019, two Philadelphia shootings stunned that city and nation. One fatality involved Nikolette Rivera, a 2-year-old shot in the head. The other shooting was that of Yazeem Jenkins, an 11-month-old, who was in the back of a car and shot four times (once in the head, once in the neck, and twice in the buttock). With a poor prognosis, if he survives, he will most likely be a quadriplegic for life (E. Shapiro, 2019). Children do not have to be targeted; they simply become collateral damage. The question of innocence or guilt is a nonquestion in instances where infants and children are killed in an exchange of gun violence. The increased numbers of gun-involved pediatric cases in emergency rooms have raised the policy questions of pediatric palliative care, which is profound in situations where lives are only just starting (Carter, Zeoli, & Goyal, 2020; Côté, Gaucher, & Payot, 2017).

We often talk about deaths and gun trafficking in the general sense. Adolescents and gun violence consequences are two subjects we generally do not equate (Dodson & Hemenway, 2015). A gun violence statistic is just a number; the context in which it occurs brings it to life and exposes the circumstances, and when the victim is a child, as in the following case, this tragedy takes on greater significance (Ali, 2019a): "Chicago has witnessed almost *2,000 homicides* since 2016, but few have shaken a city accustomed to corpses and caskets as the killing of 9-year-old Tyshawn Lee: a fourth grader shot execution-style by gang members as an act of revenge against the boy's father after being lured into an alley with the promise of a juice box."

Even by standards usually applied to urban gun fatalities, this case surpasses the norms to which hardened observers of violence are accustomed, and families of gang members are off limits, and no more so than when it involves a child member. A murder such as this has immediate and long-term ramifications, with an act of counterrevenge transpiring, making every family member feeling unsafe, or anyone else for that matter. These situations are remarkably similar to a war where the only rule is to stay alive, and casualties are the norm.

The American Pediatric Surgical Association's position paper on firearm injuries noted that the nation has reduced automobile deaths, and the same commitment must be made regarding childhood firearm injuries and deaths (Petty, Henry, Nance, & Ford, 2019). A public health approach toward gun violence takes a similar stance and emphasizes limiting access to guns (Pritchard, Parish, & Williams, 2020).

The evolutionary cause of death among youth is steady and predictable (Michigan Medicine, 2019): "A century ago, if a child or teenager died, an infectious disease was the most likely cause. A half century ago, if a child or teenager died, the most common reason was injuries from an automobile crash. Today, if an American child or teenager dies, firearm-related injuries and automobile crashes are almost equally likely to be to blame." Gun possession in homes may explain gun death increases among White, non-Latinx children (Prickett, Gutierrez, & Deb, 2019). It does not take a crystal ball to predict what the primary cause of death will be in half a century if we continue on this path, with youth of color paying the ulti-mate price (Bachier-Rodriguez, Freeman, & Feliz, 2017).

We often conceptualize shootings involving youth as transpiring in the community or in schools (Paessler-Chesterton & Green, 2019). However, shootings at sporting events have generally gone unnoticed from a na-tional perspective. Since 2013, there have been at least 108 incidents (19 killed and 100 injured) of shootings at sporting events, primarily at bas-ketball and football games that draw large crowds, and these have often transpired in the South and Midwest. As a result, many of these events have required hiring police officers to address the potential for gunfire. The sporting arenas, as a result, will necessitate site-specific interventions to prevent gun violence.

The association between guns and youth makes for deadly outcomes and a uniquely US problem, one that disproportionately impacts them and their communities (Bushman et al., 2016; Kemal, Sheehan, & Feinglass, 2018; Milam, Furr-Holden, Leaf, & Webster, 2018). Individual behavior cannot be separated from contextual settings in understanding the urban experience for youth of color (Like & Cobbina, 2019). Youth as perpetrators and victims will increase in significance for the field. Child-perpetrated (under age 14) homicides, for example, are a subcategory unto itself, usu-ally involving a gun with robbery or group assault as a motive with an urban dimension, and a category destined to expand our understanding with further research (Hemenway & Solnick, 2017). Understanding youth awareness and anticipation of experiencing violent situations provides insights into developing interventions (Schaechter & Alvarez, 2016).

The potential of becoming a victim plays an influential role in shaping the identity of these youth (youth as victims, youth as street smart, and youth action as self-defense) and their actions, such as help-seeking, avoid-ance, negotiation, or tolerance, providing insights into coping behaviors

(Zaykowski, 2019). Youth of color must contend with criminalization of daily routines, as in Baltimore, Maryland. They must contend with the constant threat of violence and a punitive culture of institutional systems of social control, adding to stress levels (Boyd & Clampet-Lundquist, 2019). Readers with a particular interest in Baltimore are recommended to read Deluca, Clampet-Lundquist, and Edin's (2016) book, *Coming of Age in the Other America,* which provides invaluable insights into the resiliency of youth against tremendous odds, including violence of various types.

Youth are disenfranchised and expendable (Giroux, 2015):

> Moreover, none of the calls to eliminate gun violence in the United States link such violence to the broader war on youth, especially poor minorities in the United States. In spite of ample reporting of gun violence, what has flown under the radar is that in the last three years 1 child under 12 years-old has been killed every other day by a firearm, which amounts to 555 children killed by guns in three years.

The youth under 18 years of age cannot vote and are dependent on adults to represent their interests in society. The institutions they attend are run by adults. The youth do not manufacture guns or ammunition. They are dependent on them for safety, but are prime victims for violence, and adults are limited in preventing this, with gun violence increases disproportionally affecting them (Ferreira et al., 2018).

Urban youth in high-violence contexts see more than their share of violence, with 26% of those participating in a violence intervention program having personally witnessed a gunshot fatality and 50% having lost a family member to this violence, for example (Purtle, Cheney, Wiebe, & Dicker, 2015). Bystanders who witness and aid shooting victims are victims also, although we do not gather data on them and rarely conduct follow-up to see how their lives have been altered as a result.

Most research and literature has focused on a singular act of gun violence resulting in a single death. However, we know very little of a family losing multiple children to gun violence. Losing one child to gun violence is a nightmare, losing more than one is beyond comprehension, and that is not uncommon, bringing self-doubt and self-blame (DeBo'rah, 2016, p. 93):

I don't know how many people you have interviewed that has had 2 sons within 2 years murdered. Living in the district, my worst nightmares came true, my 20-year-old was killed in 2007 and my younger son 17-year-old son was killed in 2009. I wonder if I had been able to move my children to the Maryland suburbs or Northern Virginia, would they still be alive! It is unfortunate, but I did not feel my wife and I were safe remaining in the district, so we have moved to out of the city.

Guns are the primary cause of premature deaths among children of color, with African Americans/Blacks 14 times more likely and 10 times more likely than their White, non-Latinx counterparts to be killed or hospitalized by shootings; Latinx youth are 10 times more likely than their White, non-Latinx, counterparts to be hospitalized and 3 times more likely to die (Centers for Disease Control and Prevention, National Center for Injury Prevention and Control, 2019; Leventhal, Gaither, & Sege, 2014). The concept of an adverse childhood experience must take into account gun violence, which typically has not been the case (Canchola, 2020; Rajan, Branas, Myers, & Agrawal, 2019), and certainly is highly applicable when discussing urban youth of color. When murder is considered senseless, as with young children being killed when playing outdoors, it not only creates public outcry but also feeds into feelings of helplessness (J. A. Fox, Levin, & Quinet, 2018).

Los Angeles Mayor Garcetti acknowledged youth bearing a tremendous burden due to gun violence (Macias, 2019):

"[Youth of color] are the ones who experience gun violence regularly. . . . They are the ones whose cousins die on their lawns. If you're not looking at the racial and age component, you're not seeing this issue clearly." In May, LA launched a youth-run "Louder Than Guns" campaign that features mock ads for insurance covering mass shootings and accidental and daily gunfire. The ads direct residents to a website where they can share their experiences with gun violence.

Readers will witness a specific focus on African American/Black and Latinx youth where appropriate. In 2010, American Indian male adolescents had the second-highest rate of gun deaths behind their African American/Black counterparts, with 19.3 gun deaths per 100,000 teens (Kaplan & Kerby, 2013). Why not include Native American youth? An urban focus finds African Americans/Blacks and Latinx youth overly represented in these geographical settings when compared to Native Americans.

The question youth can pose, "Will I make it to graduation?" is unthinkable in high-resourced. White, non-Latinx communities. The quotation, "I can tell you that I have been to more funerals that are gun-related than I've been to graduations," by a resident of Los Angeles' "Death Alley," sums up how frequent and consequential guns are among youth in urban communities (Kessler, 2015) and how life spans and major developmental achievements are measured.

We often associate urban gun violence as either gang related or involving adolescents/young adults, with their injuries and fatalities dominating public discourse. However, the very young also face this threat, as in St. Louis (Chokshi, 2019). The CNN headline covering this story says it all (Scutti, 2019): "This 7-year old was supposed to start 2nd grade this week. He's the 7th child to die by gun violence in St. Louis this year." This is a substory of St. Louis and why many are labeling this city the "murder capital" of the nation due to its gun death pace (114 compared to 105 at this same period last year 2018), an 8.6% increase from last year, and aggravated assaults (2,327 compared to 2,188). Very young children as war casualties can become the face of urban young violence and how lives are lost while they play and enjoy childhood.

Youth are vulnerable to becoming gun causalities (Parsons, Thompson, Vargas, & Rocco, 2018, p. 2/22):

On February 14, 2018, 14 students and three staff members were murdered at Marjory Stoneman Douglas High School in Parkland,

Florida, by a single shooter armed with an assault rifle. This horrific massacre galvanized the nation's attention to the issue of gun violence, particularly as it affects young people in this country. However, the scope of gun violence as it affects America's youth is much vaster than this most recent mass shooting. Gunfire has officially overtaken car accidents as one of the leading killers of young people in the U.S. Since the beginning of 2018, 820 teens ages 12 to 17 have been killed or injured with a gun. As mass shootings become more common and more deadly, a staggering 57 percent of teenagers now fear a school shooting.

States with more restrictive gun laws have fewer child fatalities (Madhavan, Taylor, Chandler, Staudenmayer, & Chao, 2019). High-capacity semiautomatics are increasingly used in crimes since the expiration of the federal ban on them, raising concerns about their increased impact on injuries and fatalities (Koper et al., 2018).

Youth killed and injured in mass school shootings receive considerable attention but represent a small percentage of overall casualties (Wong, 2019):

Seldom do those fatalities happen on school campuses at all, in fact. While comprehensive data are limited, a 2017 study *found* that the majority—85 percent—of children 12 or younger shot to death from 2003 to 2013 were killed in a home. Roughly four in 10 kids aged 13 to 17 killed with a gun also died in a home; another four in 10 were killed in the streets. Meanwhile, nearly two in three of the country's gun deaths (of all ages) are the result of suicide according to *a* FiveThirtyEight *analysis* of federal data. The remaining third are homicides, the analysis notes, and public mass shootings *make up* less than 1 percent of firearm fatalities.

Gun violence touches all age groups, from the very young to older adults. It brings an onus for the nation's youth, however, and how they socially navigate gun fears and the police in highly policed urban neighborhoods, because that is part of their operative reality and the communities where they reside (Gander, 2019b).

It is simplistic to view gun violence from a narrow fatality standpoint. Estimates have 25% of youth of color having exposure to violence, primarily in their neighborhoods, in their lifetime (Zimmerman & Pogarsky, 2011). Urban youth and guns must be examined from three points to gain insight into gun consequences: (a) gun violence; (b) gun carrying; and (c) general gun exposure (Quimby et al., 2018). These categories can be broken into subcategories, providing pieces of the challenge in addressing how guns shape the lives of urban youth and young adults and how we can conceptualize interventions.

Youth gun carrying is a dynamic event, with varying time periods of carrying and noncarrying that must be taken into account in designing interventions to reduce gun carrying. Using messaging to influence health-related behaviors such as gun carrying can be an intervention approach (Loughran, Reid, Collins, & Mulvey, 2016). Fatigue associated with violence can carry over to other spheres of the lives of urban youth. The domestic disturbance that followed Baltimore's Freddie Gray's funeral made national news and was the culmination of numerous frustrations involving the police (Boyd & Clampet-Lundquist, 2019): "As the death of Freddie Gray in Baltimore and many others illustrate, adjusting one's daily routine to manage interactions with police can truly be a matter of survival, given that men of color are disproportionately likely to be victims of officer-involved shootings." Funerals bring together people, allowing the sharing and validation that invariably occur in a crowd, and more so where there are blatant injustices.

Emotional agony takes an invisible toll and is manifest in various ways, with the fatigue associated with violence simply part of daily occurrences, with corresponding fundraisers to pay for the funeral costs (Huerta, 2018). When a victim's body is too disfigured to allow open casket viewing, it further complicates the grieving process, which for parents is a reaction hard to articulate without further eliciting soulful responses from funeral attendees.

We need more in-depth research (Hills-Evans, Mitton, & Sacks, 2018; Webster, Cerdá, Wintemute, & Cook, 2016), such as that focused on gun violence within and near schools and how educational student outcomes are impacted by this violence (Barboza, 2018), with other ramifications that often become overlooked but have deleterious outcomes. The impact of urban gun killings on schoolmates not in the immediate social network of those murdered also can cause them to experience grief and trauma that can go unrecognized (Silva, 2019).

Gun violence's ripple effects are often viewed from the obvious outcomes, but educational performance is often not part of this discussion, and it also has lifetime potential consequences. Direct and vicarious police contact involving urban youth will have the educational achievement of these youth compromised as a result, illustrating the broad reach of police contacts in altering views and behavior in areas generally not associated with them (Arnwine, 2019; Gottlieb & Wilson, 2019).

The nation's youth bear a disproportionate gun violence burden even when they only constitute a small percentage of the number of deaths overall. In 2016, for example, the top three causes of death numbered 2.7 million (heart disease, cancer, and unintentional injuries), with 2.2% for those aged 15 to 29 (Parsons et al., 2018). Gun deaths claim twice the number of children dying from cancer (M. Fox, 2018). Another way of looking at gun deaths and children is to say that in 2017 there were more children killed by guns than on-duty police officers and military personnel combined (Gander, 2019a). More specifically, this burden is greater on youth of color being victims of gun violence within their community and from police action.

Gun fatalities kill urban youth at the same rate that suicides kill rural youth (Dodson, 2016). There are over 3,000 child gun fatalities (accidental, suicides, murder) in the United States involving children under the age of 17 years old, with Black children being 10 times more likely to be victims when compared to White, non-Latinxs (Fowler, Dahlberg, Haileyesus, Gutierrez, & Bacon, 2017). Youth victimization can be defined narrowly (direct victim) or broadly, as a close friend or relative of the victimized (Z. McGee, Alexander, Cunningham, Hamilton, & James, 2017), thereby broadening the impact of gun and other forms of violence (Z. T. McGee, Logan, Samuel, & Nunn, 2019).

Is hearing gunshots considered victimization because of the fear it engenders in children (Larsen et al., 2017)? If the answer is yes, it expands the number of gun victims in a dramatic manner. I would argue that they must be considered. There is underreporting of gunshots, as evidenced in Oakland and Washington, D.C., a further indicator of the seriousness of this issue (Carr & Doleac, 2018). Systematically taking gunshot sounds into account is a step in the right direction of obtaining a comprehensive understanding of urban gun violence.

An approach related to social determinants of trauma provides a wide net for the search into the origins of various sources of trauma and their interactions and can serve as a basis for development of interventions (Mikhail, Nemeth, Mueller, Pope, & NeSmith, 2018). Gun violence's reach into a community's social fabric and its institutions is extensive, including poor school performance of its youngest students, as noted previously (Bergen-Cico et al., 2018). When gun violence disproportionately impacts children, it compromises their future, their community, and the nation. The institutions with which youth interact also feel the consequences. The daily exposure to a violent and fearful environment, including fears of death, influences psychological well-being and functioning (Singletary, 2020). However, there is a need for more extensive research and scholarship on gun violence exposure for the field to make substantive progress in this area (Aspholm, St. Vil, & Carter, 2019).

CONCLUSION

It is hoped readers have developed a deeper understanding of gun violence and its prominence nationally and in its urban centers. Statistics do not have names or faces attached to them but still tell an important story. Further, statistics are a static picture in time, requiring consistent updating because today looks different from yesterday and tomorrow. Nevertheless, there is a stark reality attached to them that paints a precarious picture of life in many urban centers.

Gun violence's reach has regional and specific neighborhood variations. However, it has more to do with the extent of the problem than whether there is a problem. We can argue that one death is too many, yet in some neighborhoods it resembles more of a war zone than a typical living situation. It is hoped this chapter captured the breadth and depth of this issue to develop gun interventions, including why self-help organizations are a potential lynchpin in solving this national disgrace.

Chapter 4 grounds statistics and narratives into the social fabric of communities and why multifaceted perspectives are needed to appreciate the complexity of gun violence causes and the range of interventions needed to be successful. These interventions, as discussed in Section II, engage (community mobilization) residents in the crafting and implementation, with self-help organizations assuming a prominent place within these approaches.

5

Social, Political, Economic, and Cultural Perspectives

What works? After twenty years of funerals and hospital visits. I do not feel like I'm much closer to knowing.

—ALEX KOTLOWITZ, *2019, p. 6*

INTRODUCTION

Starting this chapter with US Representative Pressley's (D-MA) quotation sets an appropriate tone for helping us understand the gun violence ripple effects throughout a community (Pressley, 2019):

> With every bullet that's fired, with every life that is stolen, with every community that is torn apart—we are becoming increasingly traumatized. This is about the mothers and fathers with broken spirits and broken hearts. This is about brothers with deep wounds and invisible scars. This is about children who have attended more funerals than graduation parties. This is about preserving our collective humanity. This is about ending a public health crisis. Now is the time to wage peace.

Urban Gun Violence. Melvin Delgado, Oxford University Press (2021). © Oxford University Press.
DOI: 10.1093/oso/9780197515518.003.0005.

The Pressley quotation supports Kotlowitz's quotation at the beginning of this chapter. However, attending funerals stands out for me in connecting these quotations.

Gun violence is not limited to this nation's cities, it bears noting (Morrison et al., 2015). Nevertheless, the concentration of people in urban communities, and an increased likelihood of gun violence in these areas, uplifts the importance of a geography-centric approach, taking into account local circumstances dictating how it is manifested and addressed, including its disproportionate impact on people of color. It is hoped we are in a position to appreciate gun violence's magnitude as seen through fatalities and injuries, gun sources, as well as different geographical contexts, age, and racial groups.

Gun violence acquires greater meaning when contextualized and individualized, particularly when statistics fade and narratives emerge to personalize lives and the damage caused by guns to individuals, families, neighborhoods, and the nation. It is only when the magnitude of the humanity of this issue is exposed can we truly grasp the solutions before us. Although gun violence defies an in-depth understanding without a broad canvas, there is a place for an all-encompassing view to accommodate particular practitioner interests, and this is supported by research (Becerra, 2018). This allows focusing on dimensions holding local prominence, revealing multiple manifestations of this issue, and uplifting overlooked dimensions.

Gun consequences must be couched within the broader subject of violence in general, and within very specific confines, introducing the social sciences to add depth and breadth to an analysis. Last, as in the case of social work and other helping professions and social sciences, it brings unique perspectives that aid in development of a comprehensive narrative when applied to communities of color and various subgroups, increasing our understanding of the challenge presented to us in the United States. Other countries also have gun violence challenges. However, these are typified by periods of sustained political unrest rather than a central (DNA) thread in those nation's fabric that spans multiple generations.

President Trump, at his political rallies, often talks about the murder rate in US cities, such as Baltimore, Maryland, and Chicago, Illinois, and other cities, and compares them to Honduras, El Salvador, Guatemala, and Afghanistan, with the help of audiences, neglecting to note that these countries are in the midst of major social and political upheavals, and in the case of the last country, under military occupation. President Trump's rants also disparage this nations' cities, which are heavily of color and have Democrats as elected leaders and an outlet for his racist sentiments. But just as important, the rants send a profound message to residents that they are unworthy and deserve this pain.

Four viewpoints are covered in this chapter (social, political, economic, and cultural), allowing coverage of usual and unusual aspects of urban gun violence. These perspectives are not ranked in order of importance and must be present in any analysis of urban gun violence and search for solutions, and more so when seeking a nuanced and localized approach. These perspectives interact in a highly dynamic manner; when one is particularly impacted, the others react accordingly. Gun violence permeates society, with few urban segments escaping its grasp.

SOCIAL VIEWPOINT

Providing a social canvas on which to critically examine urban gun violence is an appropriate place to start. This canvas, unlike a beautiful work of art, presents a scene that elicits feelings of anger, despair, and pain. Thus, how it is painted is extremely important in order to fully comprehend its significance and message to the world. A social perspective on gun violence is probably the most propitious place to start and a familiar viewpoint that helping professionals possess; after all, our work is about the social world, and it is an important view because of how it shapes daily life within urban communities. Our understanding cannot rely solely on this viewpoint. This viewpoint is critical because of how it sets a broad context from which to position key factors, such as urban context, people of color, gender, and youth, for example.

Carlson (2018) addressed the importance of sociology weighing in on gun violence: "How could a thorough understanding of guns in the United States proceed without some sociological sensibility?" Sociology and other professions, including social work, can provide a wide canvas from which to capture and cast other disciplines and perspectives for increasing our understanding of the social forces at work in creating gun violence.

How society views gun violence shapes the politics and funding of initiatives addressing it. If viewed as a problem in someone else's neighborhood, or simply of lawlessness gone mad, it does not have the same significance as if viewed as a local problem, and it depends if we ask gun owners or those who do not own guns (Parker, Horowitz, Igielnik, Oliphant, & Brown, 2017). There are significant differences between those living in rural areas and those in the suburbs and cities, with the latter considering gun violence far more important than those who live in other parts of the country.

Yamane (2017) argued there is no sociology of US gun culture, with this field dominated by criminological and epidemiological gun violence studies. Social sciences also have a prominent place at the table (J. Metzl, 2018):

Social science can address best approaches to stem gun mortality in the context of firearm-related attitudes, biases, and belief systems. Put another way, social science methods allow researchers to consider what guns mean in addition to what they do. Doing so helps uncover broader tensions about why certain people feel they need guns in the first place, or why others reject them out-of-hand.

No one discipline or profession dominates the discourse on urban gun violence or capture the dynamic state fulling this form of violence. Only through partnerships, including community institutions such as those that are self-help, can we hope to seek clarity and purpose in solving this form of national violence, bringing a multifaceted contextual grounding to an analysis and development of strategies. This point must be reinforced because it will take a broad coalition of professions and community partners to solve gun violence. The social dimension of urban gun violence is an essential part of the canvas on which we paint a picture of solutions.

POLITICAL VIEWPOINT

Gun violence's political manifestations are generally framed rather narrowly—pro and against gun control, with a similar viewpoint concerning elected officials in many circles. This stance must not be minimized because access to guns and ammunition has taken center stage in national debates. There are other political aspects that become lost through an exclusive focus on gun possession, particularly at a local community level, and must be taken into account in crafting localized responses.

Local politics also are influenced by gun violence, as manifested by elections and local organizational decisions to weigh in or ignore gun violence, for example. Local community organizations deciding to weigh in, or not, on gun violence are part of a dimension of politics that must not go unnoticed. Community social service agencies are impacted by gun violence, regardless of the mission of these agencies. Community gun violence is experienced throughout, with some segments (social networks) feeling its intensity more than others. The passing of local gun ordinances are an example of how political outcomes over the past 20 years have influenced gun availability (Flores, 2015; Godwin & Schroedel, 2000).

Local elections, for example, influence who becomes mayor and who city council representatives are. Mayors decide who becomes a police superintendent, and in cases where police–community relationships are strained, this decision-making power can be quite influential in shaping these relationships. If positive, it increases community cooperation in addressing gun violence. The ripple effects of increased trust can cross over into other arenas that influence well-being and engender hope.

ECONOMIC VIEWPOINT

A comprehensive economic picture on gun violence has not benefitted from the same scholarly attention compared to other perspectives in this chapter. Measuring the value of human life in economic terms is unseemly and counter to the humanistic toll it takes. However, no complete picture of gun violence is possible without understanding economic manifestations, which emerge in visible and invisible ways, with consequential outcomes at the community level. Thus, the economics of gun violence is vastly understudied (Arcas-Salvador, 2017).

Why should we be versed on the economics of gun violence? Shouldn't that be left to economists? We need to have a grasp on economics in helping us craft arguments for gun violence reduction initiatives before local governments and also at the national level. An economic argument, putting aside the human casualty aspect of gun violence, highlights the zero sum of how funds are diverted from projects that benefit the entire community rather than being devoted to a small percentage of the community. I realize that there may be some who simply will not take this stance. This problem's magnitude requires well-crafted initiatives that do not overlook any argument for sound community initiatives. Therefore, a multifaceted stance is needed.

There are many ways of conceptualizing financial costs in developing a compelling narrative on gun violence economic costs to society. The immediate and long-term financial costs of gun violence, as noted by the Giffords Law Center to Prevent Gun Violence (2017, p. 9), is staggering and diverts needed funds from other projects with community well-being implications and is considered a great moral crisis in this country, not to mention "that the law enforcement and healthcare costs alone associated with a single gun homicide are $488,000, and more than $71,000 for each non-fatal shooting." The cumulative economic costs are staggering. When we add lost employment, it further increases these costs (Koper, Johnson, Stesin, & Egge, 2019). People of color from communities with high violence rates are less likely to be hired for employment because potential employers fear them, bringing together the interplay of race, place, and crime (Mobasseri, 2019), with profound economic implications for these individuals, families, and communities.

This section addresses gun violence economics from six highly interrelated standpoints illustrative of the broad and profound reach of this standpoint: (a) the challenges in arriving at cost estimates; (b) the business of guns and ammunition; (c) health and social service costs;

(d) indirect costs to real estate taxes and similar items; (e) the cost of funerals; and (f) lost productivity. These consequences extract a much heavier price than the numerical value attributed to them, and that would be the case within low-income communities of color, where economic resources are limited. If we step back and take a zero-sum stance, there are countless losers from gun violence. There are also winners, and that may appear as odd, but cannot be ignored in crafting our research and interventions.

Challenges in Arriving at Cost Estimates

Although there are numerous hurdles to arrive at gun violence costs, we must not be dissuaded from attempting to quantify a human tragedy that is preventable, unlike other forms of death. Calculating economic costs of gun violence is an inexact science, including how to put a price on emotional agony (Muggath, 2017), which we may argue cannot be priced, particularly when transcending multiple household generations, with immense current and future economic manifestations, such as lost productivity, to look at this narrowly.

The lost productivity from gun violence is significant, with one estimate including all related costs equalizing $100 billion dollars annually, with Minnesota, for example, incurring $2.2 billion each year from the over 900 gun deaths each year (Picchi, 2017). The $100 billion figure, to put in perspective, is equal to the country's annual federal spending on education and greater than the transportation budget. Another estimate has costs even higher ($229 billion per year) when also taking into account the costs of those who are incarcerated for murder or assault. Translating gun violence costs $700 on a per capita basis every year (Giffords Law Center to Prevent Gun Violence, 2016).

Urban gun violence economics has received attention as it relates to home values and job losses. For example, each homicide in Washington, D.C., is estimated to result in the loss of two retail/service establishments. Oakland, California, in turn, experiences an average loss of $24,000 in home value for every murder that occurs, and this translates into 5% fewer jobs the next year (Irvin-Erickson, Bai, Gurvis, & Mohr, 2016). A study of home values and homicides in eight US cities (Boston, MA; Philadelphia, PA; Seattle, WA; Dallas, TX; Chicago, IL; Milwaukee, WI; Jacksonville, FL; and Houston, TX) found a 10% reduction in homicides caused an increase of 0.83% in value, and a 25% decrease translated into a 2.1% increase in home values and reductions in Boston ($11 billion); Philadelphia ($8 billion); Seattle ($7 billion); Dallas ($6 billion), and Chicago ($6 billion) (R. J. Shapiro & Hassett, 2012).

Gun violence statistics highlight its magnitude and why it is arduous to put a dollar figure on this problem (Hristova, 2017):

Since 1968, there have been 1,516,863 gun-related deaths on US territory compared to 1,396,733 war deaths since the founding of the United States. This means that up to 2015, according to data collected by Politifact, the death toll for citizens and visitors of the United States from domestic gun violence exceeds that of all the deaths from all the wars the US has participated in since its inception.

How do we cost out casualties of all this nation's wars? The past 50 years claimed more lives than all of our wars! Clearly, we struggle putting a dollar figure on the deaths, not to mention the costs for those surviving a gunshot and the emotional toll it takes.

The Business of Guns and Ammunition

The economic manifestations of the gun industry are far-reaching and multifaceted (McCann, 2019): "Gun sales have been *down* since Donald Trump won the White House, with a 6.1 percent decline in 2018 alone. And while that's good news to some, it could be a bad sign for state economies relying heavily on the firearms industry. By one *estimate*, guns contributed more than $52 billion to the U.S. economy and generated over $6.8 billion in federal and state taxes in 2018." Gun sale reductions since Trump's election may in large part be due to lessening of fears on gun control.

Forbes Magazine provides another estimate on the gun business of $28 billion annually (gun stores had revenue of about $11 billion and gun and ammunition firms generated $17 billion), but the business of protecting us from guns far exceeds these estimates (McBride, 2018). In 2018, the gun industry generated $52 billion for the US economy and over $6.8 billion in federal and state taxes (McCann, 2019). The business or industry of guns (V. M. Smith et al., 2017) has shifted in focus to an increased lethality (V. M. Smith et al., 2017), with corresponding medical and rehabilitation for survivors.

The jobs provided and local taxes paid by the gun industry represent a dimension of this business that can translate into local and political support, in similar fashion to any other multibillion dollar industry. These businesses wield considerable lobbying power at the state level, which will then translate into local political pressure.

A different perspective on local businesses is needed. Local businesses, for example, make profits from selling "Rest in Peace" T-shirts, cutouts, painting of memorial murals, burial costs, and other costs related to commemorating the life of victims, bringing another layer to financial costs and benefits, if you wish, of these deaths. Of course, we can argue that these economic benefits are not what communities want. Nevertheless, these economic ramifications must be acknowledged.

A racialized view of gun economics introduces a disturbing picture. The gun industrial complex is an underregulated manufacturing and retail industry that benefits those who are White, non-Latinx, to the detriment of communities of color, where guns and ammunition ultimately end up taking their deadly toll (Gailey, 2018). This racialized argument of how White, non-Latinx people economically have a stake in this industry will receive more attention in the future concerning who profits from these deaths. Finally, another economic manifestation of gun violence is the business of selling bulletproof gear, such as backpacks and hoodies (Chau, 2019). It is fair to say, however, that families in urban communities can ill afford purchasing these items.

Health and Social Service Costs

We are never at a loss in obtaining economic costs of certain aspects of gun violence. Service providers are cognizant of how gun violence translates into costs because we witness this on a daily basis. It is estimated that the immediate costs are $5,254 to treat a gunshot victim in an emergency room and $95,887 if they have to be admitted, which gives a sum of $2.8 billion over the course of 1 year, with estimates of $160,000 over the extended term of treatment (Myers, 2019). The economic costs of acute care of pediatric gun injuries are rising, with an estimated but dated $400 million annually, and this does not even take into account factors such as long-term medical care, lost wages, and legal costs (Allareddy, Nalliah, Rampa, Kim, & Allareddy, 2012).

Another perspective concretizes this view. A New Orleans, Louisiana, public hospital spotlighted the economic costs of gun injuries (Russo, Fury, Accardo, & Krause, 2016):

A total of 3617 patient encounters were identified that met this criteria. The total amount billed by the hospital over the study period was $141,995,682 while collecting $30,922,953. The actual hospital costs from these encounters was $73,572,892, giving the hospital a loss of $42,649,938. Of the 3617 patient encounters, 59% required orthopedic consultation. Of that consultation group, 25% required inpatient orthopedic surgical intervention. Acute gunshot wounds accounted for 23% of orthopedic trauma consultations and 13% of the orthopedic daily census.

Saving the lives of those who eventually die often takes center stage, with costs being considerable.

Gun violence costs are often cast from health and social service viewpoints (Hristova, 2017):

The findings of the investigation showed that the annual cost of fatal and non-fatal gun violence to the US was $229 billion, representing

1.4% of total G.D.P. In comparison, obesity in the US costs the country $224bn, which makes the economic impact of gun violence higher than that of obesity. These $229bn are also the equivalent of the size of Portugal's economy or the equivalent of $700 for every American citizen.

These costs necessitate that other needs go under- or uncovered, which is a side of gun violence that rarely is addressed. For example, these costs include productivity lost by the social network of those receiving services because they must take those with wounds to hospitals and rehabilitation.

Indirect Costs to Real Estate Taxes

Measuring the indirect costs of gun violence at the local level has increasingly found saliency because of how it impacts communities on a daily basis beyond the obvious focus on direct victims. In Minneapolis, Minnesota, for instance, one report concluded that for every gun homicide in a census tract within a year translates into 80 fewer jobs the following year and the reduction of an average home value by $22,000 (Hristova, 2017).

There is a strong negative relationship between local business development and gun violence, which impacts a different quality of life beyond local taxes (Matti & Ross, 2016). A study of commercial establishments in Minneapolis, Oakland, and Washington, D.C., found an increase in gun homicides translated into fewer business establishments, fewer new jobs created, and decreased sales volumes, resulting in lower generation of local taxes (Irvin-Erickson et al., 2016). Local taxes support schools, social services, law enforcement, and other services that impact the quality of life of residents, with immense implications for families and communities. Abandoning buildings and stores because of fears of guns and other forms of violence translates into blighted and abandoned lots, which in turn can be viewed as a draw for violent activities (Branas et al., 2016):

Tens of millions of vacant and abandoned properties exist in the United States. These blighted properties represent tens of billions of dollars in lost tax revenues and municipal costs. They also erode community connectedness, create stress and fear among residents, and, given the findings here, promote firearm violence. For these and other reasons, blight remediation programs have been recognized by multiple organizations interested in reducing violence and promoting urban health, including the Centers for Disease Control and Prevention, the Institute of Medicine, and the National Institutes of Health. (p. 2162)

This conclusion is not surprising, and the message it sends to residents and those outside of the neighborhood is that it is simply not worth investing in this community. Disinvestment translates into certain communities are low priority (Branas et al., 2018).

Gun violence causes higher local budgets being directed to law enforcement, as in the case of fiscal year 2017, which witnessed the following cities devoting a considerable portion of their local budgets to this activity: Oakland (41%), Chicago (39%), Minneapolis (36%), and Houston (35%). A dollar figure per resident is another way of looking at the local impact, with spending per person of $381 in Los Angeles and $772 in Baltimore (Neuhauser, 2017). Any significant reduction in costs translates into savings for projects that can alter gun violence behavior, including improving community morale.

The Cost of Funerals

Community practitioners working in marginalized urban communities are familiar with stories about how neighborhoods come together to contribute money to bury a resident whose family cannot afford to pay the costs and how businesses often assume an active role in these efforts. The funeral costs of burying their dead because of COVID-19 can be astronomical for a low-income family, and it is one reason why cremations have started to be used ($1,700), for example, even though this is not the culturally preferred way of burial (Garcia, 2020).

A review of the literature found no statistics on the costs of funerals of those killed as a result of gun violence. Although these data are not available, it is included to generate discussion because it does extract an economic cost that is invisible to the world outside the community.

We can argue that the social sciences are absent in helping us better understand how these community institutions are playing a healing role, and practitioners have not explored how to engage them on gun violence. We often think of houses of worship in coalitions, but they are often the first significant institutions engaged by the families and in a position to offer help to them in this particularly trying time.

There are, however, narratives about how funeral homes have an instrumental role in addition to an expressive one to play in the aftermath of gun killings, such as in Chicago (Sanchez, 2018) and Wilmington, Delaware, a city and state rarely associated with urban gun violence, where two funeral parlors have been particularly impacted, and how these deaths personally shaped those who work in funeral homes, which sometimes entails burying relatives and personal friends (J. Peterson, 2018):

> With record-breaking shooting deaths in recent years, Congo Funeral Home and House of Wright Mortuary have seen and handled many of the city's homicide victims, and helped their families cope with the loss. They didn't expect to see so many young adults and teens rolling through their doors when they were training for the job. "People assume death doesn't affect us because we are around it so much, but it does," Trippi Congo said. The funeral directors see the ripple effect the violence has on the family, particularly the children of the dead, as well as on the community. Both men, one a former city council member and one a current member, said it makes them want to help find a solution to the violence.

Funeral homes are often staffed and owned by residents and cannot be ignored in developing community research and initiatives on gun violence

(Cabrera & Stevenson, 2017). These institutions help families with the grieving process, bringing a distinct gun violence dimension with links to the anthropology of death (Engelke, 2019).

Lost Productivity

Lost productivity is a concept enjoying popularity. Everyone understands what it means not to be able to carry out responsibilities because of illness or some other factor. Any lost productivity discussion must not be exclusively focused on employment and must also examine it from an educational view, which is unconventional, but essential when youth are a major segment of those who are killed, injured, and exposed to violence. Their educational performance is severally compromised from a human capital perspective. This stance brings in education and health in broadening our understanding of lost productivity.

The inability to fulfill one's potential has a ripple effect that can be far-reaching because of how compromised potential impacts the families of victims; when there is a high concentration of victims, the communities where they live also are compromised. Social workers and other providers are cognizant of how a victim's family and social network also are compromised when a tragedy occurs.

CULTURAL VIEWPOINT

The concept of culture is very broad, encompassing a multitude of ways it is applied to gun violence (Contreras, 2018b). Readers may have a preffered view of bringing culture to life regarding this issue. In social work, we have a tendency to apply culture at an individual level, and on occasions apply it to organizations and other systems. Culture (racial identity, spirituality, and communalism) can be a protective factor and tapped in to developing interventions as a means of countering community violence, as in the case of African American adolescent males (C. M. Wallace, McGee, Malone-Colon, & Boykin, 2018).

Exploring gun cultural dimensions requires an expansive view, with several covered in this section illustrating its broad reach, often in unconventional ways. This view of urban gun violence brings another dimension, cultural trauma (Armstrong & Carlson, 2019): "Cultural trauma is central for understanding the broad effects of gun violence in the US. Rather than emerging in the aftermath of a close brush with a traumatic event, cultural trauma describes the processes by which collective memories are narrated as trauma to mediate collective identity."

Neighborhood as a cultural context also has taken a role at center stage (Like & Cobbina, 2019, p. 295):

> A number of criminologists have examined the association between neighborhood, culture, and violence. Research in this field has shown that structural conditions of neighborhood life, such as unemployment, poverty, alienation, inequality, and social dislocation, shape cultural processes that are conducive to male youth violence. . . . This oppositional culture emphasizes a tough identity and the use of violence, which are often perceived as necessary for acquiring respect, status, and street credibility to defer subsequent attacks in economically distressed neighborhoods.

Unfortunately, gun carrying is equated with respect and power among many, particularly youth. When these sentiments are socially ingrained, it requires a multifaceted strategy involving all community segments.

If gun carrying is part of the cultural fabric, then it takes more than an access focus or market disruption to curtail violence. It also necessitates a shift in beliefs and circumstances that lead to conflictual situations best resolved by guns (Latzer, 2019a). Culture can be manifest in a variety of ways. Bringing it to the street level is a salient way of using this construct (Burgason, Thomas, & Berthelot, 2014; Dierenfeldt, Thomas, Brown, & Walker, 2017). This view has received considerable scholarly attention, typified by E. Anderson's (1994) *The Code of the Streets*. Instead of a moral compass, there is a survival compass, and its replacement interferes with building and exercising empathy and compassion, which will prove troubling for community connectedness.

Attitudes toward gun access necessitate a major cultural change to stop violence, within and outside of urban centers, because firearms have a significant constituency in this country (Lizotte & Hendrix, 2019). Addressing attitudes will not be sufficient without changes in how to settle disputes. Trading guns for knifes is not what we think about when discussing eliminating gun violence because of how it is grounded within the broader context of violence in general.

Gun ownership is firmly embedded within this country's gun culture, and extracting it from daily life is an immense challenge, necessitating changing culture and the symbolism of what having a gun means, which is often an integral part of identity and worldview, and bringing a political dimension as manifested through our elected officials and the laws that are passed (Dunning, 2018; Egerton, 2018; Haag, 2016; Kalesan, Weinberg, & Galea, 2016; J. M. Metzl, 2019; Yamane, 2017). When gun possession is equated with masculinity, it translates into a street culture difficult to change through conventional approaches.

Gun ownership culture has received significant attention in the professional literature. Culture's power in shaping individual beliefs and behaviors makes it impossible to view any social phenomenon without paying attention to this factor. Generally, this culture is approached from a broad national perspective and one that traces gun ownership to the founding of the nation. It must also focus on gun owner social networks to shed light on the role of the group in shaping attitudes on this topic.

Introducing street culture builds on a historical understanding and use of culture as a lens to better understand consumers of services at an individual or community level. Sharing personal violence narratives helps shape youth street socialization and negotiation of daily activities (Lauger, 2014), with social sciences capturing stories and developing an understanding of why they shape street culture and, more importantly regarding gun violence, how to de-escalate injuries and fatalities (Kwak et al., 2019).

Street culture brings this lens into our worldview, helping develop a more nuanced viewpoint, which is essential for how we navigate and help structure messages about what we are hoping to accomplish in a collaborative manner with residents. RIP (Rest in Peace) shirts, which are referred to as memorial shirts, convey a variety of messages, joy as well as sorrow, are a visible form of "life writing" by sharing a narrative of the deceased and making public the private struggles with racial injustice (R. Brooks, 2018). To what extent is a code of the street operative in gun violence? Those with high code adherence will also possess low conflict management skills and be more prone to engage in violence (Erickson, Hochstetler, & Dorius, 2020).

Street memorials and artifacts memorialize the death and help their loved ones with the grieving process, bringing a much needed perspective to any effort at developing a comprehensive understanding of urban gun violence. These memorials can go by different names, such as "temporary, improvised memorials" or "spontaneous shrines" (Margry & Sanchez-Carretero, 2011). Urban memorials take many different shapes and memorialize different forms of tragedy, but those on violence remain consistent (Stevens & Ristic, 2015). Urban memorials are not limited to the United States (Kellaher & Worpole, 2016).

Chicago is home to the nation's first national memorial dedicated to gun violence victims (E. N. Brown, 2019). The prominence of gun violence in Chicago and the nation has resulted in a Chicago Cultural Center exhibition of a glass structure consisting of hundreds of personal items once belonging to gun violence victims, with the exhibition created by the Gun Violence Memorial Project. Its goal is to create a "permanent, national memorial that honors the lives and narratives of victims of gun violence."

The design of this memorial is unique (E. N. Brown, 2019):

The design team chose to create four houses, made up of 700 bricks each, symbolizing the monthly death rate from gun violence. The foundation of each house is a white, wood lattice with glass walls on either side—a design choice made because "it was important to us that people had a great sight line," Williams says. "[Another] material is the objects themselves. . . . The individuality does not show up until the objects are contributed and installed in the bricks. Having these different textures, sizes, and colors really begins to bring the personal narrative into the memorial experience." The items highlighted in each of the 2,800 total bricks range from baby shoes, to high school graduation tassels, to an heirloom tea set, and various family photographs.

Memorials can also be a target for destructive actions, with victims becoming victims again (Thomas, 2018, p. 11): "In Ferguson, after the shooting of Michael Brown, the roadside memorial that marked the site where he died was destroyed when it was run over by a car. Another roadside memorial at a nearby lamppost was burned down. These destructive acts speak to the spiritual power of these memorials, even among those who despise them." When memorials are defaced, often in cases involving rival gang members where the victim was a member, it sends a message to others that in death their death can still be disrespected. Even marking the 1-year anniversary of a gun death does not make mourners immune from gunshots, as was the case in Chicago Cultural Center Exhibit where this memorial ended up with 13 being wounded, ranging in age from 16 to 48 years old (Zaveri, 2019).

Memorials are public declarations. The clothes, photographs, and mementos remain as constant reminders of lives cut short and being at the wrong place and time. These items not only serve as a reminder of them, but also are shared with visitors. These youth did not have to be saints and may have been killed while perpetrating a crime or in retaliation for a past crime. The context surrounding their death may simply fade into the background. However, they were still someone's children. Their beds and living areas may even be left untouched in remembrance of them. The grieving process can also entail having grief displayed on the bodies of those affected by the death, such as having memorial tattoos honoring those who have been killed. Tattoos can take various forms and be located on various parts of the body (Ceballos, 2014): "Viruegas tattooed Sanchez's name on top of an hourglass on her arm. At the bottom of the hourglass, Viruegas tattooed Peraza's name. The piece of ink reminds her of her pain and her friend's forgiveness. Her life goes on."

Tattoo parlors have not received recognition for how they address customer trauma and grief. These urban parlors are nontraditional settings, as addressed previously. Street memorials and other artefacts (items of great significance to the victim) when a resident who is unarmed is killed by the police or there is the perception that the police overreacted to the situation take on added significance as resistance to what has been conceptualized as a killing without justification. These monuments are referred to as meaning making in material form (M. Walsh, 2017), providing a geographic space with symbolic meaning for gatherings. This place can be contested when law enforcement pushback creates tension-filled spaces, leading to confrontations between social activists and the police.

Violent police encounters become part of street culture narratives on how to remain safe, representing a different perspective of this cultural stance, but one that cannot be ignored (Payne, Hitchens, & Chambers, 2017). It compromises the role that police can play in reducing gun violence because of resident unwillingness to engage them because of concerns about seeking social justice from those who are supposed to serve and protect them. Unfortunately, COVID-19 and social distancing represent but the latest consequence of this distrust. In New York City, the enforcement of social distancing resulting from COVID-19 has seen comparison to that city's "stop and frisk" policies, with 35 of 45 Brooklyn arrests being arrests of African Americans/Blacks, creating tensions in African American/Latinx neighborhoods (Southall, 2020).

Spontaneous street memorials are a phenomenon that takes a variety of forms, including art projects (Delgado, 2003). Art can be an effective mechanism for expressing powerful emotions, allowing the introduction of culture and local circumstances to share how it is manifested (M. Mitchell, 2020). The degree to which they remain and are maintained becomes an indicator of the support level this victim enjoyed and the prominence of their family/social network in the community. The cultural manifestation of these memorials has deep historical roots and are dynamic to account for local context. Understanding local cultural traditions on how gun violence is conceptualized and addressed illustrates the importance of understanding the power of culture, which is dynamic, in shaping the grieving process. New Orleans has an emerging culture with a unique local element that can spread to other parts of the country (Lei & Turner, 2019):

> While photographing the funeral of Malik Braddy, an 18-year-old who was shot and killed in the Lower Ninth Ward, he noticed something striking: family and friends taking photos with, hugging and lifting into the air a life-size cutout of Malik. "When you take a selfie with the cutout, it looks like the person's there." . . . The public and communal celebrations of the dead are powerful representations of black New Orleans, and cutouts have become a modern and unique tradition of its own. Though they are also used in other celebrations, such as birthdays and graduations, "lifesize"—as they're sometimes referred to by locals—are most frequently made to remember young men, teenage to mid-20s, who died from gun violence.

New Orleans' reputation for artistic originality in handling gun violence and the emergence of cutouts is the latest example of this evolution of culture (Delgado, 2003), which will find expression in other parts of the nation.

The institutions, victims and families engage with, such as houses of worship also must contend with services involving those who are killed and how institutional culture is shaped by gun violence narratives. This influence can be purposeful or accidental with little attention to this occurring. A purposeful approach can potentially transform an institution in a manner that spreads out into the surrounding community, including participatory ways of obtaining involvement.

Houses of worship can assume meaningful roles in addressing local gun violence and trauma (Elow, 2011), as in the case of Cincinnati, Ohio's, Christ Church Cathedral (https://cincinnaticathedral.com/we-remember/):

> The Gun Violence Working Group of Christ Church Cathedral will work to identify and address the full needs of Price Hill and coordinate efforts to address the causes of gun violence there. We will identify which groups live in that area, the needs of those groups, and the challenges those groups face, and then we will utilize available

resources to implement research-based methods to prevent gun violence in that community.

Assuming a coordinating role takes on significance where there is a gap
in leadership and/or an institution that commands a wide range of social
and political support.

Houses of worship seeking a meaningful role, instead of a symbolic
one, in preventing mass shootings is the latest development because of
how these institutions have been targeted, as in the case of Charlestown,
South Carolina; Pittsburgh, Pennsylvania; and Sutherland Springs, Texas,
representing a different dimension of gun violence, but one very important for the country to address. From an urban perspective, a focus on
day-to-day gun violence episodes has the greatest saliency, however.

CONCLUSION

Urban gun violence knowledge is evolving and promises to gain steam as
it garners more attention. Interventions will necessitate a grounding in the
social sciences and the urban practice experience, positioning professions
to advance the knowledge base on how best to address gun violence at
neighborhood and social network levels. This chapter provided a broad
social-economic-political-cultural context for understanding the origins
and broad reach of gun violence in the nation and its cities and touched
on aspects rarely the focus of attention yet playing a prominent role in
helping us understand how urban gun violence emerges.

The following chapters will prove useful in expanding our "toolbox"
in deconstructing the forces encouraging urban gun violence, setting the
stage for crafting interventions with a high likelihood of achieving success. Embracing an affirming and participatory paradigm helps us socially
and politically navigate this complex field and to do so having our codes of
ethics and values as a compass guiding us through this ethical minefield,
increasing the odds of success.

6

Approaches to Preventing and Intervening With Gun Violence

There are many different kinds of dreams. But in the long tradition of African American activism, dreams have typically been linked to concrete aspirations for social reform.

—LAWRENCE RALPH, *2014, p. 6*

INTRODUCTION

Readers are well grounded on why urban gun violence is a salient issue in this country and worthy of attention from a national, urban-specific, academic, social science, and helping professions perspective, and provided case illustrations to draw lessons from in crafting urban-focused interventions. The previous chapter laid out a multifaceted picture of gun violence ramifications and how gun violence changed the nation's social fabric, often in invisible ways. The importance of local context cannot be overly emphasized in shaping how helping professions can best aid in preventing and intervening at an early point in gun violence, but that does not mean that the national picture cannot provide a broader context from to understand local situations. That chapter also started to lay out why

Urban Gun Violence. Melvin Delgado, Oxford University Press (2021). © Oxford University Press.
DOI: 10.1093/oso/9780197515518.003.0006.

certain gun violence approaches have seen acceptance throughout the country, with particular relevance to urban communities.

Interventions requiring many different institutional and community partners have garnered saliency as pathways to solve gun violence. Multifaceted interventions by their nature are complex, requiring contextual grounding to maximize success and take localized circumstances into account. A cookie-cutter approach is ill advised. Successful interventions also require cooperation of multiorganizational entities, all requiring considerable expenditure of time, energy, and other resources. In addition, these approaches require engendering trust.

Impactful interventions are predicated on strong and explicit values, underpinning how social scientists view gun violence causes (Lizotte & Hendrix, 2019) and the research questions important to answer. These values are rarely articulated in scholarly publications even though presenting them aids in understanding key assumptions, or biases, guiding the scholarship. The challenge of bringing together a multidisciplinary approach and a wide cross section of helping professions, which are understandably numerous, is minimized when concepts cross academic and professional lines. These concepts are founded on cherished values that are operationalized in addressing urban gun violence. These interventions often fail to explicate values, principles, and key concepts shaping their unfolding, missing valuable dimensions in understanding the rationales for research and strategy implementation.

This chapter seeks to correct this omission by starting with a set of intersecting values before focusing on the characteristics of successful community interventions, setting the stage for why urban self-help organizations must be a part of these efforts. These values do not receive the depth of attention because each requires a book to do justice to their importance and complexity. These values are on display throughout the book, however. Finally, this chapter discusses major national approaches to prevent urban gun violence that have shown promise, with an emphasis on examples that helping professions will typically consider in local self-help efforts.

VALUES AND CONCEPTS UNDERPINNING SUCCESSFUL
COMMUNITY INTERVENTIONS

No book on urban gun research and practice would be complete without attention to key concepts and principles, including undergirding values, that set the foundation for the development of research and interventions. An embrace of a set of guiding values can be conceptualized as DNA shaping how social interventions unfold, highlighting sociopolitical forces and therefore assuming an instrumental role in understanding the rationales for these approaches. Values, in turn, are powerful forces influencing our world outlooks and behaviors as social scientists and practitioners, and those covered in this chapter should not be surprising. How these values are operationalized, however, means turning to principles because of how they help concretize this worldview. Principles allow the integration of theory to facilitate shaping all aspects of practice and knowledge creation.

Gun-focused community interventions bring hope because of their importance as well as frustrations, particularly when we try to convert research findings and theory into action. I am fond of saying to plan is human, but to implement is simply divine. The social sciences and helping professions must bring practicality to research, scholarship, and practice. Community interventions typically require great flexibility in plan implementation, and this is no more so with gun violence. Socially navigating these rough seas requires a guidance system that has the North Star as a fixture; values are our North Star, shaping guiding principles. Staying true to one's principles is critical in navigating the turbulent social and political times associated with gun violence, gun control, and the law enforcement/ legal system.

Readers may ask about the relationship between values and guiding principles. I think of values, which are highly subjective, as a guide for creating interventions and a bridge between values and theory. When death means an instrumental member of a support system is lost, it takes on greater significance. When it is a parent, the magnitude of the consequences is immense. Five values stand out in providing a unifying vision:

1. Community empowerment
2. Participatory democracy
3. Strengths/resiliency/assets first
4. Collaboration/partnerships
5. Social justice

These values are highly interrelated. Chances are very good that if you subscribe to one, the others will follow closely, and they will cluster together, providing boundaries that shape gun violence interventions.

As a social worker, these values resonate with my profession and are ideally suited for finding multidisciplinary solutions to intentional gun violence because of how values, and the concepts that they are founded upon, are not exclusive to social work. Helping professions embracing similar values are in a propitious position to establish collaborations with urban self-help organizations. The immense problem of gun violence must bring together academic disciplines and helping professions to enhance the power of collaborations shaping public policies grounded in the operative reality of urban residents. Where the arenas of views overlap remains fertile ground for partnerships.1.

Community Empowerment

It is no surprise that empowerment starts our discussion because of its central role in the education of urban-focused social scientists and helping professionals. It is a value that can find a home in individual, family, group, organizational, and community-centered practice, facilitating the addressing of complex social problems. Life-altering violence necessitates extraordinary responses, with empowerment a central feature of these actions and is a central element in self-help efforts (Riessman & Carroll, 1995). Self-help represents self-determination, a highly attractive concept within urban communities that see external forces dictating daily activities, and it is a key aspect of empowerment.

Empowerment was originally conceptualized by Barbara Solomon (1976), a social worker, I am proud to say, as a strategy and an intervention. Empowerment has different meanings according to context, and its goal can range from lofty societal transformation focused on achieving social justice to mastering a challenging task, no matter how trivial—how I can be empowered to eat a green vegetable, for instance. How it is conceptualized and operationalized is dependent on a community's vision when applied from a collective viewpoint. Self-help initiatives primarily address need internally rather than relying on external sources (Riessman & Carroll, 1995).

What does community empowerment have to do with urban gun violence? Aiyer, Zimmerman, Morrel-Samuels, and Reischl (2015, p. 137) tied community empowerment to communities that feel safe, increasing the relevance of this value and concept to urban violence:

> Busy streets indicate safe, urban neighborhoods that exhibit a certain vibrancy, which promotes prosocial behavior. More specifically, busy streets are safe areas where businesses are flourishing, homes are occupied and well maintained, and residents are socially engaged with one another. Not only does such urban activity indicate safety, this positive energy may also influence individual behavior. Neighborhood energy determines whether people are attracted to or deterred from an area, how people behave in the area, and ultimately influences economic prosperity by encouraging or discouraging growth and expansion. Furthermore, urbanites often follow the adage of safety in numbers.

Unsafe communities equate with disempowerment and the compromising of promise and potential.

The concept of community stress has ascended in importance in understanding and addressing health and income inequities, violence, and other structural/environmental factors, with multiple manifestations of empowerment being a central goal for intervention development (Forenza, Lardier, Reid, Garcia-Reid, & Bermea, 2019). Community empowerment goes beyond urban violence, with aspects easily captured through research and others proving very challenging, but important nevertheless. Personal relationships, such as friendships, can develop through healing interactions, expanding social networks and bringing positive outcomes from tragic events (Delgado, 2017b).

Community empowerment can be operationalized in various ways, whether defined geographically or along specific group lines, such as women and how they have assumed active and leadership roles within anti–gun violence efforts (Salvi, 2019). One way that community empowerment has found relevance in urban practice consists of three components: (a) intracommunity (resident social relationships); (b) interactional (creation of trust and social capital); and (c) behavioral (collaborations between residents and organizations that result in collective actions) (Perkins & Zimmerman, 1995; N. A. Peterson & Zimmerman, 2004). These components lend themselves to gun violence interventions and engagement of self-help organizations as partners.

Community empowerment must include significant groups, such as youth (Torres-Harding, Baber, Hilvers, Hobbs, & Maly, 2018), as addressed in discussion of partnerships in this chapter. Community empowerment is a value and multifaceted construct predicated on social justice principles (Christens, 2019). Photovoice, for example, is a research and empowering intervention that urban youth can employ in understanding the causes and interventions for addressing it (Delgado, 2015; Nutt, 2019).

Trust must be an integral part of this value (Schutz, 2019) and, quite frankly, permeate the other values in this chapter. Achieving a high trust level is easier said than done, particularly in contexts where there is a long legacy of state misdeeds, making achieving this goal a long and difficult process (Delgado, 2020b). There is no substitute for trust, regardless of how arduous and lengthy a road, it is still a goal worth striving for to make progress on gun violence.

Initiatives targeting returning gang members, such as Advance Peace in Fresno, California, although proving too controversial to pass a city council vote (Charles, 2019), still holds great promise in addressing urban gun violence when seeking to empower through education and civic engagement projects (Velez, 2019):

> Foster and Gonzalez talk to gang members—young and old—to keep the peace. Fresno Police Captain Mark Salazar *told Valley Public Radio two months ago* that the work Foster's done has been effective in decreasing shootings. Foster's focus is in southwest Fresno because that's his neighborhood, or his 'hood' as he called it. Foster said he reached out to Gonzalez because he knows a different part of the city. In the gang culture, Gonzalez said, there's a racial divide and that's why working together is critical. "Like Aaron said, he can only talk to the kids in his neighborhood, the gangs he's familiar with," Gonzalez said. "I can do my part with the gangs I'm familiar with, the people I was part of." Gonzalez speaks to youth groups at Barrios Unidos monthly. He networks with families he knows so he can go into their neighborhoods to empower kids through education and civic engagement.

These types of initiatives to engage and empower communities cannot transpire without trust being present and the legitimacy of those engaged in crafting these activities, an essential element in any community-centered efforts to stem gun violence. Homeboy Industries in Los Angeles is an example of how re-entering former gang members can give back to their communities (Deuchar, 2018).

Participatory Democracy

Interventions premised on support of community residents and institutions must embrace the value of participatory democracy, which is closely connected to community empowerment. Urban participatory strategies are empowering of disenfranchised residents such as women (Frederick & Lee, 2019). We can appreciate what this value means in a democracy, although one that is flawed, such as ours. The refrain, "If you are not at the table, you are on the table," comes to mind when discussing community interventions to curb gun violence. Meaningful participation, to continue with the table metaphor, means that you are at the table, selecting the meal and music and deciding who is an invited guest. Readers get the gist about community participation, particularly with groups that historically have not played an active role in shaping policies and programs, such as youth (Schoenfeld, Bennett, Manganella, & Kemp, 2019).

Self-help is premised on participatory values and principles and fills a critical void in conventional service delivery. Self-help organizations elicit the voices and engagement of those with firsthand knowledge of violence. This may appear as simplistic, but it is far from that because of the rarity of giving legitimacy to these individuals, and those who surround them, in an atmosphere that is affirming and respectful. Victim voices, including collective testimony, must not be limited to the seeking of help but must also be systematically incorporated into programming and activities that tap their experiences and dreams, and urban self-help organizations do this.

Providing participation options increases these organizations' effectiveness. Engaging residents and decreasing their marginalization also translates into a reduction of cynicism, opens boundaries, and improves collective efficacy, all key factors in reducing neighborhood violence and making the community more amenable to outsiders being accepted for assistance (K. J. Brown & Weil, 2019). Suspicion of outsiders severely limits partnerships in reducing gun violence because these resources are essential in supporting internal efforts.

The value of participation is one that stands as a foundation for any community effort to be successful, regardless of focus. It takes on even greater significance with gun violence because of fears surrounding this urban issue. Contagious diseases usually involve some form of stigma but not fear of life, with retaliation being a very real threat when residents cooperate with law enforcement. Meaningfully bringing community participation to life will involve socially navigating a series of potential barriers.

Any resident engaging in making a community safe from gun violence must be thought of as a hero (Thompson, 2018).

Strengths/Resiliency/Assets First

The topic of strengths/resiliency/assets first, as addressed in the introductory chapter, is only touched on here. Its importance made it necessary to introduce it early, and its prominence requires reintroducing it in depth here. A strength/resiliency/assets value stance, which is emphasized throughout this book, has strong support within a wide range of social sciences and professions (Meichenbaum, 2017).

Self-help organizations embrace the importance of innovation, and tapping positive community attributes is a core element in their success. Resiliency is primarily associated with individuals and families, but has also found its way into communities (Ellis, 2019). Gun violence interventions must also systematically build community capacity, including economic dimensions (Bayouth, Lukens-Bull, Gurien, Tepas, & Crandall, 2019), introducing innovative practices in service to their communities. These efforts serve to build hope and confidence.

A sea of grief with small islands of hope is one way to describe heavily gun-scarred neighborhoods and the narratives surrounding this form of violence. Although there is a tendency to emphasize the sea of grief metaphor, the islands (assets) are extremely important and must never be lost sight of to eschew victimizing the victims even further, in similar fashion to how the media often covers the death of gun victims and rarely their lives. Victimizing the dead or the injured through negative labeling of them only further aggravates the healing process for family and friends.

High-risk and low-resourced community violence does not materialize in similar fashion in other geographical settings due to the high presence of multiple forms of lethal and nonlethal sources and high social needs (Campie, Patrosino, Fronius, & Read, 2017). Labeling entire communities as risk prone does an injustice to these communities, and those blanket statements are counterproductive to getting resident participation in gun initiatives.

Violence deters civic engagement, and it is critical that we never lose sight of a community's assets while still acknowledging a wide range of social conditions and needs that can compound gun violence. We must eschew focusing on risk factors without corresponding attention to resiliency/strength factors, and this means that only part of an equation is the focus when focus on an entire equation is in order (Bell, 2017).

Embracing a value that all human beings and communities bring indigenous resources (instrumental and expressive) that can be mobilized to help others is a fundamental foundation for exercising this value, including those with histories of involvement in the juvenile justice system (Jeffries, Myers, Kringen, & Schack, 2019). Practitioners are cognizant of the importance of not losing sight of factors that have helped those facing great adversity survive and even thrive. Building on these resources, individual as well as community, stands as a logical first choice in developing strategies focused on gun violence. This mindset and value mean that we should systematically identify these indigenous resources (Delgado & Humm-Delgado, 2013).

Family as an early and primary source of building resiliency is well embraced and does not need extensive review in this section. Resiliency is a complex construct that is far from fixed or static (Meichenbaum, 2017, p. 11): "Resilience is not a trait that a youth is born with or automatically keeps once it is achieved. Resilience is a complex interactive process that entails characteristics of the child, the family, extra familial relationships and school/community factors." Identifying and fostering resiliency, nevertheless, still brings challenges for social scientists and helping professionals.

A friendship network can be a strong buttress to family, although we rarely associate this support system among urban youth; the system can be enhanced through carefully crafted community initiatives (Delgado, 2017b). Rather, we generally equate urban youth social networks with problems. Enhancing a network can be a part of a well-coordinated gun violence prevention strategy. Getting youth involvement in community initiatives, as with self-help organizations, translates into opportunities to build resiliency and strengths in service to their community and casts youth as playing prominent roles within their communities, countering stereotypes that they are a prime cause of gun violence and have nothing to offer their communities other than pain and suffering.

Ironically, it does not have to be a stranger or enemy killing someone; it can also entail someone close killing their friend because of some concerns that they have about information getting out that could compromise or even lead to their arrest. A child's murder is complicated when it is not a stranger who kills, but rather someone who is a relative or friend (Wiebe & Bloos, 2019):

> After her son was shot to death, one Kansas City mother found her cause. But she has not chosen to advocate against guns. Rather she has chosen to focus on children, particularly those caught in what she calls a "revolving circle of brokenness and hurt and pain." Murdice Sims has heard dozens of harrowing stories from bereaved mothers since her own son died 14 years ago. One woman told her about the day her toddler shot his twin sister while playing with a gun. Another mom described the death of her daughter, whose husband shot her, then himself in front of their children. Yet another lost her son when his best friend became enraged during an argument and shot him. With each telling, Sims relives the loss of her son, Jeremey Groves, shot and killed late one spring night in 2004 while out with friends in Kansas City, Kansas.

These instances sharpen how this violence epidemic is centered on one's social network (Kotlowitz, 2019).

Tapping religious institutions unites these institutions with other community assets in addressing gun violence (Seedat et al., 2016). Houses of worship are places within the African American community, for example, where members expect to support each other during times of crisis and sadness, as in the case of women in two New Orleans, Louisiana, congregations, where they mourn and memorialize their dead sons and grandsons who have been victims of gun violence (R. L. Carter, 2018). These institutions play an important role in their community's health and can be tapped in a community-centered approach to gun violence (J. Williams et al., 2019).

When youth are viewed as assets rather than deficits and mobilized in service to their communities through civic engagement projects, they bring an often-missing dimension to efforts on violence (Jain et al., 2019, p. 26):

> Exposure to community violence and low civic engagement co-exist for many youth and are often compounded by socioeconomic disadvantage. Many have documented growing cumulative disadvantage and community violence in cities. . . . Meanwhile, others have studied the experiences of structurally marginalized urban youth, finding they are less likely to be civically engaged, but that those who do engage benefit more than their structurally supported peers.

Adolescents surviving gun violence may be more comfortable turning to peer networks than their own families, and more so when their peers have gone through a loss and grieving process.

The afterschool period provides an important setting for youth to heal (Mueller, 2017). Youth, as in Chicago, Illinois, identify the importance of engaging in positive afterschool pursuits and access to safe parks (Rigg, McNeish, Schadrac, Gonzalez, & Tran, 2019). Crime occurs throughout a community, and parks are no exception; reducing their use compromises health (lack of physical exercise) and safety (fear of being injured or killed) in multiple ways (B. Han, Cohen, Derose, Li, & Williamson, 2018).

Youth activism is a promising approach to violence prevention and integrates the values covered in this section (Aspholm & Mattaini, 2017; Wray-Lake, 2019). Having youth involved in this type of protest bodes well for communities because as they age, they bring a wealth of experience. Encouraging and investing in youth is an investment in a community's assets with immediate and long-term benefits.

It is fitting to end this section with an important reminder of cities possessing assets (McCoy, 2020):

> Urban communities are not simply bastions of violence. They are communities rich with neighbors who care about and support each other and grassroots organizers that create and implement programs to interrupt and prevent violence. However, their efforts cannot be the only or primary response. We must remember that gun violence is never normal and it impacts each of us. We must also acknowledge survivors and respond to their needs. We can no longer afford to ignore such a pervasive problem.

Collaborations/Partnerships

No one person, regardless of purpose and talents, can stop urban gun violence, although as witnessed with the establishers of self-help organizations, one person can certainly be a significant catalyst. Thus, it is appropriate to bring attention to partnerships and coalitions (Forenza et al., 2019). Interventions discussed in the section that follows in this chapter are based on partnerships and coalitions because of the immensity of the goal of reducing or stopping urban gun violence.

A literature overview shows numerous collaborations on gun violence interventions, and the following are examples: emergency rooms (Shepherd, 2001); infectious diseases physicians (Zheng & Mushatt, 2019); pediatricians (Tsou & Barnes, 2016); public health (Shepherd & Sumner, 2017); and education (E. R. Smith & Gill Lopez, 2016). Clearly, collaborations across disciplines and professions offer great potential. Collaborations must be considered from a localized perspective. Houses of worship often head or play a prominent role in these initiatives. When these partnerships involve the police, a moment of caution must be exercised if law enforcement does not enjoy the trust of the community (Brunson, Braga, Hureau, & Pegram, 2015). The same factors apply to self-help organizations because their institutional legitimacy is critical for their success and must not be compromised by the negative institutional legitimacy that law enforcement brings in cases where they are not trusted.

Seeking assistance in time of need is natural, particularly during periods of crises. Coming together can go by many different labels—partnerships, collaborations, cooperation—covering different configurations and commitments. Further, academics and practitioners can be a part of these endeavors, bringing tremendous potential for achievements and frustrations also. Urban gun violence is such an occasion. We see this value on television and other media outlets when mass shootings occur, with El Paso, Texas, and Dayton, Ohio, the latest examples. When communities experience multiple gun deaths and injuries, as in urban America, we do not witness national indignation and the marshaling of resources and goodwill that customarily accompany mass shootings.

The value undergirding establishment of a mechanism bringing together academics with helping professionals is quite common and can be found in courses and scholarly literature. It is not unusual to find funders of interventions, gun focused and otherwise, to require formal relationships between various academic and institutional entities to qualify for some grant. The same motivation must be sought in addressing urban community gun violence. These partnerships must enlist institutions and individuals we normally would not associate as part of an intervention. Neighborhood coalitions must engage local businesses because these establishments have vital economic and social interests in this issue (Irvin-Erickson et al., 2016).

Most successful efforts on urban gun violence interventions involved coalitions and partnerships and even enlisted the assistance of entities that normally would not work together, such as the police. These relationships require expenditure of considerable time and energy to overcome mistrust and stereotypes, and that is to be expected or normalized. Readers have no doubt encountered this phenomenon, and I certainly have as an academic venturing into communities where I do not live. Although we can point to multidisciplinary collaborations to achieve significant community changes, it would be disingenuous of me not to point out there are barriers that exist between collaborating partners. Different language, concepts, and historical traditions make collaborations and partnerships difficult to achieve.

Social Justice

A social justice value permeates all dimensions of developing an understanding of urban gun violence. Enacting this value as a goal and process lends itself to gun violence assessment and interventions, helping to bring together providers, academics, and community residents. Community participation can overcome despair and hopelessness through the initiation of civic engagement projects with an explicit embrace of social justice, even in war-torn countries (Grain & Land, 2017). Meaningful community participation cannot transpire without a social justice compass.

The disproportionate impact gun violence has on communities of color cannot be divorced from a racialized state tied to segregation in living area and institutions that are meant to address their needs. Self-help organizations are testaments to how inequities foster gun violence and why this problem cannot be divorced from its current day and historical contextual grounding.

MAJOR GUN VIOLENCE COMMUNITY INTERVENTIONS

I deviate from conventional wisdom of discussing successful interventions by starting this section with the unsuccessful ones. Numerous books can be written on how we failed to address gun violence, with sufficient material for a synopsis to be provided, setting an unusual context for this chapter (B. Smith, 2017):

> *A 2012 meta-study* [Makarios & Pratt, 2012] *was conducted on prior gun violence reduction* research, and offers a wealth of important takeaways. *It found that stiffer prison sentences for crime in general, waiting periods and background checks for gun purchases, gun buyback*

programs, public safety campaigns, and safe storage laws are the least effective ways to address gun violence. These findings may be surprising and counterintuitive, but we owe it to victims of gun violence to value the strength of research over our own gut-feelings. Though there are certainly studies that can be found to support any one of these approaches, such studies are like those that call climate change into question—their outlier status in meta-studies demonstrates how out of step they are with prevailing wisdom.

Lessons learned from failed attempts, which can be depressing, can still have value by informing efforts with a higher probability of achieving success. Admittedly, this is a deficit approach, but one that still has heuristic value.

How to reduce or stop gun violence has many different responses, such as using curfews, which have been found to have limited success but with controversy (Carr & Doleac, 2016), and the role severe weather plays in influencing violence (Carr & Doleac, 2018). Weather, in this instance, high heat and humidity, increases crime, explaining why summer is a high-crime/high-violence period in the nation's cities, with corresponding low police enforcement, raising implications on how climate change may influence crime in urban centers (Heilmann & Kahn, 2019).

Community interventions are not new to the gun violence field, with multiple examples achieving national prominence, such as "Concentrated Deterrence" or "Focused Deterrence," and "Operation Cease Fire." These efforts bring elements with a potential for reducing gun violence when adapted to local conditions, requiring setting aside political turf to facilitate needed collaboration.

"Concentrated Deterrence" or "Focused Deterrence": Deterrence, focused or concentrated, as manifested through Chicago's offender notification meetings, have proven successful in reducing violence by those who recently left incarceration. Studies showed that focused deterrence programs can reduce gun violence (Cook, 2017). Deterrence interventions are designed to take into account local priorities and circumstances and generally consist of six major components: (a) increased law enforcement resources target hot spots and chronic offenders; (b) there is enhanced prosecution of specific types of crimes or offenders; (c) social services are mobilized at the "nexus of the crime producing dynamics"; (d) there are concerted and targeted efforts to enlist community partners most impacted by the crime(s); (e) researchers assume an active and influential role; and (f) direct communication is made with offenders on the consequences they will face if they persist in engaging in crime (Trinkner, 2019).

Concentrated deterrence, started in Boston, Massachusetts, and adopted in other cities, showed promise by rallying on key institutions coming together, although with formidable challenges (Corsaro & Engel, 2015, p. 499):

> Focused deterrence initiatives are applauded for but also highlight longstanding tensions in our conceptualization of the very work of the criminal justice system. Balancing the objectives of due process and crime control . . . satisfying shifting public opinion and the need for political expediency . . . ; and managing the on-the-ground, day-to-day functions of complex bureaucracies with deeply embedded cultures and practices is extraordinarily complicated. Focused deterrence strategies can push police organizations out of their comfort zone in that they require surveillance and crime control functions in tandem with social support and community capacity-building activities that are still anathema to many police organizations. (p. 499)

Efforts such as concentrated deterrence highlight the need for community-based comprehensive and coordinated campaigns, bringing together public health, social, and criminal justice, although with challenges.

The formerly incarcerated are a group spotlighted in major violence-focused initiatives. Jones's (2018) *The Chosen Ones: Black Men and the Politics of Redemption* provides a detailed portrait of how San Francisco, California's African American/Black men, with histories of violence and incarceration in their lives, sought redemption for past violent deeds. The Parolee-Based Focused Deterrence Program has found success by calling attention to the importance of targeting specific groups with a high probability of engaging in violent acts, with any comprehensive effort targeting community violence needing such a component (Clark-Moorman, Rydberg, & McGarrell, 2018; Trinkner, 2019). The formerly incarcerated must be taken into account in any comprehensive urban gun violence initiative (Rossi, 2017). Targeting the formerly incarcerated takes on importance as efforts to release them take hold in the nation, with COVID-19 possibly accelerating this movement. Engaging self-help organizations helps the re-entry process for the formerly incarcerated (Anta & Men, 2018; Bellamy et al., 2019).

Concentrated attention sends a message that must be sustained over an extended period to ultimately reduce and sustain gains. This concerted effort allows a period of relief that must not be wasted, further galvanizing support and creating hope for a safer future. Using a military analogy is appropriate: winning a battle carries an understanding that this does not equate to winning a war. Going home after the battle allows networks to be re-established over a period of time, creating cynicism from residents who have seen this in the past. For those of us accustomed to funding cycles and deadlines, a concentrated effort will follow these parameters, but communities do not share this worldview.

Cynicism is not limited to community residents. Police also must contend with its presence (Abt, 2019b, pp. 68–69):

> Legal cynicism is present not only within communities but among the police, too, and with the same troubling potential for violence. While considerably less studied, it is clear that cynicism exists among many in law enforcement, and that it likely impacts their performance in problematic ways. There are many reasons why police might become cynical. Police know better than most that with regard to urban violence, today's victim is often tomorrow's perpetrator.

It is important, however, that we do not automatically consider victims to become perpetrators. We need a much more nuanced understanding of the triggers that cause this shift in roles.

Focused deterrence relies heavily on partnerships with local law enforcement, and when there is respect and trust between the police and the community, implementation is facilitated, and when not present, it meets with limited success at best (Brunson, 2015). Police killings of unarmed people of color complicates collaborations on gun violence, starting in childhood and extending into adulthood. It is inadvisable for gun initiatives to ignore the role of police in this violence (Cooper & Fullilove, 2016; Smith Lee & Robinson, 2019).

There is a need for more nuanced police enforcement approaches with communities of color; overpolicing results in a distrust of the police and reluctance to report crime and potentially dangerous developing situations. Underpolicing, in turn, causes a response detrimental to stopping gun violence because there is community reluctance to report due to the belief that law enforcement will not follow up. Local police are expected to play an important role in any comprehensive community-centered strategy.

Procedural injustice has a significant impact on crime reporting, underscoring the importance of police–community relations, "as poor perceptions of the police and reliance on oneself for protection and justice reduce cooperation with the police, especially among minorities" (Kwak et al., Dierenfeldt, & McNeeley, 2019, p. 25). Community policing, in essence, has been signaled out as a key component of any community-centered comprehensive strategy for addressing crime (Herbert, Beckett, & Stuart, 2018; Keith, 2018; D. M. Kennedy, 2019).

There is a tremendous difference between eliminating gun violence and reducing or controlling its manifestations and escalation. A focused deterrence approach is characterized by how public health has conceptualized the causes of violence and the importance of enlisting a coalition of resources with a specific focus on what are understood to be the reasons for gun violence (Braga & Weisburd, 2015):

Focused deterrence strategies are a recent addition to an emerging collection of evidence based violent gun injury prevention practices available to policy makers and practitioners. Briefly, focused deterrence strategies seek to change offender behavior by understanding underlying violence-producing dynamics and conditions that sustain recurring violent gun injury problems and by implementing a blended strategy of law enforcement, community mobilization, and social service actions. (p. 56)

Boston's success was largely due to mobilization of a wide range of resources that normally would not collaborate on gun violence (Braga, Turchan, & Winship, 2019).

This approach is also predicated on not only data grounding taking into account factors contributing to this violence but also grounding strategies within local circumstances to maximize resources by enlisting a variety of local health, educational, and social service resources, including law enforcement. Focused deterrence, as in Kansas City, may not have a lasting impact after the first year of implementation (A. M. Fox & Novak, 2018).

It is tempting to have neighborhoods as a unit of analysis and a context for interventions; we cannot ignore how social networks wield incredible influence in the presence and the unfolding of gun violence, including families playing an active role. Although our society has a propensity to romanticize families, we must not do this. We must keep in mind that families can also play a role in increasing the risk for gun violence. Parental firearm possession, for instance, increases youth having a greater propensity for firearm possession and violence risk and involvement (Sigel, Mattson, & Mercado, 2019). Being violence prone does not mean that gun absence will lead to less violence since individuals may use other weapons, such as knives, with a potential to be less lethal.

Gun violence, particularly urban centered, as in the case of the middle of summer in 2019, witnessed a series of deadly encounters, accentuating the role of weather in shaping gun use (M. A. Williams & Bassett, 2019):

This summer, U.S. cities have experienced unconscionable spikes in gun violence. Just this past weekend *12 people were* shot, one fatally, in Brooklyn, and *a mass shooting* in Gilroy, Calif., left three dead. In early June, Chicago witnessed *52 shootings during a single weekend,* including 10 fatalities. In Washington, D.C., *19 people were shot* in five days, including 11-year-old Karon Brown, killed in a car on the way to football practice. *Nine people* were *shot* during one eight-hour period in Baltimore this month. Even in Boston, which sees lower levels of gun violence than most major U.S. cities, at least 19 people have been shot since July 3, and the city's non-fatal gun injuries *have risen by nearly 20%* since 2018. After the recent spate of Boston shootings, Mayor Marty Walsh *touted the state's strong gun laws even as he lamented the city's levels of violence*: "You still have a weekend like this. And it makes you think, God, what more can you do? But there has to be more.

A seasonal dimension on urban gun use also highlights how weather becomes an instrumental factor, calling for increased initiatives during this seasonal period, and why the case illustrations highlighted in Chapter 3 show increased activities during this period.

Prevailing approaches fall into three fields—public health, criminal justice, and social work. There are dramatic differences between public health, with an emphasis on youth at particular risk and community, and a criminal justice approach (emphasis on arrests) and social work, which clearly falls within a public health stance through a participatory focus communities. A combination and coordination of these approaches has shown promise for reducing urban gun violence (Cerdá, Tracy, & Keyes, 2018). Some professions have long legacies of community involvement (Reisch & Andrews, 2014).

It bears pausing at this juncture to interject how COVID-19 has shaped the public health landscape in urban America. City mayors, for example, are confronted with the public health challenge of addressing COVID-19 and gun deaths, both taking a particularly heavy toll on people and communities of color (Donaghue, 2020):

Everytown for Gun Safety is urging mayors to prioritize gun violence intervention programs, which have seen success using outreach teams to stop violence before it starts. Gun violence has for years disproportionately impacted communities of color struggling with health care inequalities, unemployment, poverty and lower levels of education. Now, those same communities are *hardest hit by corona-virus*, and advocates say the two crises have created a "perfect storm."

COVID-19 has further exposed gross inequities in health status, care access, and precarious economic conditions. The hospital beds and equipment that are required to save the lives of gunshot victims are often the same as used to save the lives of COVID-19 victims, and sadly, they are not mutually exclusive (Kaufman, 2020):

We need I.C.U. beds, we need ventilators, we need personnel to care for the wave of Covid-19 patients. But gunshot victims are now fighting for space and resources inside America's overcrowded I.C.U.s. . . . As our I.C.U.s fill up with patients struggling to breathe, we look around and ask: Can we save a bed, can we save two beds, for the gunshot victims we know are coming next? Who can watch these ventilated patients if we have to call doctors to the operating room to give a hand?

Social distancing, we can argue, reduces the likelihood of conflicts resulting from physical contacts. However, it can also increase domestic violence because of an inability to move freely outside of the home. Shootings have increased in cities such as Philadelphia, Pennsylvania, in April 2020, where shootings were up 17% compared to the past year, most likely reflecting poor outlooks on life; Chicago also experienced an increase in shootings and deaths, with gun violence increasing by 24% compared to last year, and concomitantly experienced high numbers of COVID-19 cases and deaths (Zaru, 2020). Boston also has not escaped an increase in gun violence during this period (Ellement & Berg, 2020).

The summer of 2020 has proven to be particularly challenging for urban communities because it is during this period that the number of shootings increase and there are more people in the streets.

Understanding the process and patterns escalating from disputes to gun fatalities is critical in developing interventions that can escalate into lethal outcomes (Berg, 2019). Cure Violence, a public health antiviolence program, relies on "violence interrupters" and has many supporters because of its success (Webster, 2015). They often resemble the composition of the communities they serve and often come from those communities, helping to minimize barriers between themselves and those they hope to influence. Their goal is to de-escalate violent incidents, such as shootings, by employing individuals who understand street cultural dynamics and are able to connect with those most at risk to commit or become victims of gun violence. Interrupting incidents that can result in revenge shootings is an early intervention. The Cure Violence Campaign found an international audience, as witnessed in Trinidad and Tobago (Maguire, Oakley, & Corsaro, 2018).

Oakland's success in reducing homicides by understanding local circumstances (0.1% of residents were responsible for the majority of homicides) allowed local authorities and communities to craft intervention strategies addressing gang-related activities involving 30-year-olds, a much older cohort than expected (McLively, 2019): "We hope that many more cities will be inspired by Oakland's journey and use this report as a starting point and a roadmap for leveraging the power of partnership to address serious violence. When it comes to breaking the cycle of violence in our most impacted cities and communities, we don't have a moment to lose."

Safe Cities is program with wide recognition for success in reducing urban violence involving guns. In Baltimore, Maryland, it had success within high-violence neighborhoods, as well as bordering communities (Webster, Whitehill, Vernick, & Curriero, 2013). The Safe Streets intervention, as in Baltimore, found youth did change their attitudes in using violence to settle disputes (Milam et al., 2016), a key element in any urban-focused initiative.

A review of Project Safe Neighborhoods (PSN) across the country found promising results (McGarrell, Perez, Carter, Daffron, 2018; Petrosino et al., 2019). Chicago's PSN, considered one of the nations' longest running and most evaluated violence prevention programs, however, found mixed results, varying by time period and police districts (Grunwald &

Papachristos, 2017). A similar effort targeting Washington, D.C., found implementing community and family-focused violence prevention efforts was arduous and challenging, with the need to offer intensive services and support minimizing obstacles (Lum, Olaghere, Koper, & Wu, 2016).

Convergence of substance misuse and guns is a deadly intersection of two social issues (Abaya, Atte, Herres, Diamond, & Fein, 2019; G. Banks et al., 2017; P. M. Carter, Cranford, et al., 2020). The relationship between urban alcohol outlet density, life expectancy, and violence is particularly strong and generally escaped attention in the development of crime intervention strategies (Furr-Holden et al., 2019), even though the relationship is part of the contextual setting. These institutions are part of a neighborhood's social fabric, yet can be counterproductive and discourage community investments, although we should not automatically assume this. Thus, a case-by-case assessment is in order.

Further, gangs and drugs are a deadly combination from a gun violence standpoint (Bergen-Cico et al., 2014; McLean, Robinson, & Densley, 2018). Operation Ceasefire recognized the ramifications of these two forces coming together and mobilizing a wide range of community resources, including law enforcement, successfully in many localities, including Boston; Cincinnati, Ohio; Hempstead Village, New York; High Point, North Carolina; Minneapolis, Minnesota; Nashville, Tennessee; New Haven, Connecticut; Rockford, Illinois; Portland, Oregon; and Stockton, California (Hemenway, 2012). The focus was on gun shooting and not belonging to a gang or engaging in selling drugs. This initiative got local gang members to a forum where this operation was announced, with speakers (grandmothers, mothers, clergy, and others) sharing how gun violence dramatically altered their lives. Operation Ceasefire, unfortunately, lost funding, and in Boston, the degree of gun violence increased dramatically by 160% between 2000 and 2006 (Braga, Hureau, & Winship, 2008).

Gun interventions can be found throughout the country. Urban youth can assume meaningful roles by supporting them as peer educators and other community issues (E. Jenkins et al., 2020). This principle fits well within the self-help organizational movement, as well as other community-centered organizations. Recruiting, training, and supporting youth in this role also invests in their communities and establishes a well-prepared source of potential staff as they age out and become adults.

There are current efforts for youth of color becoming proficient in treating gunshot wound trauma, bringing a participatory/civic engagement and peer-mentoring approach to the field, premised on an empowerment and a strengths/assets perspective (Calhoun, 2019). These efforts fill an important service gap, but one with youth prepared to negotiate urban life.

Enlisting and training bystanders, particularly on hemorrhage control and scene safety, to intervene in trauma encounters increases their willingness to assist victims and saving lives, as witnessed in a Chicago initiative (Tatebe et al., 2019). Adolescents, such as in Chicago's Good Kids Mad City, are becoming first responders with training in applying tourniquets (using a jacket or shoelace) and doing cardiopulmonary resuscitation (CPR), preventing gunshot victims from bleeding out, which are viewed as life skills (Ali, 2019a):

> Darrion, a soft-spoken rising ninth-grader who lives in the South Side neighborhood of Englewood, was there to learn life-saving skills in case he comes across a shooting victim. One out of every five teens ages 15 to 17 living in Chicago's South and West Sides has witnessed a fatal shooting, according to *data* collected by the Chicago Center for Youth Violence Prevention at the University of Chicago. From September 2011 until 2018, nearly 1,700 children under the age of 17 were shot in Chicago, and 174 were killed."

In St. Louis, there is another innovative effort in this arena. There is a call for gun interventions targeting urban African American/Black males, since this form of death disproportionately impacts male individuals aged 15 to 24 years and is greater than the next nine most common causes combined. The Acute Bleeding Control (ABC) program is one such intervention and focuses on bleeding control (Andrade, Hayes, & Punch, 2019):

> The Acute Bleeding Control (ABC) program includes the entire BC course but has a strategic focus on groups most at risk of experiencing

GV. We seek to bring appropriate BC training to communities affected by GV and to equip our participants with trauma first aid (TFA) kits. Participants assemble TFA kits from provided materials, including a tourniquet, hemostatic gauze, regular gauze, adhesive compression tape, trauma shears, a permanent marker, and gloves. Kits are personalized by offering different colored materials and properly fitted gloves. By allowing participants to create their own TFA kits, we ensure that they have interacted with the materials in their kit and know where to find them if the need arises. Individually sourcing the materials and assembling the kits onsite has allowed us to significantly reduce the cost of TFA kits.

Sadly, efforts such as those discussed will increasingly find receptive audiences in other urban communities because of the realization that lives can be saved by enlisting communities. Other similar innovative efforts will no doubt follow suit.

These skill sets are more appropriate for soldiers in a war zone than in the nation's streets. There is also a call for nursing to take a leading role in promoting community bleeding control training, and bringing lessons from the battlefield, to save lives (Carman, 2019, p. 53):

Trauma victims can die from uncontrolled bleeding within minutes. Based on the amount of evidence, preparedness is nonnegotiable. This preparedness is inevitably multifactorial, and must benefit from the efforts of various stakeholders, from emergency medical services and other first responders to physicians. Nurses, with their focus on prevention and maintaining health, are natural leaders in the initiative to stop preventable deaths due to gun violence and other mass trauma events.

Summer is a time for children to play and learn gunfire lifesaving measures (Beckett, Bond Graham, & Clayton, 2019):

Abené Clayton spent a day with Elana Bolds, a local activist in Richmond, California, *teaching children how to avoid being caught in a crossfire.* In Oakland, *the work of violence prevention,* often coordinated through grassroots community organizations and churches, feels as vital as it did in the 1990s, when the city's gun violence epidemic peaked. Many of the city's neighborhoods are still stricken by shootings, despite a sharp decline over the past five years, which has been attributed to Oakland's Operation Ceasefire violence prevention initiative.

Oakland's Ceasefire was modeled on Boston.

Much fanfare has been levied on the importance of community initiatives, with local leadership and a cross section of institutions addressing a variety of social problems and crises, with gun violence being a prime example of this call for comprehensive approaches tapping local institutions with requisite legitimacy and representing their constituency regarding social justice (Abt, 2019a).

Social workers are aware of the critical role that participatory democracy plays in shaping community development, ownership of initiatives, and the empowerment that ensues (Soska & Ohmer, 2018). Social work, of course, does not have a monopoly on this stance (C. Williams, 2018): "As public health educators and researchers, we firmly believe there is no disease we cannot cure, gun violence included. But no epidemic can be eradicated without the efforts of a village." A can-do attitude is built on optimism and more powerful when it involves "we" in the sentence.

Basing community initiatives on youth of color trauma conceptualization, a subjective phenomenon but critical in shaping their sense of well-being, including using their own words, increases the likelihood of success in reaching these youth (Henderson, 2019). Self-help organizations understand this and provide professionals with requisite vocabulary and context to increase message effectiveness. Viewing community participation through a self-help lens offers great potential for expanding civic engagement. These organizations provide opportunities for reluctant resident engagement with formal organizations (Fader, VanZant, & Henson, 2019).

Addressing gun violence has taken a variety of shapes (Delgado, 2019; Frazer et al., 2018), including developing grassroots organizations specifically focused on gun violence created by the families and most likely mothers of victims leading these efforts. These organizations are invariably started by loved ones of those killed by guns. Organizations such as the Louis D. Brown Peace Institute (Boston) and Mothers With a Message (San Diego, CA), for example, typify efforts to bring solace to a victim's family and putting social and political pressure to pass legislation and support to aid families and prevent the use of guns and violence.

Enlisting local participation is widely embraced with a long tradition gaining saliency. Nevertheless, there is a counterargument to having victims and survivors not weigh in on finding solutions to their tragedies, and this cannot be ignored in understanding opposition to community-led initiatives, as reported by Somin (2019) on comments made by Kyle Kashua at the 2019 NRA Convention:

> I explained why it's a mistake to give special credence to the policy views of victims of horrible tragedies. Surviving a school shooting, or some other awful event, doesn't give you any special insight into the moral and policy questions at stake. Survivors deserve empathy and respect—but not deference to their policy views, except in rare instances where they have genuine expertise on the subject.... Often, the real reason for focusing attention on victims and survivors is not the value of their insights, but the way in which they tug at our emotional heart-strings. Opposition to policies promoted by survivors of a recent horrific event is easy to denounce as callous and unfeeling. Here, we would do well to remember that our immediate emotional reactions to tragedy *are rarely a useful guide to policy*. All too often, giving in to such feelings results in policies that create more harm and injustice than they prevent.

This stance is an antithesis of this book's values. Victims are the best experts of their lives, bringing an experiential legitimacy view in shaping policies and interventions. Slogans, and we can add self-help organization names, play an important role from a media standpoint (Gabor, 2016).

One has only to focus on the names of self-help organizations to understand the messages they convey to their broader community.

Youth must play influential roles shaping gun violence policies (Krantz, 2019; Rahamim, 2018) because this issue impacts them in particular, and they are aware of gun use the social context (Parsons, et al., 2018):

> Young people are not simply victims of gun violence in this country, they are among the leading voices calling for change to the nation's weak gun laws and deadly gun culture. Organizers of the Black Lives Matter movement; survivors of the Parkland shooting; youth organizers working in cities hardest hit by gun violence, such as Chicago, Baltimore, and St. Louis, have all lent their voices to an increasingly loud call to action. These young people do not just want to reform gun laws—they are also demanding that the issue of gun violence be examined as part of a complex and intersectional web of issues that also include community disinvestment, criminal justice reform, and policing. They are advocating not only for solutions to make schools safer from mass shootings but also for holistic and intersectional solutions that will help make all communities safer.

Not having youth at the table setting the agenda decreases the likelihood of success for any strategy hoping to influence youth behaviors. Youth benefit from positive adult engagement, but it must not be condescending and should be viewed as a partnership (Eisman, Lee, Hsieh, Stoddard, & Zimmerman, 2018).

Self-help youth-led organizations on gun violence also exist, showing how this violence is addressed when focused on this age group (Tulop, 2018): (a) March for Our Lives; (b) Students Demand Action; (c) Team Enough; (d) Orange Generation; (e) StudentsMarch.Org; (f) Youth Over Guns; and (g) National Die-In. These organizations reemphasize social action and youth, although adults can be a part of these efforts (Nishimoto, 2019). This section includes one children-focused organization to contrast with the adult-focused organizations, although the latter also involve youth programs. There is a desperate need to capture the appeal and power of the self-help movement and the lessons learned shared with other communities facing similar challenges. This book fills a knowledge gap in the puzzle.

CONCLUSION

This chapter helps us better understand the interplay of key factors shaping how gun violence is manifested and successfully addressed within urban communities, setting the stage for urban self-help organizations in any community-based strategy to address gun violence. The factors raised in this chapter are worthy of considerably more attention. The following chapter addresses what many readers have greatly anticipated—case illustrations. These cases integrate key concepts, statistics, and historical grounding and why self-help organizations will prove to be a critical element in any urban strategy on gun violence.

7

Cross-Cutting Themes

> In hot spots and for hot people, we need a range of incentives
> that promote positive associations and activities while deterring
> violence—there must be both carrot and stick.
>
> —THOMAS ABT, *2019b, p. 45*

INTRODUCTION

We are now in a position where we can pause and integrate case
illustrations highlighted in Chapter 3, and elsewhere in this book, with
the vast literature on urban gun violence. Readers no doubt bring their
own experiences to bear on the themes raised in this chapter. Bringing
together two worlds—practice and theory—allows us to garner lessons
for moving forward in crafting urban interventions with a high likelihood of achieving success for addressing this key issue. Those who are
practice oriented can take these lessons and craft interventions that take
into account local circumstances, which is a key element in best practices.
Academics, in turn, can take marching orders for furthering scholarship
on this form of violence.

Most scholarship seeks to inform or persuade gun violence strategies
(Rossi, 2017). This book seeks to both inform and persuade readers that
self-help organizations have a significant role to play in helping to solve
this nation's urban gun violence problem. These organizations' qualities

Urban Gun Violence. Melvin Delgado, Oxford University Press (2021). © Oxford University Press.
DOI: 10.1093/oso/9780197515518.003.0007.

resonate in urban centers, and we have much to learn from them in addition to partnering with them. Ethically, I cannot in all good conscience just lay out the facts without embracing an advocacy and social justice stance. Being neutral translates into taking the side of just providing information; there is a place for this stance, but a social justice stance does not allow detachment. Readers will need to make a choice.

It is hoped the cases in Chapter 3, and other illustrations covered in this book, captured the breadth of localized efforts at addressing gun violence, showing the multifaceted nature of these organizations and why they represent an essential piece of the challenge in any comprehensive approach to address violence. Other examples buttress key themes in this chapter.

Readers can see cross-cutting themes that emerged with implications for how academic disciplines and helping professions can collaborate with urban self-help organizations in helping them, and us, carry out our respective missions. Opportunities for youth to connect with caring adults are also important in efforts to interrupt gun-carrying behavior (Juan & Hemenway, 2017), and they must also be part of the equation within self-help organizations, as seen in these case illustrations and throughout the book. Changing youth attitudes and behaviors influences future gun use as these youth survive and emerge as adults. We must focus on the present with an eye toward the future and respect for the past.

Urban self-help organizations address a key aspect of youth engagement, for example, by openly affirming and welcoming the youth and providing an avenue for them to receive assistance as well as carry out projects of particular significance to them and beneficial for their communities. These organizations are also open to purposefully facilitating connections across the life span, bringing a welcoming stance that few organizations possess, with the possible exception of houses of faith. We live in a society that is heavily age segregated, and the presence of a community-based institution that brings age groups together is most welcome. Self-help organizations ascending to a more prominent position within gun violence coalitions are a goal of this book because of their potential to unify wide sectors in a common cause. The themes that follow merge the existing literature with the cases covered previously, with some perhaps a surprise to readers.

WOMEN AS ACTIVISTS AND HEALERS

Women have certainly ascended to become critical leaders of this self-help movement as highlighted throughout previous portions of this book, and their role and importance are only further reinforced here. It is no mistake that the term *mothers* will often be a part of any local self-help gun violence efforts. Further, women as healers certainly will not raise any eyebrows. There are nine themes covered in this chapter, and it is appropriate to start this chapter with one centered on women as activists and healers, and one that was a great surprise to me because of women's prominence in this movement across this country's urban centers. An in-depth treatment of this theme is a powerful revelation and bears specific attention here.

Reactions of loved ones to a killing are difficult to categorize because circumstances differ, as do possible reactions, which must take into account cultural values and traditions. Grieving has many different manifestations, making responses difficult to predict. Having others share their experiences provides an invaluable backdrop for those actively grieving to cast their pain against, and this is more so with African American/Black mothers who have had to deal with multiple stressors complicating the grieving process (Stewart, 2017, p. 355):

> One can argue that the mothers of these slain men are suffering in multiple ways. The loss of a child is truly a life-changing event and is unimaginable for any caring parent. Add to their loss, the fact that those who were supposed to be protecting their children were the ones who killed them. To compile even more grief, these mothers have to deal with an imperfect system of justice that does little to vindicate the lives of their sons.

Parents with these experiences are in a position to aid and share with others because of their experiential legitimacy that they possess. The phenomenon of shared grief is facilitated through engagement in self-help activities and projects, allowing parents to reach out to share their stories to help those in the struggles of the death of a loved one. Thus, having a constructive outlet, or action, for directing grief, and even more so when community directed, helps in making meaning of their tragic circumstances (Stewart, 2017).

Seeking explanations for what happened and why is a typical response. Some may react with compassion for other parents who have experienced a loss. Some may even react by seeking revenge. Forgiveness can translate into compassion and even an activist role, as in the case of Trayvon Martin's parents, drawing on a long African American tradition of confronting social injustices with compassion and discipline rather than revenge (Hurtado, 2018). There is a tremendous need for research on compassion, often operationalized as suffering with others, which plays a role in addressing trauma (Posada, 2019) and its developmental process.

Philadelphia's Mothers in Charge Incorporated (MIC) mission statement shows the elevated status of women in the self-help organizational movement:

We are a violence prevention, education and intervention-based organization, which advocates and supports youth, young adults, families and community organizations affected by violence. Mothers In Charge, Inc. advocates for families affected by violence and provides counseling and grief support services for families when a loved one has been murdered. We are comprised of impassioned mothers, grandmothers, aunts, sisters and others who are committed to working towards saving lives and preventing another mother from having to experience this terrible tragedy. Each mother, grandmother, aunt or sister brings a special gift to this organization and its mission. Their passion and drive comes from within because each one of these brave women has somehow found the strength to turn a personal tragedy into a medium for change. They realize that positive change cannot happen within communities without addressing the issue of senseless and random violence. They know that in the names of their lost sons, daughters, and loved ones they can and must serve as the catalyst for change. In addition, Mothers In Charge collaborates with elected officials, community leaders and other community and faith-based organizations on legislation and solutions to support safe neighborhoods and communities for children and families.

This broad response typifies how self-help organizations implement their mission and the importance of bringing together different parties, with women playing a catalyst and leading roles.

Those in social justice campaigns are often found to have suffered the greatest pain, motivating them to protest against injustices, such as police killings of unarmed people of color (Cobbina, Chaudhuri, Rios, & Conteh, 2019). Grief and loss cannot be separated from a social justice stance (Bordere, 2016). Disenfranchised grief or hidden grief (Doka, 1989), as in the case of police killing of African Americans/ Blacks and others of color, brings yet another dimension to the grieving process and introduces state-sanctioned violence (Baker, Norris, & Cherneva, 2019).

The engagement of families in addressing gun violence is another example of how these feelings are channeled into constructive actions that benefit themselves and their communities. Much can be learned by capturing their narratives and recommendations in the crafting of campaigns and interventions that are service focused.

Although most urban gun violence victims are males of color, response to this crisis is often led by women of color; men can certainly be involved, but they are the exception that proves the rule, particularly when examining leadership roles. Women have been cast into leadership roles as spokespersons and activists (Lawson, 2018, pp. 713–714): "The death of a beloved compels us to find new meanings in a permanently altered reality. For some Black mothers, grief over the violent and unexpected death of their child can lead to activism to change unjust social relations."

Nationally, gun violence activists are formidable women (T. Rothschild, 2018). Gun violence is overwhelmingly conducted by men, representing the other side of the same coin, so to speak. Heads of self-help organizations perform many functions—and one of those functions is that of activist—and are part of a national movement, either directly or indirectly. Women of color have assumed leadership roles in fighting gun violence, an underresearched aspect of violence (B. Rothschild, 2019):

> What struck me while making this film [Tamar Manasseh] documentary on was the role that grassroots activists can play when local, state and national institutions fail to address the basic needs of their constituents. America is rapidly becoming a failed state, and acutely felt in places like Chicago's inner city. In the current social and political climate with women increasingly making their voices heard and where the struggle for rights has become a unifying force, could it be that this black Jewish woman is the one person who can show us a way out of the mess that we're in?

Self- and community empowerment are valuable healing dimensions as they increase psychological well-being, introducing a resilience dimension to their participation (A. Bailey, Akhtar, Clarke, & Starr, 2015). These mothers assume a position of community assets, one specifically focused on addressing a pressing community issue; in the process, they use the energy created by a tragic event and channel it into a constructive passion and purpose. This ability to transform negative energy into constructive energy is a gift that must not be squandered and must be learned from. Academics have key roles to play in capturing the "magic" that occurs in these situations and figuring out how it can be identified and enhanced by helping professionals, which can often entail developing collaborative relationships.

Grief and loss must be contextualized to be understood, although they are universal experiences (Hooyman & Kramer, 2006, p. 2):

> Although we typically refer to grief and loss, the more appropriate term in many ways is loss and grief, since the loss precedes the

grief. Regardless of the order, grief and the pain of loss are universal human experiences that every person repeatedly encounters, although the meaning and rituals of grieving vary tremendously by culture. Loss is produced by an event that is perceived to be negative by the individuals involved and results in long-term changes to their social situation, relationships, and patterns of thought and emotions.

Of course, deaths of any kind can result in intense feelings, but when the death could have been prevented, these feelings take on even greater significance.

Al'Uqdah and Adomako (2018, p. 96) drew conclusions on gun violence activism with direct applicability for self-help organizations:

> Broadly, grief and loss can be a tumultuous experience. For African American women, their healing may be further complicated, given their experiences of racism and sexism. Because social activism is related to several positive benefits that include increased social support, positive self-identity, and healthy psychological adjustment following traumatic experiences, we assert that social activism can be used as a healing tool for grieving African American mothers.

Social activism is personally therapeutic and serves an important social goal when it transpires in marginalized urban communities and unites individuals who may feel isolated with others sharing similar social justice concerns.

Impetus for starting a self-help organization can usually follow a particular route. Detroit, Michigan's Save Our Sons and Daughters, for example, was founded by Clementine Barfield, the mother of Derick Barfield, a 16-year-old who was killed in a shooting that also left her son's friend with lifetime injuries (Price, 2017). She was approached by friends and neighbors to offer comfort and asked what she was going to do about the violence; this spurred her into action. An activist role is one way of drawing meaning from being a survivor of the experience of homicide of a loved one and a role with tremendous potential for further transforming communities beyond gun violence, empowering others to address social ills that disproportionately impact their communities.

Maternal grief has been labeled as "public motherhood" and personally transformative and mobilized into social activism (maternal protest) on gun violence (Lawson, 2018, p. 714): "In the United States, maternal activism is evidenced by Mothers of the Movement, a group comprised of African American women whose children have been unjustifiably and violently killed. Indeed, for some bereaved Black mothers, the transformative possibilities of maternal politics informed by grief often emerge from the everyday impacts of structural racial violence." The killings of their children could have been at the hands of the police or some other perpetrator.

Anyone attending a news conference or demonstration will see images of women, mothers most likely, who will be playing key roles that convey the pain and anger associated with the killing of a loved one and serve as the call to action and social justice. Mothers who have experienced this trauma have a prominent role to play in sharing their stories, assuming activist roles, and helping to broker tensions. They must be supported emotionally, socially, and politically in this roles.

The racialization of mass shootings does enter into the grieving process (Campos-Manzo, Mitobe, Ignatiadis, Rubin, & Fischer, 2019). M. Bernstein, McMillan, and Charash (2019, p. 14) made a profound observation on women of color and their grieving, highlighting the difference between individual and mass killings: "In short, the loved ones of victims of urban violence must persuade the audience of their humanity, their worthiness, and that they are not responsible for their own victimization. In contrast, victims of mass shootings are accepted as innocent victims undeserving of their fate, worthy without qualification." Mass shootings create a different reaction, regardless of race, and no one questions whether-or-not the killings were justified, such as a revenge, a drug deal gone wrong, or a "stick-up," for instance.

A belief that they must substantiate why they are grieving the loss of their child adds a tremendous burden to an act that is spontaneous, bringing a dimension that is well understood by self-help organizations and that we must incorporate into our analysis and crafting of interventions. Bridging the gap between need and resources is a major hurdle within urban communities and is done in a manner that is affirming and empowering. Urban self-help organizations can be brokers or buffers between victims and their survivors by acting as a focal point in helping communities respond to gun violence and the external (public) community, with mothers assuming prominent roles, such as the role played by Mothers Against Gun Violence (MAGV) (Dubisar, 2018):

> By acting as buffers—embodied, networked, and mediated—MAGV activists engage members of their community and offer strategies for how citizens and communities respond to gun violence. "When their children are killed, mothers are expected to say something. To help keep the peace. To help make change. But what can I possibly say? I just know we need to do something. We are taught to be peaceful, but we aren't at peace. If we mothers can't change where this is heading for these families—to public hearings, protests un-asked-for martyrdom, or worse, to nothing at all—what can we do? Failing to pay attention to activists such as MAGV members restricts our access to understand the range of strategies African American women invent and adapt, both when asked to respond to violence and to sustain attention to an issue. MAGV's buffer rhetoric's promote education and change, use rhetorical strategies to engage communities and publics, and prevent mothers' perspectives from becoming overlooked and disregarded. (p. 213)

Much can be learned on how social brokering and activism have been conceptualized and implemented by women of color. Increasing our understanding of how sexism is encountered and addressed makes us ever vigilant in preventing the undermining of women as leaders.

QUALITIES OF A LEADER

We cannot understand urban self-help organization success without putting a spotlight on their leadership, which often consists of founding

members (mothers of gun victims) because of the relatively short existence of these organizations. In the human service world, the longevity of
an organization is a typical marker of its success. Urban self-help organizations, when viewed from a life-stage perspective, can be categorized as in
their infancy-toddler stage when viewed from a conventionally standard
viewpoint. If gun violence is eliminated or significantly reduced, these organizations may be expected to close or embrace other urban issues.

Not every parent losing a child to gun violence has the qualities and
opportunities to assume a leadership role related to this issue and establish
a self-help organization. Leadership is a topic that has garnered its share
of scholarly attention and a term that is often bandied about recklessly
within the helping professions, social work included. It is a term with applicability in the discussion of the importance of community participation
in decision-making on gun violence and is relevant in the discussion of
the themes raised in the case illustrations.

Searching for other mothers, and fathers, whose child was killed is an
action that can often occur after the initial shock of losing a child. Needless
to say, this is a critical stage in a decision-making process. This may entail
contacting local houses of worship or even funeral homes for information
on a victim's family to provide outreach to them, for example. Contact can
also occur the other way around, when a mother develops a reputation as
someone who is knowledgeable, kind, and open to listening and helping.

Not having someone outside the home to listen to the affected
individuals is a serious community issue (Joe, Shillingford-Butler, & Oh,
2019, p. 74): "[Mothers] described receiving little to no empathy from
others outside of the home as well as a self-imposed masking of emotions
within the home in an effort to protect their sons. The lack of empathy
outside of the home seemed to be connected with the perceived White
privilege of coworkers and community members." These opportunities to
have this support, as a result, take on even greater significance with gun
violence. The emotional connection that transpires from mothers sharing
a tragic death and the stress accompanying these experiences, including
identifying and sharing coping strategies and strengths, must be tapped
(Joe et al., 2019):

Despite the stress they feel as mothers raising African American boys and young men, participants identified multiple ways in which they cope or care for themselves in the face of adversity. Some coping strategies were internal or individual, such as maintaining a positive outlook, engaging in self-care, journaling, and prayer or meditation. Reliance on faith was evident for many participants and for at least one participant was a means to fight oppression and liberate her son (Participant 10). Participants also discussed other ways of coping that had more of an external focus, such as connecting with other African American mothers and looking to their existent social network of family and friends for support. Several participants discussed either current involvement or a desire for future involvement in community activism to address systemic racism. These participants described a type of self-care motivated by a desire to see change and manifested in action to address the systemic racism that affected their lives and the lives of their sons. (p. 74)

Coping takes on multiple forms, necessitating that those seeking to engage these mothers be flexible in how they are identified, including the assumption of social activist roles if the opportunities are made available and desired.

Mothers who start self-help organizations invariably have an extensive social network and continue to expand it, eventually realizing that this healing is part of their life's mission. In examining the role of leader within self-help organizations, the term *servant leader* emerges to capture how these roles are conceptualized and carried out on a daily basis. It is important to emphasize that the role of leader is viewed as facilitation, as opposed to the conventional view of domination (Lacroix & Pircher Verdorfer, 2017):

One of the core tenets of servant leadership theory is that servant leaders instill in followers a desire to serve others.... Research in this field has convincingly argued that servant leaders are uniquely effective in developing and nurturing service values among followers.

More specifically, it is thought that servant leaders represent strong role models that influence followers via learning processes and vicarious experiences and, thus, eventually imbue the importance of service within their teams. Empirical support for this notion . . . found servant leadership to be positively related to service climate, which represents a "collection of behavioral features or activities of the departments all focusing explicitly on service quality." . . . Recently . . . [it was] found that servant leadership shapes a serving culture in organizations that goes even beyond the service climate with its emphasis on customer service. Rather, the notion of serving culture explicitly refers to an organizational environment in which all members, leaders and followers "share the understanding that the behavioral norms and expectations are to prioritize the needs of others above their own and to provide help and support to others."

Self-help organization leaders often live in the communities they serve, providing them with insights into a community's culture, further lending legitimacy to their roles.

Terrana (2019), in a rare study of Black women nonprofit founders, highlighted the importance of personally identifying with consumers, clients, and the urban neighborhood they serve. There is a positive influence of personal histories and experiential expertise regarding challenges facing people in neighborhoods they serve, which parallel the experiences of gun violence self-help founders so they are able to connect effortlessly, inspirationally, and charismatically.

How service professionals can support these organizations is central in this book, with the answer dependent on local circumstances. The nature and extent of this support can cover a wide range, from technical assistance to having student placements, and this topic is addressed with greater specificity in Chapter 8. We must be a constructive part of an urban gun violence prevention effort.

It will not be lost on readers that all three of the leaders of the self-help organizations featured in this book, and others, are formally educated for assuming religious leadership roles. It remains to be seen until a national study of urban self-help organizations is undertaken what percentage of these organizations is headed by directors with formal religious education. The prominence of forgiveness, a central tenet of religious training and a theme in this book, may account for its importance. This does not mean that forgiveness would not be present if the organization were headed by someone without religious training. However, it may explain why it is so significant in healing and having these individuals assume a healer role.

On a final note, self-help organizations have relied on the vision and energy of the founders. The composition of the board of directors, in turn, assumes an influential role in shaping an organization's evolution and potential to be faithful to its mission and its ability to sustain it. The composition of boards and advisory committees must be purposefully planned to bring expertise (experiential and educational) and institutional, ethical, and consumer legitimacy (Rein, 1969). This is reflective of a leader's vision and ability to garner support across a variety of social-political spheres.

The boards of the self-help organizations profiled in this chapter reflect this stance, facilitating these organizations so they are positioned to maintain and expand services as deemed necessary. Boards develop missions, executives translate missions to staff, and staff carry out the missions. When the mission is embraced by all parties, it can be implemented with minimum distractions.

PRINCIPLES OF URBAN SELF-HELP ORGANIZATIONS AND LESSONS FOR THE FIELD

It is appropriate to include in this chapter principles to integrate how urban self-help organization foci, values, and orientation coincide with the professional literature. Much can be learned from bringing together the values and principles that these self-help organizations embrace and examining the convergence of social factors that entered in their formation. These values and principles can be viewed from various standpoints: philosophical, social, political, economic, ethical, moral, and racial. They are the DNA shaping how these organizations unfold.

Six principles stand out and are presented without prioritizing their importance: (a) *forgiveness*; (b) *importance of dignity and self-worth*; (c) *broad conceptualization of victims*; (d) *multifaceted interventions whenever possible*; (e) *prominent place of self-help at the table concerning gun violence*; and (f) *community participation and empowerment permeation of all aspects of programming*. These overarching principles cross over into the world of social science and interventionists, with conceptual threads throughout this book and how they bring together communities, with social scientists and helping professionals sharing similar concerns and a desire to make a difference.

These principles are grounded within a set of values and beliefs that complement each other and represent elements of a comprehensive view of how gun violence must be seen, addressed, and evidenced in the missions of these organizations. Community interventions based on these principles are self-evident, illustrating their importance in guiding self-help organizations navigate the urban terrain and guns. This listing does not mean that tensions do not exist between them. For instance, one parent said that her faith makes her forgive, but her heart does not. Inherent tension is ever present, and seeking reconciliation, and more so among the very religious, is inherent in that declaration. This tension often requires the assistance of others who have walked on the same path and managed to forgive but not forget.

Practitioners and social scientists supporting self-help organizations in crafting initiatives must be prepared to engage in how best to bring these principles to life. Further, they must be prepared to advance knowledge of how these principles have resonated within urban communities dealing with gun violence. We can advance scholarship and give back to communities through a conscious effort to make our professions more relevant to urban life by better preparing future practitioners and academics to make contributions.

Those in the academy can open doors to resources to which we have access to aid and collaborate with urban self-help organizations to help them implement their historic missions in areas they deem necessary, and not ours, it must be emphasized (Lane et al., 2019). The academy is often criticized by community organizations because we seek their collaboration when in need of these relationships, often the result of some funding requirement; once the funding is complete, we disappear.

SUPPORT FROM MANY DIFFERENT SOURCES

One cross-cutting theme that resonated for me was the importance of gun victims emotionally connecting with others facing similar struggles, a hallmark of self-help organizations in general, but more so those involved with urban violence, and having an accessible (psychological and structural) place to turn to for help. As addressed previously, gunshot victims have a higher likelihood of becoming perpetrators of violence (Goldstick et al., 2019). Altering this potential life path from violence to healing, and enlisting these individual's participation in antigun activities, makes them individuals critical community assets. Not only does it take a village to raise a child, but also it takes a village to accomplish other life-altering events.

How to conceptualize the pain caused by guns challenges us to rethink what it means and how we should respond to it. Grief resulting from violence must not be conceptualized as an individual phenomenon or limited to the immediate family of the victim, but also must be cast into a collective context to give more universal cultural meaning and increase the likelihood of positive social change resulting from a tragedy. A murder's shadow can last a long time and cover a wide area (Hitchcock, 2019b): "Hart Howard knows the shadow that murder casts on a family. Years before she was born, her father's older sister was shot to death on the steps of a California college library by an ex-boyfriend. Six months later, her father's dad died of a broken heart. More than 70 years later, the pain still ripples through the family." These institutions are very attractive for sponsoring or being part of a network supporting other urban self-help organizations.

Enlisting co-victim participation as part of an urban self-help organization's mission extends their influence without having to expand their budgets and hire staff, further integrating these organizations into the life of a community on an issue that many formal organizations, although subject to debate, have eschewed or poorly addressed. Any social justice quest must reach out to others within one's social network and combine other social networks into one, which, if followed logically, turns into a movement of great consequence with the potential to bring communities, providers, and academics together in this quest.

C. A. Smith (2016), speaking as a Black anthropologist and addressing what is widely considered trauma but called sorrow in this context, issued a challenge for that discipline that also applies to all other disciplines and, I would also argue, helping professions:

> To think of sorrow as artifact is to consider the way that sorrow, as grief, as mourning, as longing, as suffering—is the residue, that is, the trace left behind in the wake of tragedy. As anthropologists, we typically think of artifacts as those cultural relics that we investigate from the past or present. They are things that people leave behind that leave clues as to who we are and what life means to us. Thus, to think of sorrow as artifact within the context of a discussion of Black mothering is to consider sorrow as something more than just an emotion of sentience; it is the aftermath of our social moment. Sorrow as artifact thus provides clues into what it means to mother as Black women in times of terror. (p. 6)

This challenge has profound implications for academics pursuing a scholarly agenda on this nation's marginalized groups and communities. Mothers and other loved ones may have to wait decades to see perpetrators come to justice, showing the depth of this sorrow and the emotional burden it has on them and their family (Sainz & Lush, 2019).

An immense amount of attention is paid to victims, their families, and perpetrators of gun violence. However, the families of perpetrators generally do not share in the glare of this attention, yet they also are victims, but in a rather unconventional way. Broadening the impact circle of gun violence increases the likelihood that a community-wide solution is possible.

Often, the families of perpetrators also live within the same community, if not the same building for that matter, where they commit their violent acts. Social networks have a propensity to overlap when people live in areas with a high population density, and it should not be surprising to find out that victims and perpetrators know each other. This can help or hinder the process of forgiveness.

The willingness and ability to forgive the unforgivable is an act that many would find difficult, but it plays such an instrumental role in the healing process, which when fostered through possession of understanding and empathy (internal emotional transformation of forgiveness) and evidence that the remains possible through understanding and empathy (Hourigan, 2019a). The brother of Botham Jean, the victim, in the 2019 Dallas Amber Guyer murder trial, publically forgiving her and asking permission to hug her made national news because this act of forgiveness was so profound. This act of forgiveness spoke so much about his family and the role of forgiveness, rather than embracing the burden of hate and revenge in their lives. Coming together with the perpetrator and forgiving this person, and then the perpetrator offering an apology, can be conceptualized as reconciliation, whereby these two parties do not see the future as being defined by the past.

Court proceedings are events that are emotion and tension filled and not a conducive environment for therapeutic outcomes to occur. They are settings associated with justice and not forgiveness and compassion. When parents of a dead child attend the trial of the accused killer, if apprehended and charged, their presence in court takes on terrific prominence because of the opportunity to confront the accused killer and to sit through a defense attorney's arguments seeking to present the victim as a provocateur.

The exchange that occurs when a parent of a child killed by gun violence can be the key to helping them move forward with their lives with a social justice purpose, even assuming an activist role so that no other parents go through what they have gone through. Sometimes, parents may plead with the judge to be lenient because no matter the length of the sentence, their child will not come back. It is not unusual to have parents plead for a reduced sentence for the killer as an act of compassion for killer and their family. An opportunity to share their pain is one part of this therapeutic equation. The ability to listen to the other person sitting across from them must not be overlooked in helping us understand the process of grieving. The validation and advice they provide rounds out this therapeutic exchange.

The role of forgiveness was on national display for the world to see how many of the relatives of the victims of the killings at Mother Emanuel AME Church, Charleston, South Carolina, forgave the killer, Dylann Roof, capturing a sacred moment (A. E. Johnson & Fisher, 2019, p. 8): "Despite how we might feel about the families forgiving Roof of murdering their loved ones, what was again on full display was the agony of Black pain. With the killings of Trayvon Martin, Michael Brown, Renisha McBride, Tamir Rice, and Walter Scott still fresh in the minds of many African Americans, the Charleston massacre cut deep."

This public display of forgiveness, although controversial in some circles, at the time and to this day, brings to the fore an important dimension of an act that has been highlighted in this book and is openly embraced by urban self-help organizations. This stance, which is considered moral, requires careful observation and deliberation in order to fully grasp its significance in gun violence. Jorgensen (2018), in addressing forgiveness after the Charleston killings, argued that it serves a socially constructive role beyond an individual level. Wedderburn and Carey (2017) countered that not rushing to forgive or withholding forgiveness may not be thera-peutic. There is a process we go through, some of us more quickly than others, whereby those suffering the immense pain associated with the act that caused a death must sit and contemplate, if you wish, before the act of forgiveness can transpire and be therapeutic.

Viewing perpetrators as evil interferes with the healing process by stressing punishment without forgiveness, and the engagement of the family of perpetrators in this process (Vasturia, Webster, & Saucier, 2018). It may not always be possible or advisable to seek involvement with the families of perpetrators. These families may be "crime families" where vir-tually every member has a history of criminal enterprises and violence, including an intergenerational history of gun use. Thus, seeking their involvement must be based on a case-by-case basis. Yet, the opposite is also true of never considering it.

Empathy is a personal quality that never loses appeal regardless of social circumstances, and it certainly takes on greater prominence in aiding victims of gun violence; and some would argue that no intervention can ever be successful without empathy as a key ingredient. Compassion is not possible without empathy because there is a distinction between the two. Empathy allows us to be aware of how others feel; compassion, in turn, uses empathy for mobilizing us to assist those in need. Urban self-help organizations rest on a foundation of empathy that they have transformed into compassion, which formal social service organizations are often accused of lacking, setting the stage for engaging those in pain by offering a service.

Being able to emotionally and socially connect at a particularly painful period is well understood by helping professionals and is particularly important in healing. One often hears about the need for closure. However, I do not believe closure ever really occurs with gun violence. The ability to receive emotional support from someone who looks and speaks like you, however, adds a dimension that is often missing when professionals are the source of this support. The opportunity to give back this support to others is a dimension of healing that facilitates this journey.

It would be a mistake to think that grieving children do so in a similar fashion as their adult counterparts (Nickita, 2016), and this necessitates that age-specific services be developed that take into account the unique circumstances of children, in addition to those that they share with their parents. Self-help organizations understand to this situation and have services for different age groups.

Urban adolescents can engage in deep and meaningful emotional expression with friends and adults they trust, emphasizing the importance of being able to explore underlying mechanisms and interpersonal processes that can lead to engagement in violent manifestations (Reigeluth, Pollastri, A. R., Cardemil, E. V., & Addis et al., 2016). The importance of youth of color trusting the person offering assistance cannot be overly estimated, particularly if the person offering is an adult. This ability to trust is essential in achieving behavioral changes that can de-escalate conflictual situations that in the past were resolved through violence, including use of guns. Urban children and adolescents bring unique needs because of their age and developmental stage when they encountered gun violence in their lives, and self-help organizations understand this and provide age-specific services.

Although this book has focused on self-help organizations, healing is not limited to these organizations, and such a narrow view does a disservice to the field and these communities. Social scientists and helping professionals must have an expansive view of healing sites, which can come in many different shapes and sizes, including residents who are not affiliated with any organization. Some urban community-based houses of worship, for example, have an opportunity to focus or refocus attention, as the case may be, to play an activist or leading role in gun violence as well as become a community center for healing to occur through the sharing of stories and receipt of validation and advice (M. Walsh, 2017; Wynn, 2019). Funeral homes also can assume this lofty role, as addressed in Chapter 4.

These sharing experiences parallel those found in self-help organizations covered in this book and illustrate the potential of a wide circle of healers within communities that are often thought about from a deficit perspective. The wide potential of healers and healing sites requires each community be viewed from this perspective, serving as a foundation for collaborative efforts involving helping professionals.

Some wish to label these as riots. I prefer to label them as democratic demonstrations with intense physical manifestations. It is easy for the state to label what is a demonstration as a riot, and maybe even as an act of terrorism, depending on the geographic context and characteristics of the demonstrators. The power to label is destructive and minimizes extreme sorrow and injustices in these instances (Rossi, 2019). Social activism, for example, garners victims' voices in a collective form that magnifies their plight and makes it harder to ignore by the general public and the criminal justice system (Cook, 2017).

Even the exercise of our First Amendment right has been severely impacted by COVID-19 and our right and ability to come together as a group.

Demonstrating against police brutality or indifference, or to highlight a particular shooting that has severely impacted communities, cannot transpire in the usual manner because of social distancing. This fundamental right is often perceived as one of the few ways that urban communities can draw attention to injustices, drawing media and other forms of attention to a killing, in the hopes of an intervention.

What professionals and social scientists often miss in discussing the ramifications of urban violence is that victims, narrowly or broadly defined, are able to reach out to each other and create social bonds because of this shared experience, often eschewing the assistance of professionals in helping them cope (Ralph, 2014). This ability to reach out and connect is a strength that often goes unrecognized outside of the community. Self-help organizations, in turn, provide a focal point for seeking help and forging bonds. This connection, however, may not replace the relationships developed outside of these organizations for those requiring more support. In essence, self-help organizations are never intending to replace these sources of support. They are there for those unable to find solace through their social network or wish to supplement them because these organizations provide an opportunity to engage in social activism or meet other needs.

PLACE AND SPACE

A focus on an urban context goes beyond a geographic place. It also interjects the importance of space as a concept to capture what transpires within that physical place. Self-help organizations can occupy a wide range of psychological and physical places within a community and can take a variety of shapes and sizes, bringing flexibility to how they can evolve by taking into account local circumstances. True, they may have a physical building that is geographically accessible, where meetings can transpire, and are identified as a destination for seeking solace. These places can encompass other dimensions that are emotionally centered and can aid in the healing process, introducing, or re-enforcing, the importance of co-victims having their own space, being themselves, and speaking to others who understand their pain.

Victimization can result in perpetration of violence as victims act out their anger or rage; it can also be a critical juncture or turning point resulting in a life dedicated to helping others, and this aspect has not gotten the attention it deserves, particularly when there is a pull back from a social network engaged in violence (Turanovic, 2019). This is an opportunity lost because we have lost hope in them victims. Urban self-help organizations provide a safe and affirming place and space for this transformation to occur and be supported. These organizations bring this potential as an integral part of their existence because it is so rare to find it outside of the neighborhood.

Family friends who lost their own children take on greater prominence within these social networks because of the memories and pain they share, with these friendships based on a common bond, and this dimension is recognized and fostered by self-help organizations. Providing the place and space for these engagements to transpire in a conducive atmosphere can often not be accomplished in urban neighborhoods. Filling this void is a significant public service.

Finding and creating community spaces to mourn and heal within a community ravaged by violence (Delgado, 2019; Mohn, 2018), sometimes considered as public art, is a phenomenon with tremendous potential for gun violence interventions, and these spaces can take a wide range of manifestations, including gardens as places where victims and supporters can gather, as in New Haven, Connecticut (Sharkey, 2013):

> The garden is a collaboration between members of the Survivors of Homicide support group, Yale University's Urban Resources Initiative and the City of New Haven. It's a half-acre stretch that runs along Valley Street in New Haven, nestled between a neighborhood and a block of restaurants and shops. Its positioning along a busy street is intentional, meant to draw people in. Right now, the space looks more like an open grassy field than a garden, but the mothers hold the vision of what it will become close to their hearts, busying themselves

with the beginning of its transformation. Its official name is lengthy—
The New Haven Botanical Garden of Healing Dedicated to Victims of
Gun Violence— its mission is simple: to help ease the pain.

These gardens can called "healing gardens" and can be found throughout
the world (Pouya & Demirel, 2015). A garden becomes a gathering place
for a variety of activities that address multiple aspects of gun violence,
from healing to the offering of training that can help youth socially navigate dangerous situations that can lead to becoming victims. Gardens can
assume focal points to direct energies, create fellowship, and conduct activities that can prevent gun violence. Memorial bricks and a wall add
another dimension to the site, depending on local needs. Gardens provide
flexibility on how they unfold and the nature of the art installations that
best represent local cultural norms and traditions.

Moms Demand Action (MDA) (Washington, DC) brings together
those with a significant loss in their lives and the general public wishing to
honor them (O'Connell, 2019):

> "We're planting hope and creating something hopeful," said Celia
> Slater, who handles communications for MDA. "We're planting to
> honor the people we love who've been killed. We plant seeds for
> lasting change. . . . Members of the public donated the initial flowers
> for the garden, which include sunflowers and other pollinator-
> friendly blossoms. Come fall, MDA will plant more flowers, with the
> hope of transforming the plot into a butterfly garden. . . . Children,
> students and other volunteers painted hundreds of rocks, which will
> be placed around the garden."

Boston's Peace Garden, a collaboration between the Peace Institute, one
of the three case illustrations discussed in Chapter 3, and the Massachusetts
Victim Assistance Office, is multifaceted, with a physical and virtual presence, allowing visitors to learn about those who are memorialized. The
following are three examples. The first concerns *Shawn Borden (January
12, 1975–October 25, 2016)*:

A eulogy from his daughter. . . . It's hard to find just one thing to describe him. To many people he was many things. No matter who you
spoke to, he was a kind, funny, and free-spirited soul. His friendships,
allegedly, span from a neighbor down the street to celebrities like
Mark Wahlberg alike. To know he was so well loved by many people
from different backgrounds only shows how his death was too soon.
Our city knows how heartless we as people can be, but to see such
a shining spirit as Shawn is what made Boston home to many of us.

He was the friendly neighbor making barbecues for the whole
town. He was the biker whose over the top antics made even the
rudest of drivers laugh. And his ever-growing family made this
brother, son, father, and grandfather ever so proud. As a father, he
was never afraid to show his constant love and care for all of his
family, even to the most distant. He was born into poverty as most
of us minority Boston natives are, and he managed to stay afloat in
the face of racial, socioeconomic, and familial stressors through his
light-hearted nature. His humble beginnings informed how he was
able to reach so many people. Worldly possessions were something
he and everyone enjoyed, but he found the fruitfulness of life and
living amongst those he respected much more appealing. He abided
by this ideology so much so that he stayed in front of his son when
bullets rang through the streets. Some would say he was an angel, or
at least a someone we all should strive to be. I say he was my father
who died too soon, and should be one of many examples of how our
city needs to change for the better.

The second involves Gabriel Bara-Bardo   *(July 26, 1999–August 15, 2017)*:

Gabe loved music and art and was an avid guitarist who had
aspirations of furthering his education by attending music school.
He loved the art of tattoos and was an "old soul" who often spoke
in poetic terms and anyone who knew Gabe could attest to his kind
and gentle nature. Gabe not only illuminated the lives of those he
touched while on this earth, but he now shines on through his wish

to donate life so others could live. Gabe gave the gift of life to others through his organ donation.

The pain of losing a child, especially to homicide, is unbearable. It is unrelenting. There is no reprieve. Gabe dies again every morning that we awake, every moment in between and every sleepless night. We are all broken, for the loss of Gabe permeates our family as we try to find a new normal. Please remember Gabriel. Please say his name. Gabe.

The third example is of *Barbara Jean Graham*

Barbara was born June 8, 1944 in Palm Beach County Fl. The family later moved to Sumter, SC where she grew up and graduated class of 1962 from Lincoln High with her twin Sister Betty Graham. They later moved to Boston where they shared an apartment. Barbara decided to become a professional business person and opened her own business. She was the sole proprietor of Bobbie Graham Insurance Agency. On May 7, 1979 she was taken away from her family and friends to go to the eternal resting place. "Barbara cared for family and friends and there was nothing she wouldn't do to help. She would give you her last," said her sister Rose. Her sister Jennifer said, "She was my great and loving big sister. When she left to make her career in Mass. she made sure to help her parents with the care and clothing of her younger sisters and brother. Family meant a lot to her. She built a family business that helped others and her family. She was a small woman with a Big heart. She was my sister (love)." From her sister Suzette, "Barbara had a lovely soul. She was beautiful inside and out. She loved her family as much as we loved her and that was the love of a close family." And from her sister Josephine aka Honey, "My sister was a sweet and loving person, who never hurt anyone. I miss her dearly."

These sites provide survivors with an opportunity to visit and remember their loved ones without going to a cemetery, which may be very difficult (because of geographic access and emotional pain). Geographic and psychological accessibility are minimized in these instances, facilitating a healing process (Kirk, 2019). Communities having public spaces that they control is a key indicator in the life of a community. When communities lose control over public spaces, residents face incredible challenges in uniting to counter violence, undermining self-efficacy and hope (Wilcox & Cullen, 2018). This state of social paralysis undermines their key institutions and disrupts daily lives. The presence of public art on gun violence is a good indicator that there is control over public space. Places and spaces cannot be simply developed by external sources.

DIFFERENT NEEDS FOR DIFFERENT FOLKS

Obtaining support from others is an important theme; different age groups necessitate different sources of support. Youth, often the direct target of gun violence, as addressed in this book, will have difficulty turning to adults for all of their emotional and instrumental needs. They are often very limited in seeking help outside of their social network.

Finding a place where they are welcomed and can engage in safe activities with other youth outside of their immediate social circle, who also face similar challenges, cannot be met by one or two individuals. Rather, an organization such as one that is self-help can fill this vacuum and do so in an organic manner in a response to immediate and pressing community needs. Further, it introduces the potential of youth to connect with caring adults, often a barrier in their social lives because connecting with caring adults in those institutions seems rare.

It is of paramount importance that all gun violence victims have a place to turn to for help when they need it and to receive it in a manner that is respectful, fosters trust, and is given in the language that they best can relate to, ideally by someone who looks like them. Further, being able to access this assistance within their neighborhood facilitates this help-seeking. Urban self-help organizations do meet these needs in an affirming manner. Those seeking help do not have to become involved in an organization's day-to-day or major event activities, providing flexibility on degree of involvement. All service needs cannot be met internally. Consequently, self-help organizations must establish collaborative arrangements with organizations capable of meeting these needs. These organizations serve as a central hub (brokering) for connecting those in need in an efficient manner, filling an important gap in this arena.

Loved ones must never have to legitimize their sorrow and pain to the outside world. They cannot simply put aside their experiences and move on with life. Urban self-help organizations understand this pain and the struggles of moving forward, and helping others to do so is part of this journey for some. There is no obligation that those seeking the aid of urban self-help organizations "give back" as a precondition of being assisted. This unconditional assistance allows for involvement along an entire continuum from no giveback at the beginning to playing an active role on a daily basis at the end of the continuum.

HEALING CAN TRANSPIRE IN MANY DIFFERENT URBAN PLACES

Healing can be examined from a variety of perspectives, such as the act, the individual seeking to heal, and the place where this can transpire. The concept of healing is profound because of what is required to transpire to help those in pain be able to cope and grow as a result and where it is supposed to transpire. This conclusion, of course, is shared by countless others that I have had the privilege of contacting in the course of my career as a practitioner and academic.

Healing can involve a wide range of issues, including emotional and other dimensions. One study (DeBo'rah, 2016) of African American parental experiences after the killing of their child uncovered five common themes: (a) parent blame (questioning of what they did to cause this or should have done to prevent it); (b) emotional issues (e.g., anger, posttraumatic stress disorder, uncontrollable crying, depression, inability to think about the future); (c) support systems (e.g., grief groups, compassionate friends, spiritual counseling, family support, psychiatric treatment, alcohol consumption); (d) ongoing physiological issues (e.g., cardiac problems, anxiety, stroke, ongoing medical issues); and (e) discrimination (e.g., no investigation, plea deal, judicial system). This clustering of consequences casts a wide net on how and why these life changes for parents are so profoundly consequential.

Engaging with self-help organizations takes on even greater significance for victims of color because they are able to patronize a locally based organization that reflects their backgrounds. In essence, they do not have to travel downtown or to other sections of a city. The time and cost of this travel is saved for other purposes. Urban self-help organization accessibility bears attention because it is a perennial topic among helping professions and learning how to minimize or eliminate service barriers, particularly during high-stress periods, which is often the case immediately after a shooting. Accessibility goes beyond geographic (located within the communities affected) and involves psychological (nonstigmatizing), cultural (staff who reflect the backgrounds of those seeking assistance), and logistical (services are free and available when needed, without the confines of the usual 9 to 5 workday, Monday to Friday, and holiday closures).

Urban self-help organizations have effectively overcome the following barriers to help-seeking: (a) geographical/physical (located locally); (b) psychological (trust); (c) cultural (those occupying positions in these institutions look and talk like they do and share similar concerns and experiences); and (d) operational (no costs or extensive paperwork to fill out). Each of these factors must be addressed. These barriers are of equal importance and essential in aiding gun violence victims, and self-help organizations are propitiously positioned to offer aid that is welcomed and appropriate. These barriers are of varying degrees of strength and also dynamic, increasing and decreasing in significance within local communities.

THE POWER OF THE GROUP

Using the label of self-help organization may give the mistaken impression that services are individually focused, and nothing could be further from the truth because of the importance of groups in this help-seeking and help-giving process, which often translates into great influence, or power, in shaping outcomes.

Although the seeking of support and help can involve a victim turning to others in their social network for this assistance, there is no denying that the power of belonging to a group composed of others with similar life stories brings a dimension to gun violence that has generally been overlooked. We understand the power of the group to cause individuals to do horrendous things they normally would not do by themselves; yet, the group can also be a source of power that goes beyond the abilities of one individual providing help, regardless of their competencies and how closely backgrounds are shared with those seeking help.

Not surprisingly, arts have been used with bereavement support groups for dealing with traumatic and/or unexpected losses because this vehicle allows participants to receive support, engaging in creativity, meaning making, and memorializing of the deceased (Falldien, 2019). The self-help organizations spotlighted in the previous chapter, particularly the Peace Institute and the TraRon Center, had art as a prominent feature in a broad array of activities. Those grieving are thrust into negotiating their new existence (understanding and functioning) in relation to a key missing member of their family or social network, of meaning/sense making after a significant loss (Gillies, Neimeyer, & Milman, 2015; Rozalski, Holland, & Neimeyer, 2016).

Groups can also be conceptualized as families composed of close and distant relatives. However, instead of sharing a bloodline, they share pain and a quest for healing. Group healing can go by many different names, usually ones that are affirming, such as "testimonies from the heart" and "healing circles," which have religious overtones. When healing is viewed as most favorably addressed through a group modality, as in the case St. Louis's Truth Telling Project, which focuses on violence experienced (relatives killed) by the police, with sessions taped and shared, illustrating the power of sharing of narratives (Romano & Ragland, 2018).

Self-help organizations use groups in multiple ways, from support provision, teaching, engaging in social activism, socially, and multiple other ways. This does not mean that one to one does not have a place in any healing network. Sidewalk vigils map out a space for community grieving to transpire as well as honoring and remembering those killed. These vigils are rarely silent and often involve prayer, singing, and use of religious imagery in some form of permutation or combination, engaging participants in a collective grieving process (M. Bernstein et al., 2019). Group power must be fostered whenever possible, as evidenced in vigils, for instance. This dimension requires having not only expertise in those leading these groups, but also physical space to hold them, and self-help organizations possess both.

It is not surprising that gang membership is not highly correlated with violence-related disability, with corresponding need for rehabilitation services, yet these services are underutilized, calling for targeted outreach (Dunlap & Russell, 2015). The further marginalization they experience highlights how intersectionality of race, disability, and gender occurs within urban communities of color (J. Banks, 2018). The self-help group example of Chicago's "Crippled Footprint Collective," which consisted of ex–gang members paralyzed due to gun violence, helps concretize group power in providing and receiving support, making the invisible visible, as discussed by Darius, one member of that group (Ralph, 2014, p. 127):

Darius continues, "As you can see, all of us here have wheelchairs. And the reason we have wheelchairs is because we were out in the streets gang banging, selling drugs. We got shot, and ultimately we got paralyzed." Today, Darius says, the students will learn what happens to the body when the spinal cord is injured. By educating the students about the grim realities of being wheelchair bound, the Crippled Footprint Collective speakers hope to get current gang members thinking about their lives outside the gang—specifically, if they become paralyzed and have to care for themselves. Eventually, the gang deserts gunshot victims. If this message resonates with the students, Darius and company are well on their way to achieving their primary goal: Reversing the foundational belief that the perpetuation of violence unifies the gang.

The Crippled Footprint Collective members turned a tragedy into a strength by providing members with a purpose to better the lives of residents, who, also may be facing challenges due to gun violence, and the collective has shifted to becoming a community asset when these efforts are recognized, valued, and fostered (Moser, 2014). This example substantiates the group process employed by the Mother's Healing Circle, as in Chicago, discussed in this book's introductory chapter.

Violently acquired impairments is a term that is increasing in saliency to capture the debilitating consequences of gun violence, such as use of wheelchairs and other devices (C. Green, 2019). These impairments are related to an area of service that will only increase in significance as gunshot victims are increasingly surviving, but also they are increasingly facing disability bias to go along with racism (J. Banks, 2015). In urban communities, when spinal cord injuries are secondary to gunshot wounds, it will necessitate services to be structured to take into account their living circumstances in order to maximize the potential of the patient, and this will require extensive coordination with community-based services (DiZazzo-Miller, 2015). Gun-inflicted spinal cord injuries for Latinxs, for example, severely compromise their quality of life, and more so because of the paucity of services with linguistic and cultural competencies to treat them and support their caregivers (Balcazar, Magaña, & Suarez-Balcazar, 2020).

Organized Mother's Day gun violence walks, which are purposefully planned to tap sentiments associated with this day, are increasingly becoming a vehicle for raising awareness as well as becoming a mechanism for fundraising, drawing a wide range of participants. These walks can be conceptualized in a variety of ways. Thinking of these events as group experiences, during which stories are shared and validated and expanding social networks, takes the walks out of the exclusively social activist stance to a healing experience, a dimension that further enhances these activities for community and intercommunity collaborative endeavors. This perspective illustrates the importance of embracing a nuanced approach to the cross-cutting themes in this chapter.

On a final note, youth also have an avenue for social action engagement to counter the deleterious consequences of gun violence (Wray-Lake,

2019). Self-help organizations must be welcoming of all age groups and constructively engage them in the major activities that are offered to the public, including an opportunity to engage in social change efforts. A group's power often not only goes beyond therapeutic goals but also can involve group social action causes, with therapeutic goals assuming a secondary status.

Sharing stories with others who have been through similar experiences is invaluable for people of color who find themselves isolated and living with painful feelings that often are ignored or invalidated. Social protest can be a source of emotional support for youth experiencing trauma who are reluctant to turn to conventional organizations that offer mental health services (Chavez-Diaz & Lee, 2015, p. 14):

> Both Community Healers and Community Organizers carry specialized knowledge bases that can serve as valuable assets to build more comprehensive models of community engagement and social change work. In order to foster partnerships between healers and social justice organizers, we must support the current kinship networks that exist among community healers and among organizers.

When the option of social protest is offered as part of a self-help organization's mission, it meets multiple expressive and instrumental needs, including providing a space for youth, and for that matter other adults, to obtain valuable emotional help.

DANGER AND SELF-HELP ORGANIZATIONS

It would be uplifting to highlight the important and inspirational work undertaken by self-help organizations. However, they also face challenges in achieving social change in their neighborhood, including possible death and injury while carrying out responsibilities. Danger is restricted not only to gun violence but also to the compromising of health and even possible death from COVID-19. Unlike its gun counterpart, this virus is invisible, making it that much more arduous to see and provide a response.

Gun violence and trauma know no boundaries. When women assume activist and healer roles, it does not make them immune from experiencing deadly violence themselves, which speaks so poignantly about gun violence. In July 2019, for instance, Chicago witnessed the shooting deaths of two mothers involved with Mothers/Men Against Senseless Killings (MASK) seeking to stop gun violence in their neighborhood (CBS News, 2019):

> Two women involved with a group called Mothers Against Senseless Killings were shot dead Friday on a South Side Chicago block where moms gather to help curb gun violence. Police say they don't believe the two young mothers were the intended targets. The deaths of Chantel Grant, 25, and Andrea Stoudemire, 35, in the Englewood neighborhood served as a grim reminder of the kind of violence that led them to participate in neighborhood activities organized by Mothers Against Senseless Killings. The anti-violence group launched five years ago following the shooting death of another young mother at the same corner. The group began with moms "occupying" the corner . . . hanging out and offering food and counseling for youth in response to violence in the community. "That's why we're out here seven days a week . . . trying to create a safe place where people can learn to be neighbors and not kill each other," said the group's founder, Tamar Manasseh. The gunfire on Friday night was meant for a man who is affiliated with a Chicago street gang and recently got out of prison, police spokesman Anthony Guglielmi said.

In October 2019, Jermaine Kelly, a MASK member, was injured by gunfire (Farr, 2019). The work by local activists and self-help organizations is dangerous, which makes the organizations that much more meaningful and needful of support. This dangerous aspect of their work sheds light on the immensity of their mission.

The death of a loved one often results in changing those around the victim and more so when the death is due to violence (Al'Uqdah & Adomako, 2018). This change can be negative, resulting in depression, illness, and a reduced role within a family or community. It can be a life-altering event in the opposite manner and have the individual assume an activist role for addressing gun violence. The story of those involved in self-help organizations is about the latter, but that does not make them immune from experiencing harm, however.

Practitioners and social scientists addressing urban gun violence must also contend with safety concerns, and this work is never for the faint of heart; I would argue it does not receive sufficient attention in our academic preparation. Dangerous spaces and places cannot be understood and successfully changed without a street presence from practitioners and academics. Journalists also face similar challenges.

NEVER ALONE: THE IMPORTANCE OF COLLABORATIONS

Grieving is a state of being that often necessitates not being alone, further enhancing the process and experience from a group standpoint. From a cultural stance, many urban community groups bring a preference and love for groups, be they family embracing extended family members or inclusion of friends, neighbors, and church members, to list several.

Those surviving violence should be recruited to take a central role in crafting and carrying out solutions (Sered, 2019). Self-help organizations do not exist as islands within their neighborhoods, and as a result, they broaden their influence using collaborative projects throughout their and in neighboring communities.

Cooperation and collaboration have played an influential role in expanding urban self-help organizations; they cannot be a tranquil island in a sea of intranquility. Continuing with a sea metaphor, their tentacles must touch the key institutions within the grasp. This goal is never easy to accomplish and requires a tremendous amount of time and skill and must have saliency for an organization to embrace and act on it with conviction and make it part of the mission.

These organizations' brokering role is essential in putting communities into central roles in dictating local solutions. This does exclude other local organizations assuming partnerships in coalitions. Nevertheless, urban self-help organizations bring the necessary substantial institutional, consumer, and ethical expertise to make them legitimate. This is not to say that positively changing police–community narratives with an intent to create effective partnerships is not arduous to achieve.

Urban self-help organizations, in order to increase their support and effectiveness, expand their social network to bring together conventional and unconventional settings, along with groups that have no institutional affiliation. Collaboration is often a goal that organizations proclaim as part of their mission. However, it often remains an elusive goal because collaboration is so hard to meaningfully establish and maintain. This goal, if achieved, is most impressive and bodes well for organizations such as those that are self-help focused.

Trauma reoccurring, and even death, increases after attending an emergency room, bringing forth a charge for improving medical and psychological services to interrupt a cycle of violent injury (Kao et al., 2019). Establishment of formalized collaborative partnerships with self-help organizations is one way of enhancing service delivery. The following are several examples of collaborations undertaken by Philadelphia's MIC to add further depth to the collaborations covered in the previous chapter. This organization's mission is heavily dependent on collaborative partnerships with school districts, youth and faith-based and community organizations, and government agencies, in addition to directly providing support to families:

United Way to launch 1000 WOMEN For 1000 GIRLS Mentorship Program. Mothers In Charge on site mentorship program offers group mentorship for girls from the ages of 12–17 that are currently in placement at Carson Valley Facility. MIC and The School District of Philadelphia, are partnering together to "Stop The Violence" by offering Parent, Family and Community Resources. In The School District of Philadelphia, "Parents are Our Partners" is not a slogan; it is one of the District's five Core Beliefs. . . . Mothers In Charge has partnered with MamaCita, a Mothers Cooperative in the Arts. MamaCITA's mission is to support each member in reaching her full artistic potential. MamaCITA members conduct monthly art classes during Grief Support meetings at MIC. Operation LIPSTICK is a coalition of faith and civic leaders, elected officials, social service and law enforcement professionals working to keep guns out of the hands of criminals and youth without abridging the freedoms of law-abiding Americans. LIPSTICK supports the following goals: Preventing women from being used to buy, hide or hold guns for those who can't legally own them.

The range of collaborative agreements puts a spotlight on the integration of self-help organizations into their community's social fabric and other help-providing organizations.

As noted, all three organizations discussed in Chapter 3 sought collaborations. Although time and energy consuming, there was an acknowledgment that the immensity of the problem could not be solved solely by local community resources. This theme has been echoed throughout this book. The general absence of collaboration with academic institutions is troubling, nevertheless. General suspicion of academics and their institutions is warranted because of past experiences with academics seeking to obtain funding and, once the projects ran their course, simply disappearing. Urban self-help organizations will test our purpose and trustworthiness before venturing into partnerships, and they cannot be blamed for taking this stance.

CONCLUSION

Readers, I hope, have developed a profound understanding and appreciation of how urban self-help organizations can be grounded within the existing scholarly literature. The interconnectedness of major themes covered highlights the importance of viewing urban gun violence from a comprehensive standpoint because signaling one dimension of the causes of this violence will meet with limited and short-lasting success. Stemming and preventing gun violence requires us to think about these efforts, using a track and field metaphor, as a marathon rather than a sprint. Such a view is counter to how this nation thinks about social problems. Community problems become major social problems, and are seemingly intractable, because they have taken a long time to get to that point; they, in turn, require a long-term effort to solve. This calls for a strategy that employs systematic stage sequencing that builds on each other toward a goal of eliminating gun violence.

Some of the themes raised in this chapter were not surprising to readers; others were, bringing a dimension of discovery and the excitement that this newfound knowledge often generates. I also found surprises. The importance of groups, for example, radiated throughout for me—socially, politically, and emotionally. The prominence of women also stood out in a profound manner.

8

Recommendations for Education, Research, and Community Practice

I'm not a disinterested observer. The first time I heard someone get shot, I was 8 years old. Three months later, news outlets were at my school following the brutal murder of my teacher. I lost my first friend to gun violence when I was 15 years old; two years later another friend was shot and killed on his front porch. At 18, two young girls I'd known since their birth were killed within a week of each other. My cousin was killed when I was 19. I'm now 30 years old and have lost 29 loved ones to gun violence in the Chicagoland area. Grief counseling was never offered to me or any of my friends; we weren't given any way to learn coping skills to handle the trauma we experienced.

—C. WILLIAMS, *2018*

INTRODUCTION

The quotation at the beginning of this chapter highlights why urban gun violence is such a major national issue and why its consequences are so far reaching and can often involve individuals experiencing multiple deaths

Urban Gun Violence. Melvin Delgado, Oxford University Press (2021). © Oxford University Press.
DOI: 10.1093/oso/9780197515518.003.0008.

during the early periods of their life. This recommendation chapter is a perfect time to transition from the themes raised in the previous chapter. A detailed map is in order to help us navigate the field of urban gun violence because it is so easy to get lost in the murky sea and dark skies, as represented by contradictory data, competing theories, and local political considerations; we are in desperate need of a North Star to help us get our bearings and successfully navigate to find solutions. The values outlined previously in this book help shape this North Star.

Many find motivation for moving a gun violence prevention agenda from various sources; for some, it is moral; for others, it is an academic imperative; yet for others, it is social justice. Mind you, these and other reasons are not mutually exclusive. However, turning to the warrant of the dead compels us to act on gun violence, which makes an implicit and explicit claim that the dead on those who live, requiring them to assume a voice for those who can no longer speak for themselves (Read, 2018). Not losing sight of these voices becomes imperative because it helps ensure that their lives were not lived in vain, bringing a higher purpose to tasks of stopping gun violence in future generations.

Some of us respond to gun violence from an intellectual standpoint, while others do so emotionally (Claiborne & Martin, 2019). One is not better than the other. We need passion to take on a major social cause and the intellectual honesty to direct our energies in a purposeful manner. The best laid plans are subject to the competencies and values of the personnel who ultimately carry them out. Timing, in turn, must never be understated in this quest. Understanding the factors that shape the experience of family members who have lost loved ones to violence is essential in better preparing practitioners to aid them in this very precarious period in their lives (R. G. Stevenson & Cox, 2017). Interviewing the parents of a gun fatality victim will not surprisingly uncover other family deaths due to guns, illustrating the extent of this challenge for communities and those wishing to make a difference in this realm.

Lack of trust or knowledge of existing services within urban communities of color severely limits obtaining help in a moment of crisis, such as that associated with gun fatalities and injuries, opening up opportunities for local self-help efforts to fill this critical gap. This gap in knowledge of local self-help efforts exists among us as providers and social scientists, and we also need to fill this gap. This book is an attempt to broker these two worlds that ill afford to coexist as if in different dimensions.

Planning gun violence interventions will thrust professions into pivotal relationships with self-help organizations and test us in predictable and unpredictable ways. Dramatic leaps in our knowledge base are called for to prevent the death of this and the next generation because they bear the onus of a legacy of pain and sorrow because their families will forever be incomplete. This chapter conceptualizes recommendations by focusing on education, research, and practice. Although these areas are covered as separate entities, there is overlap, with each influencing the other in a dynamic manner.

An action call provides a much needed blueprint for practitioners and academics (Abir, Nallamothu, Veneema, & Serino, 2018):

> Providers have an obligation to their patients and the communities they serve to proactively work toward injury and death prevention from *any cause*. . . . To protect our communities, we believe that prehospital providers, physicians, nurses, social workers, health educators and researchers have a professional, moral and ethical duty to take the following actions: First, we must widely share our professional experiences to bring to life the horrors of gun violence for average Americans and law makers. Second, insist upon the use of the current evidence base around gun safety and violence prevention to immediately inform strategies to reduce fire-arm related mass casualty incidents. Third, seek funds for research from private industry, foundations, and through philanthropy to expand and improve the evidence base for gun safety and injury prevention. Fourth, lobby for increased federal funding for fire-arm related research through health professional organizations such as the American Medical Association (AMA), American Nurses Association (ANA), American College of Emergency Physicians (ACEP) and advocacy groups. Finally, we must become advocates for gun safety and

injury prevention in our daily practices by starting dialogues with colleagues and patients.

A life free of gun violence is not a luxury reserved for the few, particularly when it addresses youth (Parsons et al., 2018, pp. 17/22):

Young people should not have to live in fear of being gunned down. Not in their schools, not in their churches, not in their neighborhoods—nowhere. All forms of gun violence need to be eradicated wherever present and elected leaders must heed the calls of the young people leading the movement. The solutions exist, and young people have been loud and clear in their demands. It is now time for policymakers to act.

Living life without gun violence translates into simply living. That may seem prosaic; in urban communities, it is profound!

EDUCATION

Educating professionals and social scientists takes center stage in shaping our understanding of gun violence and crafting interventions to meet the challenges that it presents and must take into account urban context to meaningfully prepare practitioners and social scientists; this may well require soul searching about relevance (M. Romero, 2020). Medical school education, for example, and that of other professions, including social work, is seriously lacking when taking into account the extent of this problem and the critical role that professions plays in treating gunshot victims (Yanes, 2017).

There is a call to have a comprehensive educational program on gun safety for pediatric residents (Hoops & Crifasi, 2019). However, it should not stop there and must also include more extensive education in helping survivors of gun violence to avoid re-injuries. This call to action, it is important to note, is not universally shared within these professions and is made more complicated because many physicians are also gun owners, as is the case with emergency room physicians, with an estimated 40% owning guns (Greene, 2019).

How best to make professional education meaningful for urban communities has necessitated the search for relevant, innovative strategies and models that can decrease the gap between professionals and the communities they seek to serve and better understand, and this observation is also applied to social work (Garay, del Toro, & Relinque, 2020). Finding ways of more meaningfully involving communities in shaping education has promising potential. We often equate community participation with interventions; a comparable call for community education is often missing.

There has been a recognition of how community members can help educate future urban teachers, and this approach can also be applied to urban self-help organizations and gun trauma through provision of field placements, civic educational projects, guest lectures, documentaries, and other means to increase the proficiency of providers by reducing the psychological distance between these parties (Lees, 2016).

Education, however, must not be limited to helping professions. How to support those involved in providing services within self-help organizations offers an opening for formal organizations, including the academy, in sharing the latest research findings and helping to decrease the possibility of burnout. This support is contingent on the willingness of these organizations to reach out and the ability of formal organizations to understand and offer services in a manner that best meets the needs of self-help organizations. This support can range from assistance in finding funding sources, trainings at the organization or academy depending on their wishes, internships for students, and assistance with evaluating services, to list several.

It must always reach community residents in high-violence situations. Providing help-saving first responder aid, as already noted, must extend to them, and this can be done with partnerships between organizations and community institutions, such as self-help organizations, houses of worship, and schools, to list three. These efforts must be modified to take into account local circumstances, including language and cultural backgrounds to make them relevant, which is enhanced when teachers share the background of those learning these life-saving approaches.

RESEARCH

Understanding community gun violence is only possible with appropriate research findings guiding approaches. Research, as a result, must play a prominent role in shaping gun violence interventions (Lizotte & Hendrix, 2019), calling for more accurate reporting methods (Post, Balsen, Spano, & Vaca, 2019) and the introduction of new approaches. Not surprisingly, losses that go unnoticed by the larger culture will also be expected to go understudied, and that is certainly the case with urban gun violence (Bordere & Larsen, 2017). Further, the advancement of the field on gun violence is only possible when communities assume an influential role in guiding the questions, analysis, and recommendations.

The need for further scholarly attention to gun violence is an understatement. Health disparities are best understood when bringing qualitative and quantitative data, probably no more so than when discussing homicides (Mastrocinque & Cerceo, 2019). Unfortunately, social work scholarship, for example, is highly deficient on gun violence, as evidenced by the paucity of articles on research, scholarship, and professional conferences (Logan-Greene, Sperlich, & Finucane, 2018, p. 1165):

In a recent meeting of the Society for Social Work and Research, the number of abstracts that contain the words "firearm" or "gun" has been very low. Between 2009 and 2016, there were no more than three per year; though the number has increased to six in 2017 and five in 2018, it still reflects a paucity of effort compared to other fields. Moreover, in the four journals produced by the National Association of Social Workers (*Children and Schools*, *Health and Social Work*, *Social Work*, and *Social Work Research*), only 35 articles have been published to date that contain either of those terms. (p. 1165)

Of course, we work in many different fields and present and publish in non–social work conferences and journals. Nevertheless, it is safe to say that we are not playing a significant role related to an issue for which we can have a strong voice. One only has to talk to colleagues recruiting senior-level social work academics on gun violence to realize we have a long way to go.

The immense impact of gun violence has resulted in a call for more research to increase intervention effectiveness (Rand Corporation, 2018). This call must not neglect how marginalized communities of color respond to gun violence, particularly how support is conceptualized, provided, re-ceived, and fostered, including self-help (L. T. Johnson, 2019). Research is not limited to social scientists and must involve helping professionals and communities. This entails quantitative and qualitative approaches, including an embrace of residents playing actives role in shaping, implementing, interpreting findings, and crafting recommendations, which is also empowering and provides capacity enhancement.

Gun violence is a generational challenge for men of color, yet it has resulted in the underfunding of research focused on this group. Carswell (2019) argued we need to use a racialized lens to better understand the federal government's underfunding research on gun violence among African Americans/Blacks. Scientific research on gun violence has declined by 60% since 1990, largely due to lobbying by the National Rifle Association to have Congress limit research spending at the Centers for Disease Control and Prevention and other government sources (Rostron, 2018).

Fortunately, there is increased interest in gun research, as evidenced by a review of scholarly publication trends (Alcorn, 2017). Developing a deeper and more nuanced understanding of how gun violence is manifested requires research, which often means use of qualitative methods. We must, however, acknowledge how urban gun violence is shaped by the methodology guiding our research questions (Ranapurwala, 2019; Vil, Richardson, & Cooper, 2018). Further, this research must involve commu-nity residents whenever possible to increase the likelihood that it answers questions relevant to their community.

Research is never apolitical and more so when it involves guns; lack of research on this subject is particularly dangerous for the nation, as pointed out by Hemenway (2017, p. 347):

> Alarmingly, the gun lobby is increasingly aligning itself with a broad political movement that sees science not as a search for truth and understanding, but as a tool for promoting partisan agendas. . . . The American Bar Association and many medical societies have spoken out on the firearm funding limitations imposed by Congress. Now all scientific associations need to add their voices. The following construction is overused, but in this context, it is felicitous: first they came after firearms research, but I did not speak up because I do not engage in firearms research. Then they came for the climatologists, but I did not speak up because I am not a climatologist. The attempt to muzzle research requires constant push-back.

There is potential for using stories (narratives) as vehicles for capturing and fostering resiliency research that requires collaboration across subdisciplines interested in this subject (Hamby, Banyard, & Grych, 2016). This line of inquiry also lends itself to community participation, increasing the prominence of a wide range of qualitative approaches. Storytelling has a long tradition within communities of color, facilitating its use on gun violence; although it brings challenges in interpreting responses, the results are indisputable in shaping our understandings of gun violence.

Bell (2017), in reviewing the lessons learned over the past 50 years of violence prevention approaches in African American communities, concluded that it has been media driven rather than based on solid research findings, and ideally using randomized, double-blind, placebo-controlled trials. We need to further our understanding and insights on urban gun violence; fortunately, we have extensive experience with urban-focused research, but only recently regarding gun violence.

Youth-led gun research has escaped attention in this field, and this is profoundly significant, for this and future generations. Oliphant et al. (2019) identified seven research priorities focused on youth that will increase our understanding of various key aspects of violence, including that which is gun related:

> examining adolescent carriage across age, gender, and racial/ethnic subgroups; (2) improving on methodological limitations of prior research, including disaggregating firearm from other weapon carriage and using more rigorous methodology (e.g., random/systematic sampling; broader population samples); (3) conducting longitudinal analyses that establish temporal causality for patterns, motives, and risk/protective factors; (4) capitalizing on m-health to develop more nuanced characterizations of underlying motives; (5) increasing the study of precursors for first-time carriage; (6) examining risk and protective factors beyond the individual-level; and, (7) enhancing the theoretical foundation for firearm carriage within future investigations. (p. 763)

Readers can see from this list that youth are not relegated to any one particular research phase. Their active involvement promises to bring exciting new ideas and approaches to this field.

Urban youth must assume significant and leadership roles in shaping the research and questions on gun violence because they bring a unique lens to this issue (Oldfield, Tinney & Dodington, 2018), and this approach can be grounded within the broad category of community-based research (M. A. Richardson, 2019). Youth-led research such as photovoice, for example, offers great potential in bringing a visual and narrative dimension to urban violence (Yang, Liller, & Coulter, 2018). When community gun violence goes unchecked, it effectively disempowers youth and is a destructive form of community trauma, potentially with lifelong consequences. Youth can lead community trauma efforts in acquiring leadership skills and trauma-informed practice in theater, documentary production, and participatory action research, all bringing their perspective on how their needs on community violence are best addressed (Harden et al., 2015).

Lessons learned by Leech, Irby-Shasanmi, and Sow (2019) on recruiting and retaining young urban Black men in a violence study (internal incentives, combination of informal and formal community recruiters, visibility and positive view of the principal investigator, and face-to-face meetings) should not be surprising to urban practitioners and social scientists and can be applied to collaborative work with self-help organizations. Resident partnerships ensure the right questions are being asked and interpreted in crafting local solutions to gun violence. Self-help organizations embrace working with residents and organizations sharing similar gun violence missions. Fostering partnerships further unifies communities in pursuit of common goals. Much can be learned from research on other forms of mutual or self-help (Mankowski, 2014).

Socially navigating gun fatalities has gotten more complicated in lives that are complicated initially. The impact of COVID-19 will no doubt see an upsurge in research from a research and treatment standpoint. However, how it impacts self-help and the grieving process must not be overlooked in importance. How does it influence help-seeking patterns? How are sources of support within houses of worship altered to aid families in putting to rest their loved ones, and how can they be supportive of each other with social distancing? Funeral parlors also will be cast into prominent roles in helping these families. Not everyone has a car to participate in a drive-by funeral, which gives new meaning to a term that is usually associated with gun violence. Findings from research, in turn, must find their way into the education and practice arenas.

COMMUNITY PRACTICE

Practice is the bottom line with urban gun violence. How we are educated and the nature of the research we undertake lead to influencing practice. For example, readers interested in how a religious background or orientation combined with a professional helper role (social work) toward urban gun violence are recommended to read Michelle Walsh's (2017), *Violent Trauma, Culture, and Power*. This book provides vivid insights into the deliberative process that an outsider (White, non-Latinx) to a Boston community of color underwent in taking a responsive and activist stance on this issue. Although based in Boston, lessons are national in scope, highlighting how violence, trauma, culture, power, and urban context converge to shape how gun violence is manifested, perceived, and addressed.

Our ability to engender trust where mistrust prevails can easily be considered one of the major challenges that we face in addressing urban gun violence. As noted throughout this book, collaboration between major institutions and self-help organizations is essential in any successful gun violence initiative. However, enhancing trust levels, particularly when involving law enforcement, stands out for me. For example, there are multiple facets to the distrust that communities of color may have toward the police, as in the case of Los Angeles. Multiple Los Angeles police officers were suspended after it was uncovered after a mother's complaint that her son was labeled as belonging to a gang, and as a result, uploaded CalGang, a state database that assists law enforcement in combatting gang violence, identified a practice that could possibly influence any future interaction with law enforcement, with potential negative consequences (Murphy, 2020). Actions such as these further alienate communities of color from law enforcement.

Of course, circumstances and local history will dictate to what degree distrust can be repaired with responsive law enforcement, with some situations more challenging than others (D'Souza, Weitzer, & Brunson, 2019). Nevertheless, regardless of circumstances, it is a goal that cannot be ignored because of the role that law enforcement resources will play in creating opportunities for initiatives to unfold involving key players. We also bring biases and various levels of distrust of law enforcement and must, as a result, come to terms with these sentiments if we are to help broker any partnerships.

On a final practice note, we must endeavor to continually seek to make sure that the lives lost to gun violence must never be forgotten and develop projects that help ensure that this does not happen. One reporter stated it quite well when discussing urban youth gun-related fatalities and how they often go unrecognized by the broader community (Baum, 2019):

I grew up believing that a violent death would make the news. What I found instead were kids who died with no public obituary, no hashtag rallying cry attached to their name. There were only gunshots ringing loudly and a death that came quietly. I found this phenomenon applied almost exclusively to gun violence victims of color. It is a testament to the ease with which our world, and our country, forgets about its dead children.

This is a sad but very insightful observation.

CONCLUSION

The themes in this chapter should not be surprising, with some taking on greater saliency, and some possibly totally unexpected. The themes also represent a journey of discovery for me. These themes, in addition, are highly interrelated in real life, although they have been treated as distinct entities to facilitate the telling of a compelling narrative on urban self-help organizations and gun violence.

The final chapter, in the form of an epilogue, is best thought of as musings of an author seeking closure on a book that simply defies closure. Readers will see a bit of me on display, as well as my concerns and hopes for the future of urban gun violence interventions. There will be hundreds of deaths between the time this book goes into production and its publication, highlighting how gun violence permeates our lives, and particularly the lives of those in the nation's urban centers.

Epilogue

Even when the truth isn't hopeful, the telling of it is.

—Poet Andrea Gibson

INTRODUCTION

I have made it a habit to have an epilogue, which goes by many different names, as a parting effort to finish a book that simply refuses to be finished, and more so on a topic such as urban gun violence. Trauma's reverberations are immediate and intergenerational, including the generation yet to be born, spanning multiple decades and becoming part of urban family and community narratives. These generational reverberations also compromise the nation's moral fabric, casting it internationally as violence prone.

Warzel (2020), in a *New York Times* opinion piece, "Will We Get Used to the Dying?" raised the provocative point of whether the country will accept deaths associated with COVID-19 as it does with gun violence. A daily tally of deaths from COVID-19 receive more publicity than a daily tally of gun deaths, although we do not have a daily reminder on television of this statistic. COVID-19 deaths, as in their gun counterparts, have fallen on urban areas of the country, as this book goes to press, and again, fall disproportionally on people of color. I hope we do not become indifferent to both types of deaths because cities, and the people who inhabit them, are destined to bear the brunt of these two diseases, so to speak.

Urban Gun Violence. Melvin Delgado, Oxford University Press (2021). © Oxford University Press.
DOI: 10.1093/oso/9780197515518.003.0009.

I personally have found the stories of COVID-19 victims that have been shared in various media outlets immensely helpful in humanizing this pandemic. It helps me to have a brief glimpse into their lives, and that of their families and loved ones in cases where a family member has gone on television to talk about them. Unfortunately, victims of gun violence do not enjoy the same treatment. Their families, accomplishments, dreams, and humanity are simply lost in a brief mention of a name and where they died. Until we take the time to understand their lives and circumstances, they will remain a numerical figure. The nation cannot blame people of color for their own deaths, be it because of COVID-19 or gunshots.

Gun violence has become a prism through which we can view and understand how this country not only tolerates but also encourages this form of violence to unfold in the nation's cities by how it funds its gun, law enforcement, and prison industries. The saying "more guns do not make communities safer" comes to mind. If guns made communities safer, we would be the safest nation in the history of the world and not the most violent!

This epilogue also summarizes and captures developments that we will encounter in our venture into this important area of practice and scholarship. It also allows my sharing of feelings and thoughts that emerged as part of the journey in writing this book and may be of interest to readers in grounding why some of the topics took on great significance. These thoughts and feelings are shared in conversation style whenever possible to facilitate engagement in this final stage. My goal is to instill hope within the context of realism. Hope within urban marginalized communities confronting gun violence, COVID-19, and food, housing, and economic insecurity can be severely tested.

A TRIP DOWN MEMORY LANE

An author is best writing about topics with personal significance in their lives, and no more so than when it is a topic that elicits a strong emotional response because writing is so much more than an academic enterprise.

Up to this point I have eschewed talking about my personal experiences with gun violence, and now is a good opportunity to share with a brief glimpse why the subject of this book was chosen. Gun violence is not just a scholarly interest for me. There is a personal side because family members and friends were on both sides of this issue, victims and perpetrators. We can argue that all families and friends have gun violence in their past or are currently living in dangerous environments. However, some communities are more violence prone, making guns a prominent part of their social history.

Have I ever fired a gun? Yes (M-16), during basic training because I spent 4 years in the US Air Force. I have never fired a gun since. Neither do I own a gun. I did not enjoy shooting because I had seen the damage a bullet can do to a human body and the victim's loved ones. The lifelong health consequences severely compromised their well-being, and they were not able to live to their potential.

Gun violence was a daily life occurrence when I grew up in the South Bronx (New York City) to Puerto Rican parents. For readers unfamiliar with this neighborhood, it has consistently been predominantly Puerto Rican/African American and ranked near the top of every major category you do not want your neighborhood associated with, such as crime, drug overdoses, poverty, school dropout rates, incarceration, and premature death due to health and, yes, gun violence. Navigating these minefields was a daily way of life for me and those in my social network.

My specific neighborhood (161st and Prospect Ave) was tough and had all of the elements found in other high-violence neighborhoods. However, there were areas, such as Kelley and Fox Avenues, for readers knowledge- able of New York, which were considered superhot ("muy caliente"), and they were to be avoided if at all possible, including not dating someone from those areas. From the outside, the South Bronx had a negative rep- utation, but internally, there was a pecking order on violence. A similar situation occurs in other cities across the country, such as in Baltimore, Chicago, Miami, and Oakland, calling for greater specificity in how we focus our resources and attention and further focusing on select social networks within these geographical areas.

This nation has discovered the value of social networks in better grasping COVID-19 contacts. The experiences in tracing this virus can further aid the use of social networking with gun violence. The most viable and effective approach will rely on local staff conducting this social network contacting in person, where feasible with the virus and definitely with gun violence. Self-help organizations are thus in propitious positions to serve as community sites for conducting this form of outreach and research. Collaborative efforts with organizations employing community health workers, which often reside within the communities they serve, represent bold initiatives to deal with both gun and COVID-19 epidemics.

Gun lethality of yesteryears (zip guns) bears no similarity to that of today, particularly with the advent of higher caliber guns. We did have a serious heroin epidemic that served as a backdrop to this violence, and gangs were certainly a reality, not to mention that the police were not viewed as providing safety but rather as an occupying force. The movie *Fort Apache, the Bronx* (1981), starring Paul Newman, for readers old enough to remember him, was based on this neighborhood and painted a portrait that was racist and classist, and the community rose to force the production to move elsewhere.

There was a section called "Little Korea," named after the convergence of local veterans returning from that conflict and the violence associated with this area of the Bronx. The eventual emergence of substance use/ misuse, gangs, and semiautomatic weapons created a highly flammable situation. A high number of liquor (bars and stores) establishments in this area did not help matters because of the lethality of alcohol and fighting, with the potential of death resulting.

Once leaving home, you needed to carefully navigate your way to your destination, which varied according to the time of day. If lucky, you went in a straight line and saved a great deal of time, which was rare; if unlucky, you had a route that was anything but straight because there were areas that needed to be avoided at all cost during particular time periods. Depending on the building you lived in, you could enter through the front entrance; if unlucky, you had to go to an adjoining building and go to the roof and cross over and then down to your apartment because of who was "hanging out" in the entranceway. Daily life was never ordinary, navigating took on significant meaning (life and death), and you developed sharp observational and instinctual skills.

I am very conscious of how urban social navigation in a highly cautious manner limits curiosity and intellectual and emotional growth, making it arduous to edit out very painful life-altering experiences, and thus becoming a victim or co-victim. These experiences, if sensitively handled, can be personally positively enhancing and transformative for their communities. However, they make you very cautious in later life.

Violence was very real for me growing up, and it has taken a considerable amount of time to write about because of the personal pain associated with it, and a key reason for becoming a social worker and eventually writing on the subject. It was not unusual to have classmates with bullet wounds or to hear about Viet Nam teenage soldiers returning to be buried. Death by heroin overdose, and the circumstances surrounding it, was yet another aspect of death for young people. Seeing death was part of daily life at a very young age, and those images remain for a lifetime and, not surprisingly, have shaped my practice, teaching, and scholarship.

IS GUN VIOLENCE A SIGNATURE ELEMENT OF AMERICAN EXCEPTIONALISM?

The past few years have proven troubling because of national politics and the almost weekly occurrence of mass shootings, against a backdrop of divisiveness. However, we can add the daily urban shootings that would equal a daily mass killing. These deaths have assumed a secondary status, a sad commentary on the state of affairs in this country when discussing race and class. Deaths due to guns must be grounded within violence in general because it is part of the national fabric. COVID-19 has resulted in states struggling with defining what establishments provide as essential services, and the emergence of gun stores, not to mention alcohol stores, falling into this category, with a corresponding increase in gun sales, says so much about how much this nation values guns and how it makes us stand apart in the world (Amnesty International, 2020; Marrow, 2020).

Interestingly, a "can-do" nation refuses to do the right thing on guns (or even finding common ground on the most insignificant aspects) and the violence they cause, and we can certainly include our inadequate response to COVID-19, and how the responses dramatically shape the national psyche (Hemenway, 2016; Husak, 2019; Rood, 2019). The past several years have witnessed intense conversations about what makes America exceptional in the world stage. This conversation has been dominated by economic and social arguments, supposedly making us the envy of the world. However, there are other elements that have escaped this discussion, and one of them has to do with gun violence and how uniquely it is American.

A comprehensive treatment of this question must also involve aspects of our country that raise serious concerns about life in this country for all and not just a small segment (S. Levine, 2019): "How is it possible that this singular country, with its enviable freedoms and achievements, its discoveries in the sciences, its *creativity* in the arts and letters, its prodigious output and wealth, its remarkable educational institutions and record number of Nobel Laureates, has a gun-caused death rate well beyond any comparison with any other civilized countries?" Clearly, there are two Americas.

Can gun violence be a prime example of American exceptionalism? This provocative statement may have little resonance to the average person in the street. However, I believe it has merit because the long legacy that guns have had in our society, and the Second Amendment of the Constitution, makes it part of our DNA and social fabric. This conclusion or illustrates the integral part guns and the violence that follows them plays in what it means to be an American in the eyes of the world.

Amnesty International (2018, p. 8) indirectly questioned America's exceptionalism regarding gun violence by introducing a human rights perspective:

The right to live free from violence, discrimination and fear has been superseded by a sense of entitlement to own a practically unlimited array of deadly weapons, without sufficient regulations on their acquisition, possession and use. In the face of clear evidence of persistent firearm violence, high rates of gun ownership, and ease of access to firearms by individuals likely to misuse them, the USA is failing to meet its obligation to protect and promote human rights pursuant to international law.

American exceptionalism must not be based on violent death. Exceptional also does not have to be positive, and this is the case with gun violence. Readers cannot be blamed to say the same about how COVID-19 has made this nation the world leader in cases and deaths, a designation to which no nation wishes to aspire. The United States is not a world leader in addressing COVID-19 regardless of what President Trump keeps telling the nation.

PLEASE CHECK YOUR EGO AT THE DOOR

Professional pride is a powerful force, including who has the legitimacy (right) to speak out on gun violence and how best to address it. We must expand the traditional stakeholders at the table on urban gun violence, and we must also think outside of the box for innovative approaches to solve this national problem. Changing how educational systems function can be compared to changing the course of a big luxury liner at sea—it takes a long time to dramatically change course. Nevertheless, if our work is to remain relevant, it must be prepared to challenge the status quo. As an academic, my biggest fear is to assume a professional station where what I do is irrelevant and a turning back on my roots and the countless number of people who contributed to my station in life.

Supporting urban self-help organizations is but one innovative approach—countless others must be tried and abandoned if unsuccessful regardless of how much time, effort, and political will were invested. Art, for example, can be a vehicle for understanding how gun violence is interpreted by children and communities, giving rise to community projects that encourage this form of expression (Samuels et al., 2018; Talwar, 2018) and how it is stressed in self-help organizations in addressing trauma.

Willingness to admit failure is an option that we must accept, although quite unpopular in professional circles for fears of how careers will be compromised. Urban violence is too important an issue to allow our vanity to stand in the way of progress; this pride translates into lives lost with pouring good money, time, and goodwill into failed efforts that we must stand by for political purposes of showing that we are making an effort. Admitting failure then requires our willingness to be bold and try new approaches because the old approaches did not solve the problem. Quite frankly, admitting failure is not such an intellectual leap if we base this failure on the number of dead and injured and our inability to make significant progress in this arena.

A RIDE UNLIKE ANY OTHER

Fighting gun violence is not a 9 to 5 effort. It is a 24 hour a day and a 7 day a week undertaking and requires a commitment and willingness to work late into the night and early morning hours, drawing on similarities with what is required to successfully address COVID-19. This virus does not rest at night or take holidays off. As readers have no doubt concluded based on the extensive review of the literature in this book, the immensity of the problem cannot be relegated into a small box limited by hours, days in the week, and weather. Immense challenges require immense and unconventional responses.

Helping professions are generally not accustomed to these hours, including holidays and weekends. It is a year-round effort but with summers taking on greater prominence because of the increase in gun injuries and fatalities. Community health workers with backgrounds similar to those of the communities they serve understand this point very clearly. Minimizing sociodemographic background differences helps increase their potential to reach out and connect during crisis periods following a shooting.

The propensity for homicides to occur during evening hours, and possibly as part of the night economy (Tomsen & Payne, 2016), sets the stage for interventions that cover this time period. This translates into having a staff presence in nightclubs, playgrounds, and crime-prone street corners, for example (Delgado, 2020a). These staff must feel comfortable in these settings and have the time availability. Just as importantly, they must have the necessary support to do this during untraditional hours.

Again, to use a war metaphor, wars are not fought on a regular schedule and comfortable terrain. When inclement weather appears, we close outdoor operations until it clears. True, inclement weather such as snowstorms do reduce violent street crime. The mission to address gun violence, in other words, is unlike any mission any of us has undertaken in the past, and this realization must be understood and embraced. This will also necessitate that we be creative.

FUNERALS AND BURIALS AS SITES FOR INTERVENTIONS

COVID-19 deaths in England's communities of color, for example, have strained the process of burying the dead and consoling the families of the dead (Yeginsu, 2020). That has also happened in the United States, but we have the added burden of burying those killed by guns, complicating the grieving process and the institutions associated with this process, such as funeral homes, graveyards, and houses of worship, for example.

Memorialization rituals and artefacts of gun violence based on shared values are an integral part of a community grieving these deaths, which can also fuel further violence (Rubinstein et al., 2018). Holding a candlelight vigil where a killing occurred, as with Mothers Against Gun Violence, brings symbolic and political meaning to these deaths (Dubisar, 2018). These artefacts, particularly when clustered, take on the semblance of an urban war memorial, but with a representation that is much more immediate and personal, increasing its significance for the community.

These sites and events help communities mourn and can become a magnet for further gun violence. Funerals, for example, are not exempt from violence, with the case of Nipsey Russell's funeral possession, an activist against gun violence and well-known singer, when four mourners were shot, with one dying (Owen, 2019). There are instances where cemeteries have started to hire off-duty police officers in an effort to prevent gun violence during burial ceremonies in cases involving gang members (Norman, 2018). Gun violence's reach goes beyond the grave in these instances. Urban gun violence is a national disgrace that undermines the principles of democracy; although far from realized in the nation's tumultuous history, it is a fight worth having. Human potential cut short, with reckless abandon and the writing off of communities and an entire generation, is disastrous for the nation.

Is it possible to address urban gun violence without addressing the structural inequities or state-sanctioned violence? That would be the equivalent of previous efforts addressing the wounds of the victim and ignoring the causes of the injury. The social sciences and helping professions have progressed to the point where we understand the causes of devaluing human life are closely tied to despair and the hurt resulting from a society that devalues the lives of millions of people of color, historically and currently.

The argument that social conditions, such as poverty, lead to gun violence is often heard in the halls of academia, and it is hard to dismiss how dire circumstance can lead to a devaluing of life itself. It takes a conceptual leap of faith that eliminating these circumstances will result in eliminating gun violence. Eliminating guns will not eliminate violence (Monteiro, 2020). It may increase use of knives, however. The causes of violent impulses are too complex to reduce to a small set of variables. Gun violence can be viewed as a national tragedy that can be averted, undermining the principles of democracy. Human potential cut short, and the writing off of an entire generation, is unacceptable.

DEEPER INSIGHT INTO THE CONSEQUENCES
OF GUN VIOLENCE

Providers understand that the event leading to a child's death is so much more than an act itself. There are numerous days in the year when the death of a child takes on even greater significance, in joy and in pain. Birthdays and anniversaries ("death days") of deaths are particularly painful for families. Parents often want to know about the last moments of their child's life before they died to add a perspective to the anniversaries of a death. One of the greatest fears urban parents have is to have a child die alone on a street without anyone there to comfort them. Capturing these last moments and words is not always possible, complicating a grieving process.

Parents often seek to talk to those who were there for their child's last moments so they can complete the narrative about their child's death. Reconstructing those moments, including visiting the site where the murder occurred, can be conceptualized as a pilgrimage that will inform the anniversaries and the story surrounding a child's life, mostly likely a son. Capturing these last moments can become a quest that impedes their healing. Bringing together these individuals, as occurs with self-help organizations, fulfills an important role in individual and community healing.

Although this section focuses on helping professionals, social scientists also have a charge to focus more on the daily consequences of guns on families of victims and perpetrators, particularly those imprisoned and eventually released. One murder radiates out extensively throughout a family and community. We need to enhance our understanding of these consequences and how best to recognize when and how professional help and initiatives are called for in helping families and communities recover in a constructive manner. Gun violence has more than its share of victims, and that includes those who pay a price for the act, their families, friends, and countless others.

A child's death, but particularly when they are very young, leaves a deep hole in the family that can never be filled, and they will never be whole again. Family celebrations will have an empty chair as a reminder. The deep and complex sadness inherent with such a death permeates across a neighborhood. This goes from the "For the grace of God there go I" to "When will death visit our family?" Destiny is not a word associated with a negative outcome; rather, within urban communities, it is, and that is such a profound view of life to hold and it is shaped by how violence and death are an almost daily occurrence. Social scientists can help providers better serve these families and communities.

KNOWLEDGE EQUALS POWER

For readers totally overwhelmed by the subject of gun violence, welcome to the club. Writing a book on this topic resulted in exploring aspects of this violence that completely surprised me. I found guns to be an overwhelming subject because of its complexity and all the information on the topic to the point where I had to stop writing. Of course, those in urban communities of color never have the luxury of pausing from life. No one is an expert on this subject and has a grasp of all of the dimensions. If anyone is an expert, it would be those who have undergone the journey of dealing with the aftermath of gun violence—they are the true experts, and their narratives must be captured and widely shared.

It is OK to select one aspect of this phenomenon and go into greater depth while maintaining a broad overview of the subject. If I were to write another book on urban gun violence, I would probably focus on gun injuries. Why? Interventions seek to prevent gun violence, often with a focus on deaths. In talking with survivors, defined very broadly, you get to see the visible and invisible scars of people attempting to pick up the pieces and continue living while embracing and even honoring the memories of those who died. Can they get closure? No, closure is not possible, but we can learn to channel our energies into worthwhile pursuits by preventing guns from altering the lives of others, as in the case of self-help organizations.

Regardless of how we proceed and focus our attention, we must never lose sight of what assets can be found in these communities. Being able to see how urban communities are resilient while not losing sight of their challenges will move the field of gun violence prevention and treatment forward; affirming strengths and assets allows social scientists and practitioners to socially navigate within these communities and enter into much needed collaborative partnerships.

THE NATION IS CHANGING

The future of people of color in this country, particularly because of demographic increases and youthfulness of this population, will be severely compromised if we take to killing each other. President Trump's stance toward people of color and cities is quite clear. Urban gun violence will be tolerated under his administration, and guns will only be discussed when mass shootings occur and require a presidential response, but no national leadership.

Communities of color are very young and are the primary perpetrators and victims of gun violence. Increased levels of residential segregation and limited upward possibilities are a formula for a disastrous future. Mind you, these communities are resilient and produce outstanding individuals who will make important contributions to their communities and country. Nevertheless, successfully addressing gun violence translates to successfully preventing gun violence in the future. COVID-19 will probably forever change the country in unimaginable ways now and in the future and may well result in greater gun violence within the nation's urban centers.

MAPPING GUN VIOLENCE AND SELF-HELP

I am fond of community asset mapping and why it must have a prominent place in any community-focused initiative. Attempts at healing and having places devoted to this act are occurring throughout the nation, and this has not received the attention it deserves in helping us better understand how urban communities deal with the pain of gunshots in a multitude of manifestations. This book shed light on this powerful topic and why gun violence cannot ignore the rainbow of efforts right before us if we take the time to look, including the efforts of self-help organizations.

Mapping local efforts is something social scientists and helping professionals can do, in the process creating a database that counters the notions that nothing is going to be done at the local level because residents simply do not care about the loss of human life in their midst. Mapping has certainly occurred to capture gun violence, and this promises to continue as more sophisticated statistical programming takes hold. This mapping has eschewed assets and efforts at dealing with gun violence. We need both maps to have a comprehensive view of gun violence. In order to develop an asset map, labor-intensive efforts are necessary because, unlike gun injuries and fatality maps, there is no systematic effort to collect these data to draw on for the maps.

GUN REFORM AND MASS KILLINGS

I avoided discussing mass killings and gun reform. As promised in the introductory chapter, I have focused on a very small slice of the gun epidemic because the vast majority of books on the subject have concentrated on both of these topics, and readers have many options in pursuing this topic, including the daily media. Readers also understand the importance of federal efforts rather than having individual states and cities instituting reforms, which is problematic because nearby states with lax laws can easily undermine the efforts.

More people die on a daily basis in a year than all of the mass killings combined, and, of course, all survivors of these tragedies are victims. However, for persons of color living in this nation's urban centers, their stories are relegated to their families, with very little attention paid outside of their families and communities. Their deaths and how they is treated by law enforcement and media, as a result, highlight their marginalized status.

FIRST STOP THE BLEEDING AND THEN . . .

It may seem odd advocating for stopping the bleeding. There is a perennial argument about what to address first—the symptoms or the causes. The structural factors shaping urban gun violence are embedded deeply in this society, necessitating them to be addressed to prevent or significantly reduce gun violence. However, we first must stop the bleeding caused by guns. One does not have to be a medical specialist to argue this point. There is an emergence of community-engaged approaches (Kang & Swaroop, 2019). The potential of community involvement if we are willing to be creative and participatory in our approaches to gun violence .

Creating social conditions that encourage major stakeholders to collaborate to prevent gun violence must overcome incredible odds and obstacles, and it may be this generation's equivalent of not putting a person on the moon, but on Mars! The cost, time, and commitment to achieve this state will be even more expensive because urban communities must have responsive school systems, excellent healthcare, employment in jobs that have a future, and housing that is not substandard. Getting rid of all guns will eliminate gun violence, but not the underlying forces leading to interpersonal conflict. Much needs to be changed to instill hope because without hope there is no belief in a future that is equitable and predicated on social justice. Such changes benefit the entire nation, not just communities of color, making your well-being tied to my well-being, and the ultimate interconnectedness of a thriving society.

A two-prong approach seems to be prudent. We do not need guns to feel comfortable and safe to function in a productive and fair society. Targeting the gun industry and severely limiting access to guns seems to be the debate of our lifetime. If I cannot access a gun, I cannot possibly use it in a dispute or in the commission of a crime. Gun access (legal and illegal), including ammunition, becomes an immediate priority. We cannot stop at that point and must address the underlying conditions leading to despair and a lack of hope for a future. A major investment in our urban youth and young adults that engages their time and bodies must also be made.

Those re-entering society from incarceration are part of the formula for success, requiring models that enhance their likelihood of assuming productive roles in society. These efforts must also be particularly sensitive to returning gang members. Substance use/misuse is one arena necessitating attention because of its role in criminal activity and because the profits that they generate must be protected by guns and corresponding violence. Incarceration due to gun violence, just like in substance use/misuse, will not solve the problem because it ignores social context and history (Sered, 2019). These two major social issues are often intertwined, illustrating the intractability of these issues.

Readers may say that these approaches are all well and good, but how will they be paid for? Gun violence initiative costs must compete for taxpayer dollars alongside other social needs that necessitate a major national social initiative, including local government taxes. The nation's debt level cannot be ignored, necessitating hard choices about what is funded beyond the national debt and entitlement programs. As noted in this book, gun violence costs billions on a yearly basis. These funds are an investment in America, particularly its urban centers, helping to ensure a future that is equitable and just for all. Urban centers that are thriving help the entire nation. When the funds are invested in youth, we get a clearer picture of this investment in the future.

A HAZARDOUS ROAD AHEAD

Embracing a mission to eliminate gun violence will result in a high price being paid. The nature and extent of that price will vary, but there is no question about the consequences. It is most appropriate to use the concept of front lines in addressing gun violence, dealing with its grasp of day-to-day consequences, and when taking a stance, expecting a political pushback (Abir et al., 2018):

Those on the frontlines of health care in communities across the U.S. are well aware of the horrors of gun violence: prehospital care providers, emergency room (ER) doctors, trauma surgeons, nurses, and so many others who have the grave misfortune to see how bullets ravage the human body and soul. The kind of tragedy that once witnessed can't be unseen. Perhaps this explains the outrage over a National Rifle Association (NRA) Tweet posted on November 8th that read *"Someone should tell self-important anti-gun doctors to stay in their lane. Half of the articles in* Annals of Internal Medicine *are pushing for gun control. Most upsetting, however, the medical community seems to have consulted NO ONE but themselves."*

Taking a social justice activist stance will cause a backlash and target academics and helping professionals, and we must be prepared for this, with immediate implications of funding for research and initiatives. When we are community based, and carry out our mission hand in hand with communities, we do not need big funding to make a difference. Broadening our coalition across disciplines and professions, and including communities, will help soften the attacks that will follow. However, any goal worth fighting for will reap untold rewards for us and the communities we aid!

CONCLUSION

We are now at the end of the journey with this book. For some of us, reading it took weeks, and others may have spent a few days doing so. A book really starts with a proposal outlining how it will unfold. In reality, it takes years because of how ideas are formulated and evolve leading up to a final product. A book, to use the metaphor of an iceberg, is the tip. What is below the water represents the bulk of the iceberg. Readers will need to make a determination of how much of this book's message is owned by you. There certainly is enough room within this issue to find saliency for all sorts of angles or topics that have relevance for all readers. This book raises the alarm while maintaining hope and providing a road map and tools for engaging in this issue.

Those who have lost loved ones to gun violence have had their share of tears of sorrow; helping others also brings tears, but they are of hope, which unite them in a very exclusive community that no members ever want to be a part of but now find themselves among. Urban self-help organizations are that vehicle or conduit that facilitates this community building, and those of us with a commitment to eliminating urban gun violence must work with them to achieve this goal.

The despair and anger that feeds urban gun violence have only gotten worse because of how COVID-19 has socially and economically impacted communities of color, making for a perfect storm of unemployment, food and housing insecurity, school closures, dismal future outlook, and increased police presence, which all combine to increase conflicts that can be explosive with hot summer weather. How urban self-help organizations respond to this pandemic while remaining focused on gun violence will prove to be a challenge that will tax their abilities to respond to emerging shootings.

It is fitting to end this epilogue with a quote since the book started with a quote (Pressley, 2019):

> We need a Survivors Bill of Rights for those robbed of loved ones and those who survived violence incidents. From funeral costs to unsolved homicides and unserved justice, the federal government has a role to play. We will continue to speak the names of those stolen from us by gun violence. We must organize and mobilize at every level of government to address the availability of guns on our streets and the underlying trauma that leads a person to pick up a gun in the first place. We need to turn towards each other, not away, and treat this like a public health crisis choking at our promise and our collective future. Long gone are the days of thoughts and prayers. Now is the time for policy and change.

REFERENCES

Abaya, R. (2019). Firearm violence and the path to prevention: What we know, what we need. *Clinical Pediatric Emergency Medicine, 20*(1), 38–47.

Abaya, R., Atte, T., Herres, J., Diamond, G., & Fein, J. A. (2019). Characteristics and behavioral risk factors of firearm-exposed youth in an urban emergency department. *Journal of Behavioral Medicine, 42*(4), 603–612.

Abir, M., Nallamothu, B., Veneema, T., & Serino, R. (2018, November 20). Health care providers and researchers have an obligation to expose the horrors of gun violence. *Health Affairs.* doi:10.1377/hblog20181119.463210. https://www.healthaffairs.org/do/10.1377/hblog20181119.463210/full/

Abt, T. (2019a, July 12). We can't end inequality until we stop urban violence. *The Trace.* https://www.thetrace.org/2019/07/we-cant-end-inequality-until-we-stop-urban-gun-violence/

Abt, T. (2019b). *Bleeding out: The devastating consequences of urban violence—and a bold new plan for peace in the streets.* New York, NY: Basic Books.

Abt, T. (2019c, July 3). To cut urban bloodshed, focus on violent hot spots. *The Wall Street Journal.* https://www.wsj.com/articles/to-reduce-the-bloodshed-in-u-s-cities-focus-on-the-violence-itself-11562171994

Ahmadi, K. S. (2018, October 8). What is a self-help group? PsychCenter. https://psychcentral.com/lib/what-is-a-self-help-group/

Ahmed, A. (2019, August 25). One handgun, 9 murders: How American firearms cause carnage abroad. *New York Times.* https://www.nytimes.com/2019/08/25/world/americas/one-handgun-9-murders-how-american-firearms-cause-carnage-abroad.html

Aiyer, S. M., Zimmerman, M. A., Morrel-Samuels, S., & Reischl, T. M. (2015). From broken windows to busy streets: A community empowerment perspective. *Health Education & Behavior, 42*(2), 137–147.

Akinleye, F. O. (2016). Violence related injuries among individuals admitted to a level I trauma center in Atlanta, 2011–2013. *Journal of the Georgia Public Health Association, 6*(2, Suppl.). https://augusta.openrepository.com/handle/10675.2/621588

Alcorn, T. (2017). Trends in research publications about gun violence in the United States, 1960 to 2014. *JAMA Internal Medicine, 177*(1), 124–126.

Alexander, C. (2018, October 30). *Why police should embrace communities—not shut them out.* The Marshall Project. https://www.themarshallproject.org/2018/10/30/why-police-should-embrace-communities-not-shut-them-out

Ali, S. S. (2019a, July 17). "They're like soldiers": Chicago's children are learning to save lives amid gunfire. *NBC News.* https://www.nbcnews.com/news/us-news/they-re- soldiers-chicago-s-children-are-learning-save-lives-n1018196

Ali, S. S. (2019b, August 7). For some in Chicago, gun violence is a daily reality, leaving the same trauma as mass shootings. *NBC News.* https://www.nbcnews.com/news/us-news/some-chicago-gun-violence-daily-reality-leaving-same-trauma-mass-n1040231

Allareddy, V., Nalliah, R. P., Rampa, S., Kim, M. K., & Allareddy, V. (2012). Firearm related injuries amongst children: Estimates from the nationwide emergency department sample. *Injury, 43*(12), 2051–2054.

Allchin, A., Chaplin, V., & Horwitz, J. (2018). Limiting access to lethal means: Applying the social ecological model for firearm suicide prevention. *Injury Prevention, 25*(Suppl. 1), 144–148.

Altheimer, I., Schaible, L. M., Klofas, J., & Comeau, M. (2019). Victim characteristics, situational factors, and the lethality of urban gun violence. *Journal of Interpersonal Violence, 34*(8), 1633–1656.

Al'Uqdah, S., & Adomako, F. (2018). From mourning to action: African American women's grief, pain, and activism. *Journal of Loss and Trauma, 23*(2), 91–98.

Alvarez, A., & Bachman, R. (2016). *Violence: The enduring problem.* Thousand Oaks, CA: Sage.

Amnesty International. (2018). In the line of fire: Human rights and the US gun crisis. https://www.amnestyusa.org/wp-content/uploads/2018/09/Gun-Report-Full_10.pdf

Amnesty International. (2020, March 31). Increased gun sales and gun stores recognized as "essential businesses" amid COVID-19 pandemic will lead to more violence. https://www.amnestyusa.org/press-releases/increased-gun-sales-and-gun-stores-recognized-as-essential-businesses-amid-covid-19-pandemic-will-lead-to-more-violence/

Anderson, B. (2019, July 19). Community-driven development: A field perspective on possibilities and limitations [Web log post]. *DevPolicyBlog.* Australian National University.

Anderson, E. (1994). The code of the streets. *Atlantic Monthly, 273*(5), 81–94.

Anderson, K. M., & Mack, R. (2019). Digital storytelling: A narrative method for positive identity development in minority youth. *Social Work With Groups, 42*(1), 43–55.

Andrade, E. G., Hayes, J. M., & Punch, L. J. (2019). Enhancement of bleeding control 1.0 to reach communities at high risk for urban gun violence: Acute bleeding control. *JAMA Surgery, 154*(6), 549–550.

Annas, G. J., & Grodin, M. A. (2017). Frozen ethics: Melting the boundaries between medical treatment and organ procurement. *The American Journal of Bioethics, 17*(5), 22–24.

Anta, F. Y., & Men, H. H. (2018). "Where we wanna be": The role of structural violence and place-based trauma for street life-oriented Black men navigating recovery and reentry. *Health & Place, 54*, 200–209.

Apelt, N., Greenwell, C., Tweed, J., Notrica, D. M., Maxson, R. T., Garcia, N. M., . . . Schindel, D. (2020). Air guns: A contemporary review of injuries at six pediatric Level I trauma centers. *Journal of surgical research, 248*, 1–6.

Arcas-Salvador, M. (2017). Capturing the economic toll of urban gun violence. *Chicago Policy Review.* Online. https://search.proquest.com/docview/1891197602?pq-origsite =gscholar&fromopenview=true. April 24, 2017.

Armstead, D. R. (2019). *Attitudes of Black Americans towards police misconduct in an urban area.* (Unpublished dissertation). Waldon University, Minneapolis, MN.

Armstrong, M., & Carlson, J. (2019). Speaking of trauma: The race talk, the gun violence talk, and the racialization of gun trauma. *Palgrave Communications, 5*(1), 1–11.

Arnwine, M., Jr. (2019). Trauma and learning: Creating a culture of educational access for inner city communities [Comment]. 53 U.S.F. L. Rev. 77.

Asher, J. (2019, December 18). How reporting practice can skew crime statistics. *The New York Times*, p. A27.

Aspholm, R. R. (2020). *Views from the streets: The transformation of gangs and violence on Chicago's South Side.* New York, NY: Columbia University Press.

Aspholm, R. R., & Mattaini, M. A. (2017). Youth activism as violence prevention. In P. Sturmey (Ed.), *The Wiley handbook of violence and aggression* (pp. 1–12). New York, NY: Wiley.

Aspholm, R. R., St. Vil, C., & Carter, K. A. (2019). Interpersonal gun violence research in the social work literature. *Health & Social Work, 44*(4), 224–231.

Astrup, J. (2019). Knife crime: Where's the public health approach? *Community Practitioner, 92*(6), 14–17.

Aufrichtig, A., Beckett, L., Diehm, J., & Lartey, J. (2017, January 9). Want to fix gun violence in America? Go local. *The Guardian.* https://bit.ly/2i6kaKw

Aviles, A. M., & Grigalunas, N. (2018). "Project awareness": Fostering social justice youth development to counter youth experiences of housing instability, trauma and injustice. *Children and Youth Services Review, 84*, 229–238.

Bachier-Rodriguez, M., Freeman, J., & Feliz, A. (2017). Firearm injuries in a pediatric population: African-American adolescents continue to carry the heavy burden. *The American Journal of Surgery, 213*(4), 785–789.

Bailey, A., Akhtar, M., Clarke, J., & Starr, S. (2015). Intersecting individual, social, and cultural factors in Black mothers resilience building following loss to gun violence in Canada. In N. Khanlou & F. Pilkington (Eds.), *Women's mental health* (pp. 311–325). New York, NY: Springer.

Bailey, A., Hannays-King, C., Clarke, J., Lester, E., & Velasco, D. (2013). Black mothers' cognitive process of finding meaning and building resilience after loss of a child to gun violence. *British Journal of Social Work, 43*(2), 336–354.

Bailey, P. (2018, September 5). Community nonprofits reduce gun violence through peer networks. *Nonprofit Quarterly.* https://nonprofitquarterly.org/community-nonprofits-reduce-gun-violence-through-peer-networks/

Baker, D., Norris, D., & Cherneva, V. (2019, May 6). Disenfranchised grief and families' experiences of death after police contact in the United States. *OMEGA-Journal of death and dying.* doi:10.1177%2F0030222819846420

Baker-Bell, A., Stanbrough, R. J., & Everett, S. (2017). The stories they tell: Mainstream media, pedagogies of healing, and critical media literacy. *English Education*, 49(2), 130–152.

Balcazar, F. E., Magaña, S., & Suarez-Balcazar, Y. (2020). Disability among the latinx population: Epidemiology and empowerment interventions. In A. Martínez & S. Rhodes (Eds.), *New and emerging issues in Latinx health* (pp. 127–143). New York, NY: Springer.

Banks, G., Hadenfeldt, K., Janoch, M., Manning, C., Ramos, K., & Wolf, D. A. P. S. (2017). Gun violence and substance abuse. *Aggression and Violent Behavior*, 34, 113–116.

Banks, J. (2015). Gangsters and wheelchairs: Urban teachers' perceptions of disability, race and gender. *Disability & Society*, 30(4), 569–582.

Banks, J. (2018). Invisible man: Examining the intersectionality of disability, race, and gender in an urban community. *Disability & Society*, 33(6), 894–908.

Barboza, G. (2018). A secondary spatial analysis of gun violence near Boston schools: A public health approach. *Journal of Urban Health*, 95(3), 344–360.

Barksky, A. (2019, April 17). Dialogues on gun violence: The role of social work values and principles. *The New Social Worker*. https://www.socialworker.com/feature-articles/ethics-articles/dialogues-on-gun-violence-role-of-social-work-values-principles/

Bartley, W. A., & Williams, G. F. (2015). *The role of gun supply in 1980s and 1990s urban violence*. Lexington. KY: Transylvania University. Available at SSRN 2623253.

Bastomski, S., & Duane, M. (2019). *Losing a loved one to homicide: What we know about homicide co-victims from research and practice evidence*. Washington, DC: Center for Victim Research.

Bauchner, H., Rivara, F. P., Bonow, R. O., Bressler, N. M., Disis, M. L. N., Heckers, S., . . . Rhee, J. S. (2017). Death by gun violence—A public health crisis. *JAMA psychiatry*, 74(12), 1195–1196.

Baum, S. E. (2019, December 23). I wrote obituaries for young gun violence victims. This is my story. *The Giffords Center*. https://giffords.org/blog/2019/12/i-wrote-obituaries-for-young-gun-violence-victims-this-is-my-story-blog/

Bayouth, L., Lukens-Bull, K., Gurien, L., Tepas, J. J., III, & Crandall, M. (2019). Twenty years of pediatric gunshot wounds in our community: Have we made a difference? *Journal of Pediatric Surgery*, 54(1), 160–164.

Beard, J. H., Resnick, S., Maher, Z., Seamon, M. J., Morrison, C. N., Sims, C. A., . . . Goldberg, A. J. (2019). Clustered arrivals of firearm-injured patients in an urban trauma system: A silent epidemic. *Journal of the American College of Surgeons*, 229(3), 236–243.

Beardslee, J., Docherty, M., Yang, V. J., & Pardini, D. (2019). Parental disengagement in childhood and adolescent male gun carrying. *Pediatrics*, 143(4), e20181552.

Becerra, C. E. (2018). Knowledge can be mightier than the gun. *Education and Culture*, 34(2), 3–16.

Beck, B., Zusevics, K., & Dorsey, E. (2019). Why urban teens turn to guns: Urban teens' own words on gun violence. *Public Health*, 177, 66–70.

Beckett, L. (2016, April 28). For black voters, gun violence a more serious problem than police misconduct. *The Guardian*. https://www.theguardian.com/world/2016/apr/28/black-voters-gun-violence-police-misconduct-poll

Beckett, L., Bond Graham, D., & Clayton, A. (2019, July 30). Gun violence is down in the Bay Area—but not everywhere. *The Guardian.* https://www.theguardian.com/us-news/2019/jul/23/guns-and-lies-bay-area-gun-violence-newsletter

Bell, C. C. (2017). Lessons learned from 50 years of violence prevention activities in the African American community. *Journal of the National Medical Association, 109*(4), 224–237.

Bellamy, C., Kimmel, J., Costa, M. N., Tsai, J., Nulton, L., Nulton, E., . . . O'Connell, M. (2019). Peer support on the "inside and outside": Building lives and reducing recidivism for people with mental illness returning from jail. *Journal of Public Mental Health, 18*(3), 188–198.

Berg, M. T. (2019). Trends in the lethality of American violence. *Homicide Studies, 23*(3), 262–284.

Bergen-Cico, D., Lane, S. D., Keefe, R. H., Larsen, D. A., Panasci, A., Salaam, N., . . . Rubinstein, R. A. (2018). Community gun violence as a social determinant of elementary school achievement. *Social Work in Public Health, 33*(7–8), 439–448.

Bergen-Cico, D. K., Haygood-El, A., Jennings-Bey, T. N., & Lane, S. D. (2014). Street addiction: A proposed theoretical model for understanding the draw of street life and gang activity. *Addiction Research & Theory, 22*(1), 15–26.

Bernstein, D. S. (2017, December 19). Americans don't really understand gun violence. *The Atlantic.* https://www.theatlantic.com/politics/archive/2017/12/guns-nonfatal-shooting-newtown-las-vegas/548372/

Bernstein, M., McMillan, J., & Charash, E. (2019, August). Once in Parkland, a year in Hartford, a weekend in Chicago: Race and resistance in the gun violence prevention movement [Special issue]. *Sociological Forum, 34*(S1), 1153–1173.

Bettencourt, G. M. (2018). Embracing problems, processes, and contact zones: Using youth participatory action research to challenge adultism. *Action Research, 18*(2), 153–170.

Betz, M. E., Bebarta, V. S., DeWispelaere, W., Barrett, W., Victoroff, M., Williamson, K., & Abbott, D. (2019). Emergency physicians and firearms: Effects of hands-on training. *Annals of Emergency Medicine, 73*(2), 210–211.

Bidgood, J. (2019, October 25). A mother wonders: Can a vote stop the guns? *The Boston Globe,* pp. A1, A6.

Bieler, S., Kijakazi, K., & Vigne, N. L. (2016). *Engaging communities in reducing gun violence.* Washington, DC: Urban Institute.

Bilgel, F. (2018, January 26). State gun control laws, gun prevalence and the supply of homicide organ donors. Available at SSRN: https://ssrn.com/abstract=3111071 or http://dx.doi.org/10.2139/ssrn.3111071

Blais, E. (2019). Focusing on places rather than guns. *American Journal of Public Health, 109*(1), 25–26.

Blakinger, K. (2019, August 15). "He just needed more time": Families grieve after spate of gun violence in Houston the same weekend as mass shootings in El Paso, Dayton. *Houston Chronicle.* https://www.houstonchronicle.com/news/houston-texas/houston/article/He-just-needed-more-time-Families-grieve-14342194.php

Blumberg, T. J., DeFrancesco, C. J., Miller, D. J., Pandya, N. K., Flynn, J. M., & Baldwin, K. D. (2018). Firearm-associated fractures in children and adolescents: trends in the United States 2003–2012. *Journal of Pediatric Orthopaedics, 38*(7), e387–e392.

Bogar, S., & Beyer, K. M. (2016). Green space, violence, and crime: A systematic review. *Trauma, Violence, & Abuse, 17*(2), 160–171.

Bordere, T. C. (2016). Social justice conceptualizations in grief and loss. In D. L. Harris & T. C. Bordere (Eds.), *Handbook of social justice in loss and grief* (pp. 29–40). New York, NY: Routledge.

Bordere, T. C. (2019). Suffocated grief, resilience and survival among African American families. In M. Hviid Jacobsen & A. Petersen (Eds.), *Exploring grief: Towards a sociology of sorrow* (pp. 188–203). New York, NY: Routledge.

Bordere, T. C., & Larsen, J. A. (2017). Grief and loss among First Nations and African American youth. In C. Arnold (Ed.), *Understanding child and adolescent grief: Supporting loss and facilitating growth* (pp. 155–166). New York, NY: Routledge.

Borg, B. A., Krouse, C. B., McLeod, J. S., Shanti, C. M., & Donoghue, L. (2019). Circumstances surrounding gun violence with youths in an urban setting. *Journal of Pediatric Surgery*. In Press. doi: https://doi.org/10.1016/j.jpedsurg.2019.09.015

Bosman, J. (2019, October 29). Chicago turns into the city of the cold shoulders. *The New York Times*, p. A17.

Bourgois, P., Hart, L. K., Karandinos, G., & Montero, F. (2019). Coming of age in the concrete killing fields of the US inner city. In J. MacClancy (Ed.), *Exotic no more: Anthropology for the contemporary world* (pp. 19–41). Chicago, IL: University of Chicago.

Bourgois, P., Holmes, S. M., Sue, K., & Quesada, J. (2017). Structural vulnerability: Operationalizing the concept to address health disparities in clinical care. *Academic Medicine: Journal of the Association of American Medical Colleges, 92*(3), 299–307.

Boyd, M. L., & Clampet-Lundquist, S. (2019). "It's hard to be around here": Criminalization of daily routines for youth in Baltimore. *Socius, 5*, 1–10.

Boyles, A. S. (2019). *You can't stop the revolution: Community disorder and social ties in post-Ferguson America*. Berkeley, CA: University of California Press.

Braga, A. A. (2017). Long-term trends in the sources of Boston crime guns. *RSF: The Russell Sage Foundation Journal of the Social Sciences, 3*(5), 76–95.

Braga, A. A., & Cook, P. J. (2018). The association of firearm caliber with likelihood of death from gunshot injury in criminal assaults. *JAMA Network Open, 1*(3), e180833–e180833.

Braga, A. A., Hureau, D., & Winship, C. (2008). Losing faith-police, black churches, and the resurgence of youth violence in Boston. *Ohio State Journal of Criminal Law, 6*, 141.

Braga, A. A., Turchan, B., & Barao, L. (2019). The influence of investigative resources on homicide clearances. *Journal of Quantitative Criminology, 35*(2), 337–364.

Braga, A. A., Turchan, B., & Winship, C. (2019). Partnership, accountability, and innovation: Clarifying Boston's experience with focused deterrence. In D. Weisburd & A. Braga (Eds.), *Police innovation: Contrasting perspectives* (pp. 227–247). New York, NY: Cambridge University Press.

Braga, A. A., & Weisburd, D. L. (2015). Focused deterrence and the prevention of violent gun injuries: Practice, theoretical principles, and scientific evidence. *Annual Review of Public Health, 36*, 55–68.

Branas, C. C., Kondo, M. C., Murphy, S. M., South, E. C., Polsky, D., & MacDonald, J. M. (2016). Urban blight remediation as a cost-beneficial solution to firearm violence. *American Journal of Public Health, 106*(12), 2158–2164.

Branas, C. C., South, E., Kondo, M. C., Hohl, B. C., Bourgois, P., Wiebe, D. J., & MacDonald, J. M. (2018). Citywide cluster randomized trial to restore blighted vacant land and its effects on violence, crime, and fear. *Proceedings of the National Academy of Sciences of the United States of America, 115*(12), 2946–2951.

Brewer, J. W., Jr., Cox, C. S., Fletcher, S. A., Shah, M. N., Sandberg, M., & Sandberg, D. I. (2019). Analysis of pediatric gunshot wounds in Houston, Texas: A social perspective. *Journal of Pediatric Surgery, 54*(4), 783–791.

Brooks, A. (2019, July 29). Survivors of violence: A life of pain and deep wounds that don't heal. *WBUR.* https://www.wbur.org/news/2019/07/29/shooting-injuries-trauma-ptsd-farm-recovery

Brooks, R. (2018). RIP shirts or shirts of the movement: Reading the death paraphernalia of Black lives. *Biography, 41*(4), 807–830.

Brooms, D. R. (2015). "We didn't let the neighborhood win": Black male students' experiences in negotiating and navigating an urban neighborhood. *The Journal of Negro Education, 84*(3), 269–281.

Brown, E. N. (2019, October 28). A new national memorial to victims of gun violence makes its debut. *FasTCompany.* https://www.fastcompany.com/90413467/a-new-national-memorial-to-victims-of-gun-violence-makes-its-debut

Brown, K. J., & Weil, F. D. (2019). Strangers in the neighborhood: Violence and neighborhood boundaries. *Journal of Contemporary Ethnograph, 41*(9), 86–117.

Brown, M. E., & Barthelemy, J. J. (2019). The aftermath of gun violence: implications for social work in communities. *Health & Social Work, 44*(4), 271–275.

Brunson, R. K. (2015). Focused deterrence and improved police-community relations: Unpacking the proverbial black box. *Criminology & Public Policy, 14*, 507–514.

Brunson, R. K., Braga, A. A., Hureau, D. M., & Pegram, K. (2015). We trust you, but not that much: Examining police–black clergy partnerships to reduce youth violence. *Justice Quarterly, 32*(6), 1006–1036.

Brunson, R. K., & Wade, B. A. (2019). "Oh hell no, we don't talk to police." Insights on the lack of cooperation in police investigations of urban gun violence. *Criminology & Public Policy, 18*(3), 623–648.

Buchanan, C. (2014). *Gun violence, disability and recovery.* Bloomington, IN: Xlibris.

Bulger, E. M., Kuhls, D. A., Campbell, B. T., Bonne, S., Cunningham, R. M., Betz, M., . . . Sakran, J. V. (2019). Proceedings from the Medical Summit on Firearm Injury Prevention: A public health approach to reduce death and disability in the US. *Journal of the American College of Surgeons, 229*(4), 415–430.

Bunting, S. R., Benjamins, M. R., & Homan, S. M. (2019, August 1–5). Gun violence and access to firearms in Chicago: Federal, state, and local legislation. Sinai Urban Health Institute. https://www.sinai.org/sites/default/files/SUHI%20Policy%20Brief_19-01_Gun%20Policies_8-19-19_Final.pdf

Burgason, K. A., Thomas, S. A., & Berthelot, E. R. (2014). The nature of violence: A multilevel analysis of gun use and victim injury in violent interpersonal encounters. *Journal of Interpersonal Violence, 29*(3), 371–393.

Burnside, A. N., & Gaylord-Harden, N. K. (2019). Hopelessness and delinquent behavior as predictors of community violence exposure in ethnic minority male adolescent offenders. *Journal of Abnormal Child Psychology, 47*(5), 801–810.

Bushman, B. J., Newman, K., Calvert, S. L., Downey, G., Dredze, M., Gottfredson, M., . . .
Romer, D. (2016). Youth violence: What we know and what we need to know.
American Psychologist, 71(1), 17–39.

Butkus, R., Doherty, R., & Bornstein, S. S. (2018). Reducing firearm injuries and deaths
in the United States: A position paper from the American College of Physicians.
Annals of Internal Medicine, 169(10), 704–707.

Butts, J. A., Roman, C. G., Bostwick, L., & Porter, J. R. (2015). Cure violence: A public
health model to reduce gun violence. *Annual Review of Public Health, 36*, 39–53.

Byrdsong, T. R., Devan, A., & Yamatani, H. (2016). A ground-up model for gun violence
reduction: A community-based public health approach. *Journal of Evidence-Informed
Social Work, 13*(1), 76–86.

Cabrera, F., & Stevenson, R. (2017). Dealing with loss and grief of minority children in
an urban setting. In R. G. Stevenson & G. R. Cox (Eds.), *Children, adolescents, and
death: Questions and answers* (pp. 203–217). New York, NY: Routledge.

Calamur, K. (2018, June 24). The normalization of gun violence in poor communities
The Atlantic. https://www.theatlantic.com/health/archive/2018/06/gun-violence/
563582/

Calhoun, T. L. (2019). *Engaging with African American youth following gunshot wound
trauma: The Calhoun cultural competency course* (Doctoral dissertation). Boston
University, Boston, MA.

Campbell, S., Nass, D., & Nguyen, M. (2018). The CDC is publishing unreliable data on gun
injuries. People are using it anyway. FiveThirtyEight. https://fivethirtyeight.com/features/
the-cdc-is-publishing-unreliable-data-on-gun-injuries-people-are-using-it-anyway/

Campie, P., Patrosino, A., Fronius, F., & Read, N. (2017). *Community based violence prevention study of the Safe and Successful Youth Initiative: An intervention to prevent gun
violence*. Washington, DC: American Institutes for Research. https://www.air.org/
sites/default/files/downloads/report/Intervention-to-Prevent-Urban-Gun-Violence-
SSYI-April-2017.pdf

Campos-Manzo, A. L., Mitobe, A. M., Ignatiadis, C., Rubin, E. W., & Fischer, J. (2019).
Collective pain: Youth of color facing the aftermath of mass school shootings. In G.
A. Crews (Ed.), *Handbook of research on school violence in American K–12 education*
(pp. 179–207). Hershey, PA: IGI Global.

Canchola, R. G. (2020). *Adverse childhood experiences, crime, and resiliency: A neu-
robiological and psychosocial review* (Doctoral dissertation). Alliant International
University, Alhambra, CA.

Cantor, J., & Haller, R. (2016, November). Developing a trauma-and resilience-focused
accountable community for health. *JSI*. https://cachi.org/uploads/resources/JSI_
trauma-resilience-ACH_2016_1130-1.pdf

Carlson, J. (2018, November 6). Why research on guns needs sociologists. And vice-
versa. Items: Insights from the Social Sciences. https://items.ssrc.org/understanding-
gun-violence/why-research-on-guns-needs-sociologists-and-vice-versa/

Carman, M. (2019). Leading the effort to promote bleeding control in our communities. *AJN The American Journal of Nursing, 119*(5), 51–53.

Carr, J. B., & Doleac, J. L. (2016). The geography, incidence, and underreporting of gun violence: New evidence using ShotSpotter data. *Incidence, and Underreporting of Gun Violence: New Evidence Using Shotspotter Data.* https://www.brookings.edu/wp-content/uploads/2016/07/Carr_Doleac_gunfire_underreporting.pdf

Carr, J. B., & Doleac, J. L. (2018). Keep the kids inside: Juvenile curfews, bad weather, and urban gun violence. *The Review of Economics and Statistics, 100*(4), 609–618.

Carswell, S. M. (2019). Have we surrendered to gun violence in urban America? Federal neglect stymies efforts to stop the slaughter among young Black men. *Race and Justice.* doi:10.1177%2F2153368719865306

Carter, P. M., Cranford, J. A., Buu, A., Walton, M. A., Zimmerman, M. A., Goldstick, J., . . . Cunningham, R. M. (2020). Daily patterns of substance use and violence among a high-risk urban emerging adult sample: Results from the Flint Youth Injury Study. *Addictive Behaviors, 101*, 106–127.

Carter, P. M., Dora-Laskey, A. D., Goldstick, J. E., Heinze, J. E., Walton, M. A., Zimmerman, M. A., . . . Cunningham, R. M. (2018). Arrests among high-risk youth following emergency department treatment for an assault injury. *American Journal of Preventive Medicine, 55*(6), 812–821.

Carter, P. M., Walton, M. A., Roehler, D. R., Goldstick, J., Zimmerman, M. A., Blow, F. C., & Cunningham, R. M. (2015). Firearm violence among high-risk emergency department youth after an assault injury. *Pediatrics, 135*(5), 805–815.

Carter, P. M., Zeoli, A. M., & Goyal, M. K. (2020). Evidence to assess potential policy-oriented solutions for reducing adolescent firearm carriage. *Pediatrics, 145*(1). https://pediatrics.aappublications.org/content/145/1/e20192334.

Carter, R. L. (2018). Life-in-death: Raising dead sons in New Orleans. *Ethnos, 83*(4), 683–705.

Cassino, D., & Besen-Cassino, Y. (2020). Sometimes (but not this time), a gun is just a gun: Masculinity threat and guns in the United States, 1999–2018. *Sociological Forum, 35*(1), 5–23.

Cazenave, N. A. (2018). *Killing African Americans: Police and vigilante violence as a racial control mechanism.* New York, NY: Routledge.

CBS 58. (2019, August 23). Mothers of gun violence victis speak outside Milwaukee county courthouse. https://www.cbs58.com/news/mothers-of-gun-violence-victims-speak-outside-milwaukee-county-courthouse

CBS News. (2019, July 31). 2 mothers working to stop gun violence shot dead. https://www.cbsnews.com/news/chantell-grant-andrea-stoudemire-chicago-mothers-working-to-stop-gun-violence-shot-dead/

Ceballos, A. (2014, April 21). Two mothers, two losses, one unexpected bond. *Voice of San Diego.* https://www.voiceofsandiego.org/topics/news/two-mothers-two-losses-one-unexpected-bond/

Center for American Progress. (2018, August 29). The dangerous racialization of crime in U.S. news media. https://www.americanprogress.org/issues/criminal-justice/news/2018/08/29/455313/dangerous-racialization-crime-u-s-news-media/

Centers for Disease Control and Prevention. (2016). *A comprehensive technical package for the prevention of youth violence and associated risks*. Atlanta, GA: Author.

Centers for Disease Control and Prevention. National Center for Injury Prevention and Control. (2019). *Web-Based Injury Statistics Query and Reporting System (WISQARS) fatal injury reports. A yearly average was developed using five years of the most recent available data: 2013 to 2017*. Atlanta, GA: Author.

Cerdá, M., Tracy, M., & Keyes, K. M. (2018). Reducing urban violence: A contrast of public health and criminal justice approaches. *Epidemiology, 29*(1), 142–150.

Charles, J. B. (2019, December 6). Advocates push California city to adopt program that pays people who don't shoot. *The Trace*. https://www.thetrace.org/2019/12/fresno-gun-violence-advocates-advance-peace/

Charlton, E. (2019, January 3). US gun deaths at their highest rate in 40 years. *World Economic Council*. https://www.weforum.org/agenda/2019/01/chart-of-the-day-us-gun-deaths-skyrocket-driven-by-a-rise-in-suicides/

Chau, M. (2019, December 16). Fear of mass shootings fuel a thriving bullet proof business. *Time*, pp. 24–25.

Chavez-Diaz, M., & Lee, N. (2015). *A conceptual mapping of healing centered youth organizing: Building a case for healing justice. Working paper*. Unpublished manuscript. Urban Peace Movement, Oakland, CA. http://urbanpeacemovement.org/wp-content/uploads/2014/02/HealingMapping_FINALVERSION.pdf

Cheng, T. (2020). Input without influence: The silence and scripts of police and community relations. *Social Problems, 67*(1), 171–189.

Chesnut, K. Y., Barragan, M., Gravel, J., Pifer, N. A., Reiter, K., Sherman, N., & Tita, G. E. (2017). Not an "iron pipeline," but many capillaries: Regulating passive transactions in Los Angeles' secondary, illegal gun market. *Injury Prevention, 23*(4), 226–231.

Chokshi, N. (2019, August 29). St. Louis seeks help in solving child deaths. *The New York Times*, p. A20.

Christens, B. D. (2019). *Community power and empowerment*. New York, NY: Oxford University Press.

Christensen, A. J., Cunningham, R., Delamater, A., & Hamilton, N. (2019). Introduction to the special issue on gun violence: Addressing a critical public health challenge. *Journal of Behavioral Medicine, 42*(4), 581–583.

Circo, G. M. (2019). Distance to trauma centres among gunshot wound victims: Identifying trauma "deserts" and "oases" in Detroit. *Injury Prevention, 25*, i39–i43.

Circo, G. M., Pizarro, J. M., & McGarrell, E. F. (2018). Adult and youth involvement in gun-related crime: Implications for gun violence prevention interventions. *Criminal Justice Policy Review, 29*(8), 799–822.

Claiborne, S., & Martin, M. (2019). *Beating guns: Hope for people who are weary of violence*. Ada, MI: Brazos Press.

Clark-Moorman, K., Rydberg, J., & McGarrell, E. F. (2018). Impact evaluation of a parolee-based focused deterrence program on community-level violence. *Criminal Justice Policy Review, 30*(9), 1408–1430.

Coates, M., & Pearson-Merkowitzz, S. (2017). Policy spillover and gun migration: The interstate dynamics of state gun control policies. *Social Science Quarterly, 98*(2), 500–512.

Cobbina, J. E., Chaudhuri, S., Rios, V. M., & Conteh, M. (2019, June). "I will be out there every day strong!" Protest policing and future activism among Ferguson and Baltimore protesters. *Sociological Forum, 34*(2), 409–433.

Cohen, L., Davis, R., & Realini, A. (2016). Violence affecting youth: Pervasive and preventable. In M. R. Korin (Ed.), *Health promotion for children and* adolescents (pp. 235–262). Boston, MA: Springer.

Cohen, R. M. (2015, October 15). Why focusing on mass shootings won't end gun violence in America. *Vice.* https://www.vice.com/en_au/article/9bgnvv/why-focusing-on-mass-shootings-wont-end-gun-violence-in-america-1012?utm_source=viceadwordsdynamicus&utm_medium=cpc

Cohen, S. (2018, December 11). 9,000 firearms and counting: Illegal guns flood Chicago. *AP.* https://www.apnews.com/1610816361014918ab6019cf93bfefef

Collins, J. W. (2019). Achieving engagement in injury and violence prevention research. *Injury Prevention, 25*(5), 472–475.

Collins, M. E., Parker, S. T., Scott, T. L., & Wellford, C. F. (2017). A comparative analysis of crime guns. *RSF: The Russell Sage Foundation Journal of the Social Sciences, 3*(5), 96–127.

Collins, R. (2019). Preventing violence: Insights from micro-sociology. *Contemporary Sociology: A Journal of Reviews, 48*(5), 487–494.

Conway, S. (2018, February). After unthinkable loss. *Politics&CityLife.* https://www.chicagomag.com/city-life/February-2018/Mothers-on-Both-Sides-of-Chicago-Violence-Find-Sisterhood-in-Loss/

Contreras, R. (2018a). From nowhere: Space, race, and time in how young minority men understand encounters with gangs. *Qualitative Sociology, 41*(2), 263–280.

Contreras, R. (2018b). Que duro! Street violence in the South Bronx. In E. B. Weininger, A. Lareau, & O. Lizardo (Eds.), *Ritual, emotion, violence* (pp. 45–63). New York, NY: Routledge.

Cook, A., Hosmer, D., Glance, L., Kalesan, B., Weinberg, J., Rogers, A., . . . Ward, J. (2019). Population-based analysis of firearm injuries among young children in the United States, 2010–2015. *The American Surgeon, 85*(5), 449–455.

Cook, B. (2017). *The efficacy of public health interventions aimed at curbing gun violence: An integrative review.* The Grace Peterson Nursing Research Colloquium. DePaul University School of Nursing. https://via.library.depaul.edu/nursing-colloquium/2017/Summer_2017/51/

Cook, E. (2018). *Bereaved family activism in the aftermath of lethal violence* (Doctoral dissertation). University of Manchester, Manchester, UK.

Cook, P. J. (2018a). Gun markets. *Annual Review of Criminology, 1*, 359–377.

Cook, P. J. (2018b). Gun theft and crime. *Journal of Urban Health, 95*(3), 305–312.

Cook, P. J., Braga, A. A., Turchan, B. S., & Barao, L. M. (2019). Why do gun murders have a higher clearance rate than gunshot assaults?. *Criminology & Public Policy. 18*(3), 525–551.

Cook, P. J., & Ludwig, J. (2002). The costs of gun violence against children. *Future of Children, 12*(2), 87–100.

Cook, P. J., Parker, S. T., & Pollack, H. A. (2015). Sources of guns to dangerous people: What we learn by asking them. *Preventive Medicine, 79*, 28–36.

Cook, P. J., Pollack, H. A., & White, K. (2019). The last link: From gun acquisition to criminal use. *Journal of Urban Health, 96*, 784–791.

Cook, P. J., Rivera-Aguirre A. E., Cerdá, M., & Wintemute G. (2017). Constant lethality of gunshot injuries from firearm assault: United States, 2003–2012. *American Journal of Public Health, 107*(8), 1324–1328.

Cooley, J. L., Ritschel, L. A., Frazer, A. L., & Blossom, J. B. (2019). The influence of internalizing symptoms and emotion dysregulation on the association between witnessed community violence and aggression among urban adolescents. *Child Psychiatry & Human Development, 50*(6), 883–893.

Cooper, H. L., & Fullilove, M. (2016). Excessive police violence as a public health issue. *Journal of Urban Health, 93*(1), 1–7.

Copeland, C., Wallin, M., & Holt, T. J. (2020). Assessing the practices and products of darkweb firearm vendors. *Deviant Behavior, 41*(8), 949–968.

Corrado, M. (2016). *Trauma narratives with inner city youth: The storiez intervention.* (Dissertation). University of Pennsylvania, Philadelphia.

Corazon, A. (2019). *Literature review on urban trauma and applying a trauma-informed approach.* (Thesis). Lesley University, Cambridge, MA.

Corsaro, N., & Engel, R. S. (2015). Most challenging of contexts: Assessing the impact of focused deterrence on serious violence in New Orleans. *Criminology & Public Policy, 14*(3), 471–505.

Cosey Gay, F. N. (2019). *Empowering high-risk males through street outreach* (Doctoral dissertation). University of Illinois, Chicago.

Côté, A., Gaucher, N., & Payot, A. (2017). P038: Does the pediatric emergency department have a role in pediatric palliative care? *Canadian Journal of Emergency Medicine, 19*(S1), S90–S91.

Crifasi, C. (2018). Gun policy in the United States: Evidence-based strategies to reduce gun violence. *Applied Health Economics and Health Policy, 16*(5), 579–581.

Cromer, K. D., D'Agostino, E. M., Hansen, E., Alfonso, C., & Frazier, S. L. (2019). After-school poly-strengths programming for urban teens at high risk for violence exposure. *Translational Behavioral Medicine, 9*(3), 541–548.

Crutcher, C. L., Fannin, E. S., & Wilson, J. D. (2016). Racial disparities in cranial gunshot wounds: Intent and survival. *Journal of Racial and Ethnic Health Disparities, 3*(4), 687–691.

Cukier, W., & Eagen, S. A. (2018). Gun violence. *Current Opinion in Psychology, 19*, 109–122.

Culyba, A. J., Ginsburg, K. R., Fein, J. A., Branas, C. C., Richmond, T. S., Miller, E., & Wiebe, D. J. (2019a). Examining the role of supportive family connection in violence exposure among male youth in urban environments. *Journal of Interpersonal Violence, 34*(5), 1074–1088.

Culyba, A. J., Miller, E., Albert, S. M., & Abebe, K. Z. (2019b). Co-occurrence of violence-related risk and protective behaviors and adult support among male youth in urban neighborhoods. *JAMA Network Open, 2*(9), e1911375–e1911375.

Cunningham, A. C. (2016). *Critical perspectives on gun control.* Berkeley Heights, NJ: Enslow.

Currie, E. (2017). Confronting the North's South: On race and violence in the United States. *International Journal for Crime, Justice and Social Democracy, 6*(1), 23–34.

Dabash, S., Gerzina, C., Simson, J. E., Elabd, A., & Abdelgawad, A. (2018). Pediatric gunshot wounds of the upper extremity. *International Journal of Orthopaedics, 5*(2), 910–915.

Davey, M., & Hassan, A. (2019, August 17). When cities try to limit guns, state laws bar the way. *The New York Times,* p. A12.

Davidoff, F. (1998). Reframing gun violence. *Annals of Internal Medicine, 128*(3), 234–235.

Deane, K. (2018). *Measuring community violence, trauma, and family functioning among youth living in low-income, urban environments* (Doctoral dissertation). Loyola University, Chicago, IL.

DeBo'rah, L. (2016). *Life after the homicide of young urban African American males: Parental experiences* (Doctoral dissertation). Capella University, Minneapolis, MN.

Delgado, M. (1999). *Social work practice in nontraditional urban settings.* New York, NY: Oxford University Press.

Delgado, M. (2000). *Community social work practice in an urban context: The potential of a capacity enhancement perspective.* New York, NY: Oxford University Press.

Delgado, M. (2003). *Death at an early age and the urban scene: The case for memorial murals and community healing.* Westport, Ct: Praeger.

Delgado, M. (2015). *Urban youth and photovoice: Visual ethnography in action.* New York, NY: Oxford University Press.

Delgado, M. (2016). *Community practice and urban youth: Social justice service-learning and civic engagement.* New York, NY: Routledge.

Delgado, M. (2017a). *Social work with Latinos: Social, economic, political, and cultural perspectives.* New York, NY: Oxford University Press.

Delgado, M. (2017b). *Urban youth friendships and community social work practice.* New York, NY: Oxford University Press. (Part of Series of Youth and Social Justice)

Delgado, M. (2018). *Music, song, dance, and theatre: Broadway meets youth community practice.* New York, NY: Oxford University Press. (Part of Series on Youth and Social Justice)

Delgado, M. (2019). *Urban youth trauma: Using community interventions to overcome gun violence.* Lanham, MD: Rowman & Littlefield.

Delgado, M. (2020a). *Community health workers in action: The efforts of "promotores de salud" in bringing health care to marginalized communities.* New York, NY: Oxford University Press.

Delgado, M. (2020b). *State sanctioned violence: Advancing a social work social justice agenda.* New York, NY: Oxford University.

Delgado, M., & Humm-Delgado, D. (2013). *Asset assessments and community social work practice.* New York, NY: Oxford University Press.

Deluca, S., Clampet-Lundquist, S., & Edin, K. (2016). *Coming of age in the other America.* New York, NY: Russell Sage Foundation.

Deng, H., Yue, J. K., Winkler, E. A., Dhall, S. S., Manley, G. T., & Tarapore, P. E. (2019). Pediatric firearm-related traumatic brain injury in United States trauma centers. *Journal of Neurosurgery: Pediatrics, 24*(5), 481–610.

Deuchar, R. (2018). Love, compassion and therapeutic communities in homeboy industries. In R. Deuchar (ed.), *Gangs and Spirituality* (pp. 89–113). New York, NY: Palgrave Macmillan.

Diamond, J. B. (2019). Unequal city: Race, schools, and perceptions of injustice; Wounded city: Violent turf wars in a Chicago barrio. *Sociology of Race and Ethnicity, 5*(1), 149–152.

DiClemente, C. M., Rice, C. M., Quimby, D., Richards, M. H., Grimes, C. T., Morency, M. M., . . . Pica, J. A. (2018). Resilience in urban African American adolescents: The protective enhancing effects of neighborhood, family, and school cohesion following violence exposure. *The Journal of Early Adolescence, 38*(9), 1286–1321.

Dierenfeldt, R., Thomas, S. A., Brown, T. C., & Walker, J. T. (2017). Street culture and gun violence: Exploring the reputation–victimization paradox. *Journal of Interpersonal Violence.* doi:10.1177%2F0886260517730028

Dierkhising, C. B., Sánchez, J. A., & Gutierrez, L. (2019). "It changed my life": Traumatic loss, behavioral health, and turning points among gang-involved and justice-involved youth. *Journal of Interpersonal Violence.* https://doi.org/10.1177%2F0886260519847779

Dill, L. J., & Ozer, E. J. (2016). "I'm not just runnin' the streets" exposure to neighborhood violence and violence management strategies among urban youth of color. *Journal of Adolescent Research, 31*(5), 536–556.

Dirlam, J. C. (2018). *Cycle of violence: Interconnections between justifiable homicides by the police and citizens and the killing of police officers* (Doctoral dissertation). The Ohio State University, Columbus.

DiZazzo-Miller, R. (2015). Spinal cord injury induced by gun shot wounds: Implications for occupational therapy. *The Open Journal of Occupational Therapy, 3*(1), 7. https://scholarworks.wmich.edu/cgi/viewcontent.cgi?article=1127&context=ojot

Docherty, M., Beardslee, J., Grimm, K. J., & Pardini, D. (2019). Distinguishing between-individual from within-individual predictors of gun carrying among Black and White males across adolescence. *Law and Human Behavior, 43*(2), 144–155.

Dockray, H. (2019, July 10). Meet the badass moms of America. *Beyond Words.* https://beyondwords.life/meet-the-most-badass-moms-of-america/

Dodson, N. A. (2016). Adolescent gun violence prevention: What we know, and what we can do to keep young people safe. *Current Opinion in Pediatrics, 28*(4), 441–446.

Dodson, N. A., & Hemenway, D. (2015). Teens and gun trafficking: A call for pediatric advocacy. *JAMA Pediatrics, 169*(2), 105–106.

Doering, J. (2020). *Us versus them: Race, crime, and gentrification in Chicago neighborhoods.* New York, NY: Oxford University Press.

Doka, K. J. (1989). *Disenfranchised grief: Recognizing hidden sorrow.* Lexington, MA: Lexington Books/DC Heath.

Donaghue, E. (2020, April 7). Coronavirus and gun violence: Mayors fight a double public health crisis. *CBS News.* https://www.cbsnews.com/news/coronavirus-gun-violence-double-public-health-crisis/

Dong, B., Branas, C. C., Richmond, T. S., Morrison, C. N., & Wiebe, D. J. (2017). Youth's daily activities and situational triggers of gunshot assault in urban environments. *Journal of Adolescent Health, 61*(6), 779–785.

Dong, B., Morrison, C. N., Branas, C. C., Richmond, T. S., & Wiebe, D. J. (2019). As violence unfolds: A space–time study of situational triggers of violent victimization among urban youth. *Journal of Quantitative Criminology, 36,* 119–152.

Dong, B., & Wiebe, D. J. (2018). Violence and beyond: Life-course features of handgun carrying in the urban United States and the associated long-term life consequences. *Journal of Criminal Justice, 54,* 1–11.

Drayton, T. (2019). *Coping with gun violence.* New York, NY: Rosen.

Driskoll, K. (2018, October 29). 5 thing to known about illegally purchased guns. *Dayton Daily News.* https://www.daytondailynews.com/news/things-know-about-illegally-purchased-guns/GqjqdPsjDyuQuKu6mqJjjL/

D'Souza, A., Weitzer, R., & Brunson, R. K. (2019). Federal investigations of police misconduct: A multi-city comparison. *Crime, Law and Social Change, 71*(5), 461–482.

Dubisar, A. (2018). Mothers against gun violence and the activist buffer. *College English, 80*(3), 195–217.

Dukmasova, M. (2015, August 14). Mothers gun violence in troubled Chicago neighborhood. *The Trace.* https://www.thetrace.org/2015/08/mothers-moms-gun-violence-prevention-chicago/

Dunlap, P. N., & Russell, V. E. (2015). Gang affiliation and disability: An initial investigation into rehabilitation counseling implications. *Journal of Rehabilitation, 81*(4), 17–24.

Dunning, M. (2018). *American gun culture: Are pro-gun tendencies ingrained in United States residents?* New York, NY: Skidmore College. https://osf.io/preprints/socarxiv/cnjpf/

Durando, S. (2018). *Under the gun: A children's hospital on the front line of an American crisis.* Self-published.

Dutil, S. (2019). Adolescent traumatic and disenfranchised grief: Adapting an evidence-based intervention for Black and Latinx youths in schools. *Children & Schools, 41*(3), 179–187.

Dzau, V. J., & Leshner, A. I. (2018). Public health research on gun violence: Long overdue. *Annals of Internal Medicine, 168*(12), 876–877.

Edmonds, R. (2019). A gun took my child. *Journal of the Motherhood Initiative for Research and Community Involvement, 10*(1/2), 273–285.

Egerton, F. N. (2018). *Guncrazy America: A history and critique of our gun culture.* Bloomington, IN: AuthorHouse.

Egley, A., Howell, J. C., & Harris, M. (2014). *Highlights of the 2012 National Young Gang Survey* (Bulletin Number NCJ 248025). Washington, DC: Office of Juvenile Justice and Delinquency Prevention, Juvenile Justice Fact Sheet, US Department of Justice.

Eisman, A. B., Lee, D. B., Hsieh, H. F., Stoddard, S. A., & Zimmerman, M. A. (2018). More than just keeping busy: The protective effects of organized activity participation on violence and substance use among urban youth. *Journal of Youth and Adolescence,* *47*(10), 2231–2242.

Ellement, J. R., & Berg, M. (2020, May 7). Activists, clergy target violence. *The Boston Globe,* p. B3.

Eligon, J., & Burch, A. D. S. (2020, May 11). Questions of bias in virus care haunt mourning Black families. *The New York Times,* pp. A1, A9.

Ellis, W. R. (2019). *Community resilience: A dynamic model for public health* (Doctoral dissertation). George Washington University, Washington, DC.

Elow, D. A. (2011). *A church based intervention and aftercare for traumatized urban youth* (Doctoral dissertation). Boston University, Boston, MA.

Emmert, A. D., Hall, G. P., & Lizotte, A. J. (2018). Do weapons facilitate adolescent delinquency? An examination of weapon carrying and delinquency among adolescents. *Crime & Delinquency, 64*(3), 342–362.

Engelke, M. (2019). The anthropology of death revisited. *Annual Review of Anthropology, 48,* 29–44.

Erickson, J. H., Hochstetler, A., & Dorius, S. F. (2020). Code in transition? The evolution of code of the street adherence in adolescence. *Deviant Behavior, 41*(3), 329–347.

Evans, E. J., & Thompson, M. (2019). Questions and answers from research centers on gun violence. *Health & Social Work, 44*(4), 221–223.

Evans, W. N., Garthwaite, C., & Moore, T. J. (2018). *Guns and violence: The enduring impact of crack cocaine markets on young Black males* (No. w24819). Cambridge, MA: National Bureau of Economic Research.

Everytown for Gun Safety. (2016, June 16). Strategies for reducing gun violence in American cities. New York City. https://everytownresearch.org/reports/strategies-for-reducing-gun-violence-in-american-cities/

Everytown for Gun Safety. (2019a, May 29). The impact of gun violence on children and teens. New York City. https://everytownresearch.org/impact-gun-violence-american-children-teens/

Everytown for Gun Safety. (2019b, April 29). Gun violence in cities. New York City. https://everytownresearch.org/gun-violence-cities/

Everytown for Gun Safety. (2019c, February 1). A nation of survivors: The toll of gun violence in America. New York City. https://everytownresearch.org/reports/nationofsurvivors/

Fader, J. J., VanZant, S. W., & Henson, A. R. (2019). Crime and justice framing in an era of reform: How the local matters. *Justice Quarterly,* 1–21. https://doi.org/10.1080/07418825.2019.1589555

Fairchild, H. H. (2016). *Solving violence in America.* New Delhi, India: Indo American Books.

Falldien, N. E. (2019). *Exploring participants' experiences in an arts-based bereavement support group for traumatic and/or unexpected losses* (Doctoral dissertation). Laurentian University of Sudbury, Sudbury, Ontario, Canada.

Farr, C. (2019, October 14). "This is a war": Chicago gun violence activist becomes victim himself. NBC. https://www.nbcchicago.com/news/local/Chicago-gun-violence-activist-victim-563091471.html

Faust, K., & Tita, G. E. (2019). Social networks and crime: Pitfalls and promises for advancing the field. *Annual Review of Criminology, 2,* 99–122.

Federal Bureau of Investigation. (2017). *Crime in the United States, 2017: Uniform crime reports, expanded homicide data.* Washington, DC: Author.

Federal Bureau of Investigation. (2019). *Uniform Crime Reporting Program, 2013–2017. Analysis of gun murders is from the Supplementary Homicide Reports.* Washington, DC: Author.

Feldman, K. A., Tashiro, J., Allen, C. J., Perez, E. A., Neville, H. L., Schulman, C. I., & Sola, J. E. (2017). Predictors of mortality in pediatric urban firearm injuries. *Pediatric Surgery International, 33*(1), 53–58.

Ferreira, A. V. P., de Macedo Bernardino, Í., Santos, L. M., da Nóbrega, L. M., Barbosa, K. G. N., & d'Avila, S. (2018). Firearms, violence-related injuries, and victimization profiles: An approach using cluster analysis. *Journal of Interpersonal Violence.* In press.

Field, K. (2019, January 23). Unusual new program seeks to cut urban crime by pushing gang members into college. *The Hechinger Report.* https://hechingerreport.org/unusual-new-program-seeks-to-cut-urban-crime-by-pushing-gang-members-into-college/

Fischer, K. R., Bakes, K. M., Corbin, T. J., Fein, J. A., Harris, E. J., James, T. L., & Melzer-Lange, M. D. (2018). Trauma-informed care for violently injured patients in the emergency department. *Annals of Emergency Medicine, 73*(2), 193–202.

Fitzpatrick, V., Castro, M., Jacobs, J., Sebro, N., Gulmatico, J., Shields, M., & Homan, S. M. (2019). Nonfatal firearm violence trends on the Westside of Chicago between 2005 and 2016. *Journal of Community Health, 44*(5), 866–873.

Fleegler, E. (2019, April 1). Mass shootings and the numbing of America. *JAMA Internal Medicine, 179*(5), 610–611. https://journals.sagepub.com/doi/pdf/10.1177/0886260518817786?casa_token=6aB5Gp_CNzcAAAAA:G2B9CVS9W3R_hjymDKpzWe7wcJXdyXkjR-cNP6uU4xirQOE7SQEsj9PC-ObNwgMhjObhd3GVORzR

Flippo, A. (2018). *Ocean of tears: An autoethnographic journey through cumulative grief and loss* (Doctoral dissertation). University of Nevada, Reno.

Flores, R. D. (2015). Taking the law into their own hands: Do local anti-ordinances increase gun sales? *Social Problems, 62*(3), 363–390.

Fontaine, J., La Vigue, N. G., Leitson, D., Erondu, K., Okeke, C., & Dwivedi, A. (2018, October 4). *"We carry guns to stay safe": Perspectives on gun violence from young adults living in Chicago's West and South Sides.* Washington, DC: Urban Institute.

Foran, C. P., Clark, D. H., Henry, R., Lalchandani, P., Kim, D. Y., Putnam, B. A., . . . Demetriades, D. G. (2019). Current burden of gunshot wound injuries at two Los Angeles County level I trauma centers. *Journal of the American College of Surgeons, 229*(2), 141–149.

Ford, E. (2019, July 10). Reducing gun violence by healing trauma. *Essence.* https://www.essence.com/op-ed/life-camp-inc-mobile-trauma-unit/

Forenza, B., Lardier, D. T., Jr., Reid, R. J., Garcia-Reid, P., & Bermea, A. (2019). Exploring community stress and empowerment among stakeholders and youth in an urban community. *Journal of Human Behavior in the Social Environment, 29*(6), 705–721.

Formica, M. K., Rajan, S., & Simons, N. (2019). Healthcare indicators and firearm homicide: an ecologic study. *Journal of Aggression, Conflict and Peace Research, 11*(2), 88–99.

Forrest, T. M., Wallace-Pascoe, D. M., Webb, M. D., & Goldstein, H. (2017). Giving the community a voice: Lessons learned from a comprehensive survey in an urban neighborhood. *Evaluation and Program Planning, 60*, 130–142.

Fowler, K. A., Dahlberg, L. L., Haileyesus, T., Gutierrez, C., & Bacon, S. (2017). Childhood firearm injuries in the United States. *Pediatrics, 140*(1), e20163486.

Fox, A. M., & Novak, K. J. (2018). Collaborating to reduce violence: The impact of focused deterrence in Kansas City. *Police Quarterly, 21*(3), 283–308.

Fox, J. A., Levin, J., & Quinet, K. (2018). *The will to kill: Making sense of senseless murder.* Thousand Oaks, CA: Sage.

Fox, M. (2018, December 19). Guns kill twice as many kids as cancer does, new study shows. *NBC News.* https://www.nbcnews.com/health/health-news/guns-kill-twice-many-kids-cancer-does-new-study-shows-n950091

Fox17. (2019, May 10). Mothers against gun violence vigil planned in GR. https://fox17online.com/2019/05/10/mothers-against-gun-violence-vigil-planned-in-gr/

Francis, M. (2018). A narrative inquiry into the experience of being a victim of gun violence. *Journal of Trauma Nursing, 25*(6), 381–388.

Franks, M. A. (2019, October 10). Far-from-innocent bystanders. *The New York Times,* p. A23.

Fraser, B. (2018, August 21). Why does violence in Chicago attract so much attention, even though it's not the murder capital of the US? *Root.* https://www.theroot.com/why-does-violence-in-chicago-attract-so-much-attention-1828327783

Frazer, E., Mitchell, R. A., Jr., Nesbitt, L. S., Williams, M., Mitchell, E. P., Williams, R. A., & Browne, D. (2018). The violence epidemic in the African American community: A call by the national medical association for comprehensive reform. *Journal of the National Medical Association, 110*(1), 4–15.

Frazier, F. (2019, October 14). Bloodshed blankets neighborhoods at heart of Jacksonville, data news. *News 4JX.* https://www.news4jax.com/enterprise/2019/10/14/bloodshed-targeted-in-neighborhoods-at-heart-of-jacksonville-data-shows/

Frederick, R. W., & Lee, M. J. (2019). The importance of dialogue: Communication strategy for empowerment of low-income African American patients via in-depth interviews of primary care providers at inner-city health clinics. *Journal of Communication in Healthcare, 12*(1), 23–31.

Fredrick, E., III. (2019). News: Death, violence, health, and poverty in Chicago. *Emergency Medical News, 41*(1), 6–8.

Free, J. L., & Macdonald, H. Z. (2019). "I've had to bury a lot of kids over the years . . . ": Violence prevention streetworkers' exposure to trauma. *Journal of Community Psychology. 47*, 1197–1209.

Freeman, J. J., Bachier-Rodriguez, M., Staszak, J., & Feliz, A. (2017). A comparison between non-powder gun and powder-gun injuries in a young pediatric population. *Injury, 48*(9), 1951–1955.

Freire-Vargas, L. (2018). Violence as a public health crisis. *AMA Journal of Ethics, 20*(1), 25–28.

Frerichs, L., Lich, K. H., Funchess, M., Burrell, M., Cerulli, C., Bedell, P., & White, A. M. (2016). Applying critical race theory to group model building methods to address community violence. *Progress in Community Health Partnerships: Research, Education, and Action*, 10(3), 443–459.

Frisby, C. M. (2017). Misrepresentations of lone shooters: The disparate treatment of Muslim, African American, Hispanic, Asian, and White perpetrators in the US news media. *Advances in Journalism and Communication*, 5(02), 162–181.

Furman, L. (2018). Firearm violence: Silent victims. *Pediatrics*, 142(4), e20182060.

Furr-Holden, C. D. M., Nesoff, E. D., Nelson, V., Milam, A. J., Smart, M., Lacey, K., . . . Leaf, P. J. (2019). Understanding the relationship between alcohol outlet density and life expectancy in Baltimore City: The role of community violence and community disadvantage. *Journal of Community Psychology*, 47(1), 63–75.

Gabor, T. (2016). *Confronting gun violence in America*. New York, NY: Springer.

Gailey, A. (2018). The racial politics of US gun policy. In M. Gardner & M. Weber (Eds.), *The ethics of policing and imprisonment* (pp. 151–167). New York, NY: Palgrave Macmillan.

Gander, K. (2019a, August 13a). US child gun deaths: Firearms are second greatest killer in America. *Newsweek*. https://www.newsweek.com/us-child-gun-death-firearms-2nd-biggest-killer-america-1264804

Gander, K. (2019b, March 21). More children were shot dead in 2017 than on-duty police officers and active duty military, study says. *Newsweek*. https://www.newsweek.com/kids-and-guns-alarming-rise-firearm-deaths-among-american-children-1370866

Garay, R. M. V., del Toro, R. G., & Relinque, C. S. (2020). Violence in adolescence from a social work perspective: A qualitative study. In J. Sarasola Sánchez-Serrano, F. Maturo, & Š. Hošková-Mayerová (Eds.), *Qualitative and quantitative models in socioeconomic systems and social work* (pp. 25–50). New York: Springer.

Garcia, M. (2020, May 14). Latinos struggle to bury their dead. *The Boston Globe*, p. A9.

Garo, L. A., & Lawson, T. (2019). My story, my way: Conceptualization of narrative therapy with trauma-exposed Black male youth. *Urban Education Research & Policy Annuals*, 6(1), 47–65.

Gay, C., & Cosey, F. N. (2019). *Empowering high-risk males through street outreach* (Doctoral dissertation). University of Illinois, Chicago.

Gellert, G. A. (2019). *Confronting violence: Answers to questions about the epidemic destroying America's homes and communities*. New York, NY: Routledge.

Giffords Law Center to Prevent Gun Violence. (2016, March 10). *Healing communities in crisis: Lifesaving solutions to the urban gun violence epidemic*. San Francisco, CA: Author. https://lawcenter.giffords.org/healing-communities-in-crisis-lifesaving-solutions-to-the-urban-gun-violence-epidemic/

Giffords Law Center to Prevent Gun Violence. (2017, December 18). *Investing in intervention: The critical role of state-level support in breaking the cycle of urban gun violence*. San Francisco, CA: Author. https://lawcenter.giffords.org/investing-intervention-critical-role-state-level-support-breaking-cycle-urban-gun-violence/

Gill, C. (2016). Community interventions. In D. Weisburd, D. P. Farrington, & C. Gill (Eds.), *What works in crime prevention and rehabilitation* (pp. 77–109). New York, NY: Springer.

Gillies, J., Neimeyer, R., & Milman, E. (2015). The grief and meaning reconstruction inventory (GMRI): Initial validation of a new measure. *Death Studies, 39*(2), 61–74.

Giovanelli, A., Hayakawa, M., Englund, M. M., & Reynolds, A. J. (2018). African-American males in Chicago: Pathways from early childhood intervention to reduced violence. *Journal of Adolescent Health, 62*(1), 80–86.

Giroux, H. (2015). America's addiction to violence. https://philosophersforchange.org/2016/01/05/americas-addiction-to-violence/

Godwin, M. L., & Schroedel, J. R. (2000). Policy diffusion and strategies for promoting policy change: Evidence from California local gun control ordinances. *Policy Studies Journal, 28*(4), 760–776.

Golden, J. N. (2019a, July 24). New Beverly Pizza Restaurant that aims to fund programs for Englewood School derailed by Metra construction. *Block Club*. https://blockclubchicago.org/2019/07/24/new-beverly-pizza-restaurant-that-aims-to-fund-programs-for-englewood-school-derailed-by-metra-construction/

Golden, J. N. (2019b, December 18). Ahead of Christmas party for kids, container full of decorations towed away from Englewood Corner. *Block Club*. https://blockclubchicago.org/2019/12/18/mask-storage-container/

Goldstick, J. E., Carter, P. M., Heinze, J. E., Walton, M. A., Zimmerman, M., & Cunningham, R. M. (2019). Predictors of transitions in firearm assault behavior among drug-using youth presenting to an urban emergency department. *Journal of Behavioral Medicine, 42*(4), 635–645.

Goolsby, C., Strauss-Riggs, K., Rozenfeld, M., Charlton, N., Goralnick, E., Peleg, K., . . . Hurst, N. (2019). Equipping public spaces to facilitate rapid point-of-injury hemorrhage control after mass casualty. *American Journal of Public Health, 109*(2), 236–241.

Gottlieb, A., & Wilson, R. (2019, August). The effect of direct and vicarious police contact on the educational achievement of urban teens. *Children and Youth Services Review, 103*, 190–199.

Goyal, M. K., Badolato, G. M., Patel, S. J., Iqbal, S. F., Parikh, K., & McCarter, R. (2019). State gun laws and pediatric firearm-related mortality. *Pediatrics, 144*(2), e20183283.

Grain, K. M., & Land, D. E. (2017). The social justice turn: Cultivating' critical hope' in an age of despair. *Michigan Journal of Community Service Learning, 23*(1). Ejournal.

Gramlich, J. (2018, December 27). *7 facts about guns in the US*. Washington, DC: PEW Research Center.

Graves, E. (2019). Moving to Improve?: A qualitative meta-analysis of neighborhood violence and residential decision-making among housing voucher holders. *Journal of Planning Literature, 34*(1), 19–37.

Green, B., Horel, T., & Papachristos, A. V. (2017). Modeling contagion through social networks to explain and predict gunshot violence in Chicago, 2006 to 2014. *JAMA Internal Medicine, 177*(3), 326–333.

Green, C. (2019). Desistance and disabled masculine identity: Exploring the role of serious violent victimization in the desistance process. *Journal of Developmental and Life-Course Criminology, 5*(3), 287–309.

Greene, J. (2019). A balancing act: The emergency physician role in firearms safety. *Annals of Emergency Medicine, 73*(1), A13–A15.

Grinshteyn, E., & Hemenway, D. (2019). Violent death rates in the US compared to those of the other high-income countries, 2015. *Preventive Medicine, 123*, 20–26.

Gross, B. W., Cook, A. D., Rinehart, C. D., Lynch, C. A., Bradburn, E. H., Bupp, K. A., . . . Rogers, F. B. (2017). An epidemiologic overview of 13 years of firearm hospitalizations in Pennsylvania. *Journal of Surgical Research, 210*, 188–195.

Grunwald, B., & Papachristos, A. V. (2017). Project safe neighborhoods in Chicago: Looking back a decade later. *Journal of Criminal Law & Criminology, 107*, 131–159.

Haag, P. (2016). *The gunning of America: Business and the making of American gun culture*. New York, NY: Basic Books.

Hagan, N. (2018, October 1). Pay attention to all gun violence, not just mass shootings. *The Pitt News*. https://pittnews.com/article/135924/opinions/pay-attention-to-all-gun-violence-not-just-mass-shootings/

Hahn, J. D. (2019, May 3). Trayvon Martin's mom is supporting her fellow grieving mothers. *People*. https://people.com/human-interest/sybrina-fulton-trayvon-martin-heal/

Hamby, S., Banyard, V., & Grych, J. (2016). Strengths, narrative, and resilience: Restorying resilience research. *Psychology of Violence, 6*(1), 1–7.

Hamby, S., Taylor, E., Jones, L., Mitchell, K. J., Turner, H. A., & Newlin, C. (2018). From poly-victimization to poly-strengths: Understanding the web of violence can transform research on youth violence and illuminate the path to prevention and resilience. *Journal of Interpersonal Violence, 33*(5), 719–739.

Han, B., Cohen, D. A., Derose, K. P., Li, J., & Williamson, S. (2018). Violent crime and park use in low-income urban neighborhoods. *American Journal of Preventive Medicine, 54*(3), 352–358.

Han, C., & Brandel, A. (2019). Genres of witnessing: Narrative, violence, generations. *Ethnos, 85*(4), 629–646.

Hannays-King, C., Bailey, A., & Akhtar, M. (2015). Social support and Black mothers' bereavement experience of losing a child to gun homicide. *Bereavement Care, 34*(1), 10–16.

Hanlon, T. J., Barber, C., Azrael, D., & Miller, M. (2019). Type of firearm used in suicides: Findings from 13 states in the National Violent Death Reporting System, 2005–2015. *Journal of Adolescent Health, 65*(1), 366–370.

Harden, T., Kenemore, T., Mann, K., Edwards, M., List, C., & Martinson, K. J. (2015). The truth n'trauma project: Addressing community violence through a youth-led, trauma-informed and restorative framework. *Child and Adolescent Social Work Journal, 32*(1), 65–79.

Hardiman, E. R., Jones, L. V., & Cestone, L. M. (2019). Neighborhood perceptions of gun violence and safety: Findings from a public health-social work intervention. *Social Work in Public Health, 34*(6), 492–504.

Hardina, D. (2012). *Interpersonal social work skills for community practice*. New York, NY: Springer.

Harris, D. (2020). *A city divided: Race, fear and the law in police confrontations*. London, UK: Anthem Press.

Haser, G., Yousuf, S., Turnock, B., & Sheehan, K. (2020). Promoting safe firearm storage in an urban neighborhood: The views of parents concerning the role of health care providers. *Journal of Community Health, 45,* 338–341.

Hayhurst, J. G., Hunter, J. A., & Ruffman, T. (2019). Encouraging flourishing following tragedy: The role of civic engagement in well-being and resilience. *New Zealand Journal of Psychology, 48*(1), 76–83.

He, K., & Sakran, J. V. (2019). Elimination of the moratorium on gun research is not enough: The need for the CDC to set a budgetary agenda. *JAMA Surgery, 154*(3), 195–196.

Heffernan, W. C. (2019). *Rights and wrongs: Rethinking the foundations of criminal justice.* London, UK: Palgrave Macmillan.

Heilmann, K., & Kahn, M. E. (2019). *The urban crime and heat gradient in high and low poverty areas* (No. w25961). Cambridge, MA: National Bureau of Economic Research.

Hemenway, D. (2012). *Don't shoot: One man, a street fellowship, and the end of violence in inner-city America.* New York, NY: Bloomsbury.

Hemenway, D. (2016). Gun exceptionalism. *Florida Law Review Forum, 68,* 45.

Hemenway, D. (2017). Fight the silencing of gun research. *Nature News, 546*(7658), 345–347.

Hemenway, D., Azrael, D., Conner, A., & Miller, M. (2019). Variation in rates of fatal police shootings across US states: The role of firearm availability. *Journal of Urban Health, 96*(1), 63–73.

Hemenway, D., Azrael, D., & Miller, M. (2017). Whose guns are stolen? The epidemiology of gun theft victims. *Injury Epidemiology, 4*(1), 11. https://injepijournal.biomedcentral.com/articles/10.1186/s40621-017-0109-8

Hemenway, D., & Solnick, S. J. (2017). The epidemiology of homicide perpetration by children. *Injury Epidemiology, 4*(1), 5. https://link.springer.com/article/10.1186/s40621-017-0102-2

Henderson, Z. (2019). In their own words: How Black teens define trauma. *Journal of Child & Adolescent Trauma, 12*(1), 141–151.

Herbert, S., Beckett, K., & Stuart, F. (2018). Policing social marginality: Contrasting approaches. *Law & Social Inquiry, 43*(4), 1491–1513.

Hickner, J. (2018). We need to treat gun violence like an epidemic. *Journal of Family Practice, 67*(4), 198.

Hill, J. R., & Adesanya, R. M. (2019). Building resilience: helping children cope with violence in their communities. *YC Young Children, 74*(4), 82–92.

Hills-Evans, K., Mitton, J., & Sacks, C. A. (2018). Stop posturing and start problem solving: A call for research to prevent gun violence. *AMA Journal of Ethics, 20*(1). doi:10.1001/journalofethics.2018.20.1.pfor1-1801. Online. https://journalofethics.ama-assn.org/article/stop-posturing-and-start-problem-solving-call-research-prevent-gun-violence/2018-01?Effort%2BCode=FBB007

Hink, A. B., Bonne, S., Levy, M., Kuhls, D. A., Allee, L., Burke, P. A., . . . Stewart, R. M. (2019). Firearm injury research and epidemiology: A review of the data, their limitations, and how trauma centers can improve firearm injury research. *Journal of Trauma and Acute Care Surgery, 87*(3), 678–689.

Hipple, N, K., & Magee, L. (2017). The difference between living and dying: Victim characteristics and motive among nonfatal shootings and gun homicides. *Violence and Victims, 32*(3), 977–997. doi:10.1891/0886-6708.VV-D-16-00150

Hipple, N. K., Thompson, K. J., Huebner, B. M., & Magee, L. A. (2019). Understanding victim cooperation in cases of nonfatal gun assaults. *Criminal Justice and Behavior, 46*(12), 1790–1811.

Hitchcock, O. (2019a, July 2). How do you curb gun violence? Jobs, healing and a village, PBC residents say. *Palm Beach Post*. https://www.palmbeachpost.com/news/20190702/how-do-you-curb-gun-violence-jobs-healing-and-village-pbc-residents-say

Hitchcock, O. (2019b, May 9). "Love me through it": These 430 moms grieve, rise and fight gun violence. *Palm Beach Post*. https://www.palmbeachpost.com/news/20190509/love-me-through-it-these-430-moms-grieve-rise-and-fight-gun-violence/1

Hoffman, A. J. (2019). Creating an edible dialogue for peace: Community gardening, horticulture, and urban fruit tree orchards. In D. Rothbart (Ed.), *The psychology of peace promotion* (pp. 267–285). New York, NY: Springer.

Holmberg, T., Jonsson, A., & Palm, F. (2019). *Death matters*. New York, NY: Springer.

Hong, J. S., Ryou, B., Wei, H. S., Allen-Meares, P., & Espelage, D. L. (2019). Identifying protective factors that potentially buffer the association between peer victimization and weapon-carrying behavior among US adolescents. *School Psychology International, 40*(4), 381–402.

Hoops, K., & Crifasi, C. (2019). Pediatric resident firearm-related anticipatory guidance: Why are we still not talking about guns? *Preventive Medicine, 124*, 29–32.

Hooyman, N. R., & Kramer, B. J. (2006). *Living through loss: Interventions across the life span*. New York, NY: Columbia University Press.

Horn, A. (2019, May 2). Louis D. Brown Peace Institute turns 25, with a call to broaden its message of healing. *The Boston Globe*. https://www.bostonglobe.com/metro/2019/05/02/louis-brown-peace-institute-turns-with-call-broaden-its-message-healing/eo6Dov2KrTcTAz4Dr4mNUI/story.html

Hourigan, K. L. (2019a). Forgiving the unforgivable: An exploration of contradictions between forgiveness-related feeling rules and lived experience of forgiveness of extreme harm. *Humanity & Society, 43*(3), 270–294.

Hourigan, K. L. (2019b). Narrative victimology: Speaker, audience, timing. In J. Fleetwood, L. Presser, S. Sandberg, & T. Ugelvik (Eds.), *The Emerald handbook of narrative criminology* (pp. 259–277). Bingley, UK: Emerald.

House, S. (2018). Addressing gun violence in the United States. *Gettysburg Social Sciences Review, 2*(2), Article 6.

Hristova, K. (2017). What is the financial impact of gun violence & mass shootings in the US? *Finance Monthly*. https://www.finance-monthly.com/2017/10/what-is-the-financial-impact-of-gun-violence-mass-shootings-in-the-us/

Huebner, B. M., Martin, K., Moule, R. K., Jr., Pyrooz, D., & Decker, S. H. (2016). Dangerous places: Gang members and neighborhood levels of gun assault. *Justice Quarterly, 33*(5), 836–862.

Huerta, A. H. (2018). Educational persistence in the face of violence: Narratives of resilient Latino male youth. *Boyhood Studies, 11*(2), 94–113.

Hureau, D. M., & Braga, A. A. (2018). The trade in tools: The market for illicit guns in high-risk networks. *Criminology, 56*(3), 510–545.

Hurtado, A. (2018). Justice forged on the bodies of children of color: Lessons of compassion from the Trayvon Martin case. *Journal of Humanistic Psychology.* Online. https://journals.sagepub.com/doi/full/10.1177/0022167818770321

Husak, D. (2019). Why Gun Control is So Hard. *Criminal Justice Ethics, 38*(1), 55–64.

Hutchison, E. D. (2018). *Dimensions of human behavior: Person and environment.* Thousand Oaks, CA: Sage Publications.

Ignatiadis, I. A., Mavrogenis, A. F., Igoumenou, V. G., Polyzois, V. D., Tsiampa, V. A., Arapoglou, D. K., & Spyridonos, S. (2019). Gunshot and blast injuries of the extremities: A review of 45 cases. *European Journal of Orthopaedic Surgery & Traumatology, 29*(2), 295–305.

Ingraham, C. (2018, June 19). There are more guns than people in the United States, according to a new study of global firearm ownership. *The Washington Post.* https://www.washingtonpost.com/news/wonk/wp/2018/06/19/there-are-more-guns-than-people-in-the-united-states-according-to-a-new-study-of-global-firearm-ownership/?utm_term=.84067a7f96e1

Irvin-Erickson, Y., Bai, B., Gurvis, A., & Mohr, E. (2016). *The effect of gun violence on local economies.* Washington, DC: Urban Institute.

"It takes the hood to heal the hood": Tackling the trauma of gun violence. (2019, December 9). *The Guardian.* https://www.theguardian.com/us-news/2019/dec/09/gun-violence-richmond-bay-area-healing

Jacobs, B. (2017). *Robbing drug dealers: Violence beyond the law.* New York, NY: Routledge.

Jacoby, S. F., Richmond, T. S., Holena, D. N., & Kaufman, E. J. (2018). A safe haven for the injured? Urban trauma care at the intersection of healthcare, law enforcement, and race. *Social Science & Medicine, 199,* 115–122.

Jaffe, S. (2018). Gun violence research in the USA: The CDC's impasse. *The Lancet, 391*(10139), 2487–2488.

Jäggi, L., & Kliewer, W. (2016). "Cause that's the only skills in school you need." A qualitative analysis of revenge goals in poor urban youth. *Journal of Adolescent Research, 31*(1), 32–58.

Jain, S., Cohen, A. K., Kawashima-Ginsberg, K., Duarte, C. D. P., & Pope, A. (2019). Civic engagement among youth exposed to community violence: Directions for research and practice. *Journal of Youth Development, 14*(1), 24–47.

Jannetta, J. (2019). *Responding to homicide and shooting scenes* (Doctoral dissertation). Urban Institute, Washington, DC.

Jasperse, N., Grigorian, A., Delaplain, P., Jutric, Z., Schubl, S. D., Kuza, C. M., & Nahmias, J. (2020). Predictors of discharge against medical advice in adult trauma patients. *The Surgeon, 18*(1), 12–18.

Jay, J., Miratrix, L. W., Branas, C. C., Zimmerman, M. A., & Hemenway, D. (2019). Urban building demolitions, firearm violence and drug crime. *Journal of behavioral medicine, 42*(4), 626–634.

Jeffries, S. R., Myers, D. L., Kringen, J. A., & Schack, R. (2019). Evaluating Project Safe Neighborhoods in Connecticut: a Youth Opportunity Initiative. *Crime Prevention and Community Safety, 21*(4), 325–345.

Jehan, F., Pandit, V., O'Keeffe, T., Azim, A., Jain, A., Tai, S. A., . . . Joseph, B. (2018). The burden of firearm violence in the United States: Stricter laws result in safer states. *Journal of Injury and Violence Research, 10*(1), 11–16.

Jenkins, E., McGuinness, L., Haines-Saah, R., Andres, C., Ziemann, M. J., Morris, J., & Waddell, C. (2020). Equipping youth for meaningful policy engagement: An environmental scan. *Health Promotion International, 35*(4), 852–865.

Jenkins, E. J. (2002). Black women and community violence: Trauma, grief, and coping. *Women & Therapy, 25*(3–4), 29–44.

Jennings-Bey, T., Lane, S. D., Rubinstein, R. A., Bergen-Cico, D., Haygood-El, A., Hudson, H., . . . Fowler, F. L. (2015). The trauma response team: a community intervention for gang violence. *Journal of Urban Health, 92*(5), 947–954.

Jennissen, C. A., Evans, E. M., Karsjens, A. A., & Denning, G. M. (2019). Social workers' determination of when children's access or potential access to loaded firearms constitutes child neglect. *Injury Epidemiology, 6*(1), 29. doi:10.1186/s40621-019-0202-2.

Jiang, T., Webster, J. L., Robinson, A., Kassam-Adams, N., & Richmond, T. S. (2018). Emotional responses to unintentional and intentional traumatic injuries among urban black men: A qualitative study. *Injury, 49*(5), 983–989.

Jiang, Y., Ranney, M. L., Sullivan, B., Hilliard, D., Viner-Brown, S., & Alexander-Scott, N. (2019). Can statewide emergency department, hospital discharge, and violent death reporting system data be used to monitor burden of firearm-related injury and death in Rhode Island? *Journal of Public Health Management and Practice, 25*(2), 137–146.

Jocson, R. M., Alers-Rojas, F., Ceballo, R., & Arkin, M. (2020). Religion and spirituality: Benefits for Latino adolescents exposed to community violence. *Youth & Society, 52*(3), 349–376.

Joe, J. R., Shillingford-Butler, M., & Oh, S. (2019). The experiences of African American mothers raising sons in the context of #BlackLivesMatter. *Professional Counselor, 9*(1), 67–79.

Johnson, A. E., & Fisher, E. J. (2019). "But, I forgive you?": Mother Emanuel, Black pain and the rhetoric of forgiveness. *Journal of Communication & Religion, 42*(1), 5–19.

Johnson, L. T. (2019). Modeling urban neighborhood violence: The systemic model and variable effects of social structure. *Urban Affairs Review*. In press.

Johnson, N. J. (2016). Us v. Them: Remnants of urban war zones. *Penn GSE Perspectives on Urban Education, 13*(1), 49–55.

Joint Economic Committee Democrats. (2017). *America can't afford gun violence*. Washington, DC: Author. https://www.jec.senate.gov/public/_cache/files/a8c89469-30a1-4b88-b3f5-0c5e54ad5df0/economic-impact-of-gun-violence-final.pdf

Jones, N. (2018). *The chosen ones: Black men and the politics of redemption* (Vol. 6). Berkeley, CA: University of California Press.

Jones-Eversley, S. D., Rice, J., Adedoyin, A. C., & James-Townes, L. (2020). Premature deaths of young Black males in the United States. *Journal of Black Studies, 51*(3), 251–272.

Jordan, M., & Oppel, R. A., Jr. (2020, May 8). In some states, an alarming disparity infection rates. *The New York Times*, p. A12.

Jorgensen, L. M. (2018). Forgiveness after Charleston: The ethics of an unlikely act. *The Good Society, 26*(2–3), 338–353.

Juan, S. C., & Hemenway, D. (2017). From depression to youth school gun carrying in America: Social connectedness may help break the link. *Cogent Social Sciences, 3*(1), 1314877.

Juarez, P. D. (2019). Screening for violent tendencies in adolescents. In V. Morelli (Ed.), *Adolescent health screening: An update in the age of big data* (pp. 115–134). Denver, CO: Elsevier.

Jumarali, S. N., Mandiyan, D., & Javdani, S. (2019). Centering justice: Transforming paradigms of approach, design and implementation. *Journal of Prevention & Intervention in the Community, 47*(2), 171–178.

Justice Policy Center. (2016, April). *Engaging communities in reducing gun violence. A road map for safer communities.* Washington, DC: Urban Institute.

Justice Policy Center. (2019, January). *Procedural justice in homicide and shooting scene response* (Doctoral dissertation). Urban Institute, Washington, DC.

Kagawa, R. M., Gary, D. S., Wintemute, G. J., Rudolph, K. E., Pear, V. A., Keyes, K., & Cerdá, M. (2019). Psychiatric disorders and gun carrying among adolescents in the United States. *The Journal of Pediatrics, 209,* 198–203.

Kalesan, B., Villarreal, M. D., Keyes, K. M., & Galea, S. (2016). Gun ownership and social gun culture. *Injury Prevention, 22*(3), 216–220.

Kalesan, B., Weinberg, J., & Galea, S. (2016). Gun violence in Americans' social network during their lifetime. *Preventive Medicine, 93,* 53–56.

Kalesan, B., Zuo, Y., Xuan, Z., Siegel, M. B., Fagan, J., Branas, C., & Galea, S. (2018). A multi-decade joinpoint analysis of firearm injury severity. *Trauma Surgery & Acute Care Open, 3*(1), e000139.

Kang, D., & Swaroop, M. (2019). Community-based approach to trauma and violence: guns, germs, and bystanders. *JAMA Surgery, 154*(3), 196–197.

Kao, A. M., Schlosser, K. A., Arnold, M. R., Kasten, K. R., Colavita, P. D., Davis, B. R., . . . Heniford, B. T. (2019). Trauma recidivism and mortality following violent injuries in young adults. *Journal of Surgical Research, 237,* 140–147.

Kaplan, M., & Kerby, S. (2013, January 17). The top ten reasons why communities-of-color should care about stricter gun violence prevention laws. *Center for American Progress.* https://www.americanprogress.org/issues/race/news/2013/01/17/49885/top-10-reasons-why-communities-of-color-should-care-about-stricter-gun-violence-prevention-laws/

Katz, A. H. (1981). Self-help and mutual aid: An emerging social movement? *Annual Review of Sociology, 7*(1), 129–155.

Katz, A. H. (1993). *Self-help in America: A social movement perspective.* New York, NY: Twayne.

Kaufman, E. (2020, April 1). Please, stop shooting, we need the beds. *The New York Times.* https://www.nytimes.com/2020/04/01/opinion/covid-gun-violence-hospitals.html

Kazemi, D. M., Jacobs, D. G., Portwood, S. G., Veach, L., Zhou, W., & Hurley, M. J. (2017). Trauma center youth violence screening and brief interventions: A multisite pilot feasibility study. *Violence and Victims, 32*(2), 251–264.

Keil, S., Beardslee, J., Schubert, C., Mulvey, E., & Pardini, D. (2020). Perceived gun access and gun carrying among male adolescent offenders. *Youth Violence and Juvenile Justice, 18*(2), 179–195.

Keith, P. E. (2018). Community policing is essential to effectively addressing violent crime. *US Attorneys Bulletin, 66*, 141.

Kellaher, L., & Worpole, K. (2016). Bringing the dead back home: Urban public spaces as sites for new patterns of mourning and memorialisation. In J. D. Sidaway (Ed.), *Deathscapes* (pp. 179–198). New York, NY: Routledge.

Kellermann, A. L., & Rivara, F. P. (2013). Silencing the science on gun research. *JAMA, 309*(6), 549–550.

Kemal, S., Sheehan, K., & Feinglass, J. (2018). Gun carrying among freshmen and sophomores in Chicago, New York City and Los Angeles public schools: The Youth Risk Behavior Survey, 2007–2013. *Injury Epidemiology, 5*(1), 12. https://link.springer.com/content/pdf/10.1186/s40621-018-0143-1.pdf.

Kennedy, D. M. (2019). Policing and the lessons of focused deterrence. In D. Weisburd & A. A. Braga (Eds.), *Police innovation: Contrasting perspectives* (pp. 205–226). New York, NY: Cambridge University Press.

Kennedy, T. M., & Ceballo, R. (2016). Emotionally numb: Desensitization to community violence exposure among urban youth. *Developmental Psychology, 52*(5), 778–789.

Kent, A. J., Sakran, J. V., Efron, D. T., Haider, A. H., Cornwell, E. E., III, Haut, E. R., & Cerdá, M. (2017). Understanding increased mortality after gunshot injury/Cook et al. respond. *American Journal of Public Health, 107*(12), E22–E23.

Kerrison, E. M., Cobbina, J., & Bender, K. (2018). "Your pants won't save you": Why Black youth challenge race-based police surveillance and the demands of Black respectability politics. *Race and Justice, 8*(1), 7–26.

Kessler, M. (2015, June 24). "I can tell you that I have been to more funerals that are gun-related than I've been to graduations." *The Trace*. https://www.thetrace.org/2015/06/i-can-tell-you-ive-been-to-more-funerals-that-are-gun-related-than-ive-been-to-graduations/

Khubchandani, J., & Price, J. H. (2018). Violent behaviors, weapon carrying, and firearm homicide trends in African American adolescents, 2001–2015. *Journal of Community Health, 43*(5), 947–955.

Killen, K. (2019). "Can you hear me now?" Race, motherhood, and the politics of being heard. *Politics & Gender, 15*(4), 623–644.

Kirk, M. (2019, March 4). A public space that commemorates victims of gun violence. *CityLab*. https://www.citylab.com/design/2019/03/healing-gardens-gun-violence-memorial-park-new-haven-svigals/583963/

Kim, D. (2019). Social determinants of health in relation to firearm-related homicides in the United States: A nationwide multilevel cross-sectional study. *PLoS Medicine, 16*(12), e1002978.

Kleck, G. (2017a). *Targeting guns: Firearms and their control*. New York, NY: Routledge.

Kleck, G. (2017b). *Point blank: Guns and violence in America*. New York, NY: Routledge.

Kleck, G. (2018, November 13). Interstate gun movement is almost entirely due to migration, not gun trafficking. *SSRN*. https://papers.ssrn.com/sol3/papers.cfm?abstract_id=3294297

Kliewer, W., Robins, J. L., & Borre, A. (2019). Community violence exposure, sleep disruption, and insulin resistance in low-income urban adolescents. *International Journal of Behavioral Medicine, 46*, 437–442.

Klofas, J., Altheimer, I., & Petitti, N. (2019). *Retaliatory violent disputes*. Phoenix, AZ: Arizona State University Watts College.

Knoll, C. (2019, November 1). A boy and his dream crumble on a Queens basketball court. *The New York Times*, pp. A1, A24.

Kochel, T. R. (2018). Applying police legitimacy, cooperation, and collective security hypotheses to explain collective efficacy and violence across neighbourhoods. *International Journal of Comparative and Applied Criminal Justice, 42*(4), 253–272.

Kochel, T. R., & Weisburd, D. (2017). Assessing community consequences of implementing hot spots policing in residential areas: Findings from a randomized field trial. *Journal of Experimental Criminology, 13*(2), 143–170.

Koepke, D. J., Thomas, D., & Manning, A. (2019). Fatal encounters. *Research in Social Sciences and Technology, 4*(1), 30–50.

Kondo, M. C., Andreyeva, E., South, E. C., MacDonald, J. M., & Branas, C. C. (2018). Neighborhood interventions to reduce violence. *Annual Review of Public Health, 39*, 253–271.

Konstam, M. A., & Konstam, A. D. (2019). Gun violence and cardiovascular health: We need to know. *Circulation, 139*(22), 2499–2501.

Koper, C. S., Johnson, W. D., Nichols, J. L., Ayers, A., & Mullins, N. (2018). Criminal use of assault weapons and high-capacity semiautomatic firearms: An updated examination of local and national sources. *Journal of Urban Health, 95*(3), 313–321.

Koper, C. S., Johnson, W. D., Stesin, K., & Egge, J. (2019). Gunshot victimisations resulting from high-volume gunfire incidents in Minneapolis: Findings and policy implications. *Injury Prevention, 25*(Suppl. 1), i9–i11.

Kotlowitz, A. (2019). *An American summer: Love and death in Chicago*. New York, NY: Talese.

Krantz, L. (2019, July 14). Youth put gun politics on agenda for 2020: Activists across nation push Democrats to address issue. *Boston Sunday Globe*, pp. A1, A8.

Kuehn, B. (2018). Suicide: The leading cause of violent death. *JAMA, 319*(10), 973.

Kuehn, B. M. (2019). Growing evidence linking violence, trauma to heart disease. *Circulation, 139*(7). 981–982.

Kukharskyy, B., & Seiffert, S. (2017). *Gun violence in the US: Correlates and causes*. Stuttgart, Germany: University of Hohenheim. http://opus.uni-hohenheim.de/volltexte/2017/1333/pdf/dp_04_2017_online.pdf

Kwak, H., Dierenfeldt, R., & McNeeley, S. (2019). The code of the street and cooperation with the police: Do codes of violence, procedural injustice, and police ineffectiveness discourage reporting violent victimization to the police? *Journal of Criminal Justice, 60*, 25–34.

Lacroix, M., & Pircher Verdorfer, A. (2017). Can servant leaders fuel the leadership fire? The relationship between servant leadership and followers' leadership avoidance. *Administrative Sciences, 7*(1), 6. http://www.mdpi.com/2076-3387/7/1/6/html

Lane, S. D., Rubinstein, R. A., Bergen-Cico, D., Jennings-Bey, T., Fish, L. S., Larsen, D. A., . . . Robinson, J. A. (2017). Neighborhood trauma due to violence: A multilevel analysis. *Journal of Health Care for the Poor and Underserved, 28*(1), 446–462.

Lane, S. D., Rubinstein, R. A., Schimpff, T. R., Keefe, R. H., Jennings-Bey, T., Leed, S. R., . . . Satterly, L. B. (2019). Bringing in the community: A university-community endeavor to teach marital and family therapy students about community-based violence and trauma. *Contemporary Family Therapy, 41*(2), 147–156.

Lanyl, B., Gonzalez, R., & Wilson, M. (2018). Tools for social workers dealing with gun violence. *Social Justice Brief.* https://www.socialworkers.org/LinkClick.aspx?fileticket =YvR20CC6ORU%3D&portalid=0

Larsen, D. A., Lane, S., Jennings-Bey, T., Haygood-El, A., Brundage, K., & Rubinstein, R. A. (2017). Spatio-temporal patterns of gun violence in Syracuse, New York 2009–2015. *PloS One, 12*(3), e0173001.

Latzer, B. (2018). Subcultures of violence and African American crime rates. *Journal of Criminal Justice, 54*, 41–49.

Latzer, B. (2019a). The futility of gun control as crime control. *Academic Questions, 32*(2), 288–292.

Latzer, B. (2019b, December 5). The need to discuss Black on Black crime. *National Review.* https://www.nationalreview.com/magazine/2019/12/22/the-need-to-discuss-black-on-black-crime/

Lauger, T. R. (2014). Violent stories: Personal narratives, street socialization, and the negotiation of street culture among street-oriented youth. *Criminal Justice Review, 39*(2), 182–200.

Lauritsen, J. L., & Lentz, T. S. (2019). National and local trends in serious violence, firearm victimization, and homicide. *Homicide Studies, 23*(3), 243–261.

Lavoie, F., & Gidron, B. (2014). *Self-help and mutual aid groups: International and multicultural perspectives.* New York, NY: Routledge.

Lawson, E. S. (2018). Bereaved Black mothers and maternal activism in the racial state. *Feminist Studies, 44*(3), 713–735.

Leasy, M., O'Gurek, D. T., & Savoy, M. L. (2019). Unlocking clues to current health in past history: Childhood trauma and healing. *Family Practice Management, 26*(2), 5–10.

Lee, B. X. (2019). *Violence: An interdisciplinary approach to causes, consequences, and cures.* New York, NY: Wiley-Blackwell.

Lee, L. K., & Schaechter, J. (2019). No silver bullet: Firearm laws and pediatric death prevention. *Pediatrics, 144*(2), e20191300.

Lee, V. J., Meloche, A., Grant, A., Neuman, D., & Tecce DeCarlo, M. J. (2019). "My thoughts on gun violence": An urban adolescent's display of agency and multimodal literacies. *Journal of Adolescent & Adult Literacy. 63*(2), 157–167.

Leech, T. G., Irby-Shasanmi, A., & Sow, H. (2019). Recruiting and retaining young urban Black men in a study of violence: Procedures used and lessons learned. *Field Methods, 31*(2), 131–149.

Lees, A. (2016). Roles of urban indigenous community members in collaborative field-based teacher preparation. *Journal of Teacher Education, 67*(5), 363–378.

Legault, R. L., Hendrix, N., & Lizotte, A. J. (2019). Caught in a crossfire: Legal and illegal gun ownership in America. In M. Krohn, N. Hendrix, G. Penly Hall, & A. Lizotte (Eds.), *Handbook on crime and deviance* (pp. 533–554). New York, NY: Springer.

Lei, C., & Turner, T. (2019, January 14). "They still take pictures with them as if the person never passed." *NPR.* https://www.npr.org/sections/pictureshow/2018/07/20/630799667/life-size-cutouts-help-extend-the-relationship-with-lost-loved-ones-in-new-orlea

Leovy, J. (2015). *Ghettoside: A true story of murder in America.* New York, NY: Spiegel & Grau.

Leventhal, J. M., Gaither, J. R., & Sege, R. (2014). Hospitalizations due to firearm injuries in children and adolescents. *Pediatrics, 133*(2): 219–225.

Levine, R. S., Salemi, J. L., de Grubb, M. C. M., Gittner, L. S., Langston, M. A., Husaini, B. A., . . . Hennekens, C. H. (2017). Infant deaths and mortality from gun violence: Causal or casual? *Journal of the National Medical Association, 109*(4), 246–251.

Levine, S. (2019, December 7). America's gun culture: Infatuation, fetish, or curse. *Psychology Today.* https://www.psychologytoday.com/us/blog/our-emotional-footprint/201912/americas-gun-culture-infatuation-fetish-or-curse

Like, T. Z., & Cobbina, J. E. (2019). Emotional girls and rational boys: The gendering of violence among urban, African American youth. *Crime & Delinquency, 65*(3), 295–321.

Lizotte, A. J., & Hendrix, N. (2019). Shoot first and ask questions later: The interplay of social science research and firearms policy and use. *American Journal of Criminal Justice, 44*, 609–627.

Loeffler, C., & Flaxman, S. (2018). Is gun violence contagious? A spatiotemporal test. *Journal of Quantitative Criminology, 34*(4), 999–1017.

LoFaso, C. A. (2020). Solving homicides: The influence of neighborhood characteristics and investigator caseload. *Criminal Justice Review, 45*(1), 84–103.

Logan, J. E., Vagi, K. J., & Gorman-Smith, D. (2016). Characteristics of youth with combined histories of violent behavior, suicidal ideation or behavior, and gun-carrying. *Crisis, 37*, 402–414.

Logan, S. (Ed.). (2018). *The Black family: Strengths, self-help, and positive change.* New York, NY: Routledge.

Logan, T. (2020, May 10). 138 more die from COVID-19. *The Boston Globe,* pp. B1, B4.

Logan-Greene, P., Sperlich, M., & Finucane, A. (2018). Social work practice and gun safety in the United States. *Advances in Social Work, 18*(4), 1165–1186.

Loggini, A., Vasenina, V. I., Mansour, A., Das, P., Horowitz, P. M., Goldenberg, F. D., . . . Lazaridis, C. (2020, April). Management of civilians with penetrating brain injury: A systematic review. *Journal of Critical Care, 56*, 159–166.

Lotan, G. T. (2019, October 20). Hard to trace, guns from Web raise fears. *The Boston Globe,* pp. A1, A19.

Lou, J. (2018, December 6). Boston homicides rate surpasses previous years *The Daily Free Press.* https://dailyfreepress.com/blog/2018/12/06/boston-homicide-rate-surpasses-previous-years/

Loughran, T. A., Reid, J. A., Collins, M. E., & Mulvey, E. P. (2016). Effect of gun carrying on perceptions of risk among adolescent offenders. *American Journal of Public Health, 106*(2), 350–352.

Lowery, W., Kelly, K., & Rich, S. (2018a, July 25). Murder with impunity: Unequal justice. *Washington Post.* https://www.washingtonpost.com/graphics/2018/investigations/black-homicides-arrests/?utm_term=.9b1439738ac7

Lowery, W., Kelly, K., & Rich, S. (2018b, July 25). Killings of Black people lead to arrests less often than when victims are white. *The Washington Post.* https://www.

macombdaily.com/news/nation-world-news/killings-of-black-people-lead-to-arrests-less-often-than/article_db68ecdb-d1aa-5536-b2e8-5e89de23b6e7.html

Lu, Y., & Temple, J. R. (2020). Gun access, ownership, gun-related experiences, and substance use in young adults: A latent class analysis. *The American Journal of Drug and Alcohol Abuse*, 1–7.

Ludwig, J. (2019). *Underground gun markets in Chicago.* National Institute of Justice, Washington, D. C.

Lum, C., Olaghere, A., Koper, C. S., & Wu, X. (2016). *Project Safe Neighborhoods youth violence and homicide prevention initiative in Washington, DC.* Washington, DC: George Mason University Center for Evidence-Based Crime Policy Department of Criminology, Law and Society.

Lurie, S. (2019, February 25). There is no such thing as a dangerous neighborhood. *CityLab.* https://www.citylab.com/perspective/2019/02/broken-windows-theory-policing-urban-violence-crime-data/583030/

Macias, M., Jr. (2019, August 22). Booker: Gun conversation must include hardest hit communities. *Courthouse News Service.* https://www.courthousenews.com/booker-gun-conversation-must-include-hardest-hit-communities/

Madhavan, S., Taylor, J. S., Chandler, J. M., Staudenmayer, K. L., & Chao, S. D. (2019). Firearm legislation stringency and firearm-related fatalities among children in the US. *Journal of the American College of Surgeons, 229*(2), 150–157.

Maghami, S., Hendrix, C., Matecki, M., Mahendran, K., Amdur, R., Mitchell, R., . . . Sarani, B. (2019). Comparison of the causes of death and wounding patterns in urban firearm-related violence and civilian public mass shooting events. *The Journal of Trauma and Acute Care Surgery.* Online. https://scholar.google.com/scholar?hl=en&as_sdt=0%2C22&q=Maghami%2C+S.%2C+Hendrix%2C+C.%2C+Matecki%2C+M.%2C+Mahendran%2C+K.%2C+Amdur%2C+R.%2C+Mitchell%2C%2C+R.%2C+...+%26++%09Sarani%2C+B.+%282019%29.+Comparison+of+the+Causes+of+Death+and+Wounding+Patterns+in++%09Urban+Firearm-Related+Violence+and+Civilian+Public+Mass+Shooting+Events.+The++%09journal+of+trauma+and+acute+care+surgery.+&btnG=

Maguire, E. R., Oakley, M. T., & Corsaro, N. (2018). *Evaluating cure violence in Trinidad and Tobago.* Washington, DC: Inter-American Development Bank.

Maguire, E. R., Telep, C. W., & Abt, T. (2018). The effectiveness of street outreach worker programs for reducing violence: A systematic review. *CampbellCollaboration.* https://campbellcollaboration.org/media/k2/attachments/CJCG_Maquire_Title.pdf

Main, F. (2018, February 19). Murder "clearance" rate in Chicago hit new low in 2017. *Chicago Sun Times.* https://chicago.suntimes.com/2018/2/9/18316995/murder-clearance-rate-in-chicago-hit-new-low-in-2017

Makarios, M. D., & Pratt, T. C. (2012). The effectiveness of policies and programs that attempt to reduce firearm violence: A meta-analysis. *Crime & Delinquency, 58*(2), 222–244.

Maki, J. (2015). *Male survivors of urban violence and trauma.* Chicago, IL: Illinois Criminal Justice Information Authority.

Mankowski, E. S. (2014). Collaborative research with a mutual help organization for men addressing masculinities: Cross cutting issues and themes. *International Journal of Self-Help & Self-Care, 8*(1), 33–40.

Manley, N. R., Croce, M. A., Fischer, P. E., Crowe, D. E., Goines, J. H., Sharpe, J. P., . . . Magnotti, L. J. (2019). Evolution of firearm violence over 20 years: Integrating law enforcement and clinical data. *Journal of the American College of Surgeons*, 228(4), 427–434.

Manojlović, A., Vnuk, D., Bottegaro, N. B., & Capak, H. (2017, January). Comparison of dogs and cats gunshot injuries in urban areas. In *7th International Congress "Veterinary Science and Profession."* Zagreb, Croatia. https://www.bib.irb.hr/923320?rad=923320

Marano, D. (2015). *Juvenile offenders and guns: Voices behind gun violence*. New York, NY: Springer.

Margry, P. J., & Sanchez-Carretero, C. (2011). Rethinking memorialization: The concept of grassroots memorials. In P. J. Margry & C. Sanchez-Carretero (Eds.), *Grassroots memorials: The politics of memorializing traumatic death* (pp. 1–48). New York, NY: Beeghahn Books.

Marrow, A. (2020, April 3). Businesses booming for US gun stores—An essential service in COVID-19 America. *The Globe and Mail*. https://www.theglobeandmail.com/world/us-politics/article-business-steady-for-us-gun-stores-an-essential-service-in-covid-1/

Masiakos, P. T., & Warshaw, A. L. (2017). Stopping the bleeding is not enough. *Annals of Surgery*, 265(1), 37–38.

Mastrocinque, J., & Cerceo, E. (2019). A trauma-informed care approach to health-care providers' interactions with families and friends of homicide victims. In D. M. Griffith, M. A. Bruce, & R. J. Thorpe Jr. (Eds.), *Men's health equity: A handbook* (pp. 433–448). New York, NY: Routledge.

Mathews, D. (2018, November 14). Living in a house with a gun increases your odds of death. *Vox*. https://www.vox.com/2015/10/1/18000520/gun-risk-death

Matoba, N., Reina, M., Prachand, N., Davis, M. M., & Collins, J. W. (2019). Neighborhood gun violence and birth outcomes in Chicago. *Maternal and Child Health Journal*, 23, 1251–1259.

Matti, J., & Ross, A. (2016). Does crime affect entrepreneurship? A discussion of the current literature. *Journal of Entrepreneurship and Public Policy*, 5(3), 254–272.

Matzat, J., & Estorff, A. (2018). On support for self help groups at the local level. In S. Humble & J. Unell (Eds.), *Self help in health and social welfare* (pp. 93–98). New York, NY: Routledge.

Mbilishaka, A. M., Mitchell, D. S., & Conyers, C. (2020). Grandma's hands: Memories of hair styling interaction with African American grandmothers. *Journal of Intergenerational Relationships*, 18(2), 139–155.

McBride, E. (2018, November 25). America's gun business is $28 billion. The gun violence business is bigger. *Forbes Magazine*. https://www.forbes.com/sites/elizabethmacbride/2018/11/25/americas-gun-business-is-28b-the-gun-violence-business-is-bigger/#6e095eeb3ae8

McCann, A. (2019, April 9). States most dependent on gun industry. *WalleThub*. https://wallethub.com/edu/states-most-dependent-on-the-gun-industry/18719/

McClatchey, I. S., King, S., & Domby, E. (2019). From grieving to giving: When former bereavement campers return as volunteers. *OMEGA-Journal of Death and Dying*, In press.

McClintock, K. A. (2019). *When trauma wounds: Pathways to healing and hope* (Vol. 7). Minneapolis, MN: Fortress Press.

McCoy, H. (2020, April 20). Gun violence in urban communities must get the same attention as suburban school shootings. *The Hill.* https://thehill.com/opinion/civil-rights/490669-gun-violence-in-urban-communities-must-get-the-same-attention-as-white

McCrea, K. T., Richards, M., Quimby, D., Scott, D., Davis, L., Hart, S., . . . Hopson, S. (2019). Understanding violence and developing resilience with African American youth in high-poverty, high-crime communities. *Children and Youth Services Review, 99*, 296–307.

McGarrell, E. F., Perez, H., Carter, R., & Daffron, H., (2018). Project Safe Neighborhoods (PSN). US Dept of Justice, . . . & United States of America. Research Foundation. Washington, D.C.

McGee, Z., Alexander, C., Cunningham, K., Hamilton, C., & James, C. (2019). Assessing the linkage between exposure to violence and victimization, coping, and adjustment among urban youth: findings from a research study on adolescents. *Children, 6*(3), 36. Online. https://www.mdpi.com/2227-9067/6/3/36

McGee, Z. T., Logan, K., Samuel, J., & Nunn, T. (2017). A multivariate analysis of gun violence among urban youth: The impact of direct victimization, indirect victimization, and victimization among peers. *Cogent Social Sciences, 3*(1), 1328772.

McLean, R., Robinson, G., & Densley, J. (2018). The rise of drug dealing in the life of the North American street gang. *Societies, 8*(3), 90–99.

McLively, M. (2019, April 19). How Oakland cut homicides in half. Giffords Law Center to Prevent Gun Violence. https://giffords.org/2019/04/how-oakland-cut-homicides-in-half/

McNeil, A. S. (2017). *The double grief phenomenon: African-American women who lost sons to gun violence.* (Dissertation). Eastern University, St. Davids, PA.

Meichenbaum, D. (2017). Bolstering resilience. The evolution of cognitive behavior therapy: A personal and professional journey with Don Meichenbaum. https://www.melissainstitute.org/documents/Bolstering_Resilience.pdf

Menger, R., Kalakoti, P., Hanif, R., Ahmed, O., Nanda, A., & Guthikonda, B. (2017). A political case of penetrating cranial trauma: The injury of James Scott Brady. *Neurosurgery, 81*(3), 545–551.

Mervosh, S. (2019, July 23). Gun ownership tied to domestic homicides, not other killings, study finds. *The New York Times,* p. A16.

Metz, T. (2019). Making sense of survivor's guilt: How to justify it with an African ethic. In G. Hull (Ed.), *Debating African philosophy: Perspectives on identity, decolonial ethics and comparative philosophy* (pp. 149–163). New York, NY: Routledge.

Metzl, J. (2018, October 2). Social science and the future of gun research. *Items: Insights From the Social Sciences.* https://items.ssrc.org/understanding-gun-violence/social-science-and-the-future-of-gun-research/

Metzl, J. M. (2019). What guns mean: The symbolic lives of firearms. *Palgrave Communications, 5*(1), 1–5.

Metzl, J. M., & MacLeish, K. T. (2015). Mental illness, mass shootings, and the politics of American firearms. *American Journal of Public Health, 105*(2), 240–249.

Michigan Medicine. (2019, August 1). How little we know: Experts document the lack of research on youth firearm injury: Review of 33 years' worth of medical studies reveals key areas for new research to explore. *Science Daily.* https://www.sciencedaily.com/releases/2019/08/190801142536.htm

Mikhail, J. N., & Nemeth, L. S. (2016). Trauma center based youth violence prevention programs: An integrative review. *Trauma, Violence, & Abuse, 17*(5), 500–519.

Mikhail, J. N., Nemeth, L. S., Mueller, M., Pope, C., & NeSmith, E. G. (2018). The social determinants of trauma: A trauma disparities scoping review and framework. *Journal of Trauma Nursing, 25*(5), 266–281.

Milam, A. J., Buggs, S. A., Furr-Holden, C. D. M., Leaf, P. J., Bradshaw, C. P., & Webster, D. (2016). Changes in attitudes toward guns and shootings following implementation of the Baltimore Safe Streets intervention. *Journal of Urban Health, 93*(4), 609–626.

Milam, A. J., Furr-Holden, C. D., Leaf, P., & Webster, D. (2018). Managing conflicts in urban communities: Youth attitudes regarding gun violence. *Journal of Interpersonal Violence, 33*(24), 3815–3828.

Miller-Graff, L., Howell, K. H., Scheid, C. R., & Schaefer, L. (2019). "Violence is everywhere": Childhood polyvictimization, perceptions of the prevalence of victimization, and posttraumatic stress symptoms. *Violence and Victims, 34*(2), 376–393.

Milliff, A. (2019). Facts before feelings: Theorizing emotional responses to violent trauma (MIT Political Science Department Research Paper No. 2019-06). Cambridge, MA: M.I.T. https://papers.ssrn.com/sol3/papers.cfm?abstract_id=3373188

Mirabile F., & Ness, D. (2019, May 15). What's the homicide capital of America? Murder rates in U. S. cities ranked. *The Trace.* https://www.thetrace.org/2018/04/highest-murder-rates-us-cities-list/

Mitchell, J. (2020). Peacebuilding through the visual arts. In J. Mitchell, G. Vincett, T. Hawksley, & H. Culbertson (Eds.), *Peacebuilding and the arts* (pp. 35–70). New York, NY: Palgrave Macmillan.

Mitchell, K. J., Jones, L. M., Turner, H. A., Beseler, C. L., Hamby, S., & Wade, R., Jr. (2019). Understanding the impact of seeing gun violence and hearing gunshots in public places: Findings from the Youth Firearm Risk and Safety Study. *Journal of Interpersonal Violence.* In press.

Mitchell, Y. T., & Bromfield, T. L. (2019, January 10). *Gun violence and the minority experiences.* St. Paul, MN: National Council on Family Relations.

Mitton, K. (2019). Public health and violence. *Critical Public Health, 29*(2), 135–137.

Mobasseri, S. (2019). Race, place, and crime: How violent crime events affect employment discrimination. *American Journal of Sociology, 125*(1), 63–104.

Mogni, B., & Maines, S. (2019). Homicide using an air weapon. *Clinical Practice and Cases in Emergency Medicine, 3*(3), 289–294.

Mohn, T. (2018, November 24). Does art have the power to heal after gun violence? One Florida town thinks so. *Forbes.* https://www.forbes.com/sites/tanyamohn/2018/11/24/does-art-have-the-power-to-heal-after-gun-violence-one-florida-town-thinks-so/#5c1ed49d3144

Moller, D. W. (Ed.). (2018). *Dying at the margins: Reflections on justice and healing for inner-city poor.* New York, NY: Oxford University Press.

Monteiro, L. H. A. (2020). More guns, less crime? A dynamical systems approach. *Applied Mathematics and Computation, 369*, 124804.

Morrison, C., Gross, B., Horst, M., Bupp, K., Rittenhouse, K., Harnish, C., . . . Rogers, F. B. (2015). Under fire: Gun violence is not just an urban problem. *Journal of Surgical Research, 199*(1), 190–196.

Morton, D. R. (2018). Improving police transparency and accountability in violent encounters with African Americans. *Journal of African American Studies, 22*(1), 125–138.

Moser, W. (2014, October 8). Q/A: Lawrence Ralph on injury and resilience in gangland Chicago. *Politics & City Life.* https://www.chicagomag.com/city-life/October-2014/Q-A-Laurence-Ralph-on-Injury-and-Resilience-in-Gangland-Chicago/

Motley, R., & Banks, A. (2018). Black males, trauma, and mental health service use: A systematic review. *Perspectives on Social Work: The Journal of the Doctoral Students of the University of Houston Graduate School of Social Work, 14*(1), 4–19.

Moyer, R., MacDonald, J. M., Ridgeway, G., & Branas, C. C. (2019). Effect of remediating blighted vacant land on shootings: A citywide cluster randomized trial. *American Journal of Public Health, 109*(1), 140–144.

Mueller, M. (2017). *Radical healing: Restoring hope in urban youth through afterschool programming.* Davis, CA: University of California, Davis.

Muggath, R. (2017, October 17). Gun violence hits all citizens with a heavy financial toll. *Guidepost.* https://www.pri.org/stories/2017-10-10/gun-violence-hits-all-citizens-heavy-financial-toll

Muller, H. A. (2019). *The role of attachment style among newcomer immigrant adolescents exposed to community violence* (Doctoral dissertation). Palo Alto University, Palo Alto, CA.

Mullings-Lawrence, S. (2017). "Silence is virtual": Youth violence, belonging, death and mourning. In K. Gildart, A. Gough-Yates, S. Lincoln, B. Osgerby, & L. Robinson (Eds.), *Youth culture and social change* (pp. 261–283). London, UK: Palgrave Macmillan.

Mullins, C. W., & Lee, S. (2020). "Like make up on a man": The gendered nature of gun norms. *Deviant Behavior, 41*(3), 294–310.

Munn-Giddings, C., Oka, T., Borkman, T., Chikoto, G. L., Matzat, J., & Montaño-Fraire, R. (2016). Self-help and mutual aid group volunteering. In D. H. Smith, R. A. Stebbins, & J. Grotz (Eds.), *The Palgrave handbook of volunteering, civic participation, nonprofit associations* (pp. 393–416). London, UK: Palgrave Macmillan.

Murphy, H. (2020, January 9). Officers suspended after boy mislabeled a gang member. *The New York Times*, p. A15.

Myers, K. (2019, August 6). Gun violence costs the United States $200 billion each year. *Yahoo Finance.* https://finance.yahoo.com/news/gun-violence-costs-the-united-states-200-billion-each-year-202527412.html

Nakamura, K., Tita, G., & Krackhardt, D. (2020). Violence in the "balance": A structural analysis of how rivals, allies, and third-parties shape inter-gang violence. *Global Crime, 21*(1), 3–27.

Narasimha, B. C., Anand, P., Ravish, K. S., Navya, S. S., & Ranganath, T. S. (2017). Role of self help groups in women empowerment and health. *International Journal of Community Medicine and Public Health, 3*(8), 2026–2028.

Neely, C. L. (2015). *You're dead—so what?: Media, police, and the invisibility of Black women as victims of homicide.* East Lansing, MI: Michigan State University Press.

Nelson, G., Ochocka, J., Griffin, K., & Lord, J. (1998). "Nothing about me, without me": Participatory action research with self-help/mutual aid organizations for psychiatric consumer/survivors. *American Journal of Community Psychology, 26*(6), 881–912.

Nelson, N. (2016, November 16). Moms against senseless killings: Unveiling the mask. *Chicago Rises.* https://chicagorises.org/moms-against-senseless-killings-unveiling-the-m-a-s-k/

Nettles, N. (2019, November 11). Where Chicago shootings go unchecked, owning a gun can feel like a necessity. *Trace.* https://www.thetrace.org/2019/11/gun-violence-chicago-self-protection-ownership/

Neville, F. G., Goodall, C. A., Gavine, A. J., Williams, D. J., & Donnelly, P. D. (2015). Public health, youth violence, and perpetrator well-being. *Peace and Conflict: Journal of Peace Psychology, 21*(3), 322–333.

Neuhauser, A. (2017, July 7). Cities spend more and more on police. Is it working? *US News and World Reports.* https://www.usnews.com/news/national-news/articles/2017-07-07/cities-spend-more-and-more-on-police-is-it-working

New York Times Editorial Board. (2015, December 4). End the gun epidemic in America. *New York Times.* https://www.nytimes.com/2015/12/05/opinion/end-the-gun-epidemic-in-america.html

Ngo, Q. M., Sigel, E., Moon, A., Stein, S. F., Massey, L. S., Rivara, F., . . . FACTS Consortium. (2019). State of the science: A scoping review of primary prevention of firearm injuries among children and adolescents. *Journal of Behavioral Medicine, 42*(4), 811–829.

Nickita, D. M. (2016). Taking action to reduce gun violence: It's just common sense. *Nursing Economics, 34*(1), 5–6.

Nishimoto, S. (2019). Insights in public health: "Youth Talk Back" leadership program promotes social change and improved community health in Hawai'i. *Hawai'i Journal of Health & Social Welfare, 78*(8), 270–273.

Nolan, T. (2019). *Perilous policing: Criminal justice in marginalized communities.* New York, NY: Routledge.

Norman, G. (2018, March 5). Shootings at Chicago's gang members' funerals getting "out of control," police say. *Fox News.* https://www.foxnews.com/us/shootings-at-chicago-gang-members-funerals-getting-out-of-control-police-say

Novich, M., & Hunt, G. (2018). Trust in police motivations during involuntary encounters: An examination of young gang members of colour. *Race and Justice, 8*(1), 51–70.

Nutt, M. (2019). *"Come here and see." Using PhotoVoice to understand youth perceptions of growing up with community violence* (Doctoral dissertation). Chicago School of Professional Psychology, Chicago, IL.

Nygaard, R. M., Marek, A. P., Daly, S. R., & Van Camp, J. M. (2018). Violent trauma recidivism: Does all violence escalate? *European Journal of Trauma and Emergency Surgery, 44*(6), 851–858.

O'Brien, D. T. (2019). The action is everywhere, but greater at more localized spatial scales: Comparing concentrations of crime across addresses, streets, and neighborhoods. *Journal of Research in Crime and Delinquency, 56*(3), 339–377.

O'Connell, M. (2019, June 4). Local nonprofit to dedicate garden honoring victims-survivors of gun violence. *ARLnow.* https://www.arlnow.com/2019/06/04/local-nonprofit-to-dedicate-garden-honoring-victims-survivors-of-gun-violence/

O'Kane, J. M. (2017). *Wicked deeds: Murder in America.* New York, NY: Routledge.

Oldfield, B. J., Tinney, B. J., & Dodington, J. M. (2018). Partnering with youth in community-based participatory research to address violence prevention. *Pediatric Research, 84*(2), 155–156.

Oliphant, S. N., Mouch, C. A., Rowhani-Rahbar, A., Hargarten, S., Jay, J., Hemenway, D., . . . FACTS Consortium. (2019). A scoping review of patterns, motives, and risk and protective factors for adolescent firearm carriage. *Journal of Behavioral Medicine, 42*(4), 763–810.

Olson, E. J., Hoofnagle, M., Kaufman, E. J., Schwab, C. W., Reilly, P. M., & Seamon, M. J. (2019). American firearm homicides: The impact of your neighbors. *Journal of Trauma and Acute Care Surgery, 86*(5), 797–802.

Olufajo, O. A., Zeineddin, A., Nonez, H., Okorie, N. C., De La Cruz, E., Cornwell, E. E., III, & Williams, M. (2020). Trends in firearm injuries among children and teenagers in the United States. *Journal of Surgical Research, 245*, 529–536.

Oppel, R. A., & Arango, T., Jr. (2019, July 31). There are loopholes in states' get-tough laws on guns: Other states. *The New York Times*, p. A24.

Oppel, R. A., & Hassan, A., Jr. (2019, August 14). Simple ways for abusers, felons and fugitives to buy a weapon. *The New York Times*, p. A14.

Ortiiz, A., & Zaveri, M. (2019, November 1). 7-year-old shot in Chicago while trick-or-treating. *The New York Times,* p. A22.

Owen, T. (2019, April 12). 4 people shot in "senseless violence" near Nipsey Russell's funeral possession. *Vice News.* https://news.vice.com/en_us/article/j5wx8b/4-people-shot-in-senseless-violence-near-nipsey-hussles-funeral-procession

Paessler-Chesterton, H. N., & Green, J. (2019). Death in the classroom: Violence in schools. In D. Capuzzi & D. R. Gross (Eds.), *Youth at risk: A prevention resource for counselors, teachers, and parents* (pp. 323–365). Philadelphia, PA: American Counseling Association.

Pallin, R., Spitzer, S. A., Ranney, M. L., Betz, M. E., & Wintemute, G. J. (2019). Preventing firearm-related death and injury. *Annals of Internal Medicine, 170*(11), ITC81–ITC96.

Papachristos, A. V., & Kirk, D. S. (2015). Changing the street dynamic. *Criminology & Public Policy, 14*(3), 525–558.

Papachristos, A. V., Wilderman, C., Roberto, E. (2015). Tragic, but not random: The social contagion of nonfatal gunshot injuries. *Social Science & Medicine, 125,* 139–150.

Parker, K., Horowitz, J. M., Igielnik, Oliphant, J. B., & Brown, A. (2017, June 22). *View of guns and gun violence.* Washington, DC: PEW Research Center.

Parsons, C., Thompson, M., Vargas, E. W., & Rocco, G. (2018). *America's youth under fire.* Washington, DC: Center for American Progress.

Patil, K., Kumar, G., Wankhede, A., Tekade, P., & Kaulaskar, S. (2019). Retrospective study of autopsied firearm fatalities over period of five years. *Medico-Legal Update*, *19*(1), 143–146.

Patton, D., Sodhi, A., Affinati, S., Lee, J., & Crandall, M. (2019). Post-discharge needs of victims of gun violence in Chicago: A qualitative study. *Journal of Interpersonal Violence*, *34*(1), 135–155.

Pavoni, A., & Tulumello, S. (2018). What is urban violence? *Progress in Human Geography*, *38*(6), 771–784.

Payne, Y. A., Hitchens, B. K., & Chambers, D. L. (2017, December). "Why I can't stand out in front of my house?": Street-identified Black youth and young adult's negative encounters with police. *Sociological Forum*, *32*(4), 874–895.

Payton, E., Thompson, A., Price, J., Sheu, J., & Dake, J. (2015). African American legislators' perceptions of firearm violence prevention legislation. *Journal of Community Health*, *40*(3), 439–447.

PBS Newshour. (2019, August 1). For Mothers/Men Against Senseless Killings, Chicago's violence strikes close to home. https://www.pbs.org/newshour/show/for-mothers-men-against-senseless-killings-chicagos-violence-strikes-close-to-home

Peetz, A. B., & Haider, A. (2018). Gun violence research and the profession of trauma surgery. *AMA Journal of Ethics*, *20*(5), 475–482.

Perez, J. (2019, February 15). Tackling gun violence as a community issue. National Institute of Justice. https://nij.ojp.gov/topics/articles/tackling-gun-violence-community-issue

Perkins, D. D., Zimmerman, M. A. (1995). Empowerment theory, research, and application. *American Journal of Community Psychology*, *23*, 569–590.

Peterson, J. (2018, August 25). "Not just a body": Funeral directors grapple with gun deaths. *AP*. https://www.apnews.com/7bb7ea3573bc409ca210c9c3a2864ddd

Peterson, N. A., Zimmerman, M. A. (2004). Beyond the individual: Toward a nomological network of organizational empowerment. *American Journal of Community Psychology*, *34*, 129–145.

Petrosino, A., Campie, P., Pace, J., Fronius, T., Guckenburg, S., Wiatrowski, M., & Rivera, L. (2015). Cross-sector, multi-agency interventions to address urban youth firearms violence: A rapid evidence assessment. *Aggression and Violent Behavior*, *22*, 87–96.

Petrosino, A., Turner, H., Hanson, T., Fronius, T., Campie, P., & Cooke, C. (2019). The impact of the Safe and Successful Youth Initiative (SSYI) on city-level youth crime victimization rates. *Journal of Multidisciplinary Evaluation*, *13*(29), 8–15.

Petty, J. K., Henry, M. C., Nance, M. L., & Ford, H. R. (2019). Firearm injuries and children: Position statement of the American Pediatric Surgical Association. *Journal of Pediatric Surgery*, *54*(7), 1269–1276.

Picchi, (2017, October 17). Can the US afford the massive cost of gun violence? *CBS News*. https://www.cbsnews.com/news/las-vegas-shooting-gun-violence-economic-costs/

Pinderhughes, H., Davis, R., & Williams, M. (2015). Adverse community experiences and resilience: A framework for addressing and preventing community trauma. Center for Victim Recovery Depository. https://ncvc.dspacedirect.org/handle/20.500.11990/988

Pineo, H., Zimmermann, N., & Davies, M. (2019). Urban planning, designing the urban planning system to shape healthy cities. In S. Galea, C. K. Ettman, & D. Vlahov (Eds.), *Urban health* (pp. 198–296). New York, NY: Oxford University Press.

Pizarro, J. M., Holt, K., & Pelletier, K. R. (2019). An examination of the situated transactions of firearm homicides. *Journal of Behavioral Medicine, 42*(4), 613–625.

Polletta, F. (2016). Storytelling in social movements. In H. Johnston (Ed.), *Culture, social movements, and protest* (pp. 43–64). New York, NY: Routledge.

Porter, R. (2018). The unique features of African-American spirituality in the context of Christian healing. *Journal of the Interdenominational Theological Center, 34*(1), 3.

Posada, G. (2019). *Examining the relationship between compassion and trauma to heal PTSD*. (Senior honors thesis). University of Toronto, Canada.

Posner, T. (2018). The development of self help organizations: Dilemmas and ambiguities. In S. Humble & J. Unell (Eds.), *Self help in health and social welfare* (pp. 51–61). New York, NY: Routledge.

Post, L. A., Balsen, Z., Spano, R., & Vaca, F. E. (2019). Bolstering gun injury surveillance accuracy using capture–recapture methods. *Journal of Behavioral Medicine, 42*(4), 674–680.

Pouya, S., & Demirel, Ö. (2015). What is a healing garden? *Akdeniz Üniversitesi Ziraat Fakültesi Dergisi, 28*(1). Online. https://www.researchgate.net/profile/Sima_Pouya2/publication/303923867_What_is_a_healing_garden/links/575e8ca808aec91374b3cd92/What-is-a-healing-garden.pdf

Prabhu, A., Parker, L. S., & DeVita, M. A. (2017). Caring for patients or organs: New therapies raise new dilemmas in the emergency department. *The American Journal of Bioethics, 17*(5), 6–16.

Pressley, A. (2019, August 9). Waging peace, healing our nation. *Bay State Banner.* https://www.baystatebanner.com/2019/08/09/waging-peace-healing-our-nation/

Preston, R., Rannard, S., Felton-Busch, C., Larkins, S., Canuto, K., Carlisle, K., . . . Yeomans, L. (2019). How and why do participatory women's groups (PWGs) improve the quality of maternal and child health (MCH) care? A systematic review protocol. *BMJ Open, 9*(9), e030461.

Price, M. J. (2017). *What would mama do? Save Our Sons and Daughters (SOSAD) and anti-violence organizing among Black Mothers of murdered children in Detroit.* Lexington, KY: University of Kentucky.

Prickett, K. C., Gutierrez, C., & Deb, S. (2019). Family firearm ownership and firearm-related mortality among young children: 1976–2016. *Pediatrics, 143*(2), e20181171.

Pritchard, C., Parish, M., & Williams, R. J. (2020). International comparison of civilian violent deaths: A public health approach to reduce gun-related deaths in US youth. *Public Health, 180*, 109–113.

Prowse, G., Weaver, V. M., & Meares, T. L. (2019). The state from below: Distorted responsiveness in policed communities. *Urban Affairs Review, 56*(5), 1423–1471.

Purtle, J., Cheney, R., Wiebe, D. J., & Dicker, R. (2015). Scared safe? Abandoning the use of fear in urban violence prevention programmes. *Injury Prevention, 21*(2), 140–141.

Quimby, D., Dusing, C. R., Deane, K., DiClemente, C. M., Morency, M. M., Miller, K. M., . . . Richards, M. (2018). Gun exposure among Black American youth residing in low-income urban environments. *Journal of Black Psychology, 44*(4), 322–346.

Rahamim, S. (2018). From dream to nightmare: Gun violence in America. *Interdisciplinary Journal of Partnership Studies, 5*(2), 7.

Rajan, S., Branas, C. C., Hargarten, S., & Allegrante, J. P. (2018). Funding for gun violence research is key to the health and safety of the nation. *American Journal of Public Health, 108*(2), 194–195.

Rajan, S., Branas, C. C., Myers, D., & Agrawal, N. (2019). Youth exposure to violence involving a gun: Evidence for adverse childhood experience classification. *Journal of Behavioral Medicine, 42*(4), 646–657.

Ralph, L. (2014). *Renegade dreams: Living through injury in gangland Chicago.* Chicago, IL: University of Chicago Press.

Ramos, J. (2019, December 7). Saying no to Trump's troops. *The New York Times,* p. A25.

Ranapurwala, S. I. (2019). Identifying and addressing confounding bias in violence prevention research. *Current Epidemiology Reports, 6,* 200–207.

Rand Corporation. (2018, July 10). *More research could help prevent gun violence in America.* Santa Monica, CA: Rand. https://www.rand.org/blog/rand-review/2018/07/more-research-could-help-prevent-gun-violence-in-america.html

Randhawa, H., Edwards, M. A., & Cantle, F. (2016). Who are our "code-red" kids? A urban major trauma centre's experience of major hemorrhage in injured children. *Emergency Medicine Journal, 33*(12), 936.

Rando, T. A. (1993). *Treatment of complicated mourning.* Champaign, IL: Research Press.

Ranney, M., Karb, R., Ehrlich, P., Bromwich, K., Cunningham, R., Beidas, R. S., & FACTS Consortium. (2019). What are the long-term consequences of youth exposure to firearm injury, and how do we prevent them? A scoping review. *Journal of Behavioral Medicine, 42*(4), 724–740.

Rawlings, W. (2019). Coffins for kids! *Kenyon Review, 41*(1), 63–72.

Read, P. (2018). Changing interpretations of the Pinochet dictatorship and its victims in Chilean memorial inscriptions since the end of the Cold War. *Quarterly Journal of Speech, 104* (1). Online. https://brill.com/view/book/edcoll/9789004361676/BP000014.xml

Reed, M. D., Dabney, D. A., Tapp, S. N., & Ishoy, G. A. (2020). Tense relationships between homicide co-victims and detectives in the wake of murder. *Deviant Behavior, 41*(3), 543–561.

Regoeczi, W. C. (2018). Solving homicides: Understanding trends and patterns in police clearances of lethal violence. In M. Deflem (Ed.), *Homicide and violent crime* (pp. 121–138). Bingley, UK: Emerald.

Reichel, C. (2018, November 8). Covering gun violence in America: Tips from German Lopez. *Journalist's Resources.* https://journalistsresource.org/tip-sheets/writing/gun-violence-mass-shootings/

Reid, J. A., Richards, T. N., Loughran, T. A., & Mulvey, E. P. (2017). The relationships among exposure to violence, psychological distress, and gun carrying among male adolescents found guilty of serious legal offenses: A longitudinal cohort study. *Annals of Internal Medicine, 166*(6), 412–418.

Reigeluth, C. S., Pollastri, A. R., Cardemil, E. V., & Addis, M. E. (2016). "Mad scared" versus "I was sad": Emotional expression and response in urban adolescent males. *Journal of Adolescence, 49,* 232–243.

Rein, M. (1969). Social planning: The search for legitimacy. *Journal of the American Institute of Planners, 35* (4), 233–244.

Reisch, M., & Andrews, J. (2014). *The road not taken: A history of radical social work in the United States*. New York, NY: Routledge.

Resnick, S., Smith, R. N., Beard, J. H., Holena, D., Reilly, P. M., Schwab, C. W., & Seamon, M. J. (2017). Firearm deaths in America: Can we learn from 462,000 lives lost? *Annals of Surgery, 266*(3), 432–440.

Reynolds, J. (2017). *Long way down*. New York, NY: Simon and Schuster.

Rich, J. A. (2009). *Wrong place, wrong time: Trauma and violence in the lives of young Black men*. Baltimore, MD: Johns Hopkins University Press.

Richards, M. H., Romero, E., Zakaryan, A., Carey, D., Deane, K., Quimby, D., . . . Burns, M. (2015). Assessing urban African American youths' exposure to community violence through a daily sampling method. *Psychology of Violence, 5*(3), 275–284.

Richardson, J. B., Jr., Van Brakle, M., & St. Vil, C. (2014). Taking boys out of the hood: Exile as a parenting strategy for African American male youth. *New Directions for Child and Adolescent Development, 2014*(143), 11–31.

Richardson, M. A. (2019). Framing community-based interventions for gun violence: A review of the literature. *Health & Social Work, 44*(4), 259–270.

Riemann, M. (2019). Problematizing the medicalization of violence: A critical discourse analysis of the "Cure Violence" initiative. *Critical Public Health, 29*(2), 146–155.

Riessman, F., & Carroll, D. (1995). *Redefining self-help: Policy and practice*. San Francisco, CA: Jossey-Bass.

Rigg, K. K., McNeish, R., Schadrac, D., Gonzalez, A., & Tran, Q. (2019). Community needs of minority male youth living in inner-city Chicago. *Children and Youth Services Review, 98*, 284–289.

Riley, S., Evans, A., Anderson, E., & Robson, M. (2019). The gendered nature of self-help. *Feminism & Psychology, 29*(1), 3–18.

Rios, M., Friedlander, S., Cardona, Y., Flores, G., & Shetgiri, R. (2019). Associations of parental monitoring and violent peers with Latino youth violence. *Journal of Immigrant and Minority Health, 22*, 240–248.

Rivers, T. (2018). *Shoot or be shot: Urban America and gun violence among African American males* (Thesis). California State University, Long Beach.

Roberto, E., Braga, A. A., & Papachristos, A. V. (2018). Closer to guns: The role of street gangs in facilitating access to illegal firearms. *Journal of Urban Health, 95*(3), 372–382.

Robertson, K. (2018, October 17). Six things we learned from young adults experiencing gun violence in Chicago. *Urban Wire*. https://www.urban.org/urban-wire/six-things-we-learned-young-adults-experiencing-gun-violence-chicagohttps://jjie.org/

Robertson, K., Bastomski, S., & Duane, M. (2018, December 26). We need to do more for homicide co-victims. *Urban Wire: Crime and Justice*. https://www.urban.org/urban-wire/we-need-do-more-homicide-co-victims

Roché, S., & Oberwittler, D. (2018). Towards a broader view of police-citizen relations: How societal cleavages and political contexts shape trust and distrust, legitimacy and illegitimacy. In D. Oberwittler & S. Roché (Eds.), *Police-citizen relations across the world. Comparing sources and contexts of trust and legitimacy* (pp. 3–26). New York, NY: Routledge.

Romano, A., & Ragland, D. (2018). Truth-telling from the margins: Exploring Black-led responses to police violence and systemic humiliation. In *Systemic humiliation in America* (pp. 145–172). New York, NY: Palgrave Macmillan.

Romero, A. P., Shaw, A. M., & Conron, K. J. (2019). *Gun violence against sexual and gender minorities in the United States.* Los Angeles, CA: UCLA. https://williamsinstitute.law.ucla.edu/wp-content/uploads/SGM-Gun-Violence-Apr-2019.pdf

Romero, M. (2020). Sociology engaged in social justice. *American Sociological Review, 85*(1), 1–30.

Romo, N. D. (2020). Gone but not forgotten: Violent trauma victimization and the treatment of violence like a disease. *Hospital Pediatrics, 10*(1), 95–97.

Rood, C. (2018). "Our tears are not enough": The warrant of the dead in the rhetoric of gun control. *Quarterly Journal of Speech, 104*(1), 47–70.

Rood, C. (2019). *After gun violence: Deliberation and memory in an age of political gridlock* (Vol. *21*). University Park, PA: Penn State Press.

Rosenberg, M. L. (2019). Let's bring the full power of science to gun violence prevention. *American Journal of Public Health, 109*(3), 396–397.

Rosenfeld, E. H., & Cooper, A. (2017). Organizing the community for pediatric trauma. In D. E. Wesson & B. Naik-Mathuria (Eds.), *Pediatric trauma* (pp. 7–27). New York, NY: CRC Press.

Rosenfeld, R., Gaston, S., Spivak, H., & Irazola, S. (2017). *Assessing and responding to the recent homicide rise in the United States.* Washington, DC: US Department of Justice, National Institute of Justice.

Rosenfeld, R., & Wallman, J. (2019). Did de-policing cause the increase in homicide rates? *Criminology & Public Policy, 18*(1), 51–75.

Rossi, P. H. (2017). *Under the gun: Weapons, crime, and violence in America.* New York, NY: Routledge.

Rossi, P. H. (2019). *Ghetto revolts.* New York, NY: Routledge.

Rostron, A. (2018). The Dickey Amendment on federal funding for research on gun violence: A legal dissection. *American Journal of Public Health, 108*(7), 805–867.

Rothschild, B. (2019, August 29). They ain't ready for her. *Jewschool.* https://jewschool.com/2019/08/171339/they-aint-ready-for-her/

Rothschild, T. (2018*). An ethnography of gun violence prevention activists: "We are thinking people."* Lanham, MD: Rowman & Littlefield.

Rowan, Z. R., Schubert, C. A., Loughran, T. A., Mulvey, E. P., & Pardini, D. A. (2019). Proximal predictors of gun violence among adolescent males involved in crime. *Law and Human Behavior, 43*(3), 250–262.

Rozalski, V., Holland, J., M., & Neimeyer, R., A. (2016). Circumstances of death and complicated grief: Indirect associations through meaning made of loss. *Journal of Loss and Trauma, 22*(1), 11–23.

Rubin, R. (2016a). Mental health reform will not reduce US gun violence, experts say. *JAMA, 315*(2), 119–121.

Rubin, R. (2016b). Tale of 2 agencies: CDC avoids gun violence research but NIH funds it. *JAMA, 315*(16), 1689–1692.

Rubinstein, R. A., Lane, S. D., Mojeed, L., Sanchez, S., Catania, E., Jennings-Bey, T., . . . Quesada, J. (2018). Blood in the Rust Belt: Mourning and memorialization in the context of community violence. *Current Anthropology, 59*(4), 439–454.

Russo, R., Fury, M., Accardo, S., & Krause, P. (2016). Economic and educational impact of firearm-related injury on an urban trauma center. *Orthopedics, 39*(1):e57–e61 https://doi.org/10.3928/01477447-20151228-02

Sacks, T. K., & Chow, J. C. C. (2018). A social work perspective on police violence: Evidence and interventions. *Journal of Ethnic & Cultural Diversity in Social Work, 27*, 215–218.

Sadat, L. N., & George, M. (2019). The US gun violence crisis: Human rights perspectives and remedies (Washington University in St. Louis Legal Studies Research Paper, 19-01-11).

Sainz, A., & Lush, T. (2019, October 11). Decades after her daughter's death, a mother gets answers. *The San Diego Union-Tribune.* https://www.sandiegouniontribune.com/news/california/story/2019-10-11/decades-after-her-daughters-death-a-mother-gets-answers

Sakran, J. V., Mehta, A., Fransman, R., Nathens, A. B., Joseph, B., Kent, A., . . . Efron, D. T. (2018). Nationwide trends in mortality following penetrating trauma: Are we up for the challenge? *Journal of Trauma and Acute Care Surgery, 85*(1), 160–166.

Salvi, N. K. (2019). Empowerment through self-help groups. *Shodhshauryam, International Scientific Refereed Research Journal, 2*(1), 69–73. http://shisrrj.com/paper/SHISRRJ192114.pdf

Sampson, R. J., Raudenbush, S. W., & Earls, F. (2019). Neighborhoods and violent crime. In F. De Maio, R. C. Shah, J. Mazzeo, & D. A. Ansell (Eds.), *Community health equity: A Chicago reader* (pp. 282–303). Chicago, IL: University of Chicago.

Samuels, J. T., Mathew, A. P., Kommanivanh, C., Kwon, D., Gomez, L., Thunder, B., . . . LaQueens, L. (2018, April). Art, human computer interaction, and shared experiences: A gun violence prevention intervention. In *Extended Abstracts of the 2018 CHI Conference on Human Factors in Computing Systems* (p. D404). ACM. http://st.sigchi.org/publications/toc/chi-2018-ea.html

Sanchez, R. (2018, October 5). She embalmed her own nephew and learned to shoot. A Chicago funeral home copes with gun violence. *CNN.* https://www.cnn.com/2018/10/01/us/chicago-violence-funeral-home/index.html

Sandoval, E. (2019, December 6). As gang-related shootings surge, a plea: "Stop the bleeding." *The New York Times*, p. A25.

Santilli, A., O'Connor Duffany, K., Carroll-Scott, A., Thomas, J., Greene, A., Arora, A., . . . Ickovics, J. (2017). Bridging the response to mass shootings and urban violence: Exposure to violence in New Haven, Connecticut. *American Journal of Public Health, 107*(3), 374–379.

Sauaia, A., Gonzalez, E., Moore, H. B., Bol, K., & Moore, E. E. (2016). Fatality and severity of firearm injuries in a Denver trauma center, 2000–2013. *JAMA, 315*(22), 2465–2467.

Saunders, J., & Kilmer, B. (2019). Changing the narrative: Police–community partnerships and racial reconciliation. *Justice Quarterly*, 1–25. doi:https://doi.org/10.1080/07418825.2019.1568520

Saxbe, D., Khoddam, H., Piero, L. D., Stoycos, S. A., Gimbel, S. I., Margolin, G., & Kaplan, J. T. (2018). Community violence exposure in early adolescence: Longitudinal associations with hippocampal and amygdala volume and resting state connectivity. *Developmental Science, 21*(6), e12686.

Scarlet, S., & Rogers, S. O., Jr. (2018). What is the institutional duty of trauma systems to respond to gun violence? *AMA Journal of Ethics, 20*(5), 483–491.

Schaechter, J., & Alvarez, P. G. (2016). Growing up–or not–with gun violence. *Pediatric Clinics, 63*(5), 813–826.

Schmidt, C. J., Rupp, L., Pizarro, J. M., Lee, D. B., Branas, C. C., & Zimmerman, M. A. (2019). Risk and protective factors related to youth firearm violence: A scoping review and directions for future research. *Journal of Behavioral Medicine, 42*(4), 706–723.

Schnell, C., Grossman, L., & Braga, A. A. (2019). The routine activities of violent crime places: A retrospective case-control study of crime opportunities on street segments. *Journal of Criminal Justice, 60*, 140–153.

Schoenfeld, E. A., Bennett, K., Manganella, K., & Kemp, G. (2019). More than just a seat at the table: The power of youth voice in ending youth homelessness in the United States. *Child Care in Practice, 25*(1), 112–125.

Schutz, A. (2019). *Empowerment: A primer.* New York, NY: Routledge.

Scutti, S. (2019, August 14). This 7-year old was supposed to start 2nd grade this week. He's the 7th child to die by gun violence in St. Louis this year. *CNN.* https://www.cnn.com/2019/08/14/us/st-louis-child-homicides/index.html

Seal, D., Nguyen, A., & Beyer, K. (2014). Youth exposure to violence in an urban setting. *Urban Studies Research, 2014*, Article ID 368047.

See, L. A. (2018). *Violence as seen through a prism of color.* New York, NY: Routledge.

Seedat, M., Taliep, N., Cochrane, J. R., Lazarus, S., Hendricks, C., Van Reenen, R., . . . Carelse, H. (2016). Community asset mapping for violence prevention: A comparison of views in Erijaville, South Africa and Memphis, USA: Original contributions. *African Safety Promotion, 14*(1), 1–25.

Sege, R. D., & Augustyn, M. (2019). Television and media violence. *UpToDate.* https://www.uptodate.com/contents/television-and-media-violence

Sered, D. (2019). *Until we reckon: Violence, mass incarceration, and a road to repair.* New York, NY: New Press.

Shafique, A., & Abdulaziz, M. (2019). Self-help groups as enhancing factor for the socio-economic development of people in modern society [Special issue]. *Journal of Economic & Social Research, 18*(1), 21–30.

Shapiro, E. (2019, October 21). 11-month old shot 4 times in grave condition, 2-year-old shot dead in mom's arms; police beg public for information. *ABC.* https://abcnews.go.com/US/11-month-shot-times-grave-condition-year-shot/story?id=66417305

Shapiro, R. J., & Hassett, K. A. (2012). *The economic benefits of reducing violent crime: A case study of 8 American cities.* Washington, DC: Center for American Progress.

Sharkey, P. (2013). *Stuck in place: Urban neighborhoods and the end of progress toward racial equality.* Chicago, IL: University of Chicago Press.

Shatan, C. F. (1973). The grief of soldiers: Vietnam combat veterans' self-help movement. *American Journal of Orthopsychiatry, 43*(4), 640–653.

Shaull, L. (2016). Substantial and unacceptable: Nearly 1300 children and adolescents aged 17 years or younger die in gun homicides and suicides each year, and a further 5790 are treated for gunshot wounds. A multifaceted approach is needed to control guns. *Lancet, 387*, 1847–1855.

Sheats, K. J., Irving, S. M., Mercy, J. A., Simon, T. R., Crosby, A. E., Ford, D. C., . . . Morgan, R. E. (2018). Violence-related disparities experienced by Black youth and young adults: Opportunities for prevention. *American Journal of Preventive Medicine, 55*(4), 462–469.

Shelley, W. W., & Peterson, D. (2019). "Sticks and stones may break my bones, but bullying will get me bangin'": Bullying involvement and adolescent gang joining. *Youth Violence and Juvenile Justice, 17*(4), 385–412.

Shelly, P., & Battista-Frazee, K. (2018). Perspectives on gun violence, mental health, and the social worker's role. *The New Social Worker.* https://www.socialworker. com/feature-articles/practice/macrosw-perspectives-on-gun-violence-mental-health-and-the-social-worker-role/

Shepherd, J. P. (2001). Emergency medicine and police collaboration to prevent community violence. *Annals of Emergency Medicine, 38*(4), 430–437.

Shepherd, J. P., & Sumner, S. A. (2017). Policing and public health—Strategies for collaboration. *JAMA, 317*(15), 1525–1526.

Shepley, M., Sachs, N., Sadatsafavi, H., Fournier, C., & Peditto, K. (2019). The impact of green space on violent crime in urban environments: An evidence synthesis. *International Journal of Environmental Research and Public Health, 16*(24), 5119.

Sher, D. (2019, July 21). Gun violence epidemic in parts of B'ham: View from UAB Trauma Center. *ComebackTown.* https://www.al.com/opinion/2019/07/gun-violence-epidemic-in-parts-of-bham-view-from-uab-trauma-center.html

Short, M. A., Bartel, K., & Carskadon, M. A. (2019). Sleep and mental health in children and adolescents. In M. A. Grandner (Ed.), *Sleep and health* (pp. 435–445). New York, NY: Academic Press.

Shute, J. (2016). Bereaved family activism in contexts of organized mass violence. In D. C. Spencer & S. Walklake (Eds.), *Reconceptualizing critical victimology* (pp. 173–190). Lanham, MD: Lexington Books.

Siegel, M., & Boine, C. (2019). *What are the most effective policies in reducing gun homicides?* Albany, NY: Rockefeller Institute of Government.

Sierra-Arévalo, M., & Papachristos, A. V. (2017). Social networks and gang violence reduction. *Annual Review of Law and Social Science, 13*, 373–393.

Sigel, E. J., Mattson, S. A., & Mercado, M. C. (2019). Increased violence involvement and other behavioral and mental health factors among youth with firearm access. *Journal of Adolescent Health, 65*(1), 63–71.

Silva, K. (2019, September 16). Black boys, grief, guns, urban schools. *PhysOrg.* https://phys.org/news/2019-09-black-boys-grief-guns-urban.html

Simon, G., Heckmann, V., Tóth, D., & Kozma, Z. (2019). Brain death of an infant caused by a penetrating air gun injury. *Legal Medicine, 144*(6), e20192739.

Sims, L. J. (2018). *Children exposed to community violence in an urban setting: A qualitative study of elementary school administrators' and principals' knowledge and practices* (Doctoral dissertation). Chicago State University, Chicago, IL.

Singletary, G. (2020). Beyond PTSD: Black male fragility in the context of trauma. *Journal of Aggression, Maltreatment & Trauma, 29*(5), 517–536.

Smith, B. (2017, November 27). Stopping gun violence in Baltimore: What works and what doesn't. *The Market Urbanism Report.* https://marketurbanismreport.com/blog/stopping-gun-violence-in-baltimore-what-works-and-what-doesnt

Smith, C. A. (2016). Sorrow as artifact: Radical Black mothering in times of terror— A prologue. *Transforming Anthropology, 24*(1), 5–7.

Smith, E. R., & Gill Lopez, P. (2016). Collaboration for a curriculum of caring: The zeitgeist is right. *Psychology in the Schools, 53*(3), 270–285.

Smith, J. R., & Patton, D. U. (2016). Posttraumatic stress symptoms in context: Examining trauma responses to violent exposures and homicide death among Black males in urban neighborhoods. *American Journal of Orthopsychiatry, 86*(2), 212–223.

Smith, K. (2018, November 9). Gun death statistics: CDC study says gun deaths are on the rise after years of decline. *CBS.* https://www.cbsnews.com/news/gun-death-statistics-cdc-study-says-gun-deaths-are-on-the-rise-after-years-of-decline/

Smith, M. (2020, January 2). After a shooting, misinformation and mistakes. *The New York Times*, p. A10.

Smith, R. N., Seamon, M. J., Kumar, V., Robinson, A., Shults, J., Reilly, P. M., & Richmond, T. S. (2018). Lasting impression of violence: Retained bullets and depressive symptoms. *Injury, 49*(1), 135–140.

Smith, V. M., Siegel, M., Xuan, Z., Ross, C. S., Galea, S., Kalesan, B., . . . Goss, K. A. (2017). Broadening the perspective on gun violence: An examination of the firearms industry, 1990–2015. *American Journal of Preventive Medicine, 53*(5), 584–591.

Smith Lee, J. R., & Robinson, M. A. (2019). "That's my number one fear in life. It's the police": Examining young Black men's exposures to trauma and loss resulting from police violence and police killings. *Journal of Black Psychology, 45*(3), 143–184.

Singer, R. M., & Gorman, G. (2018). From high street to main street: Revising and utilizing the Richter Scale for Health in an urban center in the US. *Perspectives in Public Health, 138*(3), 140–141.

So, S., Gaylord-Harden, N. K., Voisin, D. R., & Scott, D. (2018). Future orientation as a protective factor for African American adolescents exposed to community violence. *Youth & Society, 50*(6), 734–757.

Solomon, B. B. (1976). *Black empowerment: Social work in oppressed communities.* New York, NY: Columbia University Press.

Somin, I. (2019, June 19). Why we shouldn't treat victims and survivors as authorities on policy issues. *Reason.* https://reason.com/2019/06/19/why-we-shouldnt-treat-survivors-and-victims-as-authorities-on-policy-issues/

Sood, A. B., & Berkowitz, S. J. (2016). Prevention of youth violence: A public health approach. *Child and Adolescent Psychiatric Clinics, 25*(2), 243–256.

Soska, T. M., & Ohmer, M. L. (2018). Community approaches for addressing crime and violence: Prevention, intervention, and restoration. In R. Cnaan & C. Milofsky (Eds.), *Handbook of community movements and local organizations in the 21st century* (pp. 469–496). New York, NY: Springer.

Southall, A. (2020, May 8). Echo of "Stop and Frisk" is seen in social-distance crackdown. *The New York Times*, pp. A1, A15.

Soyer, M. (2018). *Lost childhoods: Poverty, trauma, and violent crime in the post-welfare era*. Berkeley, CA: University of California Press.

Spencer, Z., & Perlow, O. N. (2018). Reconceptualizing historic and contemporary violence against African Americans as savage white American terror (SWAT). *Journal of African American Studies, 22*(2–3), 155–173.

Sperlich, M., Logan-Greene, P., Slovak, K., & Kaplan, M. S. (2019). Addressing gun violence: A social work imperative. *Health & Social Work, 44*(4), 217–220.

Spinrad, M. (2017). *A public health approach to gun violence: Evaluating strategies to improve intervention and public awareness* (Doctoral dissertation). Boston University, Boston, MA.

Stein, M. B., Kessler, R. C., & Ursano, R. J. (2019). Reframing the suicide prevention message for military personnel. *JAMA Psychiatry, 76*(5), 466–468.

Stephens, A. (2019, May 17). Ghost guns are everywhere in California. *The Trace*. https://www.thetrace.org/2019/05/ghost-gun-california-crime/

Stevens, Q., & Ristic, M. (2015). Memories come to the surface: Pavement memorials in urban public spaces. *Journal of Urban Design, 20*(2), 273–290.

Stevenson, D. D. (2019). Gun violence as an obstacle to educational equality. *University of Memphis Law Review*. In press.

Stevenson, R. G., & Cox, G. R. (2017). *Perspectives on violence and violent death*. New York, NY: Routledge.

Stewart, F. R. (2017). The rhetoric of shared grief: An analysis of letters to the family of Michael Brown. *Journal of Black Studies, 48*(4), 355–372.

Stinson, P. M. (2020). *Criminology explains police violence* (Vol. 1). Berkeley, CA: University of California Press.

Stock, S., Bott, M., Villareal, M., & Carroll, J. (2016, February 16). PTSD in Oakland: Gun violence victims, families suffer continuous post-traumatic stress disorder. *NBC Bay Area*. https://www.nbcbayarea.com/investigations/Oakland-Gun-Violence-Victims-Families-PTSD-369471372.html

Stolzenberg, L., D'Alesso, S. J., & Flexon, J. L. (2019). *Eyes on the street: Police use of body-worn cameras in Miami-Dade County*. Weston, MA: Weston.

Stone, R., & Socia, K. M. (2019). Boy with toy or Black male with gun: An analysis of online news articles covering the shooting of Tamir Rice. *Race and Justice, 9*(3), 330–358.

Stroebe, W. (2016). Firearm availability and violent death: The need for a culture change in attitudes toward guns. *Analyses of Social Issues and Public Policy, 16*(1), 7–35.

Stroebe, W., Leander, N. P., & Kruglanski, A. W. (2017). Is it a dangerous world out there? The motivational bases of American gun ownership. *Personality and Social Psychology Bulletin, 43*(8), 1071–1085.

Talwar, S. K. (2018). *Art therapy for social justice*. New York, NY: Routledge.

Tasigiorgos, S., Economopoulos, K. P., Winfield, R. D., & Sakran, J. V. (2015). Firearm injury in the United States: An overview of an evolving public health problem. *Journal of the American College of Surgeons, 221*(6), 1005–1014.

Tatebe, L., Speedy, S., Kang, D., Barnum, T., Cosey-Gay, F., Regan, S., . . . Swaroop, M. (2019). Empowering bystanders to intervene: Trauma Responders Unify to Empower (TRUE) Communities. *Journal of Surgical Research, 238*, 255–264.

Team Trace. (2018, March 23). An American crisis: 18 facts about gun violence—and 6 promising ways to reduce the suffering. https://www.thetrace.org/features/gun-violence-facts-and-solutions/

Terrana, S. E. (2019). *A qualitative case study of Black women nonprofit founders: Social justice and social change in the community* (Doctoral dissertation). UCLA, Los Angeles, CA.

Thompson, C. C. (2018). *Stop the violence.* The Growth Network. http://thegrowthnetwork.org/contact

Thomas, T. (2018). *On memory and the radical Black imagination* (Thesis). City University of New York, New York, NY.

Tice, C. J., Long, D. D., & Cox, L. E. (2019). *Macro social work practice: Advocacy in action.* Thousand Oaks, CA: Sage.

Tillyer, M. S., & Walter, R. J. (2019). Low-income housing and crime: The influence of housing development and neighborhood characteristics. *Crime & Delinquency, 65*(7), 969–993.

Tita, G. E., & Barragan, M. (2018). Understanding the illicit gun market in Los Angeles. In J. Carlson, K. A. Goss, & H. Shapira (Eds.), *Gun studies: Interdisciplinary approaches to politics, policy, and practice* (pp. 75–94). New York, NY: Routledge.

Tobon, M., Ledgerwood, A. M., & Lucas, C. E. (2019). The Urban Injury Severity Score (UISS) better predicts mortality following penetrating gunshot wounds (GSW). *The American Journal of Surgery, 217*(3), 573–576.

Tomsen, S., & Payne, J. (2016). Homicide and the night-time economy. *Trends and Issues in Crime and Criminal Justice,* (*521*), 1–41.

Torres-Harding, S., Baber, A., Hilvers, J., Hobbs, N., & Maly, M. (2018). Children as agents of social and community change: Enhancing youth empowerment through participation in a school-based social activism project. *Education, Citizenship and Social Justice, 13*(1), 3–18.

Trabulsi, M. (2019, April 2). Healing a mother's pain by forgiving a killer. *KPBS.* https://www.kpbs.org/news/2019/apr/02/healing-mothers-pain-forgiving-killer/

Tracy, B. M., Smith, R. N., Miller, K., Clayton, E., Bailey, K., Gerrin, C., . . . MacNew, H. (2019). Community distress predicts youth gun violence. *Journal of Pediatric Surgery, 54*(11), 2375–2381.

Tracy, M., Braga, A. A., & Papachristos, A. V. (2016). The transmission of gun and other weapon-involved violence within social networks. *Epidemiologic Reviews, 38*(1), 70–86.

Trinkner, R. (2019). Addressing the "black box" of focused deterrence: An examination of the mechanisms of change in Chicago's Project Safe Neighborhoods. *Journal of Experimental Criminology, 15*(4), 673–683.

Tsou, P. Y. P., & Barnes, M. (2016). Pediatricians "educating kids about gun violence"—Preventing inner city youth violence through community collaboration and outreach. *Academic Pediatrics, 16*(6), e49–e50.

Tucker, D. (2019, June 13). "Army of Moms": Founder offers Mayor Lightfoot advice on city violence. *WBEZ.* https://www.wbez.org/shows/morning-shift/army-of-moms-founder-offers-mayor-lightfoot-advice-on-city-violence/d6a0556d-cea2-4d68-96f9-9e707d480573

Tuerkheimer, D. (2017). Criminal justice and the mattering of lives. *Michigan Law Review, 116*, 1145–1166.

Tulop, S. (2018, June 15). These 7 antiviolence groups are all led by youth. https://yr.media/news/7-anti-gun-violence-groups-led-by-young-people/

Turanovic, J. J. (2019). Victimization and desistance from crime. *Journal of Developmental and Life-Course Criminology, 5*(1), 86–106.

Turner, T., & Wise, A. (2019, September 14). Shattered: Life after being shot. *WAMU*. https://wamu.atavist.com/-

Ulrich, M. R. (2019). A public health approach to gun violence, legally speaking. *The Journal of Law, Medicine & Ethics, 47*(2, Suppl.), 112–115.

Universal Hub. (2018, December 27). Boston murders in 2018. https://www.universalhub.com/2018/boston-murders-2018

Uyeturk, U. (2019). Management of the scrotal trauma caused by an air-compressed gun in a child: A case report. *Pediatric Urology Case Reports, 6*(1), 17–21.

Valasik, M., Brault, E. E., & Martinez, S. M. (2019). Forecasting homicide in the red stick: Risk terrain modeling and the spatial influence of urban blight on lethal violence in Baton Rouge, Louisiana. *Social Science Research, 80*, 186–201.

Van Brocklin, E. (2019, July, 10). What gun violence prevention looks like when it focuses on the communities most hurt. *The Trace*. https://www.thetrace.org/2019/07/gun-violence-prevention-communities-of-color-funding/

van Dijk, A. J., Herrington, V., Crofts, N., Breunig, R., Burris, S., Sullivan, H., . . . Thomson, N. (2019). Law enforcement and public health: Recognition and enhancement of joined-up solutions. *The Lancet, 393*(10168), 287–294.

Vargas, R. (2016). *Wounded city: Violent turf wars in a Chicago barrio*. New York, NY: Oxford University Press.

Vasturia, D., Webster, R. J., & Saucier, D. A. (2018). Demons with firepower: How belief in pure evil relates to perceptions and punishments of gun violence perpetrators. *Personality and Individual Differences, 122*, 13–18.

Veenstra, M., Schaewe, H., Donoghue, L., & Langenburg, S. (2015). Pediatric firearm injuries: Do database analyses tell the whole story? *Current Surgery Reports, 50*(7), 1184–1187.

Velez, M. (2019, December 6). How one retired bulldog gang member is using education to combat gun violence in Fresno. *Valley Public Radio*. https://www.kvpr.org/post/how-one-retired-bulldog-gang-member-using-education-combat-gun-violence-fresno

Vella, M. A., Warshauer, A., Tortorello, G., Fernandez-Moure, J., Giacolone, J., Chen, B., . . . Reilly, P. M. (2020). Long-term functional, psychological, emotional, and social outcomes in survivors of firearm injuries. *JAMA Surgery, 155*(1), 1–9.

Vente, T. M. (2020). The impact of gun violence on those already dying: Perspectives from a palliative care physician. *Pediatrics, 145*(2). Ejournal. https://pediatrics.aappublications.org/content/145/2/e20191143

Vergano, D. (2019, May 23). Scientists showed how much guns led to more violent crime. *Buzzfeed*. https://www.buzzfeednews.com/article/danvergano/more-guns-more-crime

Vil, C. S., Richardson, J., & Cooper, C. (2018). Methodological considerations for research with black male victims of violent injury in an urban trauma unit. *Violence and Victims, 33*(2), 383–396.

Violence Policy Center. (2016). *Black homicide victimization.* Washington, DC: Author.

Violence Policy Center. (2019a). *Hispanic victimization.* Washington, DC: Author. http://vpc.org/revealing-the-impacts-of-gun-violence/hispanic-homicide-victimization/

Violence Policy Center. (2019b, February 21). *Nearly 17,000 Hispanics/Latinos killed with guns in California since 1999, new study reports.* Washington, DC: Author. http://vpc.org/press/nearly-17000-hispanics-latinos-killed-with-guns-in-california-since-1999-new-study-reports/

Vlahov, D. (2018). Building the evidence base to prevent firearm deaths and injuries. *Journal of Urban Health, 95,* 293–294.

Voisin, D., Berringer, K., Takahashi, L., Burr, S., & Kuhnen, J. (2016). No safe havens: Protective parenting strategies for African American youth living in violent communities. *Violence and Victims, 31*(3), 523–536.

Voisin, D. R. (2019). *America the beautiful and violent: Black youth and neighborhood trauma in Chicago.* New York, NY: Columbia University Press.

Walker, G. N., McLone, S., Mason, M., & Sheehan, K. (2016). Rates of firearm homicide by Chicago region, age, sex, and race/ethnicity, 2005–2010. *Journal of Trauma and Acute Care Surgery, 81*(4), S48–S53.

Wallace, C. M., McGee, Z. T., Malone-Colon, L., & Boykin, A. W. (2018). The impact of culture-based protective factors on reducing rates of violence among African American adolescent and young adult males. *Journal of Social Issues, 74*(3), 635–651.

Wallace, L. N., & Ménard, K. S. (2017). Friendships lost: The social consequences of violent victimization. *Journal of Aggression, Maltreatment & Trauma, 26*(2), 116–136.

Walsh, F. (2019). Loss and bereavement in families: A systemic framework for recovery and resilience. In B. H. Fiese, M. Celano, K. Deater-Deckard, E. N. Jouriles, & M. A. Whisman (Eds.), *APA handbook of contemporary family psychology: Foundations, methods, and contemporary issues across the lifespan* (pp. 649–663). Washington, DC: American Psychological Association.

Walsh, M. (2017). *Violent trauma, culture, and power: An interdisciplinary exploration in lived religion.* New York, NY: Springer.

Wamser-Nanney, R., Nanney, J. T., Conrad, E., & Constans, J. I. (2019). Childhood trauma exposure and gun violence risk factors among victims of gun violence. *Psychological Trauma: Theory, Research, Practice, and Policy, 11*(1), 99–106.

Warzel, C. (2020, May 6). Will we get used to the dying? *The New York Times,* p. A24.

Watts, S. J. (2019). Gun carrying and gun victimization among American adolescents: A fresh look at a nationally representative sample. *Victims & Offenders, 14*(1), 1–14.

Watts, S. J., Province, K., & Toohy, K. (2019). The kids aren't alright: School attachment, depressive symptoms, and gun carrying at school. *American Journal of Criminal Justice, 44*(1), 146–165.

Weaver, V., Prowse, G., & Piston, S. (2019). Too much knowledge, too little power: An assessment of political knowledge in highly policed communities. *The Journal of Politics, 81*(3), 1153–1166.

Webster, D. W. (2015). Commentary: Evidence to guide gun violence prevention in America. *Annual Review of Public Health, 36,* 1–4.

Webster, D. W., Cerdá, M., Wintemute, G. J., & Cook, P. J. (2016). Epidemiologic evidence to guide the understanding and prevention of gun violence. *Epidemiologic Reviews, 38*(1), 1–4.

Webster, D. W., & Vernick, J. S. (2014). *Updated evidence and policy developments on reducing gun violence in America.* Baltimore, MD: Johns Hopkins University Press.

Webster, D. W., Whitehill, J. M., Vernick, J. S., & Curriero, F. C. (2013). Effects of Baltimore's Safe Streets program on gun violence: A replication of Chicago's CeaseFire program. *Journal of Urban Health, 90*(1), 27–40.

Wedderburn, N. V., & Carey, R. E. (2017). Forgiveness in the face of hate. In A. M. Pascal (Ed.), *Multiculturalism and the convergence of faith and practical wisdom in modern society* (pp. 315–330). Hershey, PA: IGI Global.

Welch, L. (2018, May 11). Fulton is helping other mothers, and herself, heal. *Elle.* https://www.elle.com/culture/career-politics/a20663587/sybrina-fulton-trayvon-martin-circle-of-mothers-gun-violence/

Welsh, B. C., Zimmerman, G. M., & Zane, S. N. (2018). The centrality of theory in modern day crime prevention: Developments, challenges, and opportunities. *Justice Quarterly, 35*(1), 139–161.

Wheeler, A. P., Worden, R. E., & Silver, J. R. (2019). The accuracy of the violent offender identification directive tool to predict future gun violence. *Criminal Justice and Behavior, 46*(5), 770–788.

Wiebe, M., & Bloos, A. B. (2019, March 5). Mother of Kansas City gun homicide victim seeks to turn pain into purpose. *The Journal.* https://klcjournal.com/mother-of-kansas-city-gun-homicide-victim-seeks-to-turn-pain-into-purpose/

Wilcox, P., & Cullen, F. T. (2018). Community members and deterrence. In D. S. Nagin, F. T. Cullen, & C. Lero Jonson (Eds.), *Deterrence, choice, and crime* (Vol. 23, pp. 339–362). New York, NY: Routledge.

Wilkinson, A., Lantos, H., McDaniel, T., & Winslow, H. (2019). Disrupting the link between maltreatment and delinquency: How school, family, and community factors can be protective. *BMC Public Health, 19*(1), 588.

Wilkinson, D., LaMarr, F. V., Alsaada, T. F., Ahad, C., Hill, D., & Saunders Sr, J. (2018). Building an engaged community to prevent and heal from gun violence. https://pediatrics.aappublications.org/content/145/2/e20191143

Williams, C. (2018, February 9). Communities traumatized by gun violence need mental health care, not more cops. *NBC News.* https://www.nbcnews.com/think/opinion/communities-traumatized-gun-violence-need-mental-health-care-not-more-ncna846081

Williams, J., Jackson, M. S., Barnett, T., Pressley, T., & Thomas, M. (2019). Black megachurches and the provision of social services: An examination of regional differences in America. *Journal of Religion & Spirituality in Social Work: Social Thought, 38*(2), 161–179.

Williams, L. (2018, August 7). How Chicago communities are trying to stop gun violence. *PBS.* https://www.pbs.org/newshour/show/how-chicago-communities-are-trying-to-stop-gun-violence

Williams, M. A., & Bassett, M. T. (2019, July 29). Op-ed: How do we reduce gun violence? By treating it as a disease. *Los Angeles Times.* https://www.latimes.com/opinion/story/2019-07-29/gun-violence-gilroy-brooklyn-public-health-problem

Willis, J. (2018, April 30). Owning a gun in America is a luxury. *GG.* https://www.gq.com/story/gun-ownership-cost

Winfield, R. D., Crandall, M., Williams, B. H., Sakran, J. V., Shorr, K., & Zakrison, T. L. (2019). Firearm violence in the USA: A frank discussion on an American public health crisis—The Kansas City Firearm Violence Symposium. *Trauma Surgery & Acute Care Open, 4*(1). Online. https://tsaco.bmj.com/content/4/1/e000359.abstract

Wintemute, G. J. (2015). The epidemiology of firearm violence in the twenty-first century United States. *Annual Review of Public Health, 36*, 5–19.

Wise, A. (2019a, March 6). "I'm scared to die:" Children in DC cope with gun violence-trauma. *WAMU.* https://wamu.org/story/19/03/06/im-scared-to-die-children-in-d-c-cope-with-gun-violence-trauma/

Wise, A. (2019b, March 9). Lost sleep, violent outbursts: Children cope with gun violence. *KCUR.* https://www.kcur.org/post/lost-sleep-violent-outbursts-children-cope-gun-violence-trauma#stream/0

Wolf, A. (2019). *Comparison of injury severity and resource utilization in pediatric firearm and sharp force injuries* (Thesis). University of Washington, Seattle, WA.

Wong, A. (2019, February 19). The gun violence that's a bigger threat to kids than school shootings. *The Atlantic.* https://www.theatlantic.com/family/archive/2019/02/gun-violence-children-actually-experience/582964/

Wood, G., & Papachristos, A. V. (2019). Reducing gunshot victimization in high-risk social networks through direct and spillover effects. *Nature Human Behaviour, 3*, 1164–1170.

Wray-Lake, L. (2019). How do young people become politically engaged? *Child Development Perspectives, 13*(2), 127–132.

Wright, R. G. (2019). *American violence: Survival, healing, and the failure of American policy.* Lanham, MD: Lexington Books.

Wynn, A. K., Jr. (2019). *Preventing gang violence in Baltimore communities: A proposed gang prevention program for church leaders* (Doctoral dissertation). Wilmington University, Wilmington, DE.

Xu, J., & Griffiths, E. (2017). Shooting on the street: Measuring the spatial influence of physical features on gun violence in a bounded street network. *Journal of Quantitative Criminology, 33*(2), 237–253.

Xuan, Z., & Hemenway, D. (2015). State gun law environment and youth gun carrying in the United States. *JAMA Pediatrics, 169*(11), 1024–1031.

Yamane, D. (2017). The sociology of US gun culture. *Sociology Compass, 11*(7), e12497.

Yanes, A. F. (2017). Gun violence and firearm safety in medical school curricula: Missed opportunities to improve patient health. *JAMA Internal Medicine, 177*(1), 11–12.

Yang, Y., Liller, K. D., & Coulter, M. (2018). PW 2271 Photovoice and youth: A systematic review of violence and related topics. *BMJ: Injury Prevention, 24* (2, Suppl), A16.3–A117.

Yeginsu, C. (2020, May 11). Minority communities struggle to bury dead. *The New York Times,* p. A5.

Yin, A. (2019, July 29). Mothers Against Senseless Killings reclaims corner where 2 women were shot dead: "Spraying bullets on indefensible women is cowardice." *Chicago Tribune.* https://www.chicagotribune.com/news/breaking/ct-breaking-activist-mothers-grieve-2-killed-shooting-mask-20190729-g5djgygdiffevgmvn3hh3vuwry-story.html

Young, M. A. (1996). *Working with grieving children after violent death: A guidebook for crime victim assistance professionals.* Washington, DC: US Department of Justice, Office of Justice Programs, Office for Victims of Crime

Yule, K., Houston, J., & Grych, J. (2019). Resilience in children exposed to violence: A meta-analysis of protective factors across ecological contexts. *Clinical Child and Family Psychology Review, 22*(3), 406–431.

Zakarian, R. J., McDevitt-Murphy, M. E., Bellet, B. W., Neimeyer, R. A., & Burke, L. A. (2019). Relations among meaning making, PTSD, and complicated grief following homicide loss. *Journal of Loss and Trauma, 24*(3), 279–291.

Zaru, D. (2020, April 11). African Americans in Chicago face double scourge: Coronavirus and gun violence. *ABC News.* https://abcnews.go.com/Health/african-americans-chicago-face-double-scourge-coronavirus-gun/story?id=70049723

Zaveri, M. (2019, December 23). Shooting leaves 13 wounded at a house party in Chicago. *The New York Times,* p. A14.

Zaykowski, H. (2019). Victim consciousness among youth and their responses to violent encounters. *Journal of Interpersonal Violence, 34*(3), 516–544.

Zebib, L., Stoler, J., & Zakrison, T. L. (2017). Geo-demographics of gunshot wound injuries in Miami-Dade County, 2002–2012. *BMC Public Health, 17*(1), 174.

Zeoli, A. M., Goldstick, J., Mauri, A., Wallin, M., Goyal, M., Cunningham, R., & FACTS Consortium. (2019). The association of firearm laws with firearm outcomes among children and adolescents: A scoping review. *Journal of Behavioral Medicine, 42*(4), 741–762.

Zeoli, A. M., & Webster, D. W. (2019). Firearm policies that work. *JAMA, 321*(10), 937–938.

Zhang, Y., Shah, D., Foley, J., Abhishek, A., Lukito, J., Suk, J., . . . Garlough, C. (2019). Whose lives matter? Mass shootings and social media discourses of sympathy and policy, 2012–2014. *Journal of Computer-Mediated Communication, 24*(4), 182–202.

Zheng, C., & Mushatt, D. (2019, March). Let's join the lane: The role of infectious diseases physicians in preventing gun violence. *Open Forum Infectious Diseases, 6*(3), ofz026.

Zimmerman, G. M., & Pogarsky, G. (2011). The consequences of parental underestimation and overestimation of youth exposure to violence. *Journal of Marriage and Family, 73,* 194–208.

Zimmerman, G. M., Farrell, C., & Posick, C. (2017). Does the strength of the victim-offender overlap depend on the relationship between the victim and perpetrator? *Journal of Criminal Justice, 48,* 21–29.

For the benefit of digital users, indexed terms that span two pages (e.g., 52–53) may, on occasion, appear on only one of those pages.